The Hudson River in Literature

"Sunnyside," home of Washington Irving near Tarrytown. Currier & Ives, ca. 1850.

The Hudson River in Literature

An Anthology

EDITED BY

ARTHUR G. ADAMS

FORDHAM UNIVERSITY PRESS

NEW YORK

LC 79–14862
ISBN 0–8232–1202–5

This edition published by special arrangement with the State University of New York Press

First edition 1980

Second edition 1988

Second printing 1997

The Hudson River in literature : an anthology / edited by Arthur G. Adams. – New
    York : Fordham University Press, 1997.
    Includes bibliographical references.

    1. American literature – 19th century.   2. Hudson River (N.Y. and N.J.) –
Literary collections.   I. Adams, Arthur G.   II. Title.

PS509.H78 H8 1997
810/.8/032
ISBN: 0–8232–1202–5
LCCN: 79–14862

Printed in the United States of America

THIS BOOK IS DEDICATED
TO MY MOTHER WHO
ALWAYS BROUGHT THE BEST
BOOKS INTO OUR HOME

PREFACE

Whether as a bustling commercial trafficway in New York City or a tranquil expanse of water beyond the Catskills, the Hudson River has inspired American writers. This volume contains poems and excerpts from novels and essays that describe the river and life along it before the twentieth century.

Some of the writers included in this anthology are still well known, such as Washington Irving, James Fenimore Cooper, and Walt Whitman. The works of other writers, such as Joseph Rodman Drake or Nathaniel Parker Willis, are either out of print or available only as part of the collected works of the authors. In addition to excerpts from the work of both famous and less well-known authors, the anthology includes biographical paragraphs on other authors who lived and worked in the Hudson Valley.

From the river at Whitman's "mast-hemm'd Manhattan" to Nathaniel Parker Willis's "sabbath solitude" on upstate riverbanks, the modern reader will find still-accurate descriptions of the physical river itself. The many excerpts that describe particular aspects of life on the river—Indian canoes, Dutch farms, steamboat excursions, and the majestic scenery of the Hudson—allow the modern reader to imagine the people who lived along and travelled the river and how they felt about it.

Contents

CONTENTS

PART I

Early Regional Writers

Nicasius De Sille and Jacob Steendam

Early New Amsterdam produced two local writers in the Dutch language—Nicasius De Sille and Jacob Steendam. Their writings had a limited circulation among the early settlers, whose favorite poet was the Dutchman Jacob Cats (1577-1660), who was considered the Dutch national poet. His poems were didactic and moralizing in nature and dealt with such aspects of home life as the ethics of marriage and table manners. He served as spokesman for Dutch Calvinistic culture and he was affectionately called "Father Cats." Most other reading among early Dutch settlers was confined to the Bible and theological treatises of the Reformed Church.

We know relatively little about Nicasius De Sille. On July 10, 1660, he took the first census of houses in New York City, then called New Amsterdam. Jacob Steendam (1616-1672) was born in the Netherlands, and settled in the New Netherlands in 1652, as a merchant. Three volumes of poems, entitled *Den Distelvink,* were published in 1649 and 1650. He also wrote a political poem in 1659 entitled "Complaint of New Amsterdam in New Netherland to her Mother."

Cadwallader Colden

Later, under English rule, New York was the home of a distinguished scholar and statesman. Cadwallader Colden (1688-1776) was born in Ireland. He was granted an A.B. Degree at Edinburgh in 1705, and came to America in 1710, settling in New York City. By 1720, he was Surveyor General of New York, and in 1721 was serving on the New York Governor's Council. He served as Lieutenant-Governor and president of the Governor's Council between 1761 and 1776. He also served as Acting Governor for the terms: 1760-61, 1761-62, 1763-65, 1769-70, 1774-75. Needless to say, he was a staunch loyalist. During the governorship of George Clinton (1743-53), he prepared many of the governor's papers and addresses.

Aside from his political activities, Colden was a highly educated man. He had studied medicine in London and made significant contributions to the medical literature of the colonies. He was also an expert botanist and one of the earliest masters of the new Linnaean system of classifying flora. His interests were far ranging. In 1727 he wrote a *History of Five Indian Nations Depending Upon New York.* In the field of mathematics he wrote *An Explication of the First Causes of Action in Matter, and, of the Cause of Gravitation* in 1745, and *Principles of*

3

Action In Matter in 1752. Colden had extensive land holdings near Newburgh, and his name is perpetuated in the name of the village of Coldenham.

Philip Freneau

America's first important lyric poet was Philip Freneau (1752-1832). He was born in New York City and attended Princeton, from which he was graduated in 1771, a classmate of James Madison. He served as a soldier and privateer during the Revolution and in 1780 was captured and imprisoned aboard the British brig *Aurora*. This episode inspired his poem "The British Prison Ship." He returned to the sea as a captain after the war for the periods 1785-89 and 1802-04. He next became a professional journalist—one of our first. A powerful propagandist and satirist, he edited the Philadelphia-based *National Gazette,* a Jeffersonian paper between 1791 and 1793. During this period he wrote many satirical and political poems. However, his most important works were his lyrics. His most famous ones are, "The Wild Honeysuckle," "The Indian Burying Ground," and "Eutaw Springs." During his later years he lived in retirement near Monmouth, New Jersey, during which period he visited the Atlantic Highlands, which inspired his poem, "Neversink." He died when he lost his way in a snowstorm while walking between Freehold and his home.

NEVERSINK*

These Hills, the pride of all the coast,
    To mighty distance seen,
    With aspect bold and rugged brow,
    That shade the neighboring main:
These heights, for solitude design'd,
This rude, resounding shore—
    These vales impervious to the wind,
    Tall oaks, that to the tempest bend,
    Half Druid, I adore.

From distant lands, a thousand sails
    Your hazy summits greet—
    You saw the angry Briton come,

*Philip Freneau, *Poems On Several Occasions (Written Between The Years 1768 and 1794)* (Monmouth, N. J.: printed at the Press of the Author, at Mount-Pleasant, near Middletown-Point, 1795).

4

The Hills of the Neversink. Drawing by Granville Perkins, ca. 1872. From *Picturesque America* (New York: Appleton, 1872). The Twin Lights, built in 1828 to replace earlier bonfires used here since 1764, crown Beacon Hill, elevation 266 feet. Beacon fires were still used at the time of Freneau's poem, written in 1768. Sandy Hook, with the tracks of the Southern Railroad of New Jersey, is in the foreground and the mouth of the Shrewsbury River in the middle ground.

You saw him, last, retreat!
With towering crest, you first appear
The news of land to tell;
To him that comes, fresh joys impart,
To him that goes, a heavy heart,
The lover's long farewell.

Tis yours to see the sailor bold,
Of persevering mind,
To see him rove in search of care,
And leave true bliss behind;
To see him spread his flowing sails
To trace a tiresome road,
By wintry seas and tempests chas'd,
To see him o'er the ocean haste,
A comfortless abode!

Your thousand springs of waters blue
What luxury to sip,
As from the mountain's breast they flow
To moisten Flora's lip!
In vast retirements herd the deer,
Where forests round them rise,
Dark groves, their tops in aether lost,
That, haunted still by Huddy's ghost,
The trembling rustic flies.

Proud heights! with pain so often seen,
(With joy beheld once more)
On your firm base I take my stand,
Tenacious of the shore:—
Let those who pant for wealth or fame
Pursue the watery road;—
Soft sleep and ease, blest days and nights,
And health, attend these favourite heights,
Retirement's blest abode!

Sandy Hook Bay, Beacon Hill, and Twin Lights, by Granville Perkins, ca. 1870. From *Picturesque America* (New York: Appleton, 1872).

PART II

The Knickerbockers

Portrait of James Kirke Paulding. Date and artist unknown. From the editor's collection.

James Kirke Paulding

James Kirke Paulding (1779-1860) was America's first successful novelist. He was born at Millbrook, New York, but later lived in New York City, and in his later life retired to his estate Placentia, above Hyde Park. During his active life he often served in public office and was Secretary of the Navy under Martin Van Buren. In this capacity he fought against the introduction of steamships to the American Navy.

Between 1807 and 1808, he cooperated with William and Washington Irving in producing the *Salmagundi; or, The Whim-Whams and Opinions of Launcelot Langstaff & Others*, a series of satirical and humorous essays. In a similar satirical vein he wrote *John Bull in America* in 1825, and his *New Mirror for Travellers & Guide to the Springs* in 1828. Earlier, in 1818, he had tried his hand at an epic poem entitled "The Backwoodsman."

In 1828 he wrote a pastoral tale similar to Irving's *Legend of Sleepy Hollow* entitled *Cobus Yerks*, also set in Tarrytown. Another tale entitled *Dyspepsy* was written in 1829. He wrote a total of seventy tales, a *Life of George Washington*, and several novels. His most popular novels were *Koningsmarke* of 1834, and *The Dutchman's Fireside* of 1831. This later novel has an exciting episode descriptive of the Hudson above Albany.

From *New Mirror for Travellers; and Guide to the Springs* by An Amateur (James Kirke Paulding)*

The Narrows and New York Bay

O its delightful to travel, Maria! We had such a delightful sail in the steam boat, though we were all sick; and such a delightful party, if they only had been well. Only think of sailing without sails, and not caring which way the wind blows; and going eight miles an hour let what would happen. It was quite charming; but for all this I was glad when it was over, and we came into still water. Coming into the Narrows, as they are called, was like entering a Paradise. On one side is Long Island, with its low shores, studded with pretty houses, and foliage of various kinds, mixed up with the dark cedars. On the other, Staten Island, with its high bluff, crowned by the telegraph and signal poles; and beyond, the great fort that put me in mind of the old castles which Stephen talks about. We kept close to the Long Island shore, along which we glided, before wind and tide with the swiftness of wings. Every moment some new beauty

*James Kirke Paulding, *New Mirror For Travellers; and Guide to the Springs* (New York: G & C. Carvill, 1828).

opened to our view. The little islands of the bay crowned with castles; the river beyond terminated by the lofty ledge of perpendicular rocks, called the palisades; and lastly, the queen of the west, the beautiful city, with its Battery and hundred spires, all coming one after the other in succession, and at last all combined in one beautiful whole, threw me almost into raptures, and entirely cured my sea sickness. Add to this, the ships, vessels and boats, of all sizes, from the seventy-four to the little thing darting about, like a feather, with a single person in it; and the grand opening of the East River, with Brooklyn and the charming scenery beyond, and you can form some little idea of my suprise and delight. . . .

NEW YORK CITY

Of the other occupations or mysteries, such as spending a great deal of money, without having any; and running in debt, without possessing any credit; our limits will not allow us to dilate so copiously as we could wish. Suffice it to say, that New York is in this respect by no means behind hand with its neighbours, inasmuch as it is not uncommon to see people riding in splendid carriages, living in splendid houses, and owning a whole street, who when they come to settle with death, or their other creditors, pay the former and that is all. For the benefit of all fashionable tourists, we would wish to enter upon a full development of this the most valuable secret of the whole art of living, which may possibly one day stand them in stead. But it would require volumes of illustrations, and a minuteness of detail irreconcilable with the plan of this work. And even then it is doubtful whether the tourist would be able to put the system in practice, since many are of opinion, that nothing but a regular apprenticeship in the arts of stock jobbing, stock companies, hypothecation, blowing bubbles and bursting them, as practised *par excellence* in the *beau monde* of New York, will qualify a person for living upon nothing, unless he has an extraordinary natural genius.

Among the many modes however of raising the wind in New York, that of buying lottery tickets is one of the most infallible. It is amazing what a number of prizes every lottery office keeper has sold either in whole or in shares, and what is yet more extraordinary, as well as altogether out of fashion, paid them too if you will take his word for it. The whole insides and large portion of the outsides of many houses in Broadway, are covered with the vast sums thus liberally dispensed to the public, and what is very remarkable, among all those who have made their fortunes in this way, we never heard of a single person who was brought to ruin by it! People need have no scruples of conscience about trying their luck in this way, since if it were really gambling, the legislature of New York state, which is a great enemy to horse racing—save in one consecrated spot—and all other kinds of gambling, would certainly never have authorized a series of lotteries, of which some people may recollect the beginning, but nobody

The Lower Bay, from Staten Island. Drawing by Granville Perkins, from *Picturesque America* (New York: Appleton, 1872). This view is looking southeastward toward the Highlands of the Neversink and the open sea. The view looking northward up the Narrows is shown in William Bartlett's drawing entitled View from the Telegraph Signal, New York Bay, shown facing page 271. A complementary view entitled The Narrows, from Fort Hamilton (Brooklyn, Long Island), also by William Bartlett, faces page 284. Both of Bartlett's drawings appeared in *American Scenery* (London: Virtue, 1836). All three scenes present the vicinity as seen by Paulding in 1828.

Steamboat *Chancellor Livingston* of 1816. Drawing by Samuel Ward Stanton, ca. 1890, from the editor's collection. This type of early steamboat also carried auxiliary sails and was used in both coastal and river service. It is likely that Paulding's passengers entered New York Bay on this or one of a very few similar sister ships.

can predict the end. Nothing can exceed the philanthropic earnestness with which the dispensers of fortune's favours, in the lotteries, strive to allure the ignorant and unwary, who are not aware of the certainty of making a fortune in this way, into a habit of depending on the blind goddess, instead of always stupidly relying upon the labour of their hands, and the sweat of their brows. Nor ought the unwearied pains of these liberal hearted persons, to coax them into parting with all they have, in the moral certainty of getting back a hundred, yea a thousand fold, pass without due commendation, for certain it is, that if any body in New York is poor, it must be owing to their own obstinate stupidity in refusing these disinterested invitations. N. B. There are very severe laws against gambling in New York.

There are many other ways of living and getting money here, and spending it too, which it is not necessary to enumerate. We have premised sufficient to enable the enlightened tourist, who peradventure may have been left destitute in a strange place, by a run at cards, a failure of remittances or any other untoward accident, to retrieve his fortune, if he possesses an ordinary degree of intrepidity and enterprise. A complete knowledge of the world is the first requisite for living in the world, and the first step to the attainment of this, is to know the difference between catching and being caught, as aptly exemplified in the fable of the fox and the oyster.

Once upon a time—it was long before the foxes had their speech taken from them lest they should get the better of man—as Reynard was fishing for oysters with his tail, he had the good luck to put the end of it into the jaws of a fine *Blue Pointer* that lay gaping with his mouth wide open, by reason of his having drank too much salt water at dinner. "Ah ha!" cried the oyster, shutting his mouth as quickly as his corpulent belly would permit—"Ah ha! have I caught you at last!" Reynard tickled to death at this wise exclamation, forthwith set off full tilt for his hole, the oyster holding on with all his might, though he got most bitterly bethumpt against the rocks, and exclaiming all the while, "Ah ha! my honest friend, dont think to escape me—I've got you safe enough—ah ha!" All which he uttered without opening his mouth, as was the custom of speaking in those days. Reynard who had well nigh killed himself with laughing, at length came safe to his lodgings with the clumsy oyster still fast to his tail. After taking a little breath, he addressed it thus, "Why thou aquatic snail—thou non-descript among animals, that art neither fish, flesh, nor fowl—hadst thou but one single particle of brains in all that fat carcase of thine, I would argue the matter with thee. As it is, I will soon teach thee the difference between catching and being caught." So saying, he broke the shell of the honest oyster, with a stone, and swallowed his contents with great satisfaction.

Having seen every thing worth seeing, and eaten of every thing worth eating, in New York, the traveller may begin to prepare for the ineffable delights of the springs. After the month of April, oysters become unlawful, and canvass backs are out of season. There is then nothing to detain the inquisitive tourist, and there are many things that render his speedy departure highly expedient. . . .

SAFETY BARGES AND STEAMBOATS

These principal requisites being procured you take the steam boat for Albany. If you are in a great hurry, or not afraid of being drowned in going ashore at West Point, or blown up by the way, take one of the fastest boats you can find. But if you wish to travel pleasantly, eat your meals in comfort, associate with genteel company, sleep in quiet, and wake up alive, our advice is to take one of the SAFETY BARGES, where all these advantages are combined. It grieves us to the soul to see these sumptuous aquatic palaces, which constitute the very perfection of all earthly locomotion almost deserted, by the ill advised traveller—and for what? that he may get to Albany a few hours sooner, as if it were not the distinguishing characteristic of a genteel man of pleasure to have more time on his hands than he knows what to do with. Let merchants, and tradesmen, and brokers, and hand-icraft people, and all those condemned to the labour of hands, to whom time is as money, patronize the swift boats; and let those who are running away from justice affect these vehicles; but for the man of leisure, whose sole business is to kill time pleasantly, enjoy himself at his ease, and dine free from the infamous proximity of hungry rogues, who devour with their eyes what they cant reach with their hands, the safety barges are preferable even to the chariot of the sun. N. B. We dont mean to discourage people who may cherish the harmless propensity to be blown up—every one to their taste.

PASSAGE UP THE HUDSON

The following hints will be found serviceable to all travellers in steam boats.
In the miscellaneous melange usually found in these machines, the first duty of a man is to take care of himself—to get the best seat at table, the best location on deck; and when these are obtained to keep resolute possession in spite of all the significant looks of the ladies.
If your heart yearns for a particularly comfortable seat which is occupied by a lady, all you have to do is to keep your eye steadily upon it, and the moment she gets up, dont wait to see if she is going to return, but take possession without a moment's delay. If she comes back again, be sure not to see her.
Keep a sharp look out for meals. An experienced traveller can always tell when these amiable conveniences are about being served up, by a mysterious move-ment on the part of the ladies, and a mysterious agitation among the male species, who may be seen gradually approximating towards the cabin doors. Whenever you observe these symptoms, it is time to exert yourself by pushing through the

Hudson River Steamboat typical of 1828 era, with a view of Manhattan in the background. The view is looking east. Anonymous print, courtesy of Claire Tholl. Paulding traveled up the Hudson in a sidewheeler such as this.

crowd to the place of flagons. Never mind the sour looks, but elbow your way with resolution and perseverance, remembering that a man can eat but so many meals in his life, and that the loss of one can never be retrieved.

The most prudent and infallible arrangement, however, is that generally pursued by your knowing English travellers, which is as follows: As soon as you have seen your baggage disposed of, and before the waiters have had time to shut the cabin doors, preparatory to laying the tables, station yourself in a proper situation for action at one of them. The inside is the best, for there you are not in the way of the servants. Resolutely maintain your position in spite of the looks and hints of the servants about, "Gentlemen being in the way," and "No chance to set the tables." You can be reading a book or a newspaper, and not hear them; or the best way is to pretend to be asleep.

Keep a wary eye for a favourite dish, and if it happens to be placed at a distance, or on another table, you can take an opportunity to look hard at an open window, as if there was too much air for you, shrug your shoulders, and move opposite the dish aforesaid.

The moment the bell rings, fall to; you need not wait for the rest of the company to be seated, or mind the ladies, for there is no time to be lost on these occasions. For the same reason, you should keep your eyes moving about, from one end of the table to the other, in order that if you see any thing you like, you can send for it without losing time. Call as loudly and as often as possible for the waiter; the louder you call, the more consequence you will gain with the company. If he dont mind you, dont hesitate to snatch whatever he has got in his hands, if you happen to want it.

Be sure to have as many different things on your plate at one time as possible, and to use your own knife in cutting up all the dishes within your reach, and particularly in helping yourself to butter, though there may be knives on purpose. N. B. It is of no consequence whether your knife is fishy or not.

Dont wait for the dessert to be laid, but the moment a pudding or a pie is placed within your reach, fall to and spare not. Get as much pudding, pie, nuts, apples, raisins, &c. on your plate as it will hold, and eat all together.

Pay no attention to the ladies, who have or ought to have friends to take care of them, or they have no business to be travelling in steam boats.

The moment you have eaten every thing within your reach, and are satisfied nothing more is forthcoming, get up and make for the cabin door with a segar in your hand. No matter if you are sitting at the middle of the inner side of the table, and disturb a dozen or two of people. They have no business to be in your way. If it is supper time and the candles lighted, you had best light your segar at one of them, and puff a little before you proceed for fear it should go out. N. B. If you were to take an opportunity to find fault with the meals, the attendants, and the boat, in an audible tone, as Englishmen do, it will serve to give people an idea you have been used to better at home.

13

Never think of pulling off your hat on coming into the cabin, though it happens to be full of ladies. It looks anti-republican; and besides has the appearance of not having been used to better company.

Never miss an opportunity of standing in the door way, or on the stairs, or in narrow passages, and never get out of the way to let people pass, particularly ladies.

If there happens to be a scarcity of seats, be sure to stretch yourself at full length upon a sopha or a cushion, and if any lady looks at you as if she thought you might give her a place, give her another look as much as to say, "I'll see you hanged first."

If the weather is cold get directly before the stove, turn your back, and open the skirts of your coat behind as wide as possible, that the fire may have fair play.

If you happen to be better dressed than your neighbour, look at him with an air of superiority; and dont hear him if he has the impudence to speak to you. If it is your ill fortune to be dressed not so well, employ a tailor as soon as possible to remedy the inferiority.

Be sure to pay your passage, if you have any money. If you have none, go to sleep in some out of the way corner, and dont wake till the last trumpet blows.

Dont pay any attention to the notification that "no smoking is allowed abaft the wheel;" but strut about the quarter deck, and the upper gallery, among the ladies with a segar on all occasions. There are so many ignorant people that smoke on board steam boats, that it will naturally be supposed you cant read, and of course dont know of the prohibition. If you can get to the windward of a lady or two, so much the better.

Whenever you are on deck by day, be sure to have this book in your hand, and instead of boring yourself with the scenery, read the descriptions which will be found infinitely superior to any of the clumsy productions of nature.

N.B. These rules apply exclusively to gentlemen, the ladies being allowed the liberty of doing as they please, in all respects except six.

They are not permitted to eat beef steaks and mutton chops at breakfast, unless they can prove themselves past fifty.

They must not sit at table more than an hour, unless they wish to be counted hungry, which no lady ought ever to be.

They must not talk so loud as to drown the noise of the engine, unless their voices are particularly sweet.

They must not enact the turtle dove before all the company, unless they cant help it.

They must not jump overboard, at every little noise of the machinery.

They must not be always laughing, except they have very white teeth.

With these exceptions, they may say and do just what they like, in spite of papa and mama, for this is a free country.

"This magnificent river,* which taking it in all its combinations of magnitude and beauty, is scarcely equalled in the new, and not even approached in the old world, was discovered by Hendrick Hudson in the month of September, 1609, by accident, as almost every other discovery has been made. He was searching for a northwest passage to India, when he first entered the bay of New York, and imagined the possibility that he had here found it, until on exploring the river upwards, he came to fresh water, ran aground, and abandoned his hopes.

"Of this man, whose name is thus identified with the discovery, the growth, and the future prospects of a mighty state, little is known; and of that little the end is indescribably melancholy. He made four voyages in search of this imaginary northwest passage, and the termination of the last is in the highest degree affecting, as related in the following extract from his Journal, as published in the collections of the New York Historical Society."

"You shall understand," says Master Abacuk Pricket, from whose Journal this is taken, "that our master kept in his house in London, a young man named Henrie Greene, borne in Kent, of worshipfull parents, but by his lewd life and conversation hee lost the good will of all his friends, and spent all that hee had. This man our master (Hudson) would have to sea with him, because hee could write well: our master gave him meate, and drinke and lodgeing, and by means of one Master Venson, with much ado got four pounds of his mother to buy him clothes, wherewith Master Venson would not trust him, but saw it laid out himself. This Henry Greene was not set down in the owners' bookes, nor any wages made for him. Hee came first on board at Gravesend, and at Harwich should have gone into the field with one Wilkinson. At Island, the surgeon and hee fell out in Dutch, and hee beat him ashore in English, which set all the company in a rage; so that wee had much ado to get the surgeon aboarde. I told the master of it, but hee bade mee let it alone, for (said hee,) the surgeon had a tongue that would wrong the best friend hee had. But Robert Juet (the master's mate) would needs burn his fingers in the embers, and told the carpenter a long tale (when hee was drunk) that our master had brought in Greene to worke his credit that should displease him; which words came to the master's ears, who when he understood it would have gone back to Island, when he was forty degrees from thence, to have sent home his mate, Robert Juet, in a fisherman. But being otherwise persuaded, all was well. So Henry Greene stood upright and very inward with the master, and was a serviceable man every way for manhood: but for religion, he would say he was cleane paper whereon he might write what hee would. Now when our gunner was dead, (and as the order is in such cases) if the company stand in need of any thing that belonged to the man deceased, then it is brought to the mayne mast, and there sold to him that will give most for the same. This gunner had a graye cloth gowne which Greene prayed the master to friend

*We quote from the unpublished *ana* of Alderman Janson.

him so much to let him have it, paying for it as another would give. The master saith he should, and therefore he answered some that sought to have it, that Greene should have it, and none else, and so it rested.

"Now out of season and time the master calleth the carpenter to go in hand with a house on shore, which at the beginning our master would not heare when it might have been done. The carpenter told him that the snow and frost were such, as he neither could or would go in hand with such worke. Which when our master heard, he ferretted him out of his cabbin, to strike him, calling him by many foule names, and threatening to hang him. The carpenter told him that hee knew what belonged to his place better than himselfe, and that hee was no house carpenter. So this passed, and the house was (after) made with much labour, but to no end.

"The next day after the master and the carpenter fell out, the carpenter took his peece and Henry Greene with him, for it was an order that none should go out alone, but one with a peece, and the other with a pike. This did moove the master so much the more against Henry Greene, that Robert Billet, his mate, must have the gowne, and had it delivered to him; which when Henry Greene saw he challenged the master's promise; but the master did so raile on Greene with so many words of disgrace, telling him that all his friends would not trust him with twenty shillings, and therefore why should hee? As for wages hee had none, nor none should have if he did not please him well. Yet the master had promised him to make his wages as good as any man's in the ship; and to have him one of the prince's guard when he came home. But you shall see how the devil out of this so wrought with Greene, that hee did the master what mischiefe hee could in seeking to discredit him, and to thrust him and many other honest men out of the ship in the end."

It appears that Greene having come to an understanding with others whom he had corrupted, a plot was laid to seize Hudson and those of the crew that remained faithful to him, put them on board a small shallop which was used in making excursions for food or observations, and run away with the ship. Of the manner in which this was consummated the same writer gives the following relation:

"Being thus in the ice on Saturday the one and twentieth day of June, (1610,) at night Wilson the boatswayne and Henry Greene came to mee lying in my cabbin lame, and told me that they and the rest of their associates would shift the company and turne the master and all the sick men into the shallop, and let them shift for themselves. For there was not fourteen daies victuals left for all the company, at that poor allowance they were at, and that there they lay, the master not caring to goe one way or other: and that they had not eaten any thing these three dayes, and therefore were resolute either to mend or end, and what they had begun would go through with it, or dye." Pricket refuses and expostulates with Wilson and Greene. "Henry Greene then told me I must take my chance in the shallop. If there be no remedy, (said I,) the will of God be done." Pricket tries to persuade them to put off their design for two days, nay for twelve hours, that he might persuade Hudson to return home with the ship; but, to this they would not consent, and proceeded to execute their plot as follows:

"In the mean time, Henry Greene and another went to the carpenter, and held him with a talke till the master (Hudson) came out of his cabbin; (which he soon did;) then came John Thomas and Bennett before him, while Wilson bound his arms behind him. He asked them what they meant? They told him he should know when he was in the shallop. Now Juet while this was doing, came to John King into the hold, who was provided for him, for he had got a sword of his own and kept him at bay, and might have killed him, but others came to help him, and so he came up to the master. The master called to the carpenter and told him he was bound; but I heard no answer he made. Now Arnold Lodlo and Michael Bute rayled at them, and told them their knaverie would shewe itselfe. Then was the shallop haled up to the ship's side, and tho poore sick and lame men were called upon to get them out of their cabbins into the shallop. The master called to mee, who came out of my cabbin as well as I could to the hatch waye to speak to him: where on my knees, I besought them for the love of God to remember themselves, and to doe as they would be done unto. They bade me keepe myselfe well, and get me into my cabbin, not suffering the master to speake to me. But when I came into my cabbin, againe he called to me at the horne that gave light into my cabbin, and told me that Juet would overthrow us all. Nay, says I, it is that villaine Henry Greene, and I spake it not softly.

"Now were all the poore men in the shallop, whose names are as followeth: Henrie Hudson, John Hudson, Arnold Lodlo, Sidrach Faner, Phillip Staffe, Thomas Woodhouse, (or Wydhouse,) Adam Moore, Henrie King, and Michael Bute. The carpenter got of them a peece, and powder and shot, and some pikes, an iron pot, with some meale and other things. They stood out of the ice, the shallop being fast to the sterne of the shippe, and so when they were nigh out, for I cannot say they were cleane out, they cut her head fast from the sterne of the ship, then out with theire topsayles, and towards the east they stood in a cleare sea."

The mutineers being on shore, some days after, were attacked by a party of indians.

"John Thomas and William Wilson had their bowels cut, and Michael Pearce and Henry Greene being mortally wounded, came tumbling in the boat together. When Andrew Moter saw this medley, hee came running down the rockes, and leaped into the sea, and soe swamme to the boat, hanging on the sterne thereof, till Michael Pearce took him in, who manfully made good the head of the boat against the savages that pressed sore upon us. Now Michael Pearce had got an hatchet, wherewith I saw him strike one of them, that he lay sprawling in the sea. Henry Greene crieth coragio, and layeth about him with his truncheon. The savages betook themselves to their bowes and arrows which they sent among us, wherewith Henry Greene was slaine outright, and Michael Pearce received many wounds, and so did the rest. Michael Pearce and Andrew Moter rowed the boat away, which when the savages saw they ranne to their boats, and I feared they would have launched them to have followed us, but they did not, and our ship was in the middle of the channel, and did not see us.

"Now when they had rowed a good way from the shore, Michael Pearce fainted and could row no more. Then was Andrew Moter driven to stand in the boat's head and waft to the ship, which at the first saw us not, and when they did, they could not tell what to make of us; but in the end they stood for us, and so took us up. Henry Greene was thrown out of the boat into the sea, and the rest were had on board. But they died all three that day, William Wilson swearing and cursing in the most fearful manner. Michael Pearce lived two days after and then died. Thus you have heard the tragicale of Henry Greene and his mates, whom they called the captaine, these four being the only lustie men in all the ship."

After this, Robert Juet took the command, but "died for meere want," before they arrived at Plymouth, which is the last we hear of them, except that Pricket was taken up to London to Sir Thomas Smith. Neither was the unfortunate Hudson and his companions ever heard of more. Doubtless they perished miserably, by famine, cold, or savage cruelty. The mighty river which he first explored, and the great bay to the north, alone by bearing his name, carry his memory, and will continue to carry it down to the latest posterity. We thought we could do no less than call the attention of the traveller a few moments, to the hard fate of one to whom they are originally indebted, for much of the pleasures of the tour to the springs.

After the traveller has paid tribute to the memory of honest Henry Hudson, by reading the preceding sketch of his melancholy end, he may indulge himself in contemplating the beautiful world expanding every moment before him, appearing and vanishing in the rapidity of his motion, like the creations of the imagination. Every object is beautiful, and its beauties heightened by the eye having no time to be palled with contemplating them too long. Nature seems in merry motion hurring by, and as she moves along displays a thousand varied charms in rapid succession, each one more enchanting than the rest. If the traveller casts his eyes backwards, he beholds the long perspective waters gradually converging to a point at the Narrows, fringed with the low soft scenery of Jersey and Long Island, and crowned with the little buoyant islands on its bosom. If he looks before him, on one side the picturesque shore of Jersey, its rich strip of meadows and orchards, sometimes backed by the wood crowned hills, and at others by perpendicular walls of solid rock; on the other, York Island with its thousand little palaces, sporting its green fields and waving woods, by turns allure his attention, and make him wish either that the river had but one side, or that he had more eyes to admire its beauties.

As the vessel wafts him merrily, merrily along, new beauties crowd upon him so rapidly as almost to efface the impressions of the past. That noble ledge of

The Palisades, as described by Paulding. From an old postal card, ca. 1890. Claire Tholl collection.

rocks which is worthy to form the barrier of the noble river, and which extends for sixteen miles, shows itself in a succession of sublime bluffs, projecting out one after the other, looking like the fabled creations of the giants, or the Cyclops of old. High on these cliffs, may be seen the woodman, pitching his billet from the very edge down a precipice of hundreds of feet, whence it slides or bounds to the water's edge, and is received on board its destined vessel. At other points, half way up its sides you will see the quarriers, undermining huge masses of rocks that in the lapse of ages have separated from the cliff above, and setting them rolling down with thundering crashes to the level beach below. Here and there under the dark impending cliff, where nature has formed a little green nook or flat, some enterprising skipper who owns a little pettiauger, or some hardy quarrier, has erected his little cot. There when the afternoon shadows envelope the rocks, the woods and the shores, may be seen little groups of children sporting in all the glee of youthful idleness. Some setting their little shaggy dog to swimming into the river after a chip, others worrying some patient pussy, others wading along the white sands knee deep in the waters, and others perhaps stopping to stare at the moving wonder champing by, then chasing the long ripple created by its furious motion as it breaks along the sands. Contrasting beautifully with this long mural precipice on the west, the eastern bank exhibits a charming variety of waving outline. Long graceful curving hills, sinking into little vales, pouring forth a gurgling brook—then rising again into wood crowned heights, presenting the image of a mighty succession of waves, suddenly arrested in their rolling career, and turned into mingled woods, and meadows, and fertile fields, animated with all the living emblems of industry; cattle, sheep, waving fields of grain, and whistling ploughmen.

These precipices are said to be of the trap formation, a most important species of rock in geology, as whoever "understands trap," may set up for a master of the science. In many places, this trap formation is found apparently based on a horizontal stratum of primitive rock. This has somewhat shaken the trap theory and puzzled geologists. But we leave them to settle the affair, and pass on to objects of more importance to the tourist, in a historical point of view at least.

At Sneden's Landing, opposite Dobb's Ferry, the range of perpendicular trap rocks, disappears until you again detect it, opposite Sing Sing, where it exhibits itself in a most picturesque and beautiful manner at intervals, in the range of mountains bordering the west side of the river, between Nyack and Haverstraw. At Sneden's, commences a vast expanse of salt meadows, generally so thickly studded with barracks and haystacks, as to present at a distance the appearance of a great city rising out of the famed Tappan Sea, like Venice from out the Adriatic. Travellers, who have seen both, observe a great similarity—but on the whole prefer the haystacks. Here commences Tappan Sea, where the river expands to a breadth of three miles, and where in the days of log canoes and pine skiffs, full many an adventurous navigator is said to have encountered dreadful perils in crossing over from the Slote to Tarrytown. At present its dangers are all traditionary.

The western border of this beautiful expanse is mountainous; but the hills rise in such gradual ascent that the whole is cultivated to the very top, and exhibits a charming display of variegated fields. That the soil was once rich, is established by the fact of this whole district being settled by the Dutch, than whom there never was a people better at smelling out rich vales and fat alluvions. Here the race subsists unadulterated to the present time. The sons are cast in the same moulds with the father and grandfather; the daughters depart not from the examples of their mothers and grandmothers. The former eschew the mysteries of modern tailoring, and the latter borrow not the fashion of their bonnets from the French milliners. They travel not in steam boats, or in any other new fangled inventions; abhor canals and rail roads, and will go five miles out of the way to avoid a turnpike. They mind nobody's business but their own, and such is their inveterate attachment to home, that it is credibly reported there are men now living along the shores of the river, who not only have never visited the renowned Tarrytown, directly opposite, but who know not even its name.

They are deplorably deficient in the noble science of gastronomy, and such is their utter barbarity of taste, that they never eat but when they are hungry, nor after they are satisfied, and the consequence of this barbarous indifference to the chief good of life, is that they one and all remain without those infallible patents of high breeding, gout and dyspepsia. Since the period of the first settlement of this region, the only changes that have ever been known to take place, are those brought about by death, who if report says true has sometimes had his match with some of these tough old copperheads; in the aspect of the soil, which from an interminable forest has become a garden; and in the size of the loaves of bread, which from five feet long have dwindled down into the ordinary dimensions. For this unheard of innovation, they adduce in their justification the following undoubted tradition, which, like their hats and their petticoats, has descended down from generation to generation without changing a syllable.

"Sometime in the autumn of the year 1694, just when the woods were on the change, Yffrow, or Vrouw Katrinchee Van Noorden, was sitting at breakfast, surrounded by her husband and family, consisting of six stout boys, and as many strapping girls, all dressed in their best, for it was of a Sunday morning. Vrouw Katrinchee, had a loaf of fresh rye bread between her knees, the top of which was about on a line with her throat, the other end resting upon a napkin on the floor; and was essaying with the edge of a sharp knife to cut off the upper crust for the youngest boy, who was the pet; when unfortunately it recoiled from the said crust, and before the good Vrouw had time to consider the matter, sliced off her head as clean as a whistle, to the great horror of Mynheer Van Noorden, who actually stopt eating his breakfast. This awful catastrophe, brought the big loaves

An early Periauger, or Pettiauger as spelled by Paulding. Woodcut by S. Cozzens, undated. Claire Tholl collection. These freight-carrying boats were the ancestors of the later, more graceful, Hudson River sloops. They were also used for passenger ferryboats.

into disrepute, but such was their attachment to good old customs, that it was not until Domine Koontzie denounced them as against the law and the prophets, that they could be brought to give them up. As it is, the posterity of the Van Noordens to this day keep up the baking of big loaves, in conformity to the last will and testament of their ancestor, who decreed that this event should be thus preserved immortal in his family."*

On the opposite side of the river, snugly nestling in a little bay, lies Tarrytown, famous for its vicinity to the spot where the British spy, Andre, was intercepted by the three honest lads of Westchester. If the curious traveller is inclined to stop and view this spot, to which a romantic interest will ever be attached, the following directions will suffice.

"Landing at Tarrytown,† it is about a quarter of a mile to the post road, at Smith's tavern. Following the post road due north, about half a mile, you come to a little bridge over a small stream, known by the name of Clark's Kill, and sometimes almost dry. Formerly the wood on the left hand south of the bridge, approached close to the road, and there was a bank on the opposite side, which was steep enough to prevent escape on horseback that way. The road from the north, as it approaches the bridge, is narrowed between two banks of six or eight feet high, and makes an angle just before it reaches it. Here, close within the copse of wood on the left, as you approach from the village, the three militia lads, for lads they were, being hardly one and twenty, concealed themselves, to wait for a suspicious stranger, of whom they had notice from a Mrs. Read, at whose house they had stopt on their way towards Kingsbridge. A Mr. Talmadge, a revolutionary officer, and a member of the house of representatives, some years since took occasion to stigmatize these young men, as *Cow Boys,* out on a plundering expedition. The imputation was false; they were in possession of passes from General Philip Van Courtlandt, to proceed beyond the lines, as they were called, and of course by the laws of war, authorized to be where they were.

"As Major Andre approached, according to the universal tradition among the old people of Westchester, John Paulding, darted out upon him and seized his horse's bridle. Andre was exceedingly startled at the suddenness of this rencontre, and in a moment of unguarded surprise, exclaimed—'Where do you belong?'

"'Below,' was the reply, which was the phrase commonly used to designate the British, who were then in possession of New York.

"'So do I,' was the rejoinder of Andre in the joyful surprise of the moment. It has been surmised that this hasty admission sealed his fate. But when we reflect that he was suspected before, and that afterwards not even the production of his pass from General Arnold, could prevail upon the young men to let him go, it will appear sufficiently probable that this imprudent avowal was not the original

*We quote from the manuscript *ana* of Alderman Janson, to which we shall frequently refer in the course of this work.
†Vide *ana* of Alderman Janson.

cause of his being detained and searched. After some discussion and exhibiting his pass, he was taken into the wood, and searched, not without a good deal of unwillingness on his part; it is said he particularly resisted the pulling off his right boot, which contained the treasonable documents. When these were discovered, it is also said, Andre unguardedly exclaimed, 'I'm lost!' but presently recollecting himself, he added, 'No matter—they dare not hang me.'

"Finding himself discovered, Andre offered his gold watch and a purse of guineas for his release. These were rejected. He then proposed that they should take and secrete him, while one of the party carried a letter, which he would write in their presence, to Sir Henry Clinton, naming the ransom necessary to his discharge, and which they might themselves specify, pledging his honour that it should accompany their associate on his return. To this they likewise refused their assent. Andre then threatened them with a severe punishment for daring to disregard a pass from the commanding general at West Point; and bade them beware of carrying him to head quarters, for they would only be tried by a court martial and punished for mutiny. Still the firmness of these young men sustained them against all these threats and temptations, and they finally delivered him to Colonel Jameson. It is no inconsiderable testimony to the motives and temptations thus overcome, that Colonel Jameson, an officer of the regular army, commanding a point of great consequence, so far yielded to the production of this pass, as to permit Andre to write to General Arnold a letter, which enabled that traitor to escape the ignominious fate he deserved.

"While in custody of the three Westchester volunteers, Andre is said gradually to have recovered from his depression of spirits, so as to sit with them after supper, and chat about himself and his situation, still preserving his incognito of John Anderson. In the course of the evening which he passed in their company, he related the following singular little anecdote. It seems the evening before he left London to embark for America, he was in company with some young ladies of his familiar acquaintance, when it was proposed, that as he was going to a distant country on a perilous service, he should have his fortune told by a famous sybil, at that time fashionable in town, in order that his friends might know what had become of him while away. They went accordingly, when the old beldam, after the usual grimace and cant, on examining his palms, gravely announced, 'That he was going a great distance, and would either be hanged, or come very near it, before he returned.' All the company laughed at this awful annunciation, and joked with him on the way back. 'But,' added Andre, smiling, 'I seem in a fair way of fulfilling the prophecy.'

"It was not till Andre arrived at head quarters, and concealment became no longer possible, that he wrote the famous letter to General Washington, avowing his name and rank. He was tried by a court martial, found guilty on his own confession, was hanged at Tappan, where he met his fate with dignity, and excited in the bosoms of the Americans that sympathy as a criminal, which has since been challenged for him as a hero and a martyr. A few years since the British consul at New York, caused his remains to be disinterred and sent to England, where to perpetuate if possible the delusion of his having suffered in an honourable enterprize, they were buried in Westminster Abbey, among heroes, statesmen, and poets. The thanks of congress, with a medal, an annuity, and a farm, were bestowed on the three young volunteers, and lately a handsome monument has been erected by the corporation of New York, to John Paulding, at Peekskill, where his body was buried. The other two, Isaac Van Wart and David Williams, still survive.

"About half a quarter of a mile south of Clark's Kill Bridge, on the high road, formerly stood the great tulip, or whitewood tree, which being the most conspicuous object in the immediate vicinity, has been usually designated as the spot where Andre was taken and searched. It was one of the most magnificent of trees, one hundred and eleven feet and a half high, the limbs projecting on either side more than eighty feet from the trunk, which was ten paces round. More than twenty years ago it was struck by lightning, and its old weather beaten trunk so shivered that it fell to the ground, and it was remarked by the old people, that on the very same day, they for the first time read in the newspapers the death of Arnold. Arnold lived in England on a pension, which we believe is still continued to his children. His name was always coupled even there with infamy; insomuch that when the Duke of Richmond, Lord Shelburne, and other violent opponents of the American revolutionary war, were appointed to office, the late Duke of Lauderdale remarked, that 'If the king wished to employ traitors, he wondered that he should have overlooked Benedict Arnold.' For this he was called out by Arnold, and they exchanged shots, but without effect. Since then we know nothing of Arnold's history, till his death. He died as he lived the latter years of his life, an object of detestation to his countrymen, of contempt to the rest of the world.

"There is a romantic interest attached to the incidents just recorded, which will always make the capture of Andre a popular story; and the time will come when it will be chosen as the subject of poetry and the drama, as it has been of history and tradition. There is already a play founded upon it by Mr. William Dunlap, the writer and translator of many dramatic works. Mr. Dunlap has however we think committed a mistake in which however he is countenanced by most other writers—that of making Andre his hero. There is also extant a history of the whole affair, written by Joshua Hett Smith, the person who accompanied Andre across the river from Haverstraw, and whose memory is still in some measure implicated in the treason of Arnold. It is written with much passion and prejudice, and abounds in toryisms. Neither Washington, Greene, nor any of the members of the court martial escape the most degrading imputations: and the three young men who captured Andre are stigmatized with cowardice, as well as treachery! The history is the production of a man, who seems to have had but one

23

object, that of stigmatizing the characters of others, with a view of bolstering up his own. Washington and Greene require no guardians to defend their memory, at one time assailed by women and dotards, on the score of having, the one presided at the just condemnation of a spy; the other of having refused his pardon to the threats and bullyings of the enemy. The reputations of the three young captors of Andre have also been attacked, where one would least of all expect it—in the congress of the United States, where some years ago an honourable member, denounced them as *Cow Boys*; and declared to the house that Major Andre had assured him, he would have been released, could he have made good his promises of great reward from Sir Henry Clinton. The characters of these men, were triumphantly vindicated by the publication of the testimony of nearly all the aged inhabitants of Westchester who bore ample testimony to the purity of their lives and the patriotism of their motives. The slander is forgotten, and if its author be hereafter remembered, no one will envy him his reputation."

Tarrytown is still farther distinguished, by being within a mile or two of *Sleepy Hollow*, the scene of a pleasant legend of our friend Goeffrey Crayon, with whom in days long past we have often explored this pleasant valley, fishing along the brooks, though he was beyond all question the worst fisherman we ever knew. He had not the patience of Job's wife—and without patience no man can be a philosopher or a fisherman.

SING SING.

Sing Sing is a pleasant village, on the east side of the river, about six miles above Tarrytown. It is a very musical place (as its name imports,) as all the birds sing charmingly; and is blessed with a pure air, and delightful prospects. There is a silver mine a couple of hundred yards from the village, to which we recommend the adventurers in the South American and North Carolinian mines to turn their attention. They will certainly lose money by working it, but the money will be spent at home and the village will benefit by their patriotism. If they get ruined, there is a state prison close by where they will find an asylum. There is an old lady living in the neighbourhood, who recollects hearing her father say, that he had once before the revolutionary war, been concerned in this mine, and there is a sixpence still preserved in the family, coined from its produce, that only cost him two hundred pounds. There is a new state prison building here, from marble procured on the spot, in which the doleful experiment of solitary confinement is to be tried. It will not do. It will only be substituting lingering torments for those of sudden death. Without society, without books, without employment, without anticipations, and without the recollection of any thing but crimes, madness or death must be the consequence of a protracted seclusion of this sort. A few days will be an insufficient lesson, and a few months would be worse than death— madness or idiotism. It is a fashionable Sunday excursion with a certain class of idlers in New York, to visit this prison in the steam boat. It is like going to look at their lodgings before they are finished. Some of them will get there if they dont mind. After all, we think those philanthropists are in the right who are for abolishing the criminal code entirely, and relying on the improved spirit of the age and the progress of moral feeling.

Three or four miles east of Sing Sing, is the CHAPPAQUA SPRING, which at one time came very nigh getting the better of Ballston, Saratoga and Harrowgate, for it is a fact well authenticated that one or two persons of good fashion came very near to be cured of that incurable disease called "I dont know what," by drinking these waters. Upon the strength of this, some "public spirited individuals" erected a great hotel for the public accommodation. We wish we knew their names, as we look upon every man who builds a tavern, as a public benefactor, upon the authority of the famous prize poet, heretofore quoted, who says—

> "Thrice happy land! to glorious fates a prey,
> Where taverns multiply, and cots decay!
> And happy they, the happiest of their kind,
> Who ease and freedom in a tavern find!
> No household cares molest the chosen man
> Who at the tavern tosses off his can,
> Who far from all the irksome cares of life,
> And most of all that care of cares, a wife,
> Lives free and easy, all the livelong year,
> And dies without the tribute of a tear,
> Save from some Boniface's bloodshot eye,
> Who grieves that such a liberal soul should die,
> And on that 'Canongate of Chronicles,' the door,
> Leave such a long unliquidated score."

POINT NO POINT.

Directly opposite to Sing Sing is Point no Point, a singular range of highlands of the trap formation, which are extremely apt to deceive the traveller who dont "understand trap" as the geologists say. In sailing along up the river, a point of land appears at all times, (except in a dense fog or a dark night, when we advise the reader not to look out for it,) projecting far into the river. On arriving opposite, it seems to recede, and to appear again a little beyond. Some travellers compare this Point no Point, to a great metaphysician, who reasons through a whole quarto, without coming to a conclusion. Others liken it to the great Dr.——— who plays round his subject like children round a bonfire, but never ventures too near, lest he should catch it, and belike burn his fingers. Others again approximate it, to the speech of a member of congress, which always seems coming to the point, but never arrives at it. The happiest similitude

25

however in our opinion, was that of a young lady, who compared a dangling dandy admirer of hers, to Point no Point, "Because," said she, "he is always pointing to his game, but never makes a dead point."

If the traveller should happen to go ashore here, by following the road from Slaughter's Landing, up the mountain about half a mile, he will come suddenly upon a beautiful sheet of pure water nine miles in circumference, called Snedecker's Lake, a name abhorred of Poetry and the Nine. The southern extremity is bounded by a steep pine clad mountain, which dashes headlong down almost perpendicularly into the bosom of the lake, while all the other portions of its graceful circle are rich in cultivated rural beauties. The Brothers of the Angle may here find pleasant sport, and peradventure catch a pike, the noblest of all fishes, because he has the noblest appetite. Alas!—how is the pride of human reason, mortified at the thought, that a pike not one tenth the bulk of a common sized man, can eat as much as half a score of the most illustrious gourmands!— and that too without dyspepsia, or apoplexy. Let not man boast any longer of his being the lord of the creation. Would we were a pike and lord of Snedecker's Lake, for as the great prize poet sings in a fit of hungry inspiration—

"I sing the Pike! not him of lesser fame,
At Little York, who gained a deathless name,
And died a martyr to his country's weal,
Instead of dying of a glorious meal—
But thee, O Pike! lord of the finny crew,
King of the waters, and of eating too.
Imperial glutton, that for tribute takes
The glittering small fry of a hundred lakes;
No surfeits on thy ample feeding wait,
No apoplexy shortens thy long date,
The patriarch of eating, thou dost shine;
A century of gluttony is thine.
Sure the old tale of transmigration's true,
The soul of Heliogababus dwells in you!"

STONY POINT.

This is a rough picturesque point pushing boldly out into the river, directly opposite to Verplanck's Point on the east side. The remains of a redoubt are still to be seen on its brow, and here was the scene of one of the boldest exploits of one of the boldest spirits of a revolution fruitful in both. The fort was carried at midnight at the point of the bayonet, by a party of Americans under General Anthony Wayne, the fire eater of his day. In order to judge of this exploit, it is necessary to examine the place and see the extreme difficulty of its approach. The last exploit of "Mad Anthony," as he was christened by his admiring soldiers who would follow him any where, was the decisive defeat of the indians at the battle of Miami in 1794, which gave rest to a long harassed and extensive frontier, and led to the treaty of Greenville, by which the United States acquired an immense accession of territory. He died at Presque Isle on Lake Erie, in the fifty-second year of his age. It is believed that Pennsylvania yet owes him a monument.

There is a light house erected here on the summit of the point. We have heard peoplé laugh at it as entirely useless, but doubtless they did not know what they were talking about. Light houses are of two kinds, the useful and the ornamental. The first are to guide mariners, the others to accommodate the lovers of the picturesque. The light house at Stony Point is of this latter description. It is a fine object either in approaching or leaving the Highlands, and foul befall the carping Smelfungus, who does not thank the public spirited gentleman, (whoever he was,) to whom we of the picturesque order are indebted for the contemplation of this beautiful superfluity. Half the human race, (we mean no disparagement to the lasses we adore,) and indeed half the world, is only made to look at, and why not a light house? The objections are untenable, for if a light house be of no other use, it affords a snug place for some lazy philosopher to loll out the rest of his life on the feather bed of a snug sinecure.

We now approach the Highlands, and advise the reader to shut himself up in the cabin and peruse the following pages attentively, as it is our intention to give a sketch of this fine scenery, so infinitely superior to the reality, that Nature will not be able to recognise herself in our picture.

Genius of the picturesque sublime, or the sublime picturesque, inspire us! Thou that didst animate the soul of John Bull, insomuch that if report says true, he did once get up from dinner, before it was half discussed, to admire the sublime projection of Antony's Nose. Thou that erewhile didst allure a first rate belle and beauty from adjusting her curls at the looking glass, to gaze for more than half a minute, at beauties almost equal to her own. Thou that dost sometimes actually inspirit that last best work of the ninth part of a man—the dandy— actually to yawn with delight at the Crow's Nest, and pull up his breeches at sight of Fort Putnam. Thou genius of travellers, and tutelary goddess of bookmaking, grant us a pen of fire, ink of lightning, and words of thunder, to do justice to the mighty theme!

First comes the gigantic Donderbarrack—all mountains are called gigantic, because the ancient race of giants was turned into mountains, which accounts for the race being extinct—first comes the mighty Donderbarrack, president of hills—we allow of no king mountains in our book—whose head is hid in the clouds, whenever the clouds come down low enough; at whose foot dwells in all the feudal majesty (only a great deal better) of a Rhoderick Dhu, the famous highland chieftain, Caldwell, lord of Donderbarrack, and all the little hills that grow out of his ample sides like warts on a giant's nose. To this mighty chieftain, all the steam boats do homage, by ringing of bells, stopping their machinery, and sending their boats ashore to carry him the customary tribute, to wit, store of visitors, who it is his delight to entertain at his hospitable castle. This stately pile is of great antiquity; its history being lost in the dark ages of the last century, when the indian prowled about these hills, and shot his deer, ere the rolling wave of the white man swept him away forever. Above—as the prize poet sings—

> "High on the cliffs the towering eagles soar—
> But hush my muse—for poetry's a bore."

Turning the base of Donderbarrack, the nose of all noses, Antony's Nose, gradually displays itself to the enraptured eye, which must be kept steadily fixed on these our glowing pages. Such a nose is not seen every day. Not the famous hero of Slawkemburgius, whose proboscis emulated the steeple of Strasburg, ever had such a nose to his face. Taliacotius himself never made such a nose in his life. It is worth while to go ten miles to hear it blow—you would mistake it for a trumpet. The most curious thing about it is, that it looks no more like a nose than my foot. But now we think of it, there is still something more curious connected with this nose. There is not a soul born within five miles of it, but has a nose of most jolly dimensions—not quite as large as the mountain, but pretty well. Nay, what is still more remarkable, more than one person has recovered his nose, by regularly blowing the place where it ought to be, with a white pocket handkerchief, three times a day, at the foot of the mountain, in honour of St. Antony. In memory of these miraculous restorations, it is the custom for the passengers in steam boats, to salute it in passing with a universal blow of the nose: after which, they shake their kerchiefs at it, and put them carefully in their pockets. No young lady ever climbs to the top of this stately nose, without affixing her white cambric handkerchief to a stick, placing it upright in the ground, and leaving it waving there, in hopes that all her posterity may be blessed with goodly noses.

Immediately on passing the Nose the Sugar Loaf appears; keep your eye on the book for your life—you will be changed to a loaf of sugar if you dont. This has happened to several of the followers of Lot's wife, who thereby became even sweeter than they were before. Remember poor Eurydice, whose fate was sung in burlesque by an infamous outcast bachelor, who it is said was afterwards punished, by marrying a shrew who made him mix the mustard every day for dinner.

WEST POINT.

"If the traveller," observes Alderman Janson, "intends stoppping here to visit the military academy, and its admirable superintendent, I advise him to make his will, before he ventures into the landing boat. That more people have not been drowned, in this adventurous experiment, can only be accounted for on the supposition that miracles are growing to be but every day matters. There is I believe a law regulating the mode of landing passengers from steam boats, but it is a singular fact that laws will not execute themselves notwithstanding all the wisdom of the legislature. Not that I mean to find fault with the precipitation with which people and luggage are tumbled together into the boat, and foisted ashore at the rate of fifteen miles an hour. At least five minutes is saved in this way in the passage to Albany, and so much added to the delights of the tourist, who is thereby enabled to spend five minutes more at the springs. Who would not risk a little drowning, and a little scalding for such an object? Certainly the most precious of all commodities is time, especially to people who dont know what to do with it, except indeed it be money to a miser who never spends any. It goes to my heart to find fault with any thing in this best of all possible worlds, where the march of mind is swifter than a race horse or a steam boat, and goes hand in hand with the progress of public improvement, like Darby and Joan, or Jack and Jill, blessing this fortunate generation, and preparing the way for a world of steam engines, spinning jennies, and machinery: insomuch that there would be no use at all for such an animal as man in this world any more, if steam engines and spinning jennies would only make themselves. But the reader will I trust excuse me this once, for venturing to hint with a modesty that belongs to my nature, that all this hurry—this racing—this tumbling of men, women, children and baggage into a boat, helter skelter—and sending them ashore at the risk of their lives—might possibly be excusable if it were done for the public accommodation. But the fact is not so. It is nothing but the struggle of interested rivalry; the effort to run down a rival boat, and get all, instead of sharing with others. The public accommodation requires that boats should go at different times of the day, yet they prefer starting at the same hour; nay, the same moment; eager to sweep off the passengers along the river, and risking the lives of people at West Point, that they may take up the passengers at Newburgh. The truth is, in point of ease and comfort, convenience and safety, the public is not now half so well off, as during the existence of what the said public was persuaded to call a great grievance—the exclusive right of Mr. Fulton.

"There is a most comfortable hotel at West Point, kept by Mr. Cozens, a most obliging and good humoured man, to whom we commend all our readers, with an assurance that they need not fear being *cozened* by him. Nothing can be more interesting than the situation of West Point, the grand object to which it is devoted, and the magnificent views it affords in all directions. If there be any inspiration in the sublime productions of nature, or if the mind as some believe, receives an impulse or direction from local situation, there is not perhaps in the world, a spot more favourable to the production of a race of heroes, and men of science. Secluded from the effeminate, or vitious allurements of cities, both mind and body, preserve a vigorous strength and freshness, eminently favourable to the development of each without enfeebling either. Manly studies and manly exercise go hand in hand, and manly sentiments are the natural consequence. Their bodies are invigorated by military exercise and habits, while their intellects are strengthened, expanded and purified by the acquirement of those high branches of science, those graces of literature, and those elegant accomplishments, which when all combined constitute the complete man. No one whose mind is susceptible of noble emotions, can see these fine young fellows going through their exercises on the plain of West Point, to the sound of the bugle repeated by a dozen echoes of the mountains, while all the magnificence of nature combines to add beauty and dignity to the scene and the occasion, without feeling his bosom swell and glow with patriotic pride.

"If these young men require an example to warn or to stimulate, they will find it in the universal execration heaped upon the name, and the memory of Benedict Arnold, contrasted with the reverential affection, that will forever descend to the latest posterity as an heirloom, with which every American pronounces the name of Washington. It was at West Point that Arnold betrayed his country and it was on the hills opposite West Point, that Washington, wintered with his army, during the most gloomy period of our revolution, rendered still more gloomy by the treason of Arnold, so happily frustrated by the virtue of the American yeomanry. The remains of the huts are still to be seen on Redoubt Hill, and its vicinity, and there is a fine spring on the banks of a brook, nigh by, to this day called Washington's, from being the spring whence the water was procured for his drinking. It issues from the side of a bank, closely embowered with trees and is excessively cold. The old people in the vicinity who generally live a hundred years, still cherish the tradition of its uses, and direct the attention of inquirers to it, with a feeling than which nothing can more affectingly indicate the depth of that devotion implanted in the heart of America for her good father. Close to the spring are two of the prettiest little cascades to be found any where. Indeed the whole neighbourhood abounds in beautiful views and romantic associations, worthy the pen or pencil, and it is worth while to cross over in a boat from West Point to spend a morning here in rambling, during which the West Point foundry, the most complete establishment of its kind in the new world, may be visited."

On the opposite side of the river from West Point, and about two miles distant, lies COLD SPRING, a pleasant thriving little village, from whence, to Fishkill, is perhaps the pleasantest ride in the whole country. A road has been made along the foot of the mountains. On one hand it is washed by the river—on the other overhung by Bull and Breakneck Hills, whose bases have been blown up in many places to afford room for it to pass. The prospects on every hand are charming, and at the turning at the base of Breakneck Hill, there opens to the north and northwest a view, which when seen will not soon be forgotten.

Nearly opposite Cold Spring, at the foot of two mountains inaccessible except from the river, lies the CITY OF FAITH—a city by brevet; founded by an enterprising person, with the intention of cutting out Washington, and making it the capital of the United States—and indeed of the new world. He has satisfied himself that the spot thus aptly selected, is the nearest possible point of navigation, to the great Northern Pacific, and contemplates a rail road, from thence to the mouth of Columbia River. This must necessarily concentrate the intercourse on this fortunate spot. After which his intention is to dig down the Crow's Nest and Butter Hill, or decompose the rocks with vinegar, in order that travellers may get at his emporium, by land, without breaking their necks. He has already six inhabitants to begin with, and wants nothing to the completion of this great project, but a bank—a subscription of half a dozen millions from the government—a loan of "the credit of the state," for about as much, and a little more faith in the people. We think the prospect quite cheering, and would rejoice in the prospective glories of the City of Faith, were it not for the apprehension that it will prove fatal to the Ohio and Chesapeake Canal, and swallow up the Mamakating and Lacawaxan. This business of founding cities in America is considered a mere trifle. They make a great noise about Romulus the founder of Rome, and Peter the founder of St. Petersburg! We knew a man who had founded twelve great cities, some of which like Rome are already in ruins, and yet he never valued himself on that account.

As you emerge from the Highlands, a noble vista expands itself gradually to the view. The little towns of NEW CORNWALL, NEW WINDSOR, and NEWBURGH, are seen in succession along the west bank of the river, which here as if rejoicing at its freedom from the mountain barrier expands itself into a wide bay, with Fishkill and Matteawan on the east, and the three little towns on the west, the picturesque shores of which rise gradually into highlands, bounded in the distance to the northwest by the blue summits of the Kaatskill Mountains. Into this bay on the east enters Fishkill Creek, a fine stream which waters some of the richest and most beautiful vallies of Dutchess County. Approaching the Hudson, it exhibits several picturesque little cascades, which have lately been spoiled by dams and manufactories, those atrocious enemies to all picturesque beauty, as the prize poet exclaims in a fine burst of enthusiasm—poetical enthusiasm, consisting in swearing roundly.

> "Mill dams be d——d, and all his race accurs'd,
> Who d——d a stream by damming it the first!"

On the west and nearly opposite, enters Murderer's Creek, which after winding its way through the delightful vale of Canterbury, as yet unvisited and undescribed, by tourist or traveller, tumbles over a villanous mill dam into the river. If the traveller has a mind for a beautiful ride in returning from the springs, let him land at Newburgh, and follow the turnpike road through the village of

3 1

Canterbury, on to the *Clove,* a pass of the great range of mountains, through which the Ramapo plunges its way, among the rocks. The ride through this pass is highly interesting, and the spot where the Ramapo emerges from the southern side of the mountains and joining the Mauwy, courses its way through a narrow vale of exquisite beauty, till it is lost in the Pompton Plains in the river of that name, is highly worthy of attention. The roads are as good as usual, but the accommodations are not the best in the world, and those who love good eating and good beds, better than nature's beauties, (among which we profess ourselves,) may go some other way. Those who choose this route by way of variety, must by no means forget the good house of Mynheer Roome at Pompton village, famed in song, where they will meet with mortal store of good things; sweetmeats of divers sorts, cakes innumerable and unutterable, and hear the Dutch language spoken in all its original purity, with the true Florentine accent.

But let the traveller beware of talking to him about turnpikes, rail ways or canals, all which he abhorreth. In particular avoid the subject of the MORRIS CANAL, as the very name of which the Mynheer's pipe will be seen to pour forth increasing volumes of angry smoke, and like another Vesuvius, he will disgorge whole torrents of red hot Dutch lava. In truth Mynheer Roome has an utter contempt for modern improvements, and we dont know but he is half right— "Dey always cost more dan dey come to," he says, and those who contemplate the sober primitive independence of the good Mynheer, and see his fat cattle, his fat negroes, and his fat self, encompassed by rich meadows and smiling fields, all unaided by the magic of modern improvements, will be apt to think with Mynheer "dat one half dese tings dey call improvements," add little if any, to human happiness, or domestic independence.

Within a couple of hundred yards of Mynheer Roome's door, the Pompton, Ramapo and Ringwood, three little rivers, in whose very bottoms you can see your face unite their waters, gathered from the hills to the north and west, and assuming the name of the first, wind through the extensive plain in many playful meanders, almost out of character for Dutch rivers, till they finally disappear, through a break in the hills towards the south. From Pompton there is a good road to Hoboken, by diverging a little from which, the traveller may visit the falls of Passaic, which were once the pride of nature, who has lately resigned them to her rival art and almost disowns them now. But it is high time to return to Murderer's Creek and Canterbury Vale, which hath been sung by the prize poet so often quoted, in the following strains, which partake of the true mystical metaphysical sublime.

"As I was going to Canterbury,
I met twelve hay cocks in a fury,
When as I gaz'd a hieroglyphic bat
Skimm'd o'er the zenith in a slip shod hat."

From which the intelligent traveller will derive as clear an idea of the singular charms of this vale, as from most descriptions in prose or verse.

The name of Murderer's Creek is said to be derived from the following incidents.

Little more than a century ago, the beautiful region watered by this stream, was possessed by a small tribe of indians, which has long since become extinct or been incorporated with some other savage nation of the west. Three or four hundred yards from where the stream discharges itself into the Hudson, a white family of the name of Stacey, had established itself, in a log house, by tacit permission of the tribe, to whom Stacey had made himself useful by his skill in a variety of little arts highly estimated by the savages. In particular a friendship subsisted between him and an old indian called Naoman, who often came to his house and partook of his hospitality. The indians never forgive injuries or forget benefits. The family consisted of Stacey, his wife, and two children, a boy and girl, the former five, the latter three years old.

One day Naoman, came to Stacey's log hut, in his absence, lighted his pipe and sat down. He looked very serious, sometimes sighed deeply, but said not a word. Stacey's wife asked him what was the matter, and if he was sick. He shook his head, sighed, but said nothing, and soon went away. The next day he came again, and behaved in the same manner. Stacey's wife began to think strange of this, and related it to her husband, who advised her to urge the old man to an explanation the next time he came. Accordingly when he repeated his visit the day after, she was more importunate than usual. At last the old indian said, "I am a red man, and the pale faces are our enemies—why should I speak?" But my husband and I are your friends: you have eaten salt with us a thousand times, and my children have sat on your knee as often. If you have any thing on your mind tell it me. "It will cost me my life if it is known, and the white-faced women are not good at keeping secrets," replied Naoman. Try me, and see. "Will you swear by your Great Spirit, you will tell none but your husband?" I have none else to tell. "But will you swear?" I do swear by our Great Spirit, I will tell none but my husband. "Not if my tribe should kill you for not telling?" Not if your tribe should kill me for not telling.

Naoman then proceeded to tell her that, owing to some encroachments of the white people below the mountains, his tribe had become irritated, and were resolved that night to massacre all the white settlers within their reach. That she must send for her husband, inform him of the danger, and as secretly and speedily as possible take their canoe, and paddle with all haste over the river to Fishkill for safety. "Be quick, and do nothing that may excite suspicion," said Naoman as he departed. The good wife sought her husband, who was down on the river fishing, told him the story, and as no time was to be lost, they proceeded to their boat, which was unluckily filled with water. It took some time to clear it out, and meanwhile Stacey recollected his gun which had been left behind. He

33

proceeded to the house and returned with it. All this took up considerable time, and precious time it proved to this poor family.

The daily visits of old Naoman, and his more than ordinary gravity, had excited suspicion in some of the tribe, who had accordingly paid particular attention to the movements of Stacey. One of the young indians who had been kept on the watch, seeing the whole family about to take their boat, ran to the little indian village, about a mile off, and gave the alarm. Five indians collected, ran down to the river side where their canoes were moored, jumped in, and paddled after Stacey, who by this time had got some distance out into the stream. They gained on him so fast, that twice he dropt his paddle and took up his gun. But his wife prevented his shooting, by telling him, that if he fired, and they were afterwards overtaken, they would meet no mercy from the indians. He accordingly refrained, and plied his paddle, till sweat rolled in big drops down his forehead. All would not do; they were overtaken within a hundred yards of the shore, and carried back with shouts of yelling triumph.

When they got ashore, the indians set fire to Stacey's house, and dragged himself, his wife and children, to their village. Here the principal old men, and Naoman among the rest, assembled to deliberate on the affair. The chief among them, stated that some one of the tribe had undoubtedly been guilty of treason, in apprising Stacey the white man of the designs of the tribe, whereby they took the alarm, and had well nigh escaped. He proposed to examine the prisoners, as to who gave the information. The old men assented to this; and Naoman among the rest. Stacey was first interrogated by one of the old men, who spoke English, and interpreted to the others. Stacey refused to betray his informant. His wife was then questioned, while at the same moment, two indians stood threatening the two children with tomahawks in case she did not confess. She attempted to evade the truth, by declaring that she had a dream the night before which had alarmed her, and that she had persuaded her husband to fly. "The Great Spirit never deigns to talk in dreams to a white face," said the old indian: "Woman, thou hast two tongues and two faces. Speak the truth, or thy children shall surely die." The little boy and girl were then brought close to her, and the two savages stood over them, ready to execute their bloody orders.

"Wilt thou name," said the old indian, "the red man who betrayed his tribe. I will ask thee three times." The mother answered not. "Wilt thou name the traitor? This is the second time." The poor mother looked at her husband, and then at her children, and stole a glance at Naoman, who sat smoking his pipe with invincible gravity. She wrung her hands and wept; but remained silent. "Wilt thou name the traitor? 'tis the third and last time." The agony of the mother waxed more bitter; again she sought the eye of Naoman, but it was cold and motionless; a pause of a moment awaited her reply, and the next moment the tomahawks were raised over the heads of the children, who besought their mother not to let them be murdered.

"Stop," cried Naoman. All eyes were turned upon him. "Stop," repeated he, in a tone of authority. "White woman, thou hast kept thy word with me to the last moment. I am the traitor. I have eaten of the salt, warmed myself at the fire, shared the kindness of these Christian white people, and it was I that told them of their danger. I am a withered, leafless, branchless trunk; cut me down if you will. I am ready." A yell of indignation sounded on all sides. Naoman descended from the little bank where he sat, shrouded his face with his mantle of skins and submitted to his fate. He fell dead at the feet of the white woman by a blow of the tomahawk.

But the sacrifice of Naoman, and the firmness of the Christian white woman, did not suffice to save the lives of the other victims. They perished— how it is needless to say; and the memory of their fate has been preserved in the name of the pleasant stream on whose banks they lived and died, which to this day is called Murderer's Creek.

NEW CORNWALL, AND NEW WINDSOR.

It is bad policy to call places new. The name will do very well for a set out, but when they begin to assume an air of antiquity, it becomes quite unsuitable. It is too much the case with those who stand godfathers to towns in our country. They seem to think because we live in a new world, every thing must be christened accordingly. The most flagrant instance of this enormity is New York, which although ten times as large, and ten times as handsome as York in England, is destined by this infamous cognomen of "new," to play second to that old worn out town, which has nothing in it worth seeing except its great minster. The least people can do after condemning a town to be called *new,* is to paint their houses every now and then, that the place may do honour to its christening. But between ourselves, Monsieur Traveller, the whole thing is absurd. Some score of centuries hence, we shall have a dozen clutterheaded antiquaries, disputing whether New York and old York, were not one and the same city; and it is just as likely as not, that the latter will run away with all the glories of the queen of the new world. Why not call our cities by a name utterly new to human ears. Conecocheague, Amoonoosuck, Chabaquidick, Ompompanoosuck, or Kathtippakamuck; there would then be no danger of their being confounded with those of the old world, and they would stand by themselves in sesquipedalian dignity, till the end of time, or till people had not breath to utter their names.

"NEW CORNWALL," as Alderman Janson truly observes, "is assuredly not one of the largest towns on the river; but it might be so, and it is not its fault that it is not six times as large as Pekin, London, Paris or Constantinople, as it can be clearly proved that it might have extended half a dozen leagues towards any of the four quarters of the world without stumbling over any thing of consequence except a river and a mountain. If its illustrious founders (whose names are unknown) instead of confining their energies to building a few wooden houses, which they forgot to paint even with Spanish brown, had cut a canal to the Pacific Ocean, made a rail road to Passamaquoddy, and a tunnel under the Atlantic, and erected three hundred thousand handsome brick houses with folding doors, and marble mantel pieces, without doubt it might have been at this moment the greatest city in the known world. I know that a certain ignoramus of a critic denies all this, inasmuch as the river is in the way towards the east and therefore it cannot extend that way. But I suppose this blockhead never heard of turning the course of the Hudson into the channel of Fishkill Creek, and so at the same time improving the navigation of both, and affording ample space for the growth of the city by digging down Fishkill Mountains. Nay, we dare affirm he is totally ignorant of the mode of sucking a river. . . .

HUDSON.

"A very respectable town, or rather city," says Alderman Janson: "so called after the renowned Hendrick Hudson of blessed memory. It is opposite to Athens, and ought to have been noticed immediately after it. But if the traveller wishes particularly to view the city, he has only to mention his desire, and the steam boat will turn back with him, for they are very obliging. Hudson furnishes one of those examples of rapid growth so common and so peculiar to our country. It goes back no farther than 1786, and is said now to contain nearly 2000 inhabitants. But towns, like children, are very apt to grow more in the few first years, than all their lives after. But Hudson has a bank, which is a sort of wet nurse to these little towns, giving them too often a precocious growth, which is followed by a permanent debility. The town is beautifully situated, and the environs of the most picturesque and romantic description. There are several pretty country seats in the neighbourhood. Here ends, according to the law of nature, the ship navigation of the river; but by a law of the legislature, a company has been incorporated with a capital of 1,000,000 of dollars—how easy it is to coin money in this way!—to make a canal to New Baltimore; for what purpose, only legislative wisdom can explain. There was likewise an incorporated company, to build a mud machine for deepening the river. But the river is no deeper than it was, and the canal to New Baltimore is not made, probably because the million of dollars is not forthcoming. One may pay too dear for a canal as well as a whistle. That canals are far better than rivers, is not to be doubted; but as we get our rivers for nothing, and pay pretty dearly for our canals, I would beg leave to represent in behalf of the poor rivers, that they are entitled to some little consideration, if it is only on the score of coming as free gifts. Hudson is said to be very much infested with politicians, a race of men, who though they have never been classed among those who live by their own wits, and the little wit of their neighbours, certainly belong to the genus."

From hence to Albany the Hudson gradually decreases in magnitude, changing its character of a mighty river for that of a pleasant pastoral stream. The high banks gradually subside into rich flats, portentous of Dutchmen, who light on them as certainly as do the snipes and plovers. "Wisely despising," observes Alderman Janson, "the barren mountains which are only made to look at, they passed on up the river from Fort Amsterdam, till they arrived hereabouts, and here they pitched their tents. Their descendants still retain possession of the seats of their ancestors, though sorely beset by the march of the human mind, and the progress of public improvement on one hand, and on the other by interlopers from the modern Scythia, the cradle of the human race in the new world, Connecticut. These last, by their pestilent scholarship, and mischievous contrivances of patent ploughs, patent threshing machines, patent corn shellers, and patent churns, for the encouragement of domestic industry, have gone near to overset all the statutes of St. Nicholas. The honest burghers of Coeymans; Coxsackie and New Paltz, still hold out manfully; but alas! the women—the women are prone to backslidings, and hankering after novelties. A Dutch damsel cant, for her heart, resist a Connecticut schoolmaster with his rosy cheeks and store of scholarship; and even honest yffrow herself chuckles a little amatory Dutch at his approach; simpering mightily thereat and stroking down her apron. A goose betrayed—no I am wrong—a goose once saved the capitol of Rome; and it is to be feared a woman will finally betray the citadels of Coeymans, Coxsackie and New Păltz, to the schoolmasters of Connecticut, who circumvent them with outlandish scholarship. . . .

ALBANY.

Leaving Coxsackie, the traveller gradually approaches those rich little islands and *flats,* beloved by the honest Dutchmen of all parts of the world, and elsewhere, in the midst of which are seen the long comfortable brick mansions of the Cuylers, the Schuylers, the Van Rensselaers, and others of the patroons of ancient times. "I never see one of these," quoth Alderman Janson, "without picturing to myself the plentiful breakfasts, solid dinners, and manifold evening repasts, which have been and still are discussed in these comfortable old halls, guiltless of folding doors and marble mantel pieces, and all that modern trumpery which starves the kitchen to decorate the parlour, and robs the stranger of his hospitable welcome to bestow upon superfluous trumpery. I never think of the picture so delightfully drawn by Mrs Grant, in the 'Memoirs of an American Lady,' of the noble patriarchal state of 'Uncle Schuyler' and his amiable wife, without contrasting it with the empty, vapid, mean, and selfish pageantry of the present time, which satiates itself with the paltry vanity of display, and stoops to all the dirty drudgery of brokerage and speculation, to gather wealth, only to

37

excite the gaping wonder, or secret envy of vulgar rivals. By St. Nicholas, the patron of good fellows, but the march of the human intellect is sometimes like a crab, backwards!"

"The city of Albany," continues the worthy alderman, "was founded, not by Mars, Neptune, Minerva, or Vulcan, nor any of the wandering vagabond gods of ancient times. Neither does it owe its origin to a runaway hero like Æneas, nor a runaway debtor, like a place that shall be nameless. Its first settlers were a race of portly burghers from old Holland, who sailing up the river in search of a resting place, and observing how the rich flats invited them as it were to their fat and fruitful bowers, landed thereabouts, lighted their pipes, and began to build their tabernacles without saying one word. Tradition also imports, that they were somewhat incited to this, by seeing divers large and stately sturgeons jumping up out of the river as they are wont to do, most incontinently in these parts. These sturgeons are, when properly disguised by cookery, so that you cannot tell what they are, most savoury and excellent food, although there is no truth in the story hatched by the pestilent descendants of Philo Longfellow, that the flesh of the sturgeon is called Albany beef, and that it is sometimes served up at Rockwell's Cruttenden's, and other favourite resorts of tourists, as veal cutlets. Out upon such slanders! By St. Nicholas, the Longfellows lie most immoderately. The worthy burghers of Albany never deceived a Christian in their lives. As their old proverb says:

> " 'Twould make an honest Dutchman laugh,
> To say a sturgeon is a calf.'

"The indians according to the learned Knickerbocker, perceiving that the new comers, were like themselves great smokers, took a vast liking to them, and sat down and smoked with them, without saying a word, and presently a cloud of smoke overspread the land, like the haze of the indian summer. An old chief at length looked at Mynheer Van Wezel, the leader of the party, and gave a significant grunt. Mynheer Van Wezel looked at the old indian and gave another grunt equally significant. Thus they came to a mutual good understanding, and a treaty was concluded without exchanging a single word, or any other ceremony than a good sociable smoking party. Some of the descendants of Philo Longfellow, insinuate that Mynheer Van Wezel took an opportunity of presenting his pistol, well charged with Schiedam, to the old chief and his followers, and that it operated marvellously in bringing about the treaty. But there is not a word of truth in the story. This good understanding was produced by the magic virtues of silence and tobacco. This example shows how easy it is to be good friends, if people will only hold their tongues; and it moreover forever rescues the excellent practice of smoking from the dull jests of effeminate puppies, who affect to call it

38

vulgar. If modern negotiators would only sit down and smoke a sociable pipe together every day for five or six months, my life upon it there would be less ink shed, and blood shed too in this world. By St. Nicholas! the saint of smokers, there is nothing comparable to the pipe, for soothing anger, softening down irritation, solacing disappointment, and disposing the mind to balmy contemplation, poetical flights, and lofty soarings of the fancy; insomuch that any young bard, who will tie his shirt with a black ribbon and take to smoking and drinking gin and water like my Lord Byron, will in a short time write equal to his lordship, allowing for accidents."

"Thus," continues the alderman, "was the city of Albany founded, and originally called *All-bonny,* as the Dutch people still pronounce it, from the bonny river, the bonny woods, bonny pastures, and bonny landscapes by which it was environed. But blessed St. Nicholas! how is it sophisticated, since, by the posterity of Philo Longfellow, by politicians, tourists, lobby members, widening streets, building basins, and digging canals! The old Dutch church, where the followers of Mynheer Van Wezel, first offered up their simple orisons, is pulled down, and in its room a non-descript with two tin steeples erected, wherein they preach nothing but English. The young men who descend from the founders, are Dutchmen no more, and the damsels are nought. Not one in a hundred can read a Dutch Bible! In a little while the children of that roving Ishamelite, Philo Longfellow, will sweep them from their inheritance, and the land shall know them no more. The very houses have changed their position, and it is written, that an old mansion of Dutch brick which whilom projected its end in front, on Pearl Street, did one night incontinently turn its broadside to the street, as if resolved like its master to be in the fashion, and follow the march of public improvement." As the prize poet sings—corroborating the sentiments of the worthy alderman—

> "All things do change in this queer world;
> Which world is topsy-turvy hurl'd!
> Tadpoles to skipping bull frogs turn,
> And whales in lighted candles burn;
> The worm of yesterday, to day
> A butterfly is, rich and gay;
> The city belles all turn religious,
> And say their prayers in hats prodigious;
> St. Tammany becomes Clintonian,
> And Adams-men downright Jacksonian.
> Thus all our tastes are wild and fleeting,
> And most of all our taste in eating:
> I knew a man—or rather savage,
> Who went from ducks* to beef and cabbage!"

*Quere.—Canvass backs?—if so, there is no hope for him.

As Albany is a sort of depot, where the commodities of the fashionable world are warehoused as it were a night or two, for exportation to Saratoga, Niagara, Montreal, Quebec, and Boston, we shall here present to our readers a short system of rules and regulations, for detecting good inns, and generally for travelling with dignity and refinement. And first, as to smelling out a comfortable inn.

Never go where the stage drivers or steam boat men advise you.

Never go to a newly painted house. Trap for the green horns. A butcher's cart, with a good fat butcher, handing out turkeys, venison, ducks, marbled beef, celery, and cauliflowers, is the best sign for a public house.

Never go to a hotel, that has a fine gilt framed picture of itself hung up in the steam boat. Good wine needs no bush—a good hotel speaks for itself, and will be found out without a picture.

Never yield implicit obedience to a puff in the newspapers in praise of any hotel. It is a proof that the landlord has been over civil to one guest at the expense of all the others. No man is ever particularly pleased any where, or with any body, unless he has received more attention than he deserves. Perhaps you may be equally favoured, particularly if you hint that you mean to publish your travels. Even publicans sigh for immortality.

Never seem anxious to get lodgings at any particular place. The landlord will put you in the garret if you do, unless you come in your own carriage.

If you have no servant of your own, always hire one of the smartest dressed fellows of the steam boat to carry your baggage, and pass him off if possible till you are snugly housed at the hotel, as your own. Your accommodations will be the better for it. . . .

Before we leave Albany, we would caution the traveller against anticipating any thing extraordinary in the way of eating at this place. In vain may he sigh for canvass backs, or terrapins. A turtle sometimes finds its way there, and now and then a cargo of oysters; but in general there is little or nothing to detain the enlightened, travelled gourmand. The fare will do well enough for legislators and lobby members, but for a refined and cultivated palate, what can be expected from a people who are said to follow the antiquated maxim of the old song:

"I eat when I'm hungry, and drink when I'm dry,"—

a maxim in itself so utterly vulgar and detestable, that it could only have originated in the fancy of some half starved ballad monger, who considered the mere filling of his stomach, as the perfection of human happiness. Any fool can eat when he is hungry, and drink when he is dry, provided he can get any thing to eat or drink; this is the bliss of a quadruped, devoid of the reasoning faculty. But to enjoy the delight of eating without appetite, to be able to bring back the sated palate to a relish of some new dainty, to reanimate the exhausted energies of the

40

fainting stomach, and waken it to new exstacies of fruition; to get dyspepsias, and provoke apoplexies, is the privilege of man alone, whose reason has been refined, expanded, and perfected by travel and experience. The happiest man, in our opinion, we ever knew, was a favoured being who possessed the *furor* of eating in greater perfection than all the rest of his species. He would eat a whole turkey, a pair of canvass backs, and a quarter of mutton, at a sitting, and finish with a half bushel of peaches. He was indeed an example to his species; but he was too good for this world, and was maliciously taken off by an unlucky bone, at a turtle feast at Hoboken,where he excelled even himself, and died a blessed martyr. The ony consolation remaining to his friends, is that he was afterwards immortalized in the following lines of the famous prize poet, who happened to be at the feast which proved so disastrous.

> "Here lies a man whom flesh could ne'er withstand,
> But bone alas! did get the upper hand.
> Death in the shape of turtle, venison, fowl,
> Oft came and shook his scythe with ghastly scowl,
> But hero like he d——d him for a bore,
> And cried undaunted 'waiter bring us more!'
> At last death came in likeness of a bone,
> And the pot-valiant champion was o'erthrown.
> If death one single ounce of flesh had had,
> 'Twould have been all over with him there, egad;
> A broth of him, our hungry friend had made
> And turtle-clubs been never more dismay'd,
> By the gaunt imp of chaos and old night,
> Who spoils full many a glorious appetite."

"At Albany," as Alderman Janson observes, "ends the proper sloop navigation of the Hudson. It is true they do manage to get them up as far as Troy, and Lansingburgh, and even Waterford. But nature never intended they should go farther than Albany. It was in full confidence of this that the first colony pitched upon Albany, as the site of a great city which was destined in a happy hour, to become the capital of the state. Unfortunate adventurers! they never dreamed of the march of the human mind, and the progress of public improvements; or of companies incorporated for the performance of miracles. They never surmised the possibility of a great river like the Hudson, the masterpiece of the Creator of the universe, being improved by an act of the legislature; nor did it ever enter into their matter of fact brains that the posterity of Philo Longfellow would found a city as it were right over their heads at Troy, and thus interrupt the rafts coming down the river to Albany. What a pity it is people cannot see a little farther into millstones! what glorious speculations we should all make, except that every body being equally enlightened as to the future, there would be no speculation at all, which would be a terrible thing for those useful people, who having no money themselves, disinterestedly go about manufacturing excellent projects, to drain the pockets of those who have. Money is in truth like an eel, it is easy to catch it, but to hold it fast afterwards, is rather a difficult matter. And here I am reminded of the fate of an honest codger of my acquaintance, who had become rich by a long course of industry and economy, and at the age of forty-five set himself down in a smart growing town, not a hundred miles, from I forget where, to enjoy the life of a gentleman. . . .

NORTH OF ALBANY.

We would advise the fashionable tourist, and to none other is this work addressed, who of course is hurrying directly to the springs, to go by the way of the Cohoes, Waterford, and as far as possible keep the banks of the Hudson. "Leaving Albany," says Alderman Janson, "you come upon those rich flats, that present a soft arcadian scene, beautified with all the products of nature, and industrious man. The meadows are peopled with luxurious Dutch cattle, basking in the shade of spreading elms that dot the landscape here and there. The fields of golden wheat just ripening in the sunny month of July, the dark green leaves of the blessed corn, flaunting like ribbons about the brow of youth—bounded on one side by the swelling, rolling hills, on the other by the glassy river, all present together a scene worthy of the golden age, and of the simple virtuous patriarchs who yet inhabit there, smoking their pipes, and talking Dutch, in spite of the changes of fashion, the vagaries of inflated vanity, which instill into the hearts of the foolish, that alteration is improvement, and that one generation of man is wiser than another. It is thus that youth laughs at age, and that the forward urchin, who knows nothing of the world but its vices and follies, thinks himself wiser, than his grandfather of fourscore."

"One day the Caliph Almansor, one of the vainest of the Arabian monarchs, was conversing familiarly with the famous poet Fazelli, with whom he delighted to talk, when retired from the cares of his empire. 'Thou thinkest,' said he to Fazelli, 'that I am not wiser than my father. Why is it so; doth not every succeeding generation add to the wisdom of that which preceded it?' 'Dost thou think thyself wiser, than the prophet?' answered the poet, bowing his head reverentially. 'Assuredly not,' answered the caliph. 'Dost thou think thyself wiser than Solomon?' asked the poet, bowing still lower. 'Assuredly not,' again answered the caliph. 'Dost thou think thyself wiser than Moses who communed with Allah himself?' a third time asked the poet bowing to the ground. Almansor was for a moment very thoughtful and held down his head. 'Assuredly not,' replied he at length, 'I were foolishly presumptuous to think so.'

"'Then how,' resumed Fazelli, 'canst thou prove that each succeeding generation is wiser than another that is past?' 'The aggregate of knowledge is certainly increased,' replied the caliph. 'True O my king,' replied Fazelli, 'but knowledge is not wisdom. Wisdom points out the road to happiness and virtue; knowledge, is only an acquaintance with a mass of facts, which are not necessarily connected, with either wisdom, virtue or happiness, the only objects worthy the pursuit of a wise man. The knowledge of things has certainly increased, but O king! remember that wisdom is always the same; as much so as the great power by whom it is dispensed. Thou mayest perhaps know more of the moon, the stars, the earth, and the seas, than thy father; but of thy organization, thy soul, thy passions, appetites, the power to direct them, and the Being who bestowed them upon thee, thou knowest no more than the meanest of thy father's slaves.' 'Thou sayest true,' replied the Caliph bowing his head reverently—'Allah teach me humility.' 'Great king,' said Fazelli, 'lament not thine ignorance. Every thing we cannot comprehend, furnishes proof of the existence of a Being wiser than ourselves.'"

Infandum regina—we despise Latin scraps ever since the publication of the dictionary of quotations. But who has not heard of Troy—not that famous city which Jacob Bryant maintained never had an existence, although it has made more noise in the world, than the greatest matter of fact cities extant—not the city which thousands of travellers have gone to see, and come away, without seeing—not the city which sustained a ten years siege, and was at last taken by a wooden horse; no verily, but the indubitable city of Troy, on the banks of the Hudson, which is worth three thousand beggarly Scamanders, and six thousand Hellesponts. We are aware that this excellent town, which contains at this moment Helens enough to set the whole world on fire, is pronounced by that great geographer and traveller, Lieutenant De Roos, to be in New England. Perish the thought! New England never had such a town to its back; so full of enterprizing people, continually plotting against the repose of dame nature. Alexander once seriously contemplated cutting Mount Athos into a statue; King Stephanus Bombastes, lost his wits with the idea of making Bohemia a maritime power; whence it was, that Corporal Trim very properly called him, 'This unfortunate king of Bohemia;' and a great advocate of public improvements, is now so unluckily mad on the subject, that he fancies himself a great chip, floating all weathers on the great northern canal. But all these are nothing to the Trojans, who it is said seriously contemplate a canal, parallel with the Hudson, from Troy to New York, if they can only get the legislature to pass an act against its freezing. Alas! poor river gods! what will become of them, as sings the famous prize poet, whom we hereby solemnly affirm, in our opinion, deserves to have his whiskers curled on the very pinnacle of Parnassus:

> "Noah be hang'd, and all his race accurst,
> Who in sea brine did pickle timber first!"

Meaning to say, that your salt water rivers are no longer to be tolerated, and ought to be forthwith legislated out of their waters as soon as possible. It is a great thing to know what poets mean now a days. They are the true "children of mist." But to continue our quotation:

> "O Trojan Greeks! who dwell at Ida's foot,
> Pull up this crying evil by the root;
> Rouse in the mighty majesty of mind,
> Pull up your mighty breeches tight behind,
> Then stretch the red right arm from shore to shore,
> And swear that rivers shall endure no more!"

"It is almost worth while," says Alderman Janson, "to sacrifice a few hours of the delights of the springs, to ascend Mount Ida, and see the romantic little cascade, a capital place for manufactories. In the opinion of some people, this is all that water falls are good for now a days. I would describe it, but for fear of drawing the attention of some prowling villain, who would perhaps come and build a cotton mill, and set all the pretty little rosy cheeked Helens of Troy tending spinning jennies, from sunrise to sunset, and long after, at a shilling a day, instead of leaving them to the enjoyment of the few hours of rest and careless hilarity which God in his wisdom hath appropriated to the miserable pack horses of this age of improvements. The domestic industry of females, is at home, by the fireside, in the society of their families, surrounded and protected by their household gods; not in woollen and cotton mills, herded together by hundreds, and toiling without intermission at the everlasting spinning jenney, without leisure to cultivate the domestic virtues, or opportunity for mental improvement. Of all the blockheads this side of the moon, in my opinion the farmers of these United States are the greatest, considering the pains taken by the members of congress and others to enlighten them. What in the name of all the thick sculled wiseacres past, present and to come, do they want of a 'woollen bill,' and what do the blockheads expect, from getting a penny or two more perhaps a pound for their wool, except to pay twice as much a yard for the cloth which is made out of it? Why dont they learn wisdom from their own sheep? . . .

TROY.

It will hardly be worth the traveller's while to visit Troy, except to partake of these good dinners; for after reading our book, he will know more about it than he could learn in ten visits, and being now so near the focus of all worldly delights, the springs, every moment becomes precious. Let him therefore keep on the west side of the river, crossing the Mohawk just below the Cohoes Falls, of which he will have a fine view from the bridge. Here he may stop fifteen minutes to look at the locks which connect the great canal with the Hudson, as a flight of steps connects the upper and lower stories of a house. "Without doubt," observes our old fashioned friend, Alderman Janson, whom we quote as the great apostle of antediluvian notions, "without doubt canals and locks are good things in moderation; but some how or other, I think I have a prejudice in favour of rivers, where they are to be had, and where they are not, people may as well make up their minds to do without them. In sober truth, it is my firm opinion, and I dont care whether any body agrees with me or not, that the great operation of a canal is, merely to concentrate on its line, and within its immediate influence, that wealth, population, and business, which, if let alone, would diffuse themselves naturally, equally, and beneficially through every vein and artery of the country. The benefits of a canal are confined to a certain distance, while all beyond is actually injured, although all pay their proportion of the expenses of its construction."

NORTH OF TROY.

The ride along the glorious Hudson, from the Mohawk to where the road turns westward to the springs, presents a perpetual succession of enchanting scenery. But by this time the inquisitive traveller is doubtless full of anticipations of the delights of these Castalian fountains, where a thousand nymphs more beautiful, or at least better dressed, than ever haunted enchanted stream, or chrystal fount of yore, quaff the inspiring beverage, till—till one is astonished what becomes of it! We will therefore delay him no longer. Perish the beauties of nature! What are they all when compared with those exquisite combinations of art and nature, which puzzle the understanding to decide which had the most to do in their production, the milliner or the goddess.

BALLSTON.

The first view of Ballston, generally has the same effect upon visiters, that matrimony is said to have upon young lovers. It is very extraordinary, but the first impression derived from the opening scene—we mean of Ballston—is that it is the ugliest, most uninviting spot in the universe. But this impression soon wears away, as he daily associates with beautiful damsels, the lustre of whose unfading, and ineffable charms, as it were, diffuses itself over the whole face of nature, converting the muddy swamp into a green meadow, the muddy brook into a chrystal stream meandering musically along, the sand hills into swelling, full bosomed protuberances of nature, and Sans Souci, into the palace of the fairy Feliciana, where, as every body knows, people were so happy they did not know what to do with themselves. We defy any man to be surrounded by beautiful women, even though it were in utter darkness, without having his imagination exclusively saturated with ideas of beauty, let the surrounding objects be what they may. For as the poet has it—

45

"The eye of beauty, like the glorious sun,
Casts a reflected lustre all around,
Making deformity itself partake
In its wide glowing splendours."

The localities of Ballston and Saratoga, are ennobled and illustrated, by this singular influence of beauty; otherwise, it must be confessed, if they depended only on their own intrinsic capabilities they would be no way extraordinary. Yet, to do them justice, they are not altogether desperate as to pretensions. If the marshes were only green meadows, dotted with stately elms; the sand hills richly cultivated with fields of golden wheat, and stately corn, waving its green ribbons to the breeze; the muddy brook a pastoral, purling river; the pine trees stately forests of oak and hickory, and their stumps were a little more picturesque, neither Ballston or Saratoga, need be ashamed to show themselves any day in the week, not excepting Sunday. As it is, candour itself must admit, that their beauties are altogether reflected from the ladies' eyes.

From *The Dutchman's Fireside**

CHAPTER I. RURAL SCENES AND RURAL MANNERS.

"Somewhere about the time of the old French war," there resided on the rich border that skirts the Hudson, not a hundred miles from the good city of Albany, a family of some distinction, which we shall call Vancour, consisting of three brothers whose names were Egbert Dennis, and Ariel, or Auriel as it was pronounced by the Dutch of that day. They were the sons of one of the earliest as well as most respectable of the emigrants from Holland, and honourably sustained the dignity of their ancestry, by sturdy integrity, liberal hospitality, and a generous public spirit.

On the death of the old patriarch, who departed this life almost a century old, according to the custom of those early times, the estate was amicably divided among his three sons; the portion of the eldest being alone distinguished from that of the others by comprising the old mansion-house. This was the sole compliment paid to the right of primogeniture, which in almost every other Christian country swallows up the inheritance of the younger offspring, and enables one man to wallow in overgrown luxury, at the expense of all the rest of his blood and name. This concession was rather a voluntary acknowledgment of the younger, than claimed by the elder brother. Neither at this early period of our infancy was it the general custom for people that had children to make their wills; and however singular it may seem, there were fewer lawsuits concerning the division of property among heirs, than there is now, when such particular care is taken in the

*James Kirke Paulding, *The Dutchman's Fireside—A Tale* (New York: J. & J. Harper, 1831).

Schuyler House at the Flats, also known as De Vlackte. Sketch by Benson J. Lossing from his *The Hudson from the Wilderness to the Sea* (Troy: Nims, 1866), p. 117.

In 1664 or 1670, Richard Van Rensselaer built this house on the Flats on the west bank of the Hudson River opposite Breaker Island south of Watervliet. This house was the prototype of the Vancour Mansion in Paulding's "The Dutchman's Fireside."

devising of estates, that it generally takes three or four courts, six or eight lawyers, and the like number of years to interpret the oracle. And how can it be otherwise, since I once heard a great pleader affirm, that there never were three words put together, in any language, that would not admit of three different interpretations. Here, however, there was no necessity for the interference of strangers; the children knew the wishes of their parents, and for the most part complied without a murmur.

The settlement of Mr. Vancour's affairs was actually made without consulting a lawyer; partly, perhaps, for the reason that there was no person of that description within less than one hundred and sixty miles, at New-York. According to Pliny, Rome subsisted five hundred years without a physician; which fact, however incredible it may appear, is equalled by the miracle of the city of Albany and the surrounding country having flourished for the best part of a century without the aid of a single lawyer. People can no more go to law without lawyers, than to war without arms; deprive them of both, and there would be no more occasion for peace societies. But to return.

Among the many good old fashions that prevailed in the days of ignorance and simplicity among our forefathers, was that of paying their debts themselves, instead of leaving it to their posterity. They knew little or nothing of the virtues of the *post obit*; nor, I believe, did it ever happen to occur to them, that it was a capital speculation to revel in luxuries and support a splendid establishment during life, leaving the penalty to be paid by their offspring. When old Mr. Vancour died, he paid the only debt he owed—the debt of nature.

In the division of the estate, Egbert, the elder brother, received the third part, which occupied the centre, with the old mansion-house; Dennis, that on the right, and Ariel, that on the left-hand. Each of these occupied the space which lay between a range of hills and the banks of the Hudson, on which they bordered about two miles equally. With a view to this arrangement, Mr. Vancour had erected, at different times, a comfortable mansion on either of the extremities of his estate; so that the two younger brothers were saved the expense of building.

At the period in which our history commences, the old gentleman had been dead many years, and Ariel, the youngest of the three brothers, was fast verging towards that stage of life in which a man runs imminent risk of being set down as an old bachelor by the young ladies. Dennis, the second brother, was a widower without issue; and Egbert was blessed with a most notable wife, the mother of an only daughter verging towards womanhood, and finishing her education at a boarding-school in New-York. The house occupied by Mr. Vancour was built when it was customary for men to anticipate the possibility of their descendants', some one of them at least, inheriting and dwelling in their old nestling places. It was a large four square mansion of two low stories, built of little yellow Dutch bricks, imported from Holland, as much from veneration for the "Faderland," as from a certain unconsciousness of the capacity to do any thing out of the ordinary way, that long beset and still in some degree besets the occupants of this western world. Right through the centre ran a wide and stately hall, wainscotted with oak; from the farther end of which a broad staircase rose in such a gentle ascent as to be almost as easy as a railway. This staircase was defended on the outerside by a row of chubby mahogany banisters, ranged so as almost to touch each other, and presenting in their plump exuberance fit models for the legs of all the gallant burghers of the country round. We know not whether it was in sympathy with these classical patterns, or from some other more occult influence, but certain it is, there hath not, since the fashion of them changed, been seen so goodly a set of legs, not even in the picture of the Declaration of our Independence, as was exhibited every Sabbath-day in summer-time, in woollen hose, at the little eight-square stone church of the Flats, at the time of which we are treating.

The furniture of the mansion corresponded with its Doric dignity and simplicity. There was nothing too fine for use, or which was not used whenever occasion required; although we are willing to confess, there was one hallowed room, dignified with the name of the spare room, which was difficult of access, and into which no one intruded except on very particular occasions. Here was the sacred deposite of ancestral heirlooms. Chairs with high and haughty backs and worked satin bottoms, from the old country; a Brussels carpet; two vast china jars, on either side of the chimney, nearly five feet high; and the treasure of all treasures, a Dutch cabinet, exactly such a one as is now to be seen at Hampton Court, left there by King William, so exuberantly and yet so tastefully and richly ornamented with brass hinges and a lock covering almost half its front, that when properly rubbed, as it was every day, it was dazzling to behold. The brass had a silvery whiteness, a delicate lustre, such as is never exhibited by the bastard imitation of these degenerate days. But the most valued and valuable part of the embellishments, were a number of fine pictures of the Flemish school, which the elder Mr. Vancour had brought with him from Holland, and which have since been lost by the burning of the mansion of one of his later descendants.

The house stood about a quarter of a mile from the river, in the midst of a rich meadow, dotted here and there with a vast primeval elm, standing like a wide umbrella, under which the lazy herds lay ruminating free from the midday sun. Four of these surrounded and almost hid the mansion, all but its front, and furnished retreats for a host of twittering birds. Within a hundred yards on one side ran a brook, which descended from the hills about a mile in the rear, and which in the course of ages had made a deep ravine, skirted on either side with a wilderness of various woods, and plants, and briers, and wild flowers, and vines of every sort, where was, in the genial season, a perpetual concert of nature's nevertiring and never-tired songsters. This copse was wide enough to shelter an invisible road, the only passage to and from the home; so that all around it was nothing but one fair carpet of delicious green, unbroken by road or pathway.

The river in front slept between its verdant banks, for its course was so slow, so quiet, so almost imperceptible, that it seemed to partake in that repose which it diffused all around. Besides the elms and sycamores which the rich alluvion fostered into majestic exuberance, its borders were fringed at intervals with silvery willows drinking its pure moisture, and other dwarfish fry, from whose branches hung grape vines and vines of various other names, forming canopies, through which the pattering shower could scarcely win its way. The stream was about a quarter of a mile wide, so that every rural sight and rural sound could be clearly distinguished from side to side; and at the extremity of the rich meadows on the opposite shore, there rose a bold precipice of gray-beard rocks, enamelled with light green mosses, and bearing on its summit a crown of towering pines of everlasting verdure.

There is certainly in the majesty of nature, its hoary rocks, its silent shadowy glens, foaming torrents, and lofty mountains, something that awakens the soul to high contemplation and rouses its slumbering energies. But there is in her gentler beauties, her rich and laughing meadows enamelled with flowers, and joyous with sprightly birds, her waving fields of grain, her noiseless glassy streams, a charm not less delightful and far more lasting than the high wrought enthusiasm of the other. Both have, without doubt, their influence on the human character. He who dwells in the rude regions of the mountain solitude will generally prefer dangerous and fatiguing enterprise to easy and wholesome labours. He would rather risk his safety for a meal, or go without it entirely, than earn it by the sweat of his brow in the cultivation of the earth. But the inhabitant of the rich plain, that pours from its generous bosom an ample reward for every hour of labour he bestows, is enamoured of security; he hates all changes but those of the revolving seasons; is seldom buffeted by extremes of passion, never elevated to enthusiasm, or depressed to despair. If let alone, his life will probably glide away as noiselessly, if not as pure, as the gentle stream that winds its way unheard through his lowland domain. It has been said a thousand times, that the inhabitants of mountains are more attached to their homes than those of the lowlands; but I doubt the truth of the observation. Take any man away from his home and his accustomed routine of life, and he will sigh to return to them, the native of the plain, as well as the sojourner among the hills. The former we doubt would be as wretched among the rocks and torrents, the wild beasts, and hunters equally wild, as the latter in the laborious quiet of the fruitful valleys.

However this may be, the brothers to whom the reader has just been introduced, partook in a great degree of the character of the scene of their birth and of their inheritance, but modified in some particulars by certain peculiarities in their situation. Peaceful as was the abode they inhabited, and the aspect of all around them, they were not always reposing in the lap of security. Within thirty or forty miles, in almost every direction, roamed various tribes of Indians, whose fierce, unsteady, and revengeful nature made their friendship as precarious as their enmity was terrible. True, they were now at peace, or rather they had begun to submit to their inevitable destiny; yet still their friendship could not be relied on, and they not unfrequently approached the neighbouring settlements in the dead of the night, where they committed the most horrible atrocities. This state of things contributed to keep up a warlike spirit and habits of dangerous enterprise, among the early settlers, and they partook of the opposite characters of husbandman and soldier, in a degree which has seldom been known in the inhabitants of the rest of the world. The Vancours and their neighbours all found it necessary to mingle the arts of peace and war together; all had their arms at hand, and all knew how to use them.

The Vancours were people of fashion, as well as fortune. The elder more especially, from inhabiting the family mansion, and having a regularly established household, saw a great deal of company at times from Albany, New-York, and elsewhere. His house, indeed, was open to all respectable visitors, and was seldom without the presence of some stranger, friend, or relative from a distance. They were received and treated with that plain, unostentatious, quiet hospitality which always bespeaks a welcome. Madame Vancour, as she was called by way of eminence, was a New-York lady, born and bred, partaking almost equally in the blood of the genuine Hollander, the Englishman, and the Huguonot. New-York, being at that time the residence of the English governor, was of course, the focus of fashion. The governor affected somewhat of the kingly state; and there being always a considerable number of troops in garrison, the place swarmed with red coats, as some of our eating cellars now do with boiled lobsters. These ruddy sons of Mars were the prime objects of the ambition of our city belles, and happy was the damsel and proud the mother that could unite their fate and family with the lieutenant of a company of British grenadiers. His excellency, like most other excellencies, had plenty of aids-de-camp to keep up his state, write his invitations, pick up news, and carve at his table. These important functions, of course, entitled them to great distinction among our provincial belles, and it is on record in the traditions of those times, that the good matrons of the capital could never sleep quietly the night before a ball at the government-house, for thinking whether their daughters would dance with an aid-de-camp. They occasionally demeaned themselves by marrying a provincial heiress, and many of the largest estates in the province, with a blooming damsel at the back of them, were exchanged for a red coat and a pair of gorgeous epaulettes, to the infinite contentment of the mothers, who partook largely in the dignity of the connexion. I cannot affirm that the fathers and brothers shared in these triumphs; for already the fine airs of the pompous intruders, and their undisguised assumptions of superiority, had awakened in the bosoms of these homely provincials a feeling, which, in after-times mingling with others equally powerful, produced a revolution, of which the world yet feels, and will long feel the influence. The Vancours had many connexions in New-York, among the most wealthy and fashionable of the inhabitants, and seldom missed paying them a visit of a few weeks in the course of every autumn. They were always well received, and as the governor never came to Albany, without partaking in their hospitalities, he thought himself bound to repay them when they visited the place of his residence. This intercourse with the gay world kept up certain feelings and habits, which seldom fail to accompany it; but still, in the main, their characters partook largely of the simplicity of the country where they resided. In manners they might not be particularly distinguished from the polite and well-bred people of the world; but in habits and modes of thinking they were essentially different. There was a certain doric simplicity in their mode of life, which has long since passed away, leaving behind what I sometimes feel inclined to doubt is but an inadequate compensation for its loss.

Dennis and Ariel, the two younger brothers, being the one a lonely widower, the other an equally lonely bachelor, spent a good deal of their time at the old mansion, where they were as much at home as at their own houses. The two elder brothers were greatly attached to each other, and fond of being together in their own quiet way. They sometimes passed a whole morning without exchanging half a dozen words. They had a way of communicating their thoughts by certain little expressive inarticulate sounds and unobtrusive gestures, which each one understood as well as he did his mother tongue. Ariel, on the contrary, was ungovernably impatient of idleness, and never could sit still fifteen minutes at a time without falling into a doze. He was a great hand at grafting and inoculating fruit-trees; an industrious seeker after mushrooms; and mighty in all undertakings which had for their object the furtherance of good eating. In truth, he was one of those persons who are seldom without a project for the benefit of their neighbours, and who, though they never by any chance succeed in their own undertakings, can always tell to a nicety what will be most for the advantage of others. Dennis, on the other hand, had a horror of all innovation and improvement in rural economy; he despised labour-saving machines from the bottom of his soul, and held it as incontrovertible, that the human hand was the most perfect instrument ever invented. Ariel one year spent the proceeds of a whole crop in devising inventions for exterminating field mice; while Egbert secured half of his by labour and attention. Somehow or other, so it was, that one grew richer every year, and the other was always in want of money.

"They won't be here to-day," said Dennis, one morning, after his elder brother and himself had been sitting with their heads inclined towards each other about two hours, without exchanging a word.

"They won't be here to-day," echoed Egbert, and there ended the conversation for an hour at least.

"I think it will clear up before noon," quoth Dennis, eyeing the clouds as they separated above, disclosing a little piece of clear blue sky.

"I think it will," responded Egbert, and the matter was settled.

The expected arrivals were Colonel Vancour's wife and daughter, the latter of whom, having finished her education at the boarding-school, was now on her way home from New-York with her mother. The reader will be pleased to recollect that this was long before the invention of steamboats, and when a genuine Albany packet never dreamed of sailing but with a fair wind, nor scarcely ever passed the Overslaugh without paying it the compliment of running high and dry aground. We ourselves well remember, in long after-times, having once lain there seven days within seven miles of Albany; yet such appeared the immeasurable distance, that no one on board ever dreamed of leaving the vessel and going to the city by land. All waited patiently for an easterly-wind or a heavy rain, to float them off again; and spent the time pleasantly in eating and smoking. In truth, there is no greater help to patience than a pipe of Blaze Moore's tobacco. But the fact is, people were neither so much in a hurry, nor was their time half so precious as it is now. In those days a man was all his life in making a fortune; at present he cannot spare so much time, because he has not only to make, but to spend a fortune before he dies. It would have been next to an impossibility to persuade a man to risk a quick passage to the other world, for the sake of shortening his journey in this.

The daughter, accompanied by her mother and Tjerck, an old black servant, had been expected more than a week, every day of which precisely the same colloquy as that we have just recorded passed between the two brothers. We ought to mention, that Mr. Egbert Vancour was prevented attending the ladies home by having been appointed a commissioner to hold a treaty with the Five Nations at Schenectady. The past week had been one of almost continual rain, and the three brothers each began to manifest impatience in his own way. The two elder by frequent emigrations from the chimney corner to the window; and the younger by marching out every five minutes, in the intervals between his naps, squaring himself with his thick short legs wide apart, and reconnoitring the weathercock, which, I ought to mention, was an iron shad, through whose sides were cut the letters D. V., in honour of the family.

At length, towards evening the yellow sun broke through the opening western clouds, most gorgeously gilding the weeping landscape, and turning the cold drops of rain which had condensed on the grass and waving branches of the trees to sparkling diamonds bright. A brisk yet mellow south wind sprung up, and a fleet of sloops with snow white sails appeared below, ploughing their merry way up the river. All turned out to see if they could distinguish the "Patroon," the vessel in which the ladies had taken passage. The indefatigable Ariel was down at the wharf, in front of the mansion-house, making a prodigious noise, and calling out to every vessel that passed to know if the Patroon was coming, every now and then clearing his throat, as was his custom, with "a-hem!" that at length startled a flock of black ducks, which had maintained its station in a little neighbouring cove for several days past. Sloop after sloop passed on, without stopping, until Ariel got out of all patience; he stamped about from one side of the wharf to the other; the Patroon was the worst of all vessels, and the captain the most lazy, slow motioned, stupid of all blockheads.

"I knew it; d——n him, I knew it. I'll bet my life he is high and dry on the Overslaugh.—No! hey! no: d——n it, there she comes—there she is at last;" and he darted across the wharf towards her with such enthusiasm, that he broke his shins against a post; whereat he gave the Patroon and her captain another broadside, not forgetting the post.

Ariel was not mistaken: it was the Patroon, and in a few minutes, Madame Vancour and her daughter Catalina were welcomed once more at the fireside of their best friends, with a quiet speechless warmth which nature dictated and nature understood. All but Ariel spoke through their eyes; but it was the characteristic of that worthy bachelor, to make a noise on all occasions of merriment or sadness; the more he felt, the more noise he made, and this propensity followed him even in his sleep; he being a most sonorous and indefatigable snorer, in all its varieties. He paraded round the young woman, crying, "A-hem! bless me, how you have grown; a-hem! zounds, I should'nt have known you; why, ahem! d——n it you're almost as tall as I am!" And then he measured his little square stumpy figure with that of the tall graceful girl. Finally, having exhausted all his waking noises, he placed himself in an arm chair and fell into a sleep, from which he was only roused by the music of setting the supper-table, which above all others was most agreeable to his ear. "Hey!— d——n it, what have you got for supper—hey!" and he marched round, taking special cognizance of the ample board.

"But where is Sybrandt!" asked Madame Vancour, "I expected, to be sure, he would be here to welcome us home."

"Oh, that's true, Dennis," said Egbert, "what has become of the boy?"

"I can't tell."

Ariel broke into one of his inspiring laughs, "I can," said he; "the poor fellow sneaked away home, as soon as he knew the Patroon was in sight."

Egbert shrugged his shoulders; Dennis twisted a piece of celery with such a petulant jerk, that he overturned the whole arrangement of the dish, the pride of Dame Phillis, presiding goddess of the kitchen. Ariel cried, "A-hem!" like a stentor, and madame and her daughter exchanged significant looks, and smiled. Sybrandt appeared not that night, and nothing more was said on the subject.

As this young gentleman is destined to make some figure in our story, we will take this opportunity to introduce him more particularly to the reader's notice.

CHAPTER IV. *The Morning's smiles, the Evening's tears.*

The next morning Ariel came over, and found Sybrandt half-willing, half-afraid to accompany the party to the island, of which he was to be the commander-in-chief. Never man was so busy, so important, and so happy as the good

Ariel, at having something to do for a whole day. Blessed, indeed, yea, thrice blessed is he whom trifles can make happy. It is this which forms the bliss of childhood and the consolation of old age, each of which finds its appropriate enjoyments in an exemption from the serious labours and oppressive anxieties of the world's great business.

It was a cheerful and inspiring morning as ever shone upon the rich plains of the happy Hudson—happy in being the chosen river on whose bosom floats the tide of fashion to and fro; on whose delicious borders dwell in rustic competency thousands of contented human beings, enjoying the fruits of their labours amid the fruitions of a blameless life and a quiet spirit. The day was such a one as I myself prefer to all others; when the sun diffuses his influence through a gauzy veil of semi-transparent clouds, which temper his rays into a mild genial warmth, that, while it takes, perhaps, from the vigour of the body, communicates to the mind a delicious and luxurious aptitude for the indulgence of the gentler emotions. In such days, and through such a medium, the beauties of nature exhibit only their softest features; and display their greatest varieties of shade and colouring; the winds are hushed; the waters smooth and glassy; the foliage wears a fleecy softness; the hills appear more beautiful; the mountains, magnified in the misty vagueness of distance, seem blended with the skies; the different shades of green that deck the bosom of the earth become more distinct yet more harmonious than when basking in the glare of the sun; and every sound that meets the ear, like every object that attracts the eye, partakes in the gentle harmony that reigns all around. It is in the remembrance of such scenes in after-life, and amid the struggles, hopes, and disappointments which checker the course of manhood, that we are apt to contrast our present cares with our former enjoyments, exaggerating both, and giving a false estimate of the different periods of an existence, which, if we fairly hold the balance, will be found pretty much the same in all its various changes, from the cradle to the grave.

Our little party consisted of Master-commandant Ariel, chief manager, factotum, &c., as busy as a bee, as noisy as a caty-did, and as merry as a cricket; Catalina, Sybrandt, and some half a score of the beaux and belles of Albany, who had come to the mansion-house bright and early in the morning, all dressed in neat and simple attire, befitting a ramble among the wild roses and clambering vines of the happy island. This little paradise, to speak in learned phrase, was an alluvial formation of times long past, composed of the rich spoils of the surrounding lands, deposited by the river. It was as level as the surface of the stream in which it was embosomed, and covered with a carpet of rich, luxuriant verdure, which, when it was not pastured, gave to the scythe a glorious harvest three times a year. On every side and all around, the banks were fringed with the light silvery foliage of the water-willows, mingled with tufts of wild roses, and growths of nameless wild flowers of every hue and various odours; and canopied at intervals with clambering vines, whose long tendrils sometimes bent down and waved to and fro on the gliding waters as they passed slowly by. Within this leafy barrier was nothing but a green sward, shaded at various intervals by the vast giants of the alluvial growth—elms and plane-trees, of such towering majesty, that they overlooked the gentle eminences which bounded the flats on either side. The witching murmurs of the waters, as they glided along under the willow branches and nodding vines, mingled with the chorus of a thousand birds, who remained all summer in undisturbed possession; and though the pipe of the shepherd was never heard in these pleasant abodes, it was aptly supplied by the music of harmonious nature, the murmuring waters, and the warblers of the woodlands.

Under the skilful guidance of the active, indefatigable Ariel, the little party arrived at the scene of their anticipated pleasures, all gay and happy, save our friend Sybrandt, who, from the moment he joined the group, felt the spell of the demon besetting him sorely. His gayety was repressed, his faculties benumbed, and his youthful vigour changed to a leaden inertness by that habitual shyness and awkwardness the very consciousness of which prevented all efforts to shake it off. He was always either behind or before the party, and generally too far from it to hear what was said. Thus, when the hilarity of the youthful spirit effervesced into a sprightly laugh, the demon of pride, suspicion, and consciousness, whispered that the laugh was at him. The other young men were, indeed, quite as awkard, and without his knowledge and acquirements; but they made an excellent figure, notwithstanding, and performed their parts with a gay, gallant frankness, such as woman in all situations loves. They had lived in the world at Albany, mixed in its business, and dissipated their self-love in the pursuit of various objects, while poor Sybrandt had passed his youth in nursing the offspring of solitude—sensibility, pride, and selfishness. It is social intercourse alone that, by calling us off from self-contemplation, and making it necessary to remember and to administer to the wants or the enjoyments of others, can make man happy himself, and an instrument of happiness to others.

When they came to the river-side, where lay the little boat which was to take them to the island, Sybrandt had sworn to himself that he would offer his hand to Catalina to assist her in embarking. But he was so long before he could screw himself up to the direful feat, that one of the Albany lads, more gallant as well as alert, was beforehand with him. A bashful man is like a tiger; he makes but one effort, and if that fails, slinks away to his jungle, and essays not another. I myself have my own experience to vouch for this; having in the far-off days of my gallantry, full many a time and oft, in dining out, gathered myself together with a gallant ferocity to ask the lady of the feast for the honour of a glass of wine with her. But alas! if peradventure the lady listened not to my first demonstration, I was prone to relapse into an utter and incurable incapacity to repeat the mighty effort. The sound of my voice died suddenly, and word spoke I nevermore. So was it with master Sybrandt, who, having expended his powder in a flash of the pan, sunk only the lower for the exertion he had made.

The little party landed, and pursued their pleasures in separate groups, or couples, as chance or inclination prompted. In those days of Doric innocence and simplicity—and thanks to Heaven, it is so still in our happy country—young people of different sexes could enjoy the pleasures of a rural ramble, in parties or in pairs, without the remotest idea of impropriety, and without waking a single breath of scandal. If there be any thing in the music, the repose, the fascinating and quiet beauties of nature that excites to love, it is gentle and virtuous love; an awakening impulse rather than an ungovernable passion; and if perchance it works to final mischief, it is rather from accident than purpose—nature than depravity. It is not here that the sensual passions acquire their overpowering energies; but at midnight revels, where dazzling lights, artificial splendours, seducing music, high-seasoned viands, and luxurious wines, pamper the senses into lascivious longings, and swell the imagination to exaggerated conceptions of pleasure, which carry us away we know not and we care not whither. Long may it be before it is the fashion to abridge the freedom of virgins, and extend that of wives, in our country.

Catalina having carried her point in making Sybrandt one of the party, was rather in a better humour with him than usual. She plagued him now and then in various sly ways, and sometimes raised a laugh at his expense. The first fine edge of the feelings, fortunately for mankind, both in pleasure and pain, is worn off by the first enjoyment and the first suffering. Were it not so—but I am insensibly becoming a moralist, when I only aspire to story-telling. Sybrandt by degrees already felt like a musical instrument, in better tune for being played upon, and two or three times caught himself actually enjoying the scene and the festivity of his companions. The ridicule of women sometimes makes bold men only more bold and confident; and I have known a most exemplary modest person made downright saucy by the freedoms of others. Indeed there is not in the world so impudent a being, as a shy man forced out of his shyness. The very impulse carries him to the opposite extreme. The bent of Sybrandt's mind had, however, been too long and too rigid to be relaxed all at once.

I pity the most exalted of all created beings who cannot feel the inspiration of the balmy air, the music and the smiles of nature; for he can have neither sensibility nor imagination. It was not so with Sybrandt; though apparently a most unpromising pupil for the school of romance, there were, if we mistake not, certain springs of action and certain latent fires hidden and buried in his head and heart, which only required to be touched or lighted to make him a far other being than he seemed just now. As the morning passed, he insensibly began to feel less awkward, and his shyness gradually wore away. He ventured to speak to some of the young damsels, and finally had the unparalleled intrepidity to attach himself to the side of his cousin in a stroll under the vines and willows that skirted the shores of the little island.

By degrees the feelings which nature had implanted in his heart opened and expanded, like the seeds which lay dormant in the deep shades of the forest for years, until the trees being cut down, the warm sunbeams waken them to life and vegetation. The emotions of his heart for a while overpowered his long-cherished timidity, and lent to his tongue an eloquence that pleased, while it surprised Catalina. The rich stores of imagery which long reading and contemplation had gathered in his mind, where they had lain enchained in the icy fetters of timidity, were let loose by the new-born warmth that thrilled through his frame, and flowed forth without study or effort into striking observations, tender associations, and sparkles of a rich and glowing fancy. Catalina listened with astonishment to the animated statue; and as she looked him in the face while pouring forth the treasures of his mind, and saw the divinity that sparkled in his eyes, she once or twice detected herself in thinking Sybrandt almost as handsome as an aid-de-camp. He, too, felt elevated in his own estimation; for the first time in his life he had listened to his own voice without feeling his heart beat with apprehension, and for the first time he could look back upon an hour spent in the society of a female, without a pang of the keenest mortification.

"Sybrandt," at length said Catalina, "why don't you talk so every day?"

"Because every day is not like to-day; nor are you, my cousin, always what you are now."

A silence ensued, from which they were roused by the cheerful, joy-inspiring shouts of Ariel, who had prepared his collation, and was summoning all the rambling lads and lasses to come and partake of the blessings of his prudent forethought. To him eating was an affair of the first consequence; he never joined a party, either of business or pleasure, without first reducing it to a certainty that there would be no starvation attending it; and it was almost as affecting as a last dying speech to hear him relate the melancholy story of the ruin of a brace of the finest woodducks he ever saw, by the "d——d stupid folly" of his cook, who roasted them in a pot instead of before the fire. The good Ariel had spread his stores on a snow-white tablecloth of ample dimensions, laid upon the rich greensward beneath a canopy of vines, that clambered over the tops of a clump of sassafras, whose aromatic buds sent forth a grateful fragrance. Here he marshalled his forces with great discretion, placing the lads and lasses alternately around the rural repast, and enjoining upon the former the strictest attention to his nearest neighbour. As to himself, he could never sit still where there was room for action. He curvetted around the little circle like a merry spaniel; cracked his jokes, and laughed only the louder when nobody joined him; helped himself, and ate and talked, all at the same time, with a zest, an hilarity, and honest frankness that communicated themselves to all about him, infecting them with a contagious merriment. The birds chirped over their heads, the flowers grew beneath their feet, the mild summer breezes played upon their cheeks, hope glowed in their hearts, and youth and health were their handmaids; why then should they not laugh and be merry?

But a plague on Nature! she is a female, after all, and there is no trusting her. As thus they sat unheeding all but themselves and the present moment, Nature had been at work unnoticed by the little crew, gathering into one great mass a pack of dark rolling clouds along the western horizon. The banks of the little isle were, as we said before, fringed all around by trees and shrubbery, and tangled vines, that quite hid the opposite shores, making it a little world within itself. The dark tempest gathering in the west had therefore escaped the notice of the party, until the moment when a burst of merriment was interrupted by a flash of lightning, and a quick, sharp crash of thunder. When the Creator speaks, all nature is silent; and if, as some suppose, the leaping lightning is the quick glancing of his angry eye, the thunder the threatening of his voice, no wonder if every sound is hushed when they break forth from the pitchy darkness of the heavens. The laugh ceased; the birds became silent in their leafy bowers; the trees stilled their sweet whisperings; the insects chirped no longer, and the river murmured no more. There was a dead pause in the air, the earth, and the waters, save when the Creator of them all spoke from the depths of his vast obscurity.

The merrymakers looked at each other in silence, and in silence sat, until Ariel ventured to clear his voice with "a-hem!" which, to say the truth, lacked much of its wonted vigorous energy and clearness. Sybrandt gained a position whence he could overlook the island barrier, and came back running to announce that a thunderstorm was coming on rapidly—so rapidly that it would be impossible to cross the river and gain the nearest house in time to escape its fury. The damsels looked at the young men, and the young men looked at the damsels. One had on her best hat, another a new shawl, a third her holyday chintz gown, and each and all wore some favourite piece of finery, which, though peradventure Dolly the cook and Betty the chambermaid would scorn to wear, even on week-days, in this age of rapid unparalleled improvement, was still dear to their simple, innocent affections. The boys too, as they were called, and still are called among the old lords of the land, had on their Sunday gear, which, as they never ran in debt to the tailor, it behooved them to nurse with special care. What was to be done in this sore dilemma; for now the quick, keen flashes, the equally keen crashes that came with them, and the dead, dull calm that intervened, announced that the rain and the tempest was nigh.

Ariel was as busy as an assistant-alderman at a fire, and about as useful. Being a man that was always in a hurry when there was no occasion, it may be naturally supposed, that when there was occasion he would be in such a great hurry that his resolves would tread upon one another's heels, or impede their operations by running athwart each other, and breaking their heads. And so, indeed, it happened; he was ten times more busy than when he had nothing to do; swore at the lads for not doing something; suggested a hundred impracticable things; and concluded, good man! by wishing with all his soul they were safe housed in the old mansion.

Catalina had been brought up at the boarding-school in the fear of thunder. The schoolmistress, indeed, always encouraged the young ladies by precept not to be frightened; but she never failed to disappear in a thunderstorm, and was one time discovered between two featherbeds almost smothered to death. It is to be regretted that this natural and proper feeling of awe which accompanies the sublime phenomena of nature should degenerate into abject fear or irrational superstition. Divested of these, the approach of a thunderstorm is calculated to waken the mind to the most lofty associations with the great Being who charges and discharges this vast artillery, and to exalt the imagination into the highest regions of lofty contemplation. But fear is an abject, soul-subduing sentiment, which monopolizes the mind, debases the physical man, and shuts out every feeling allied to genuine piety and faith.

Suddenly an idea struck Sybrandt, which was instantly adopted and put into execution. The boat, a broad, flat skiff, was drawn up the bank, and placed bottom upwards, with one side supported by sticks, and the other reclining on the ground towards the west, so that the rain might run off in that direction. The few minutes which intervened between this operation and the bursting of the torrent of rain were employed by the young men in covering the open spaces about the sides of the boat with grass and branches, as well as the time would admit. There was only space enough under this shelter for the young women, though Ariel managed to find himself a place among them. He was in the main a good-natured, kind-hearted man, but he did not like being out in a storm any more than his neighbours. The young men stood cowering under a canopy of thick vines, which shaded the boat and a little space besides. It was observed that Sybrandt placed himself nearest that end of the boat under which Catalina was sheltered, and that he was particular in the disposition of the grass and branches in that quarter.

A few, a very few minutes of dead silence on the part of our little group intervened before the tempest sent forth its hoards of wind and rain, smiting the groaning trees, and deluging the thirsty earth till it could drink no more, but voided the surplus into the swelling stream, that began anon to rise and roar in angry violence. This storm was for a long time traditionary for its terrible violence; and for more than half a century people talked of the incessant flashes of the lightning, the stunning and harsh violence of the thunder, the deluge of rain, the hurricane which accompanied it, the lofty trees that were either split with lightning or torn up by the roots by the wind, and the damage done by the sudden swelling of the river on that remarkable day.

The party that found shelter under the boat fared indifferently well; but the others were in a few moments wet to the skin. The little flexible willows bent down to let the storm pass over them; but the sturdy elms and plane-trees stood stiff to the blast that wrung their arms from their bodies, and scattered them in the air like straws and feathers. The rushing winds, the roaring of the troubled waters, were mingled with incessant flashings of lightning, accompanied by

59

those quick, sharp explosions of thunder that proclaim the near approach of the electric power. At length the little party was roused by a peal that seemed to have rent the vault of heaven, and beheld with terror and dismay a vast plane-tree, within a hundred yards' distance, directly in front of them, shivered from top to bottom like a reed. The explosion for a moment stilled the tempest of rain, during which interval the vast dissevered trunk stood trembling and nodding, like one suddenly struck by the hand of death. Another moment, and the winds resumed their empire, the vast monarch of the isle fell to the ground with a tremendous crash, and the force of Omnipotence was demonstrated in the instantaneous destruction of a work which long ages had brought to maturity.

The young women screamed, and the youths shuddered, as they beheld this vast giant of nature yielding in an instant to a mightier power. But soon they were drawn off to the contemplation of a new danger. It is well known how sudden, nay, almost instantaneous, is the swelling of our rivers, especially near their sources, and where they traverse a hilly or mountainous region. The little isle where our scene is laid was but a few feet above the ordinary level of the stream, and its surface as flat as the stream itself, which now began to dash its waves beyond the usual barrier, until at length the situation of the little party became extremely critical. The land had become less safe than the waters, and immediate measures were taken to prepare for the inundation, by turning the boat upon her bottom again. The party was arranged on the benches to the best advantage, and the young men stood prepared to ply the oars the moment the boat was floated off. Soon the tremendous torrent rolled over the surface of the whole island in one mighty mass of dark waters, speckled with white foam; and the boat was carried down the stream with the swiftness of an arrow. The difficulty was to escape the trees and bushes, which still reared their heads above the waters, since it was obvious that nothing could preserve the boat but her being kept from the slightest interruption in her course. The great object, therefore, was to avoid every obstacle, and to keep her head directly down the stream, till they met with some little nook or cove, where the current was less violent. In times of danger the master spirit instinctively takes the lead, and the lesser ones instinctively yield obedience.

Ever since the coming of the storm Sybrandt had seemed a new being, animated by a newly-awakened soul. The excitement of the scene had by degrees caused him to forget his shyness; and now the presence of danger and the necessity of exertion roused into action those qualities which neither himself nor others were conscious he possessed. He who had trembled at the idea of being introduced into a drawing-room, and shrunk from the encounter of a smiling female eye, now stood erect in the composure of unawed manhood, with a steady hand and a steady eye, guiding the little skiff through roaring whirlpools and angry currents, furiously conflicting with each other, almost as skilfully as a veteran Mississippi boatman. All else sat still in the numbness of irrepressible apprehension. Even the busy Ariel was motionless in his seat, and his active tongue silent as the grave. But neither human skill nor human courage could struggle any length of time with the power of the waters, every moment aggravated by new accessions. In turning a projecting point, round which the current whirled with increased impetuosity, the boat struck the edge of an old stump of a tree just beneath the surface, and was upset in a single instant. Forunately for some, though, alas! not for all, the current made a sudden inflexion immediately below the projecting point into a little shallow cove, where it subsided into repose. It was in making for this harbour that the boat unfortunately encountered the stump, which, as I stated, was not visible above the waters. It is with sorrowful emotions I record that the accident was fatal to two of the innocent girls and one of the young men, who sat in the bow of the boat, which unfortunately, as she overturned, sheered out into the stream, and launched them into the whole force of the current. They were carried away and their bodies found a day or two afterward many miles below. The others, with the exception of Catalina, were shot directly, and in an instant, by the sudden angle made by the current, into the little shallow, quiet cove, where they were all preserved. Catalina was not one of these. Less strong, and less inured to the sports and perils of rural life, she became insensible the moment the accident occurred, and would have quickly perished, had not Sybrandt swam into the edge of the turbulent whirlpool where she was floating, and brought her safely to the land.

Sadly the remant of our little party returned to their respective homes without their lost companions, and sadly they contrasted the beauty of the quiet genial morning, and the happy anticipations that beckoned them forward to sportful revelry, with the uproar of nature, and the gloomy shadows of the evening, which closed in darkness, sorrow, and death. The remembrance of this scene, and of the conduct of Sybrandt, not only before but during the storm, and in the hour of her extreme peril, was often afterward called to mind by Catalina, and not unfrequently checked her inclination to laugh sometimes, and sometimes to be downright angry with her sheepish, awkward cousin.—We need not dwell upon the anxiety of the father and mother of our heroine, nor of the good Dennis, who, in the midst of his fears, could not help crying out against and sparing not this new-fangled custom of making parties for the island, though both tradition and history avouch that these sports were coeval with the commencement of our happy era of honest simplicity. Suffice it to say, that the good parents received their only child as one a second time bestowed upon them by the bounty of Heaven, and that they were full of gratitude to Sybrandt,—whose inspiration seemed now departed from him. The crisis that awakened his sleeping energies having passed away, his long-cherished habits again beset him; instead of expressing his joy at having been instrumental in preserving Catalina, and showing his sensibility to the parents' gratitude, he became embarrassed, silent, awkward, stultified—and finally vanished away no one knew whither. We must not omit to record that from this time forward the worthy Ariel attended the Dominie's sermons regularly twice every Sabbath; a custom he had never followed before, inasmuch as he had a most sovereign propensity to falling asleep and disturbing the congregation by snoring.

Washington Irving

The most famous of the Knickerbockers was Washington Irving (1783-1859). Irving was both a professional diplomat and author. He studied law and amused himself by writing essays on New York society for various periodicals. The *Letters of Jonathan Oldstyle, Gent.* written in 1802 and 1803 are in this category. Between 1804 and 1806 he took a tour of France and Italy. Upon return home, he collaborated with his brother William Irving and James Kirke Paulding in producing the *Salmagundi Papers* (1807-08). He first gained notoriety in 1809 with his *A History of New York,* written under the pen name of Diedrich Knickerbocker. This book was highly satirical of the early Dutch settlers and was both loathed and loved by the New Yorkers of Irving's time. It was a great comic success.

In 1815, Irving went to England to run the Liverpool branch of the family hardware business, but he did not take kindly to commerce. After making the acquaintance of Sir Walter Scott, he turned seriously to literature. His first efforts at romantic tales were collected in *The Sketch Book of Geoffrey Crayon, Gent.,* published in London in 1820 and serially in New York between 1819-20. This effort was a great success and finally decided Irving on a literary career. The *Sketch Book* included such popular tales as *The Spectre Bridegroom, The Legend of Sleepy Hollow,* and *Rip Van Winkle,* and served to introduce Europeans to the romance of American scenery. Actually *Rip Van Winkle* derives, from an old legend of the long sleep of the Emperor Frederick Barbarossa. The immediate inspiration may have come from the tale *Karl Katz* in *Grimm's Fairy Tales* (1812-15), collected by the noted German philologists and folklorists Jakob Ludwig Karl Grimm (1785-1863) and his brother Wilhelm Karl Grimm (1786-1859).

The story of Rip Van Winkle struck a sympathetic note with the general public. In 1865, the actor Joseph Jefferson (1829-1905), in conjunction with the British playwright and actor Dion Boucicault (1822-1890), turned this tale into a play which was popular on British and American stages for many years. In 1884 it was turned into a very popular operetta by Robert Planquette (1850-1903) entitled *Rip.* It was treated more seriously as an opera by the American composer

Washington Irving. Oil portrait by Henry F. Darby, ca. 1858. Courtesy of Historic Hudson Valley.

The Catskill Mountains as seen from the Hudson River off Saugerties and described by Irving in his *Autobiography*. Photograph taken by Arthur G. Adams from steamer *Martha's Vineyard*, Captain Lynn Bottum, on Saturday, October 15, 1977, on the last trip of a classic steamboat from New York to Albany.

Reginald De Koven (1859-1920) in 1920 and the Italo-British composer Franco Leoni (1864-1937) in 1897.

The *Sketch Book* was followed in 1822 by *Bracebridge Hall*, another collection of tales, including that of *Dolph Heyliger*. *Bracebridge Hall* was followed by *Tales of a Traveller* in 1824. However, by this time the vein had been worked out and the public was less enthusiastic. In 1826, Irving became attached to the American embassy in Madrid. While in Spain, Irving wrote his *Biography of Columbus* (1828), *The Conquest of Granada* (1829), and *The Alhambra* (1832), which remains very popular in Spain even today. Irving thereafter served briefly in a diplomatic capacity in London, before returning to New York.

After visiting the American frontier, he wrote *A Tour of the Prairies* in 1835 and *Astoria* in 1836. *Astoria* was written from records furnished by John Jacob Astor. In 1837 he joined with Pierre Irving in writing *The Adventures of Captain Bonneville, U.S.A.* At this time he purchased his estate at Sunnyside near Tarrytown, where he was to spend the remainder of his life, except for a term as Minister to Spain at Madrid, between 1842 and 1846. Back at home he wrote a biography of Goldsmith in 1849, a book of sketches entitled *Wolfert's Roost* in 1855, and his monumental *Life of George Washington* between 1855 and 1859. This last great work runs to five volumes.

Irving never married. He cherished the memory of his fiancée, Matilda Hoffman, who had died during their engagement. However, his later years were made comfortable and happy by his nieces who lived with him at Sunnyside. Irving was very sensitive to the natural beauty of the Hudson River and was very concerned about the aesthetic damage done by the building of the Hudson River Railroad along the waterfront in 1852 and the building of the Erie Railroad pier at Piermont, across the river from his home.

Although derivative and lacking in dramatic depth, Irving's tales have an indefinable charm, and in several of his characters he has created immortal legends.

From *Autobiography**

Of all the scenery of the Hudson, the Kaatskill Mountains had the most witching effect on my boyish imagination. Never shall I forget the effect upon me of my first view of them, predominating over a wide extent of country—part wild, woody and rugged: part softened away into all the graces of cultivation. As we slowly floated along, I lay on the deck and watched them through a summer's day, undergoing a thousand mutations under the magical effects of atmosphere; sometimes seeming to approach; at other times to recede; now almost melting

*Washington Irving, *Autobiography*, Fulton Edition of *The Works of Washington Irving* (New York: 1909).

into hazy distance, now burnished by the setting sun, until in the evening they printed themselves against the glowing sky in the deep purple of an Italian landscape.

From *The Sketch Book of Geoffrey Crayon, Gent.**

RIP VAN WINKLE A Posthumous Writing of Diedrich Knickerbocker.

> By Woden, God of Saxons,
> From whence comes Wensday, that is
> Wodensday,
> Truth is a thing that ever I will keep
> Unto thylke day in which I creep into
> My sepulchre—
>
> CARTWRIGHT

[The following Tale was found among the papers of the late Diedrich Knickerbocker, an old gentleman of New York, who was very curious in the Dutch history of the province, and the manners of the descendants from its primitive settlers. His historical researches, however, did not lie so much among books as among men; for the former are lamentably scanty on his favorite topics; whereas he found the old burghers, and still more their wives, rich in that legendary lore, so invaluable to true history. Whenever, therefore, he happened upon a genuine Dutch family, snugly shut up in its low-roofed farmhouse, under a spreading sycamore, he looked upon it as a little clasped volume of black-letter, and studied it with the zeal of a book-worm.

The result of all these researches was a history of the province during the reign of the Dutch governors, which he published some years since. There have been various opinions as to the literary character of his work, and, to tell the truth, it is not a whit better than it should be. Its chief merit is its scrupulous accuracy, which indeed was a little questioned on its first appearance, but has since been completely established; and it is now admitted into all historical collections, as a book of unquestionable authority.

The old gentleman died shortly after the publication of his work, and now that he is dead and gone, it cannot do much harm to his memory to say that his time might have been much better employed in weightier labors. He, however, was apt to ride his hobby his own way; and though it did now and then kick up the dust a little in the eyes of his neighbors, and grieve the spirit of some friends, for whom he felt the truest deference and affection; yet his errors and follies are remembered "more in sorrow than in anger," and it begins to be suspected, that

---

*Washington Irving, Author's Revised Edition, included in *The Works of Washington Irving*, The Kinderhook Edition (New York: G. P. Putnam's Sons, 1880).

64

he never intended to injure or offend. But however his memory may be appreciated by critics, it is still held dear by many folks, whose good opinion is well worth having: particularly by certain biscuit-bakers, who have gone so far as to imprint his likeness on their new-year cakes; and have thus given him a chance for immortality, almost equal to the being stamped on a Waterloo Medal, or a Queen Anne's Farthing.]

Whoever has made a voyage up the Hudson must remember the Kaatskill Mountains. They are a dismembered branch of the great Appalachian family, and are seen away to the west of the river, swelling up to a noble height, and lording it over the surrounding country. Every change of season, every change of weather, indeed, every hour of the day, produces some change in the magical hues and shapes of these mountains, and they are regarded by all the good wives, far and near, as perfect barometers. When the weather is fair and settled, they are clothed in blue and purple, and print their bold outlines on the clear evening sky; but, sometimes, when the rest of the landscape is cloudless, they will gather a hood of gray vapors about their summits, which, in the last rays of the setting sun, will glow and light up like a crown of glory.

At the foot of these fairy mountains, the voyager may have descried the light smoke curling up from a village, whose shingle-roofs gleam among the trees, just where the blue tints of the upland melt away into the fresh green of the nearer landscape. It is a little village of great antiquity, having been founded by some of the Dutch colonists, in the early times of the province, just about the beginning of the government of the good Peter Stuyvesant, [may he rest in peace!] and there were some of the houses of the original settlers standing within a few years, built of small yellow bricks brought from Holland, having latticed windows and gable fronts, surmounted with weather-cocks.

In that same village, and in one of these very houses [which, to tell the precise truth, was sadly time-worn and weather-beaten], there lived many years since, while the country was yet a province of Great Britain, a simple good-natured fellow of the name of Rip Van Winkle. He was a descendant of the Van Winkles who figured so gallantly in the chivalrous days of Peter Stuyvesant, and accompanied him to the siege of Fort Christina. He inherited, however, but little of the martial character of his ancestors. I have observed that he was a simple, good-natured man; he was, moreover, a kind neighbor, and an obedient, hen-pecked husband. Indeed, to the latter circumstance might be owing that meekness of spirit which gained him such universal popularity; for those men are most apt to be obsequious and conciliating abroad, who are under the discipline of shrews at home. Their tempers, doubtless, are rendered pliant and malleable in the fiery furnace of domestic tribulation; and a curtain lecture is worth all the sermons in the world for teaching the virtues of patience and long-suffering. A termagant wife may, therefore, in some respects, he considered a tolerable blessing; and if so, Rip Van Winkle was thrice blessed.

Certain it is, that he was a great favorite among all the good wives of the village, who, as usual, with the amiable sex, took his part in all family squabbles; and never failed, whenever they talked those matters over in their evening gossipings, to lay all the blame on Dame Van Winkle. The children of the village, too, would shout with joy whenever he approached. He assisted at their sports, made their playthings, taught them to fly kites and shoot marbles, and told them long stories of ghosts, witches, and Indians. Whenever he went dodging about the village, he was surrounded by a troop of them, hanging on his skirts, clambering on his back, and playing a thousand tricks on him with impunity; and not a dog would bark at him throughout the neighborhood.

The great error in Rip's composition was an insuperable aversion to all kinds of profitable labor. It could not be from the want of assiduity or perseverance; for he would sit on a wet rock, with a rod as long and heavy as a Tartar's lance, and fish all day without a murmur, even though he should not be encouraged by a single nibble. He would carry a fowling-piece on his shoulder for hours together, trudging through woods and swamps, and up hill and down dale, to shoot a few squirrels or wild pigeons. He would never refuse to assist a neighbor even in the roughest toil, and was a foremost man at all country frolics for husking Indian corn, or building stone fences; the women of the village, too, used to employ him to run their errands, and to do such little odd jobs as their less obliging husbands would not do for them. In a word Rip was ready to attend to anybody's business but his own; but as to doing family duty, and keeping his farm in order, he found it impossible.

In fact, he declared it was of no use to work on his farm; it was the most pestilent little piece of ground in the whole country; everything about it went wrong, and would go wrong, in spite of him. His fences were continually falling to pieces; his cow would either go astray, or get among the cabbages; weeds were sure to grow quicker in his fields than anywhere else; the rain always made a point of setting in just as he had some out-door work to do; so that though his patrimonial estate had dwindled away under his management, acre by acre, until there was a little more left than a mere patch of Indian corn and potatoes, yet it was the worst conditioned farm in the neighborhood.

His children, too, were as ragged and wild as if they belonged to nobody. his son Rip, an urchin begotten in his own likeness, promised to inherit the habits, with the old clothes of his father. He was generally seen trooping like a colt at his mother's heels, equipped in a pair of his father's cast-off galligaskins, which he had much ado to hold up with one hand, as a fine lady does her train in bad weather.

Rip Van Winkle, however, was one of those happy mortals, of foolish, well-oiled dispositions, who take the world easy, eat white bread or brown, whichever can be got with least thought or trouble, and would rather starve on a penny than work for a pound. If left to himself, he would have whistled life away

The famous American actor Joseph Jefferson (1829–1905) in the role of Rip Van Winkle. Undated photo. From the editor's collection.

"Rip Berated by Dame Van Winkle," by American artist Felix
Darley (1822–1888). Print from the editor's collection.

in perfect contentment; but his wife kept continually dinning in his ears about his idleness, his carelessness, and the ruin he was bringing on his family. Morning, noon, and night, her tongue was incessantly going, and everything he said or did was sure to produce a torrent of household eloquence. Rip had but one way of replying to all lectures of the kind, and that, by frequent use, had grown into a habit. He shrugged his shoulders, shook his head, cast up his eyes, but said nothing. This, however, always provoked a fresh volley from his wife; so that he was fain to draw off his forces, and take to the outside of the house—the only side which, in truth, belongs to a hen-pecked husband.

Rip's sole domestic adherent was his dog Wolf, who was as much hen-pecked as his master; for Dame Van Winkle regarded them as companions in idleness, and even looked upon Wolf with an evil eye, as the cause of his master's going so often astray. True it is, in all points of spirit befitting an honorable dog, he was as courageous an animal as ever scoured the woods—but what courage can withstand the ever-during and all-besetting terrors of a woman's tongue? The moment Wolf entered the house his crest fell, his tail drooped to the ground, or curled between his legs, he sneaked about with a gallows air, casting many a sidelong glance at Dame Van Winkle, and at the least flourish of a broomstick or ladle, he would fly to the door with yelping precipitation.

Times grew worse and worse with Rip Van Winkel as years of matrimony rolled on; a tart temper never mellows with age, and a sharp tongue is the only edged tool that grows keener with constant use. For a long while he used to console himself, when driven from home, by frequenting a kind of perpetual club of the sages, philosophers, and other idle personages of the village; which held its sessions on a bench before a small inn, designated by a rubicund portrait of His Majesty George the Third. Here they used to sit in the shade through a long lazy summer's day, talking listlessly over village gossip, or telling endless sleepy stories about nothing. But it would have been worth any statesman's money to have heard the profound discussions that sometimes took place, when by chance an old newspaper fell into their hands from some passing traveller. How solemnly they would listen to the contents, as drawled out by Derrick Van Bummel, the schoolmaster, a dapper learned little man, who was not to be daunted by the most gigantic word in the dictionary; and how sagely they would deliberate upon the public events some months after they had taken place.

The opinions of this junto were completely controlled by Nicholas Vedder, a patriarch of the village, and landlord of the inn, at the door of which he took his seat from morning till night, just moving sufficiently to avoid the sun and keep in the shade of a large tree; so that the neighbors could tell the hour by his movements as accurately as by a sun-dial. It is true he was rarely heard to speak, but smoked his pipe incessantly. His adherents, however [for every great man has his adherents], perfectly understood him, and knew how to gather his opinions. When anything that was read or related displeased him, he was observed to smoke his pipe vehemently, and to send forth short, frequent and angry puffs; but when pleased, he would inhale the smoke slowly and tranquilly, and emit it in light and placid clouds; and sometimes, taking the pipe from his mouth, and letting the fragrant vapor curl about his nose, would gravely nod his head in token of perfect approbation.

From even this stronghold the unlucky Rip was at length routed by his termagant wife, who would suddenly break in upon the tranquillity of the assemblage and call the members all to naught; nor was that august personage, Nicholas Vedder himself, sacred from the daring tongue of this terrible virago, who charged him outright with encouraging her husband in habits of idleness.

Poor Rip was at last reduced almost to despair; and his only alternative, to escape from the labor of the farm and clamor of his wife, was to take gun in hand and stroll away into the woods. Here he would sometimes seat himself at the foot of a tree, and share the contents of his wallet with Wolf, with whom he sympathized as a fellow-sufferer in persecution. "Poor Wolf," he would say, "thy mistress leads thee a dog's life of it; but never mind, my lad, whilst I live thou shalt never want a friend to stand by thee!" Wolf would wag his tail, look wistfully in his master's face, and if dogs can feel pity I verily believe he reciprocated the sentiment with all his heart.

In a long ramble of the kind on a fine autumnal day, Rip had unconsciously scrambled to one of the highest parts of the Kaatskill Mountains. He was after his favorite sport of squirrel shooting, and the still solitudes had echoed and re-echoed with the reports of his gun. Panting and fatigued, he threw himself, late in the afternoon, on a green knoll, covered with mountain herbage, that crowned the brow of a precipice. From an opening between the trees he could overlook all the lower country for many a mile of rich woodland. He saw at a distance the lordly Hudson, far, far below him, moving on its silent but majestic course, with the reflection of a purple cloud, or the sail of a lagging bark, here and there sleeping on its glassy bosom, and at last losing itself in the blue highlands.

On the other side he looked down into a deep mountain glen, wild, lonely, and shagged, the bottom filled with fragments from the impending cliffs, and scarcely lighted by the reflected rays of the setting sun. For some time Rip lay musing on this scene; evening was gradually advancing; the mountains began to throw their long blue shadows over the valleys; he saw that it would be dark long before he could reach the village, and he heaved a heavy sigh when he thought of encountering the terrors of Dame Van Winkle.

As he was about to descend, he heard a voice from a distance, hallooing, "Rip Van Winkle! Rip Van Winkle!" He looked round, but could see nothing but a crow winging its solitary flight across the mountain. He thought his fancy must have deceived him, and turned again to descend, when he heard the same cry ring through the still evening air: "Rip Van Winkle! Rip Van Winkle!" At the same time Wolf bristled up his back, and giving a low growl, skulked to his master's side, looking fearfully down into the glen. Rip now felt a vague apprehension stealing over him; he looked anxiously in the same direction, and perceived a strange figure slowly toiling up the rocks, and bending under the weight of something he carried on his back. He was suprised to see any human being in this lonely and unfrequented place, but supposing it to be someone of the neighborhood in need of his assistance, he hastened down to yield it.

On nearer approach he was still more surprised at the singularity of the stranger's appearance. He was a short square-built old fellow, with thick bushy hair, and a grizzled beard. His dress was of the antique Dutch fashion—a cloth jerkin strapped round the waist—several pair of breeches, the outer one of ample volume, decorated with rows of buttons down the sides, and bunches at the knees. He bore on his shoulder a stout keg, that seemed full of liquor, and made signs for Rip to approach and assist him with the load. Though rather shy and distrustful of this new acquaintance, Rip compiled with his usual alacrity; and mutually relieving one another, they clambered up a narrow gully, apparently the dry bed of a mountain torrent. As they ascended, Rip every now and then heard long rolling peals, like distant thunder, that seemed to issue out of a deep ravine, or rather cleft, between lofty rocks, toward which their rugged path conducted. He paused for an instant, but supposing it to be the muttering of one of those transient thunder-showers which often take place in mountain heights, he proceeded. Passing through the ravine, they came to a hollow, like a small amphitheatre, surrounded by perpendicular precipices, over the brinks of which impending trees shot their branches, so that you only caught glimpses of the azure sky and the bright evening cloud. During the whole time Rip and his companion had labored on in silence; for though the former marvelled greatly what could be the object of carrying a keg of liquor up this wild mountain, yet there was something strange and incomprehensible about the unknown, that inspired awe and checked familiarity.

On entering the amphitheatre, new objects of wonder presented themselves. On a level spot in the centre was a company of odd-looking personages playing at ninepins. They were dressed in a quaint outlandish fashion; some wore short doublets, other jerkins, with long knives in their belts, and most of them had enormous breeches, of similar style with that of the guide's. Their visages, too, were peculiar: one had a large beard, broad face, and small piggish eyes; the face of another seemed to consist entirely of nose, and was surmounted by a white sugar-loaf hat set off with a little red cock's tail. They all had beards, of various shapes and colors. There was one who seemed to be the commander. He was a stout old gentleman, with a weather-beaten countenance; he wore a laced doublet, broad belt and hanger, high-crowned hat and feather, red stockings, and high-heeled shoes, with roses in them. The whole group reminded Rip of the figures in an old Flemish painting, in the parlor of Dominie Van Shaick, the village parson, and which had been brought over from Holland at the time of the settlement.

What seemed particularly odd to Rip was, that though these folks were evidently amusing themselves, yet they maintained the gravest faces, the most mysterious silence, and were, withal, the most melancholy party of pleasure he had ever witnessed. Nothing interrupted the stillness of the scene but the noise of the balls, which, whenever they were rolled, echoed along the mountains like rumbling peals of thunder.

As Rip and his companion approached them, they suddenly desisted from their play, and stared at him with such fixed statue-like gaze, and such strange, uncouth, lack-lustre countenances, that his heart turned within him, and his knees smote together. His companion now emptied the contents of the keg into large flagons, and made signs to him to wait upon the company. He obeyed with fear and trembling; they quaffed the liquor in profound silence, and then returned to their game.

By degrees Rip's awe and apprehension subsided. He even ventured, when no eye was fixed upon him, to taste the beverage, which he found had much of the flavor of excellent Hollands. He was naturally a thirsty soul, and was soon tempted to repeat the draught. One taste provoked another; and he reiterated his visits to the flagon so often that at length his senses were overpowered, his eyes swam in his head, his head gradually declined, and he fell into a deep sleep.

On waking, he found himself on the green knoll whence he had first seen the old man of the glen. He rubbed his eyes—it was a bright sunny morning. The birds were hopping and twittering among the bushes, and the eagle was wheeling aloft, and breasting the pure mountain breeze. "Surely," thought Rip, "I have not slept here all night." He recalled the occurrences before he fell asleep. The strange man with a keg of liquor—the mountain ravine—the wild retreat among the rocks—the woe-begone party at ninepins—the flagon—"Oh! That flagon! That wicked flagon!" thought Rip. "What excuse shall I make to Dame Van Winkle!"

He looked round for his gun, but in place of the clean well-oiled fowling-piece, he found an old firelock lying by him, the barrel incrusted with rust, the lock falling off, and the stock worm-eaten. He now suspected that the grave roysters of the mountain had put a trick upon him, and, having dosed him with liquor, had robbed him of his gun. Wolf, too, had disappeared, but he might have strayed away after a squirrel or partridge. He whistled after him and shouted his name, but all in vain; the echoes repeated his whistle and shout, but no dog was to be seen.

He determined to revisit the scene of the last evening's gambol, and if he met with any of the party, to demand his dog and gun. As he rose to walk, he found himself stiff in the joints, and wanting in his usual activity. "The mountain beds do not agree with me," thought Rip, "and if this frolic should lay me up with a fit of the rheumatism, I shall have a blessed time with Dame Van Winkle." With some difficulty he got down into the glen: he found the gully up which he and his companion had ascended the preceding evening; but to his astonishment a mountain stream was now foaming down it, leaping from rock to rock, and filling the glen with babbling murmurs. He, however, made shift to scramble up its sides, working his toilsome way through thickets of birch, sassafrass, and witch-hazel, and sometimes tripped up or entangled by the wild grapevines that twisted their coils or tendrils from tree to tree, and spread a kind of network in his path.

At length he reached to where the ravine had opened through the cliffs to the amphitheatre; but no traces of such opening remained. The rocks presented a high impenetrable wall, over which the torrent came tumbling in a sheet of feathery foam, and fell into a broad deep basin, black from the shadows of the surrounding forest. Here, then, poor Rip was brought to a stand. He again called and whistled after his dog; he was only answered by the cawing of a flock of idle crows, sporting high in air about a dry tree that overhung a sunny precipice; and who, secure in their elevation, seemed to look down and scoff at the poor man's perplexities. What was to be done? The morning was passing away, and Rip felt famished for want of his breakfast. He grieved to give up his dog and gun; he dreaded to meet his wife; but it would not do to starve among the mountains. He shook his head, shouldered the rusty firelock, and, with a heart full of trouble and anxiety, turned his steps homeward.

As he approached the village he met a number of people, but none whom he knew, which somewhat surprised him, for he had thought himself acquainted with everyone in the country round. Their dress, too, was of a different fashion from that to which he was accustomed. They all stared at him with equal marks of surprise, and whenever they cast their eyes upon him, invariably stroked their chins. The constant recurrence of this gesture induced Rip, involuntarily, to do the same, when, to his astonishment, he found his beard had grown a foot long!

He had now entered the skirts of the village. A troop of strange children ran at his heels, hooting after him, and pointing at his gray beard. The dogs, too, not one of which he recognized for an old acquaintance, barked at him as he passed. The very village was altered; it was larger and more populous. There were rows of houses which he had never seen before, and those which had been his familiar haunts had disappeared. Strange names were over the doors—strange faces at the windows—everything was strange. His mind now misgave him; he began to doubt whether both he and the world around him were not bewitched. Surely this was his native village, which he had left but the day before. There stood the Kaatskill Mountains—there ran the silver Hudson at a distance—there was every hill and dale precisely as it had always been. Rip was sorely perplexed—"That flagon last night," thought he, "has addled my poor head sadly!"

It was with some difficulty that he found the way to his own house, which he approached with silent awe, expecting every moment to hear the shrill voice of Dame Van Winkle. He found the house gone to decay—the roof fallen in, the windows shattered, and the doors off the hinges. A half-starved dog that looked like Wolf was skulking about it. Rip called him by name, but the cur snarled, showed his teeth, and passed on. This was an unkind cut indeed—"My very dog," sighed poor Rip, "has forgotten me!"

He entered the house, which, to tell the truth, Dame Van Winkle had always kept in neat order. It was empty, forlorn, and apparently abandoned. This desolateness overcame all his connubial fears—he called loudly for his wife and children—the lonely chambers rang for a moment with his voice, and then all again was silence.

He now hurried forth, and hastened to his old resort, the village inn—but it too was gone. A large rickety wooden building stood in its place, with great gaping windows, some of them broken and mended with old hats and petticoats, and over the door was painted, "the Union Hotel, by Jonathan Doolittle." Instead of the great tree that used to shelter the quiet little Dutch inn of yore, there now was reared a tall naked pole, with something on the top that looked like a red night-cap, and from it was fluttering a flag, on which was a singular assemblage of stars and stripes—all this was strange and incomprehensible. He recognized on the sign, however, the ruby face of King George, under which he had smoked so many a peaceful pipe; but even this was singularly metamorphosed. The red coat was changed for one of blue and buff, a sword was held in the hand instead of a sceptre, the head was decorated with a cocked hat, and underneath, was painted in large characters, GENERAL WASHINGTON.

There was, as usual, a crowd of folk about the door, but none that Rip recollected. The very character of the people seemed changed. There was a busy, bustling, disputatious tone about it, instead of the accustomed phlegm and drowsy tranquillity. He looked in vain for the sage Nicholas Vedder, with his broad face, double chin, and fair long pipe, uttering clouds of tobacco-smoke instead of idle speeches; or Van Bummel, the schoolmaster, doling forth the contents of an ancient newspaper. In place of these, a lean, bilious-looking fellow, with his pockets full of handbills, was haranguing vehemently about rights of citizens—elections—members of Congress—liberty—Bunker's Hill—heroes of seventy-six—and other words, which were a perfect Babylonish jargon to the bewildered Van Winkle.

The appearance of Rip, with his long grizzled beard, his rusty fowling-piece, his uncouth dress, and an army of women and children at his heels, soon attracted the attention of the tavern politicians. They crowded round him, eying him from head to foot with great curiosity. The orator bustled up to him, and, drawing him partly aside, inquired "On which side he voted?" Rip stared in vacant stupidity.

"The Return of Rip Van Winkle to His Ruined Home," print by Felix Darley. Editor's collection.

"Rip Not Recognized by His Former Tavern Cronies," print by
Felix Darley. Editor's collection.

Another short but busy little fellow pulled him by the arm, and, rising on tiptoe, inquired in his ear, "Whether he was Federal or Democrat?" Rip was equally at a loss to comprehend the question; when a knowing, self-important old gentleman, in a sharp cocked hat, made his way through the crowd, putting them to the right and left with his elbows as he passed, and planting himself before Van Winkle, with one arm akimbo, the other resting on his cane, his keen eyes and sharp hat penetrating, as it were, into his very soul, demanded in an austere tone, "What brought him to the election with a gun on his shoulder, and a mob at his heels, and whether he meant to breed a riot in the village?"—"Alas! Gentlemen," cried Rip, somewhat dismayed, "I am a poor quiet man, a native of the place, and a loyal subject of the king, God bless him!"

Here a general shout burst from the bystanders—"A tory! A tory! A spy! A refugee! Hustle him! Away with him!" It was with great difficulty that the self-important man in the cocked hat restored order; and, having assumed a tenfold austerity of brow, demanded again of the unknown culprit, what he came there for, and whom he was seeking? The poor man humbly assured him that he meant no harm, but merely came there in search of some of his neighbors, who used to keep about the tavern.

"Well—who are they? Name them."

Rip bethought himself a moment, and inquired, "Where's Nicholas Vedder?"

There was a silence for a little while, when an old man replied in a thin piping voice, "Nicholas Vedder! Why, he is dead and gone these eighteen years! There was a wooden tombstone in the church-yard that used to tell all about him, but that's rotten and gone too."

"Where's Brom Dutcher?"

"Oh, he went off to the army in the beginning of the war; some say he was killed at the storming of Stony Point—others say he was drowned in a squall at the foot of Antony's Nose. I don't know—he never came back again."

"Where's Van Bummel, the schoolmaster?"

"He went off to the wars too, was a great militia general, and is now in Congress."

Rip's heart died away at hearing of these sad changes in his home and friends, and finding himself thus alone in the world. Every answer puzzled him too, by treating of such enormous lapses of time, and of matters which he could not understand: war—congress—Stony Point; he had no courage to ask after any more friends, but cried out in despair, "Does nobody here know Rip Van Winkle?"

"Oh, Rip Van Winkle!" exclaimed two or three, "Oh, to be sure! That's Rip Van Winkle yonder, leaning against the tree."

Rip looked, and beheld a precise counterpart of himself, as he went up the mountain: apparently as lazy, and certainly as ragged. The poor fellow was now completely confounded. He doubted his own identity, and whether he was himself or another man. In the midst of his bewilderment, the man in the cocked hat demanded who he was, and what was his name?

"God knows," exclaimed he, at his wit's end; "I'm not myself—I'm somebody else—that's me yonder—no—that's somebody else got into my shoes—I was myself last night, but I fell asleep on the mountain, and they've changed my gun, and everything's changed, and I'm changed, and I can't tell my name or who I am!"

The bystanders began now to look at each other, nod, wink significantly, and tap their fingers against their foreheads. There was a whisper, also, about securing the gun, and keeping the old fellow from doing mischief, at the very suggestion of which the self-important man in the cocked hat retired with some precipitation. At this critical moment a fresh, comely woman pressed through the throng to get a peep at the graybearded man. She had a chubby child in her arms, which, frightened at his looks, began to cry. "Hush, Rip," cried she, "Hush, you little fool; the old man won't hurt you." The name of the child, the air of the mother, the tone of her voice, all awakened a train of recollections in his mind. "What is your name, my good woman?" asked he.

"Judith Gardenier."

"And your father's name?"

"Ah, poor man, Rip Van Winkle was his name, but it's twenty years since he went away from home with his gun, and never has been heard of since—his dog came home without him; but whether he shot himself, or was carried away by the Indians, nobody can tell. I was then but a little girl."

Rip had but one question more to ask; but he put it with a faltering voice: "Where's your mother?"

"Oh, she too had died but a short time since; she broke a blood-vessel in a fit of passion at a New England peddler."

There was a drop of comfort, at least, in this intelligence. The honest man could contain himself no longer. He caught his daughter and her child in his arms. "I am your father!" cried he, "Young Rip Van Winkle once—old Rip Van Winkle now! Does nobody know poor Rip Van Winkle?"

All stood amazed, until an old woman, tottering out from among the crowd, put her hand to her brow, and peering under it in his face for a moment, exclaimed, "Sure enough! It is Rip Van Winkle—it is himself! Welcome home again, old neighbor. Why, where have you been these twenty long years?"

Rip's story was soon told, for the whole twenty years had been to him but as one night. The neighbors stared when they heard it; some were seen to wink at each other, and put their tongues in their cheeks; and the self-important man in the cocked hat, who, when the alarm was over, had returned to the field, screwed down the corners of his mouth, and shook his head—upon which there was a general shaking of the head throughout the assemblage.

74

It was determined, however, to take the opinion of old Peter Vanderdonk, who was seen slowly advancing up the road. He was a descendant of the historian of that name, who wrote one of the earliest accounts of the province. Peter was the most ancient inhabitant of the village, and well versed in all the wonderful events and traditions of the neighborhood. He recollected Rip at once, and corroborated his story in the most satisfactory manner. He assured the company that it was a fact, handed down from his ancestor the historian, that the Kaatskill Mountains had always been haunted by strange beings. That it was affirmed that the great Hendrick Hudson, the first discoverer of the river and country, kept a kind of vigil there every twenty years, with his crew of the Half-Moon; being permitted in this way to revisit the scenes of his enterprise, and keep a guardian eye upon the river, and the great city called by his name. That his father had once seen them in their old Dutch dresses playing at ninepins in a hollow of the mountain; and that he himself had heard one summer afternoon, the sound of their balls, like distant peals of thunder.

To make a long story short, the company broke up, and returned to the more important concerns of the election. Rip's daughter took him home to live with her; she had a snug, well-furnished house, and a stout cheery farmer for a husband, whom Rip recollected for one of the urchins that used to climb upon his back. As to Rip's son and heir, who was the ditto of himself, seen leaning against the tree, he was employed to work on the farm; but evinced an hereditary disposition to attend to anything else but his business.

Rip now resumed his old walks and habits; he soon found many of his former cronies, though all rather the worse for the wear and tear of time, and preferred making friends among the rising generation, with whom he soon grew into great favor.

Having nothing to do at home, and being arrived at that happy age when a man can be idle with impunity, he took his place once more on the bench at the inn door, and was reverenced as one of the patriarchs of the village, and a chronicle of the old times "before the war." It was some time before he could get into the regular track of gossip, or could be made to comprehend the strange events that had taken place during his torpor. How that there had been a revolutionary war—that the country had thrown off the yoke of old England—and that, instead of being a subject of his Majesty George the Third, he was now a free citizen of the United States. Rip, in fact, was no politician; the changes of states and empires made but little impression on him; but there was one species of despotism under which he had long groaned, and that was—petticoat government. Happily that was at an end; he had got his neck out of the yoke of matrimony, and could go in and out whenever he pleased, without dreading the tyranny of Dame Van Winkle. Whenever her name was mentioned, however, he shook his head, shrugged his shoulders, and cast up his eyes; which might pass either for an expression of resignation to his fate, or joy of his deliverance.

He used to tell his story to every stranger that arrived at Mr. Doolittle's hotel. He was observed, at first, to vary on some points every time he told it, which was, doubtless, owing to his having so recently awaked. It at last settled down precisely to the tale I have related, and not a man, woman, or child in the neighborhood, but knew it by heart. Some always pretended to doubt the reality of it, and insisted that Rip had been out of his head, and that this was one point on which he always remained flighty. The old Dutch inhabitants, however, almost universally gave it full credit. Even to this day they never hear a thunderstorm of a summer afternoon about the Kaatskill, but they say Hendrick Hudson and his crew are at their game of ninepins; and it is a common wish of all henpecked husbands in the neighborhood, when life hangs heavy on their hands, that they might have a quieting draught out of Rip Van Winkle's flagon.

Note

The foregoing Tale, one would suspect, had been suggested to Mr Knickerbocker by a little German superstition about the Emperor Frederick der Rothbart, and the Kypphäuser mountain: the subjoined note, however, which he had appended to the tale, shows that it is an absolute fact, narrated with his usual fidelity:

"The story of Rip Van Winkle may seem incredible to many, but nevertheless I give it my full belief, for I know the vicinity of our old Dutch settlements to have been very subject to marvellous events and appearances. Indeed, I have heard many stranger stories than this, in the villages along the Hudson; all of which were too well authenticated to admit of a doubt. I have even talked with Rip Van Winkle myself, who, when last I saw him, was a very venerable old man, and so perfectly rational and consistent on every other point, that I think no conscientious person could refuse to take this into the bargain; nay, I have seen a certificate on the subject taken before a country justice and signed with a cross, in the justice's own handwriting. The story, therefore, is beyond the possibility of doubt.

D.K."

Postscript

The following are travelling notes from a memorandum-book of Mr. Knickerbocker:

The Kaatsberg, or Catskill mountains, have always been a region full of fable. The Indians considered them the abode of spirits, who influenced the weather, spreading sunshine or clouds over the landscape, and sending good or bad hunting seasons. They were ruled by an old squaw spirit, said to be their mother. She dwelt on the highest peak of the Catskills, and had charge of the doors of day and night to open and shut them at the proper hour. She hung up the new moons in the skies, and cut up the old ones into stars. In times of drought, if properly propitiated, she would spin light summer clouds out of cobwebs and morning dew, and send them off from the crest of the mountain, flake after flake, like flakes of carded cotton, to float in the air; until, dissolved by the heat of the sun, they would fall in gentle showers, causing the grass to spring, the fruits to ripen, and the corn to grow an inch an hour. If displeased, however, she would brew up clouds black as ink, sitting in the midst of them like a bottle-bellied spider in the midst of its web; and when these clouds broke, woe betide the valleys!

In old times, say the Indian traditions, there was a kind of Manitou or Spirit, who kept about the wildest recesses of the Catskill Mountains, and took a mischievous pleasure in wreaking all kinds of evils and vexations upon the red men. Sometimes he would assume the form of a bear, a panther, or a deer, lead the bewildered hunter a weary chase through tangled forests and among ragged rocks; and then spring off with a loud ho! ho! leaving him aghast on the brink of a beetling precipice or raging torrent.

The favorite abode of this Manitou is still shown. It is a great rock or cliff on the loneliest part of the mountains, and, from the flowering vines which clamber about it, and the wild flowers which abound in its neighborhood, is known by the name of the Garden Rock. Near the foot of it is a small lake, the haunt of the solitary bittern, with water-snakes basking in the sun on the leaves of the pond-lilies which lie on the surface. This place was held in great awe by the Indians, insomuch that the boldest hunter would not pursue his game within its precincts. Once upon a time, however, a hunter who had lost his way, penetrated to the garden rock, where he beheld a number of gourds placed in the crotches of trees. One of these he seized and made off with it, but in the hurry of his retreat he let if fall among the rocks, when a great stream gushed forth, which washed him away and swept him down precipices, where he was dashed to pieces, and the stream made its way to the Hudson, and continues to flow to the present day; being the identical stream known by the name of the Kaaters-kill.

From *The Sketch Book of Geoffrey Crayon, Gent.**

THE LEGEND OF SLEEPY HOLLOW. FOUND AMONG THE PAPERS OF THE LATE DIEDRICH KNICKERBOCKER.

> A pleasing land of drowsy head it was,
>   Of dreams that wave before the half shut eye;
> And of gay castles in the clouds that pass,
>   For ever flushing round a summer sky.
>   CASTLE OF INDOLENCE

The Works of Washington Irving, The Kinderhook Edition (New York: G. P. Putnam's Sons, 1880).

In the bosom of one of those spacious coves which indent the eastern shore of the Hudson, at that broad expansion of the river denominated by the ancient Dutch navigators the Tappan Zee, and where they always prudently shortened sail, and implored the protection of St. Nicholas when they crossed, there lies a small market-town or rural port, which by some is called Greensburgh, but which is more generally and properly known by the name of Tarry Town. This name was given, we are told, in former days, by the good housewives of the adjacent country, from the inveterate propensity of their husbands to linger about the village tavern on market days. Be that as it may, I do not vouch for the fact, but merely advert to it, for the sake of being precise and authentic. Not far from this village, perhaps about two miles, there is a little valley, or rather lap of land, among high hills, which is one of the quietest places in the whole world. A small brook glides through it, with just murmur enough to lull one to repose; and the occasional whistle of a quail, or tapping of a woodpecker, is almost the only sound that ever breaks in upon the uniform tranquillity.

I recollect that, when a stripling, my first exploit in squirrel-shooting was in a grove of tall walnut-trees that shades one side of the valley. I had wandered into it at noon time, when all nature is peculiarly quiet, and was startled by the roar of my own gun, as it broke the Sabbath stillness around, and was prolonged and reverberated by the angry echoes. If ever I should wish for a retreat, whither I might steal from the world and its distractions, and dream quietly away the remnant of a troubled life, I know of none more promising than this little valley.

From the listless repose of the place, and the peculiar character of its inhabitants, who are descendants from the original Dutch settlers, this sequestered glen has long been known by the name of SLEEPY HOLLOW, and its rustic lads are called the Sleepy Hollow Boys throughout all the neighboring country. A drowsy, dreamy influence seems to hang over the land, and to pervade the very atmosphere. Some say that the place was bewitched by a high German doctor, during the early days of the settlement; others, that an old Indian chief, the prophet or wizard of his tribe, held his pow-wows there before the country was discovered by Master Hendrick Hudson. Certain it is, the place still continues under the sway of some witching power, that holds a spell over the minds of the good people, causing them to walk in a continual reverie. They are given to all kinds of marvellous beliefs; are subject to trances and visions; and frequently see strange sights, and hear music and voices in the air. The whole neighborhood abounds with local tales, haunted spots, and twilight superstitions; stars shoot and meteors glare oftener across the valley than in any other part of the country, and the nightmare, with her whole nine fold, seems to make it the favorite scene of her gambols.

The dominant spirit, however, that haunts this enchanted region, and seems to be commander-in-chief of all the powers of the air, is the apparition of a figure on horseback without a head. It is said by some to be the ghost of a Hessian trooper, whose head had been carried away by a cannon-ball, in some nameless battle during the revolutionary war; and who is ever and anon seen by the country folk, hurrying along in the gloom of night, as if on the wings of the wind. His haunts are not confined to the valley, but extend at times to the adjacent roads, and especially to the vicinity of a church at no great distance. Indeed, certain of the most authentic historians of those parts, who have been careful in collecting and collating the floating facts concerning this spectre, allege that the body of the trooper, having been buried in the church-yard, the ghost rides forth to the scene of battle in nightly quest of his head; and that the rushing speed with which he sometimes passes along the Hollow, like a midnight blast, is owing to his being belated, and in a hurry to get back to the church-yard before daybreak.

Such is the general purport of this legendary superstition, which has furnished materials for many a wild story in that region of shadows; and the spectre is known, at all the country firesides, by the name of the Headless Horseman of Sleepy Hollow.

It is remarkable that the visionary propensity I have mentioned is not confined to the native inhabitants of the valley, but is unconsciously imbibed by every one who resides there for a time. However wide awake they may have been before they entered that sleepy region, they are sure, in a little time, to inhale the witching influence of the air, and begin to grow imaginative—to dream dreams, and see apparitions.

I mention this peaceful spot with all possible laud; for it is in such little retired Dutch valleys, found here and there embosomed in the great State of New-York, that population, manners, and customs, remain fixed; while the great torrent of migration and improvement, which is making such incessant changes in other parts of this restless country, sweeps by them unobserved. They are like those little nooks of still water which border a rapid stream; where we may see the straw and bubble riding quietly at anchor, or slowly revolving in their mimic harbor, undisturbed by the rush of the passing current. Though many years have elapsed since I trod the drowsy shades of Sleepy Hollow, yet I question whether I should not still find the same trees and the same families vegetating in its sheltered bosom.

In this by-place of nature, there abode, in a remote period of American history, that is to say, some thirty years since, a worthy wight of the name of Ichabod Crane; who sojourned, or, as he expressed it, "tarried," in Sleepy Hollow, for the purpose of instructing the children of the vicinity. He was a native of Connecticut; a State which supplies the Union with pioneers for the mind as well as for the forest, and sends forth yearly its legions of frontier woodsmen and country schoolmasters. The cognomen of Crane was not inapplicable to his person. He was tall, but exceedingly lank, with narrow shoulders, long arms and legs, hands that dangled a mile out of his sleeves, feet that might have served for shovels, and his whole frame most loosely hung together. His head was small, and flat at top, with huge ears, large green glassy eyes, and long snipe nose, so that it looked like a weather-cock, perched upon his spindle neck, to tell which way the wind blew. To see him striding along the profile of a hill on a windy day, with his clothes bagging and fluttering about him, one might have mistaken him for the genius of famine descending upon the earth, or some scarecrow eloped from a cornfield.

His school-house was a low building of one large room, rudely constructed of logs; the windows partly glazed, and partly patched with leaves of old copybooks. It was most ingeniously secured at vacant hours, by a withe twisted in the handle of the door, and stakes set against the window shutters; so that, though a thief might get in with perfect ease, he would find some embarrassment in getting out; an idea most probably borrowed by the architect, Yost Van Houten, from the mystery of an eel-pot. The school-house stood in a rather lonely but pleasant situation, just at the foot of a woody hill, with a brook running close by, and a formidable birch tree growing at one end of it. From hence the low murmur of his pupils' voices, conning over their lessons, might be heard in a drowsy summer's day, like the hum of a bee-hive; interrupted now and then by the authoritative voice of the master, in the tone of menace or command; or, peradventure, by the appalling sound of the birch, as he urged some tardy loiterer along the flowery path of knowledge. Truth to say, he was a conscientious man, and ever bore in mind the golden maxim, "Spare the rod and spoil the child."—Ichabod Crane's scholars certainly were not spoiled.

I would not have it imagined, however, that he was one of those cruel potentates of the school, who joy in the smart of their subjects; on the contrary, he administered justice with discrimination rather than severity; taking the burthen off the backs of the weak, and laying it on those of the strong. Your mere puny stripling, that winced at the least flourish of the rod, was passed by with indulgence; but the claims of justice were satisfied by inflicting a double portion on some little, tough, wrong-headed, broad-skirted Dutch urchin, who sulked and swelled and grew dogged and sullen beneath the birch. All this he called "doing his duty by their parents;" and he never inflicted a chastisement without following it by the assurance, so consolatory to the smarting urchin, that "he would remember it, and thank him for it the longest day he had to live."

When school hours were over, he was even the companion and playmate of the larger boys; and on holiday afternoons would convoy some of the smaller ones home, who happened to have pretty sisters, or good housewives for mothers, noted for the comforts of the cupboard. Indeed it behooved him to keep on good terms with his pupils. The revenue arising from his school was small, and would have been scarcely sufficient to furnish him with daily bread, for he was a huge feeder, and though lank, had the dilating powers of an anaconda; but to help out his maintenance, he was, according to country custom in those parts, boarded and lodged at the houses of the farmers, whose children he instructed. With these he lived successively a week at a time; thus going the rounds of the neighborhood, with all his worldly effects tied up in a cotton handkerchief.

That all this might not be too onerous on the purses of his rustic patrons, who are apt to consider the costs of schooling a grievous burden, and schoolmasters as mere drones, he had various ways of rendering himself both useful and agreeable. He assisted the farmers occasionally in the lighter labors of their farms; helped to make hay; mended the fences; took the horses to water; drove the cows from pasture; and cut wood for the winter fire. He laid aside, too, all the dominant dignity and absolute sway with which he lorded it in his little empire, the school, and became wonderfully gentle and ingratiating. He found favor in the eyes of the mothers, by petting the children, particularly the youngest; and like the lion bold, which whilom so magnanimously the lamb did hold, he would sit with a child on one knee, and rock a cradle with his foot for whole hours together.

In addition to his other vocations, he was the singing-master of the neighborhood, and picked up many bright shillings by instructing the young folks in psalmody. It was a matter of no little vanity to him, on Sundays, to take his station in front of the church gallery, with a band of chosen singers; where, in his own mind, he completely carried away the palm from the parson. Certain it is, his voice resounded far above all the rest of the congregation; and there are peculiar quavers still to be heard in that church, and which may even be heard half a mile off, quite to the opposite side of the mill-pond, on a still Sunday morning, which are said to be legitimately descended from the nose of Ichabod Crane. Thus, by divers little make-shifts in that ingenious way which is commonly denominated "by hook and by crook," the worthy pedagogue got on tolerably enough, and was thought, by all who understood nothing of the labor of headwork, to have a wonderfully easy life of it.

The schoolmaster is generally a man of some importance in the female circle of a rural neighborhood; being considered a kind of idle gentlemanlike personage, of vastly superior taste and accomplishments to the rough country swains, and, indeed, inferior in learning only to the parson. His appearance, therefore, is apt to occasion some little stir at the tea-table of a farmhouse, and the addition of a supernumerary dish of cakes or sweet-meats, or, peradventure, the parade of a silver tea-pot. Our man of letters, therefore, was peculiarly happy in the smiles of all the country damsels. How he would figure among them in the church-yard, between services on Sundays! gathering grapes for them from the wild vines that overrun the surrounding trees; reciting for their amusement all the epitaphs on the tombstones; or sauntering, with a whole bevy of them, along the banks of the adjacent mill-pond; while the more bashful country bumpkins hung sheepishly back, envying his superior elegance and address.

From his half itinerant life, also, he was a kind of travelling gazette, carrying the whole budget of local gossip from house to house; so that his appearance was always greeted with satisfaction. He was, moreover, esteemed by the women as a man of great erudition, for he had read several books quite through, and was a perfect master of Cotton Mather's history of New England Witchcraft, in which, by the way, he most firmly and potently believed.

He was, in fact, an odd mixture of small shrewdness and simple credulity. His appetite for the marvellous, and his powers of digesting it, were equally extraordinary; and both had been increased by his residence in this spellbound region. No tale was too gross or monstrous for his capacious swallow. It was often his delight, after his school was dismissed in the afternoon, to stretch himself on the rich bed of clover, bordering the little brook that whimpered by his school-house, and there con over old Mather's direful tales, until the gathering dusk of the evening made the printed page a mere mist before his eyes. Then, as he wended his way, by swamp and stream and awful woodland, to the farmhouse where he happened to be quartered, every sound of nature, at that witching hour, fluttered his excited imagination: the moan of the whip-poor-will* from the hill-side; the boding cry of the tree-toad, that harbinger of storm; the dreary hooting of the screech-owl, or the sudden rustling in the thicket of birds frightened from their roost. The fire-flies, too, which sparkled most vividly in the darkest places, now and then startled him, as one of uncommon brightness would stream across his path; and if, by chance, a huge blockhead of a bettle came winging his blundering flight against him, the poor varlet was ready to give up the ghost, with the idea that he was struck with a witch's token. His only resource on such occasions, either to drown thought, or drive away evil spirits, was to sing psalm tumes;— and the good people of Sleepy Hollow, as they sat by their doors of an evening, were often filled with awe, at hearing his nasal melody, "in linked sweetness long drawn out," floating from the distant hill, or along the dusky road.

Another of his sources of fearful pleasure was, to pass long winter evenings with the old Dutch wives, as they sat spinning by the fire, with a row of apples roasting and spluttering along the hearth, and listen to their marvellous tales of ghosts and goblins, and haunted fields, and haunted brooks, and haunted bridges, and haunted houses, and particularly of the headless horseman, or galloping Hessian of the Hollow, as they sometimes called him. He would delight them equally by his anecdotes of witchcraft, and of the direful omens and portentous sights and sounds in the air, which prevailed in the earlier times of Connecticut; and would frighten them wofully with speculations upon comets and shooting stars; and with the alarming fact that the world did absolutely turn round, and that they were half the time topsy-turvy!

But if there was a pleasure in all this, while snugly cuddling in the chimney corner of a chamber that was all of a ruddy glow from the crackling wood fire,

---

*The whip-poor-will is a bird which is only heard at night. It receives its name from its note, which is thought to resemble those words.

and where, of course, no spectre dared to show his face, it was dearly purchased by the terrors of his subsequent walk homewards. What fearful shapes and shadows beset his path amidst the dim and ghastly glare of a snowy night!—With what wistful look did he eye every trembling ray of light streaming across the waste fields from some distant window!—How often was he appalled by some shrub covered with snow, which, like a sheeted spectre, beset his very path!—How often did he shrink with curdling awe at the sound of his own steps on the frosty crust beneath his feet; and dread to look over his shoulder, lest he should behold some uncouth being tramping close behind him!—and how often was he thrown into complete dismay by some rushing blast, howling among the trees, in the idea that it was the Galloping Hessian on one of his nightly scourings!

All these, however, were mere terrors of the night, phantoms of the mind that walk in darkness; and though he had seen many spectres in his time, and been more than once beset by Satan in divers shapes, in his lonely perambulations, yet daylight put an end to all these evils; and he would have passed a pleasant life of it, in despite of the devil and all his works, if his path had not been crossed by a being that causes more perplexity to mortal man than ghosts, goblins, and the whole race of witches put together, and that was—a woman.

Among the musical disciples who assembled, one evening in each week, to receive his instructions in psalmody, was Katrina Van Tassel, the daughter and only child of a substantial Dutch farmer. She was a blooming lass of fresh eighteen; plump as a partridge; ripe and melting and rosy cheeked as one of her father's peaches, and universally famed, not merely for her beauty, but her vast expectations. She was withal a little of a coquette, as might be perceived even in her dress, which was a mixture of ancient and modern fashions, as most suited to set off her charms. She wore the ornaments of pure yellow gold, which her great-great-grandmother had brought over from Saardam; the tempting stomacher of the olden time; and withal a provokingly short petticoat, to display the prettiest foot and ankle in the country round.

Ichabod Crane had a soft and foolish heart towards the sex; and it is not to be wondered at, that so tempting a morsel soon found favor in his eyes; more especially after he had visited her in her paternal mansion. Old Baltus Van Tassel was a perfect picture of a thriving, contented, liberal-hearted farmer. He seldom, it is true, sent either his eyes or his thoughts beyond the boundaries of his own farm; but within those every thing was snug, happy, and well-conditioned. He was satisfied with his wealth, but not proud of it; and piqued himself upon the hearty abundance, rather than the style in which he lived. His stronghold was situated on the banks of the Hudson, in one of those green, sheltered, fertile nooks, in which the Dutch farmers are so fond of nestling. A great elm-tree spread its broad branches over it; at the foot of which bubbled up a spring of the softest and sweetest water, in a little well, formed of a barrel; and then stole sparkling away through the grass, to a neighboring brook, that bubbled along among alders and dwarf willows. Hard by the farmhouse was a vast barn, that might have served for a church; every window and crevice of which seemed bursting forth with the treasures of the farm; the flail was busily resounding within it from morning to night; swallows and martins skimmed twittering about the eaves; and rows of pigeons, some with one eye turned up, as if watching the weather, some with their heads under their wings, or buried in their bosoms, and others swelling, and cooing, and bowing about their dames, were enjoying the sunshine on the roof. Sleek unwieldly porkers were grunting in the repose and abundance of their pens; whence sallied forth, now and then, troops of sucking pigs, as if to snuff the sir. A stately squadron of snowy geese were riding in an adjoining pond, convoying whole fleets of ducks; regiments of turkeys were gobbling through the farmyard, and guinea fowls fretting about it, like ill-tempered housewives, with their peevish discontented cry. Before the barn door strutted the gallant cock, that pattern of a husband, a warrior, and a fine gentleman, clapping his burnished wings, and crowing in the pride and gladness of his heart—sometimes tearing up the earth with his feet, and then generously calling his ever-hungry family of wives and children to enjoy the rich morsel which he had discovered.

The pedagogue's mouth watered, as he looked upon this sumptuous promise of luxurious winter fare. In his devouring mind's eye, he pictured to himself every roasting-pig running about with a pudding in his belly, and an apple in his mouth; the pigeons were snugly put to bed in a comfortable pie, and tucked in with a coverlet of crust; the geese were swimming in their own gravy; and the ducks pairing cosily in dishes, like snug married couples, with a decent competency of onion sauce. In the porkers he saw carved out the future sleek side of bacon, and juicy relishing ham; not a turkey but he beheld daintily trussed up, with its gizzard under its wing, and, peradventure, a necklace of savory sausages; and even bright chanticleer himself lay sprawling on his back, in a side-dish, with uplifted claws, as if craving that quarter which his chivalrous spirit disdained to ask while living.

As the enraptured Ichabod fancied all this, and as he rolled his great green eyes over the fat meadow-lands, the rich fields of wheat, or rye, of buckwheat, and Indian corn, and the orchards burthened with ruddy fruit, which surrounded the warm tenement of Van Tassel, his heart yearned after the damsel who was to inherit these domains, and his imagination expanded with the idea, how they might be readily turned into cash, and the money invested in immense tracts of wild land, and shingle palaces in the wilderness. Nay, his busy fancy already realized his hopes, and presented to him the blooming Katrina, with a whole family of children, mounted on the top of a wagon loaded with household trumpery, with pots and kettles dangling beneath; and he beheld himself bestriding a pacing mare, with a colt at her heels, setting out for Kentucky, Tennessee, or the Lord knows where.

84

When he entered the house the conquest of his heart was complete. It was one of those spacious farmhouses, with high-ridged, but lowly-sloping roofs, built in the style handed down from the first Dutch settlers; the low projecting eaves forming a piazza along the front, capable of being closed up in bad weather. Under this were hung flails, harness, various utensils of husbandry, and nets for fishing in the neighboring river. Benches were built along the sides for summer use; and a great spinning-wheel at one end, and a churn at the other, showed the various uses to which this important porch might be devoted. From this piazza the wondering Ichabod entered the hall, which formed the centre of the mansion and the place of usual residence. Here, rows of resplendent pewter, ranged on a long dresser, dazzled his eyes. In one corner stood a huge bag of wool ready to be spun; in another a quantity of linsey-woolsey just from the loom; ears of Indian corn, and strings of dried apples and peaches, hung in gay festoons along the walls, mingled with the gaud of red peppers; and a door left ajar gave him a peep into the best parlor, where the claw-footed chairs, and dark mahogany tables, shone like mirrors; and irons, with their accompanying shovel and tongs, glistened from their covert of asparagus tops; mock-oranges and conch-shells decorated the mantel-piece; strings of various colored birds' eggs were suspended above it: a great ostrich egg was hung from the centre of the room, and a corner cupboard, knowingly left open, displayed immense treasures of old silver and well-mended china.

From the moment Ichabod laid his eyes upon these regions of delight, the peace of his mind was at an end, and his only study was how to gain the affections of the peerless daughter of Van Tassel. In this enterprise, however, he had more real difficulties than generally fell to the lot of a knight-errant of yore, who seldom had any thing but giants, enchanters, fiery dragons, and such like easily-conquered adversaries, to contend with; and had to make his way merely through gates of iron and brass, and walls of adamant, to the castle keep, where the lady of his heart was confined; all which he achieved as easily as a man would carve his way to the centre of a Christmas pie; and then the lady gave him her hand as a matter of course. Ichabod, on the contrary, had to win his way to the heart of a country coquette, beset with a labyrinth of whims and caprices, which were for ever presenting new difficulties and impediments; and he had to encounter a host of fearful adversaries of real flesh and blood, the numerous rustic admirers, who beset every portal to her heart; keeping a watchful and angry eye upon each other, but ready to fly out in the common cause against any new competitor.

Among these the most formidable was a burly, roaring, roystering blade, of the name of Abraham, or, according to the Dutch abbreviation, Brom Van Brunt, the hero of the country round, which rang with his feats of strength and hardihood. He was broad-shouldered and double-jointed, with short curly black hair, and a bluff, but not unpleasant countenance, having a mingled air of fun and arrogance. From his Herculean frame and great powers of limb, he had received the nickname of BROM BONES, by which he was universally known. He was famed for great knowledge and skill in horsemanship, being as dexterous on horseback as a Tartar. He was foremost at all races and cock-fights; and, with the ascendency which bodily strength acquires in rustic life, was the umpire in all disputes, setting his hat on one side, and giving his decisions with an air and tone admitting of no gainsay or appeal. He was always ready for either a fight or a frolic; but had more mischief than ill-will in his composition; and, with all his overbearing roughness, there was a strong dash of waggish good humor at bottom. He had three or four boon companions, who regarded him as their model, and at the head of whom he scoured the country, attending every scene of feud or merriment for miles round. In cold weather he was distinguished by a fur cap, surmounted with a flaunting fox's tail; and when the folks at a country gathering descried this well-known crest at a distance, whisking about among a squad of hard riders, they always stood by for a squall. Sometimes his crew would be heard dashing along past the farmhouses at midnight, with whoop and halloo, like a troop of Don Cossacks; and the old dames, startled out of their sleep, would listen for a moment till the hurry-scurry had clattered by, and then exclaim, "Ay, there goes Brom Bones and his gang!" The neighbors looked upon him with a mixture of awe, admiration, and good will; and when any madcap prank, or rustic brawl, occurred in the vicinity, always shook their heads, and warranted Brom Bones was at the bottom of it.

This rantipole hero had for some time singled out the blooming Katrina for the object of his uncouth gallantries, and though his amorous toyings were something like the gentle caresses and endearments of a bear, yet it was whispered that she did not altogether discourage his hopes. Certain it is, his advances were signals for rival candidates to retire, who felt no inclination to cross a lion in his amours; insomuch, that when his horse was seen tied to Van Tassel's paling, on a Sunday night, a sure sign that his master was courting, or, as it is termed, "sparking," within, all other suitors passed by in despair, and carried the war into other quarters.

Such was the formidable rival with whom Ichabod Crane had to contend, and, considering all things, a stouter man than he would have shrunk from the competition, and a wiser man would have despaired. He had, however, a happy mixture of pliability and perseverance in his nature; he was in form and spirit like a supple-jack—yielding, but tough; though he bent, he never broke; and though he bowed beneath the slightest pressure, yet, the moment it was away—jerk! he was as erect, and carried his head as high as ever.

To have taken the field openly against his rival would have been madness; for he was not a man to be thwarted in his amours, any more than that stormy lover, Achilles. Ichabod, therefore, made his advances in a quiet and gently-insinuating manner. Under cover of his character of singing-master, he made frequent visits at the farmhouse; not that he had any thing to apprehend from the meddlesome interference of parents, which is so often a stumbling-block in the path of lovers. Balt Van Tassel was an easy indulgent soul; he loved his daughter better even than his pipe, and, like a reasonable man and an excellent father, let her have her way in every thing. His notable little wife, too, had enough to do to attend to her housekeeping and manage her poultry; for, as she sagely observed, ducks and geese are foolish things, and must be looked after, but girls can take care of themselves. Thus while the busy dame bustled about the house, or plied her spinning-wheel at one end of the piazza, honest Balt would sit smoking his evening pipe at the other, watching the achievements of a little wooden warrior, who, armed with a sword in each hand, was most valiantly fighting the wind on the pinnacle of the barn. In the mean time, Ichabod would carry on his suit with the daughter by the side of the spring under the great elm, or sauntering along in the twilight, that hour so favorable to the lover's eloquence.

I profess not to know how women's hearts are wooed and won. To me they have always been matters of riddle and admiration. Some seem to have but one vulnerable point, or door of access; while others have a thousand avenues, and may be captured in a thousand different ways. It is a great triumph of skil! to gain the former, but a still greater proof of generalship to maintain possession of the latter, for the man must battle for his fortress at every door and window. He who wins a thousand common hearts is therefore entitled to some renown; but he who keeps undisputed sway over the heart of a coquette, is indeed a hero. Certain it is, this was not the case with the redoubtable Brom Bones; and from the moment Ichabod Crane made his advances, the interests of the former evidently declined; his horse was no longer seen tied at the palings on Sunday nights, and a deadly feud gradually arose between him and the preceptor of Sleepy Hollow.

Brom, who had a degree of rough chivalry in his nature, would fain have carried matters to open warfare, and have settled their pretensions to the lady, according to the mode of those most concise and simple reasoners, the knights-errant of yore—by single combat; but Ichabod was too conscious of the superior might of his adversary to enter the lists against him: he had overheard a boast of Bones, that he would "double the schoolmaster up, and lay him on a shelf of his own school-house;" and he was too wary to give him an opportunity. There was something extremely provoking in this obstinately pacific system; it left Brom no alternative but to draw upon the funds of rustic waggery in his disposition, and to play off boorish practical jokes upon his rival. Ichabod became the object of whimsical persecution to Bones, and his gang of rough riders. They harried his hitherto peaceful domains; smoked out his singing school, by stopping up the chimney; broke into the school-house at night, in spite of its formidable fastenings of withe and window stakes, and turned every thing topsy-turvy: so that the poor schoolmaster began to think all the witches in the country held their meetings there. But what was still more annoying, Brom took all opportunities of turning him into ridicule in presence of his mistress, and had a scoundrel dog whom he taught to whine in the most ludicrous manner, and introduced as a rival of Ichabod's to instruct her in psalmody.

In this way matters went on for some time, without producing any material effect on the relative situation of the contending powers. On a fine autumnal afternoon, Ichabod, in pensive mood, sat enthroned on the lofty stool whence he usually watched all the concerns of his little literary realm. In his hand he swayed a ferule, that sceptre of despotic power; the birch of justice reposed on three nails, behind the throne, a constant terror to evil doers; while on the desk before him might be seen sundry contraband articles and prohibited weapons, detected upon the persons of idle urchins; such as half-munched apples, popguns, whirligigs, fly-cages, and whole legions of rampant little paper game-cocks. Apparently there had been some appalling act of justice recently inflicted, for his scholars were all busily intent upon their books, or slyly whispering behind them with one eye kept upon the master; and a kind of buzzing stillness reigned throughout the school-room. It was suddenly interrupted by the appearance of a negro, in tow-cloth jacket and trowsers, a round-crowned fragment of a hat, like the cap of Mercury, and mounted on the back of a ragged, wild, half-broken colt, which he managed with a rope by way of halter. He came clattering up to the school door with an invitation to Ichabod to attend a merry-making or "quilting frolic," to be held that evening at Mynheer Van Tassel's; and having delivered his message with that air of importance, and effort at fine language, which a negro is apt to display on petty embassies of the kind, he dashed over the brook, and was seen scampering away up the hollow, full of the importance and hurry of his mission.

All was now bustle and hubbub in the late quiet school-room. The scholars were hurried through their lessons, without stopping at trifles; those who were nimble skipped over half with impunity, and those who were tardy, had a smart application now and then in the rear, to quicken their speed, or help them over a tall word. Books were flung aside without being put away on the shelves, inkstands were overturned, benches thrown down, and the whole school was turned loose an hour before the usual time, bursting forth like a legion of young imps, yelping and racketing about the green, in joy at their early emancipation.

The gallant Ichabod now spent at least an extra half hour at his toilet, brushing and furbishing up his best, and indeed only suit of rusty black, and arranging his looks by a bit of broken looking-glass, that hung up in the school-house. That he might make his appearance before his mistress in the true style of a cavalier, he borrowed a horse from the farmer with whom he was domiciliated, a choleric old Dutchman, of the name of Hans Van Ripper, and, thus gallantly mounted, issued forth, like a knight-errant in quest of adventures. But it is meet I should, in the true spirit of romantic story, give some account of the looks and equipments of my hero and his steed. The animal he bestrode was a broken-down plough-horse, that had outlived almost every thing but his viciousness. He was gaunt and

"Ichabod Crane in his Classroom," drawing by Felix Darley. Editor's collection.

shagged, with a ewe neck and a head like a hammer; his rusty mane and tail were tangled and knotted with burrs; one eye had lost its pupil, and was glaring and spectral; but the other had the gleam of a genuine devil in it. Still he must have had fire and mettle in his day, if we may judge from the name he bore of Gunpowder. He had, in fact, been a favorite steed of his master's, the choleric Van Ripper, who was a furious rider, and had infused, very probably, some of his own spirit into the animal; for, old and broken-down as he looked, there was more of the lurking devil in him than in any young filly in the country.

Ichabod was a suitable figure for such a steed. He rode with short stirrups, which brought his knees nearly up to the pommel of the saddle; his sharp elbows stuck out like grasshoppers'; he carried hs whip perpendicularly in his hand, like a sceptre, and, as his horse jogged on, the motion of his arms was not unlike the flapping of a pair of wings. A small wool hat rested on the top of his nose, for so his scanty strip of forehead might be called; and the skirts of his black coat fluttered out almost to the horse's tail. Such was the appearance of Ichabod and his steed, as they shambled out of the gate of Hans Van Ripper, and it was altogether such an apparition as is seldom to be met with in broad daylight.

It was, as I have said, a fine autumnal day, the sky was clear and serene, and nature wore that rich and golden livery which we always associate with the idea of abundance. The forests had put on their sober brown and yellow, while some trees of the tenderer kind had been nipped by the frosts into brilliant dyes of orange, purple, and scarlet. Streaming files of wild ducks began to make their appearance high in the air; the bark of the squirrel might be heard from the groves of beech and hickory nuts, and the pensive whistle of the quail at intervals from the neighboring stubble-field.

The small birds were taking their farewell banquets. In the fulness of their revelry, they fluttered, chirping and frolicking, from bush to bush, and tree to tree, capricious from the very profusion and variety around them. There was the honest cock-robin, the favorite game of stripling sportsmen, with its loud querulous note; and the twittering blackbirds flying in sable clouds; and the golden-winged woodpecker, with his crimson crest, his broad black gorget, and splendid plumage; and the cedar bird, with its red-tipt wings and yellow-tipt tail, and its little monteiro cap of feathers; and the blue-jay, that noisy coxcomb, in his gay light-blue coat and white under-clothes; screaming and chattering, nodding and bobbing and bowing, and pretending to be on good terms with every songster of the grove.

As Ichabod jogged slowly on his way, his eye, ever open to every symptom of culinary abundance, ranged with delight over the treasures of jolly autumn. On all sides he beheld vast store of apples; some hanging in oppressive opulence on the trees; some gathered into baskets and barrels for the market; others heaped up in rich piles for the cider-press. Farther on he beheld great fields of Indian corn, with its golden ears peeping from their leafy coverts, and holding out the promise of cakes and hasty pudding; and the yellow pumpkins lying beneath them, turning up their fair round bellies to the sun, and giving ample prospects of the most luxurious of pies; and anon he passed the fragrant buckwheat fields, breathing the odor of the bee-hive, and as he beheld them, soft anticipations stole over his mind of dainty slapjacks, well buttered, and garnished with honey or treacle, by the delicate little dimpled hand of Katrina Van Tassel.

Thus feeding his mind with many sweet thoughts and "sugared suppositions," he journeyed along the sides of a range of hills which look out upon some of the goodliest scenes of the mighty Hudson. The sun gradually wheeled his broad disk down into the west. The wide bosom of the Tappan Zee lay motionless and glassy, excepting that here and there a gentle undulation waved and prolonged the blue shadow of the distant mountain. A few amber clouds floated in the sky, without a breath of air to move them. The horizon was of a fine golden tint, changing gradually into a pure apple green, and from that into the deep blue of the mid-heaven. A slanting ray lingered on the woody crests of the precipices that overhung some parts of the river, giving greater depth to the dark-gray and purple of their rocky sides. A sloop was loitering in the distance, dropping slowly down with the tide, her sail hanging uselessly against the mast; and as the reflection of the sky gleamed along the still water, it seemed as if the vessel was suspended in the air.

It was toward evening that Ichabod arrived at the castle of the Heer Van Tassel, which he found thronged with the pride and flower of the adjacent country. Old farmers, a spare leathern-faced race, in homespun coats and breeches, blue stockings, huge shoes, and magnificent pewter buckles. Their brisk withered little dames, in close crimped caps, long-waisted short-gowns, home-spun petti-coats, with scissors and pincushions, and gay calico pockets hanging on the outside. Buxom lasses, almost as antiquated as their mothers, excepting where a straw hat, a fine ribbon, or perhaps a white frock, gave symptoms of city innovation. The sons, in short square-skirted coats with rows of stupendous brass buttons, and their hair generally queued in the fashion of the times, especially if they could procure an eel-skin for the purpose, it being esteemed, throughout the country, as a potent nourisher and strengthener of the hair.

Brom Bones, however, was the hero of the scene, having come to the gathering on his favorite steed Daredevil, a creature, like himself, full of mettle and mischief, and which no one but himself could manage. He was, in fact, noted for preferring vicious animals, given to all kinds of tricks, which kept the rider in constant risk of his neck, for he held a tractable well-broken horse as unworthy of a lad of spirit.

Fain would I pause to dwell upon the world of charms that burst upon the enraptured gaze of my hero, as he entered the state parlor of Van Tassel's mansion. Not those of the bevy of buxom lasses, with their luxurious display of red and white; but the ample charms of a genuine Dutch country tea-table, in the sumptuous time of autumn. Such heaped-up platters of cakes of various and almost indescribable kinds, known only to experienced Dutch housewives! There was the doughty dough-nut, the tenderer oly kock, and the crisp and crumbling cruller; sweet cakes and short cakes, ginger cakes and honey cakes, and the whole family of cakes. And then there were apple pies and peach pies and pumpkin pies; besides slices of ham and smoked beef; and moreover delectable dishes of preserved plums, and peaches, and pears, and quinces; not to mention broiled shad and roasted chickens; together with bowls of milk and cream, all mingled higgledy-piggledy, pretty much as I have enumerated them, with the motherly tea-pot sending up its clouds of vapor from the midst—Heaven bless the mark! I want breath and time to discuss this banquet as it deserves, and am too eager to get on with my story. Happily, Ichabod Crane was not in so great a hurry as his historian, but did ample justice to every dainty.

He was a kind and thankful creature, whose heart dilated in proportion as his skin was filled with good cheer; and whose spirits rose with eating as some men's do with drink. He could not help, too, rolling his large eyes round him as he ate, and chuckling with the possibility that he might one day be lord of all this scene of almost unimaginable luxury and splendor. Then, he thought, how soon he'd turn his back upon the old school-house; snap his fingers in the face of Hans Van Ripper, and every other niggardly patron, and kick any itinerant pedagogue out of doors that should dare to call him comrade!

Old Baltus Van Tassel moved about among his guests with a face dilated with content and good humor, round and jolly as the harvest moon. His hospitable attentions were brief, but expressive, being confined to a shake of the hand, a slap on the shoulder, a loud laugh, and a pressing invitation to "fall to, and help themselves."

And now the sound of the music from the common room, or hall, summoned to the dance. The musician was an old grayheaded negro, who had been the itinerant orchestra of the neighborhood for more than half a century. His instrument was as old and battered as himself. The greater part of the time he scraped on two or three strings, accompanying every movement of the bow with a motion of the head; bowing almost to the ground, and stamping with his foot whenever a fresh couple were to start.

Ichabod prided himself upon his dancing as much as upon his vocal powers. Not a limb, not a fibre about him was idle; and to have seen his loosely hung frame in full motion, and clattering about the room, you would have thought Saint Vitus himself, that blessed patron of the dance, was figuring before you in person. He was the admiration of all the negroes; who, having gathered, of all ages and sizes, from the farm and the neighborhood, stood forming a pyramid of shining black faces at every door and window, gazing with delight at the scene, rolling their white eye-balls, and showing grinning rows of ivory from ear to ear. How could the flogger of urchins be otherwise than animated and joyous? the lady of his heart was his partner in the dance, and smiling graciously in reply to all his amorous oglings; while Brom Bones, sorely smitten with love and jealousy, sat brooding by himself in one corner.

When the dance was at an end, Ichabod was attracted to a knot of the sager folks, who, with old Van Tassel, sat smoking at one end of the piazza, gossiping over former times, and drawing out long stories about the war.

This neighborhood, at the time of which I am speaking, was one of those highly-favored places which abound with chronicle and great men. The British and American line had run near it during the war; it had, therefore, been the scene of marauding, and infested with refugees, cow-boys, and all kinds of border chivalry. Just sufficient time had elapsed to enable each storyteller to dress up his tale with a little becoming fiction, and, in the indistinctness of his recollection, to make himself the hero of every exploit.

There was the story of Doffue Martling, a large blue-bearded Dutchman, who had nearly taken a British frigate with an old iron nine-pounder from a mud breastwork, only that his gun burst at the sixth discharge. And there was an old gentleman who shall be nameless, being too rich a mynheer to be lightly mentioned, who, in the battle of White-plains, being an excellent master of defence, parried a musket ball with a small sword, insomuch that he absolutely felt it whiz round the blade, and glance off at the hilt: in proof of which, he was ready at any time to show the sword, with the hilt a little bent. There were several more that had been equally great in the field, not one of whom but was persuaded that he had a considerable hand in bringing the war to a happy termination.

But all these were nothing to the tales of ghosts and apparitions that succeeded. The neighborhood is rich in legendary treasures of the kind. Local tales and superstitions thrive best in these sheltered long-settled retreats; but are trampled under foot by the shifting throng that forms the population of most of our country places. Besides, there is no encouragement for ghosts in most of our villages, for they have scarcely had time to finish their first nap, and turn themselves in their graves, before their surviving friends have travelled away from the neighborhood; so that when they turn out at night to walk their rounds, they have no acquaintance left to call upon. This is perhaps the reason why we so seldom hear of ghosts except in our long-established Dutch communities.

The immediate cause, however, of the prevalence of supernatural stories in these parts, was doubtless owing to the vicinity of Sleepy Hollow. There was a contagion in the very air that blew from that haunted region; it breathed forth an atmosphere of dreams and fancies infecting all the land. Several of the Sleepy Hollow people were present at Van Tassel's, and, as usual, were doling out their wild and wonderful legends. Many dismal tales were told about funeral trains, and mourning cries and wailings heard and seen about the great tree where the unfortunate Major André was taken, and which stood in the neighborhood. Some mention was made also of the woman in white, that haunted the dark glen at

Raven Rock, and was often heard to shriek on winter nights before a storm, having perished there in the snow. The chief part of the stories, however, turned upon the favorite spectre of Sleepy Hollow, the headless horseman, who had been heard several times of late, patrolling the country; and, it was said, tethered his horse nightly among the graves in the church-yard.

The sequestered situation of this church seems always to have made it a favorite haunt of troubled spirits. It stands on a knoll, surrounded by locust-trees and lofty elms, from among which its decent whitewashed walls shine modestly forth, like Christian purity beaming through the shades of retirement. A gentle slope descends from it to a silver sheet of water, bordered by high trees, between which, peeps may be caught at the blue hills of the Hudson. To look upon its grass grown yard, where the sunbeams seem to sleep so quietly, one would think that there at least the dead might rest in peace. On one side of the church extends a wide woody dell, along which raves a large brook among broken rocks and trunks of fallen trees. Over a deep black part of the stream, not far from the church, was formerly thrown a wooden bridge; the road that led to it, and the bridge itself, were thickly shaded by overhanging trees, which cast a gloom about it, even in the daytime; but occasioned a fearful darkness at night. This was one of the favorite haunts of the headless horseman; and the place where he was most frequently encountered The tale was told of old Brouwer, a most heretical disbeliever in ghosts, how he met the horseman returning from his foray into Sleepy Hollow, and was obliged to get up behind him; how they galloped over bush and brake, over hill and swamp, until they reached the bridge; when the horseman suddenly turned into a skeleton, threw old Brouwer into the brook, and sprang away over the tree-tops with a clap of thunder.

This story was immediately matched by a thrice marvellous adventure of Brom Bones, who made light of the galloping Hessian as an arrant jockey. He affirmed that, on returning one night from the neighboring village of Sing Sing, he had been overtaken by this midnight trooper; that he had offered to race with him for a bowl of punch, and should have won it too, for Daredevil beat the goblin horse all hollow, but, just as they came to the church bridge, the Hessian bolted, and vanished in a flash of fire.

All these tales, told in that drowsy undertone with which men talk in the dark, the countenances of the listeners only now and then receiving a casual gleam from the glare of a pipe, sank deep in the mind of Ichabod. He repaid them in kind with large extracts from his invaluable author, Cotton Mather, and added many marvellous events that had taken place in his native State of Connecticut, and fearful sights which he had seen in his nightly walks about Sleepy Hollow.

The revel now gradually broke up. The old farmers gathered together their families in their wagons, and were heard for some time rattling along the hollow roads, and over the distant hills. Some of the damsels mounted on pillions behind their favorite swains, and their light-hearted laughter, mingling with the clatter of hoofs, echoed along the silent woodlands, sounding fainter and fainter until they gradually died away—and the late scene of noise and frolic was all silent and deserted. Ichabod only lingered behind, according to the custom of country lovers, to have a tête-à-tête with the heiress, fully convinced that he was now on the high road to success. What passed at this interview I will not pretend to say, for in fact I do not know. Something, however, I fear me, must have gone wrong, for he certainly sallied forth, after no very great interval, with an air quite desolate and chop-fallen.—Oh these women! these women! Could that girl have been playing off any of her coquettish tricks?—Was her encouragement of the poor pedagogue all a mere sham to secure her conquest of his rival?—Heaven only knows, not I!—Let it suffice to say, Ichabod stole forth with the air of one who had been sacking a hen roost, rather than a fair lady's heart. Without looking to the right or left to notice the scene of rural wealth, on which he had so often gloated, he went straight to the stable, and with several hearty cuffs and kicks, roused his steed most uncourteously from the comfortable quarters in which he was soundly sleeping, dreaming of mountains of corn and oats, and whole valleys of timothy and clover.

It was the very witching time of night that Ichabod, heavy-hearted and crest-fallen, pursued his travel homewards, along the sides of the lofty hills which rise above Tarry Town, and which he had traversed so cheerily in the afternoon. The hour was as dismal as himself. Far below him, the Tappan Zee spread its dusky and indistinct waste of waters, with here and there the tall mast of a sloop, riding quietly at anchor under the land. In the dead hush of midnight, he could even hear the barking of the watch dog from the opposite shore of the Hudson; but it was so vague and faint as only to give an idea of his distance from this faithful companion of man. Now and then, too, the long-drawn crowing of a cock, accidentally awakened, would sound far, far off, from some farmhouse away among the hills—but it was like a dreaming sound in his ear. No signs of life occurred near him, but occasionally the melancholy chirp of a cricket, or perhaps the guttural twang of a bull-frog, from a neighboring marsh, as if sleeping uncomfortably, and turning suddenly in his bed.

All the stories of ghosts and goblins that he had heard in the afternoon, now came crowding upon his recollection. The night grew darker and darker; the stars seemed to sink deeper in the sky, and driving clouds occasionally hid them from his sight. He had never felt so lonely and dismal. He was, moreover, approaching the very place where many of the scenes of the ghost stories had been laid. In the centre of the road stood an enormous tulip-tree, which towered like a giant above all the other trees of the neighborhood, and formed a kind of landmark. Its limbs were gnarled, and fantastic, large enough to form trunks for ordinary trees, twisting down almost to the earth, and rising again into the air. It was connected with the tragical story of the unfortunate André, who had been taken prisoner hard by; and was universally known by the name of Major André's tree. The common people regarded it with a mixture of respect and superstition, partly out of sympathy for the fate of its ill-starred namesake, and partly from the tales of strange sights and doleful lamentations told concerning it.

As Ichabod approached this fearful tree, he began to whistle: he thought his whistle was answered—it was but a blast sweeping sharply through the dry branches. As he approached a little nearer, he thought he saw something white, hanging in the midst of the tree—he paused and ceased whistling; but on looking more narrowly, perceived that it was a place where the tree had been scathed by lightning, and the white wood laid bare. Suddenly he heard a groan—his teeth chattered and his knees smote against the saddle: it was but the rubbing of one huge bough upon another, as they were swayed about by the breeze. He passed the tree in safety, but new perils lay before him.

About two hundred yards from the tree a small brook crossed the road, and ran into a marshy and thickly-wooded glen, known by the name of Wiley's swamp. A few rough logs, laid side by side, served for a bridge over this stream. On that side of the road where the brook entered the wood, a group of oaks and chestnuts, matted thick with wild grapevines, threw a cavernous gloom over it. To pass this bridge was the severest trial. It was at this identical spot that the unfortunate André was captured, and under the covert of those chestnuts and vines were the sturdy yeomen concealed who surprised him. This has ever since been considered a haunted stream, and fearful are the feelings of the schoolboy who has to pass it alone after dark.

As he approached the stream his heart began to thump; he summoned up, however, all his resolution, gave his horse half a score of kicks in the ribs, and attempted to dash briskly across the bridge; but instead of starting forward, the perverse old animal made a lateral movement, and ran broadside against the fence. Ichabod, whose fears increased with the delay, jerked the reins on the other side, and kicked lustily with the contrary foot: it was all in vain; his steed started, it is true, but it was only to plunge to the opposite side of the road into a thicket of brambles and alder bushes. The schoolmaster now bestowed both whip and heel upon the starveling ribs of old Gunpowder, who dashed forward, snuffling and snorting, but came to a stand just by the bridge, with a suddenness that had nearly sent his rider sprawling over his head. Just at this moment a plashy tramp by the side of the bridge caught the sensitive ear of Ichabod. In the dark shadow of the grove, on the margin of the brook, he beheld something huge, misshapen, black and towering. It stirred not, but seemed gathered up in the gloom, like some gigantic monster ready to spring upon the traveller.

The hair of the affrighted pedagogue rose upon his head with terror. What was to be done? To turn and fly was now too late; and besides, what chance was there of escaping ghost or goblin, if such it was, which could ride upon the wings of the wind? Summoning up, therefore, a show of courage, he demanded in stammering accents—"Who are you?" He received no reply. He repeated his demand in a

95

still more agitated voice. Still there was no answer. Once more he cudgelled the sides of the inflexible Gunpowder, and, shutting his eyes, broke forth with involuntary fervor into a psalm tune. Just then the shadowy object of alarm put itself in motion, and, with a scramble and a bound, stood at once in the middle of the road. Though the night was dark and dismal, yet the form of the unknown might now in some degree be ascertained. He appeared to be a horseman of large dimensions, and mounted on a black horse of powerful frame. He made no offer of molestation or sociability, but kept aloof on one side of the road, jogging along on the blind side of old Gunpowder, who had now got over his fright and waywardness.

Ichabod, who had no relish for this strange midnight companion, and bethought himself of the adventure of Brom Bones with the Galloping Hessian, now quickened his steed, in hopes of leaving him behind. The stranger, however, quickened his horse to an equal pace. Ichabod pulled up, and fell into a walk, thinking to lag behind—the other did the same. His heart began to sink within him; he endeavored to resume his psalm tune, but his parched tongue clove to the roof of his mouth, and he could not utter a stave. There was something in the moody and dogged silence of this pertinacious companion, that was mysterious and appalling. It was soon fearfully accounted for. On mounting a rising ground, which brought the figure of his fellow-traveller in relief against the sky, gigantic in height, and muffled in a cloak, Ichabod was horror-struck, on perceiving that he was headless!—but his horror was still more increased, on observing that the head, which should have rested on his shoulders, was carried before him on the pommel of the saddle: his terror rose to desperation; he rained a shower of kicks and blows upon Gunpowder, hoping, by a sudden movement, to give his companion the slip—but the spectre started full jump with him. Away then they dashed, through thick and thin; stones flying, and sparks flashing at every bound. Ichabod's flimsy garments fluttered in the air, as he stretched his long lank body away over his horse's head, in the eagerness of his flight.

They had now reached the road which turns off to Sleepy Hollow; but Gunpowder, who seemed possessed with a demon, instead of keeping up it, made an opposite turn, and plunged headlong down hill to the left. This road leads through a sandy hollow, shaded by trees for about a quarter of a mile, where it crosses the bridge famous in goblin story, and just beyond swells the green knoll on which stands the whitewashed church.

As yet the panic of the steed had given his unskilful rider an apparent advantage in the chase; but just as he had got half way through the hollow, the girths of the saddle gave way, and he felt it slipping from under him. He seized it by the pommel, and endeavored to hold it firm, but in vain; and had just time to save himself by clasping old Gunpowder round the neck, when the saddle fell to the earth, and he heard it trampled under foot by his pursuer. For a moment the terror of Hans Van Ripper's wrath passed across his mind—for it was his Sunday saddle; but this was no time for petty fears; the goblin was hard on his haunches;

and (unskilful rider that he was!) he had much ado to maintain his seat; sometimes slipping on one side, sometimes on another, and sometimes jolted on the high ridge of his horse's back-bone, with a violence that he verily feared would cleave him asunder.

An opening in the trees now cheered him with the hopes that the church bridge was at hand. The wavering reflection of a silver star in the bosom of the brook told him that he was not mistaken. He saw the walls of the church dimly glaring under the trees beyond. He recollected the place where Brom Bones's ghostly competitor had disappeared. "If I can but reach that bridge," thought Ichabod, "I am safe." Just then he heard the black steed panting and blowing close behind him; he even fancied that he felt his hot breath. Another convulsive kick in the ribs, and old Gunpowder sprang upon the bridge; he thundered over the resounding planks; he gained the opposite side; and now Ichabod cast a look behind to see if his pursuer should vanish, according to rule, in a flash of fire and brimstone. Just then he saw the goblin rising in his stirrups, and in the very act of hurling his head at him. Ichabod endeavored to dodge the horrible missile, but too late. It encountered his cranium with a tremendous crash—he was tumbled headlong into the dust, and Gunpowder, the black steed, and the goblin rider, passed by like a whirlwind.

The next morning the old horse was found without his saddle, and with the bridle under his feet, soberly cropping the grass at his master's gate. Ichabod did not make his appearance at breakfast—dinner-hour came, but no Ichabod. The boys assembled at the school-house, and strolled idly about the banks of the brook; but no schoolmaster. Hans Van Ripper now began to feel some uneasiness about the fate of poor Ichabod, and his saddle. An inquiry was set on foot, and after diligent investigation they came upon his traces. In one part of the road leading to the church was found the saddle trampled in the dirt; the tracks of horses' hoofs deeply dented in the road, and evidently at furious speed, were traced to the bridge, beyond which, on the bank of a broad part of the brook, where the water ran deep and black, was found the hat of the unfortunate Ichabod, and close beside it a shattered pumpkin.

The brook was searched, but the body of the schoolmaster was not to be discovered. Hans Van Ripper, as executor of his estate, examined the bundle which contained all his worldly effects. They consisted of two shirts and a half; two stocks for the neck; a pair or two of worsted stockings; an old pair of corduroy small-clothes; a rusty razor; a book of psalm tunes, full of dogs' ears; and a broken pitchpipe. As to the books and furniture of the school-house, they belonged to the community, excepting Cotton Mather's History of Witchcraft, a New England Almanac, and a book of dreams and fortune-telling; in which last was a sheet of foolscap much scribbled and blotted in several fruitless attempts to make a copy of verses in honor of the heiress of Van Tassel. These magic books and the poetic scrawl were forthwith consigned to the flames by Hans Van Ripper; who from that time forward determined to send his children no more to school; observing, that he never knew any good come of this same reading and writing. Whatever money the schoolmaster possessed, and he had received his quarter's pay but a day or two before, he must have had about his person at the time of his disappearance.

The mysterious event caused much speculation at the church on the following Sunday. Knots of gazers and gossips were collected in the churchyard, at the bridge, and at the spot where the hat and pumpkin had been found. The stories of Brouwer, of Bones, and a whole budget of others, were called to mind; and when they had diligently considered them all, and compared them with the symptoms of the present case, they shook their heads, and came to the conclusion that Ichabod had been carried off by the galloping Hessian. As he was a bachelor, and in nobody's debt, nobody troubled his head any more about him. The school was removed to a different quarter of the hollow, and another pedagogue reigned in his stead.

It is true, an old farmer, who had been down to New York on a visit several years after, and from whom this account of the ghostly adventure was received, brought home the intelligence that Ichabod Crane was still alive; that he had left the neighborhood, partly through fear of the goblin and Hans Van Ripper, and partly in mortification at having been suddenly dismissed by the heiress; that he had changed his quarters to a distant part of the country; had kept school and studied law at the same time, had been admitted to the bar, turned politician, electioneered, written for the newspapers, and finally had been made a justice of the Ten Pound Court. Brom Bones too, who shortly after his rival's disappearance conducted the blooming Katrina in triumph to the altar, was observed to look exceedingly knowing whenever the story of Ichabod was related, and always burst into a hearty laugh at the mention of the pumpkin; which led some to suspect that he knew more about the matter than he chose to tell.

The old country wives, however, who are the best judges of these matters, maintain to this day that Ichabod was spirited away by supernatural means; and it is a favorite story often told about the neighborhood round the winter evening fire. The bridge became more than ever an object of superstitious awe, and that may be the reason why the road has been altered of late years, so as to approach the church by the border of the mill-pond. The school-house being deserted, soon fell to decay, and was reported to be haunted by the ghost of the unfortunate pedagogue; and the ploughboy, loitering homeward of a still summer evening, has often fancied his voice at a distance, chanting a melancholy psalm tune among the tranquil solitudes of Sleepy Hollow.

Postscript, Found in the Handwriting of Mr. Knickerbocker.

The preceding Tale is given, almost in the precise words in which I heard it related at a Corporation meeting of the ancient city of Manhattoes, at which were present many of its sagest and most illustrious burghers. The narrator was a pleasant, shabby, gentlemanly old fellow, in pepper-and-salt clothes, with a sadly humorous face; and one whom I strongly suspected of being poor,—he made such efforts to be entertaining. When his story was concluded, there was much laughter and approbation, particularly from two or three deputy aldermen, who had been asleep a greater part of the time. There was, however, one tall, dry-looking old gentleman, with beetling eyebrows, who maintained a grave and rather severe face throughout; now and then folding his arms, inclining his head, and looking down upon the floor, as if turning a doubt over in his mind. He was one of your wary men, who never laugh, but upon good grounds—when they have reason and the law on their side. When the mirth of the rest of the company had subsided, and silence was restored, he leaned one arm on the elbow of his chair, and, sticking the other akimbo, demanded, with a slight but exceedingly sage motion of the head, and contraction of the brow, what was the moral of the story, and what it went to prove?

The story-teller, who was just putting a glass of wine to his lips, as a refreshment after his toils, paused for a moment, looked at his inquirer with an air of infinite deference, and, lowering the glass slowly to the table, observed, that the story was intended most logically to prove:—

"That there is no situation in life but has its advantages and pleasures— provided we will but take a joke as we find it:

"That, therefore, he that runs races with goblin troopers is likely to have rough riding of it.

"Ergo, for a country schoolmaster to be refused the hand of a Dutch heiress, is a certain step to high preferment in the state."

The cautious old gentleman knit his brows tenfold closer after this explanation, being sorely puzzled by the ratiocination of the syllogism; while, methought, the one in pepper-and-salt eyed him with something of a triumphant leer. At length, he observed, that all this was very well, but still he thought the story a little on the extravagant—there were one or two points on which he had his doubts.

"Faith, sir," replied the story-teller, "as to that matter, I don't believe one-half of it myself."

D.K.

From *Tales of a Traveller**

WOLFERT WEBBER, OR GOLDEN DREAMS.

In the year of grace one thousand seven hundred and—blank—for I do not remember the precise date; however, it was somewhere in the early part of the last century, there lived in the ancient city of the Manhattoes a worthy burgher, Wolfert Webber by name. He was descended from old Cobus Webber of the

---

The Works of Washington Irving, Fulton Edition (New York: Century Company, 1909).

Brille in Holland, one of the original settlers, famous for introducing the cultivation of cabbages, and who came over to the province during the protectorship of Oloffe Van Kortlandt, otherwise called the Dreamer.

The field in which Cobus Webber first planted himself and his cabbages had remained ever since in the family, who continued in the same line of husbandry, with that praiseworthy perseverance for which our Dutch burghers are noted. The whole family genius, during several generations, was devoted to the study and development of this one noble vegetable; and to this concentration of intellect may doubtless be ascribed the prodigious renown to which the Webber cabbages attained.

The Webber dynasty continued in uninterrupted succession; and never did a line give more unquestionable proofs of legitimacy. The eldest son succeeded to the looks, as well as the territory of his sire; and had the portraits of this line of tranquil potentates been taken, they would have presented a row of heads marvellously resembling in shape and magnitude the vegetables over which they reigned.

The seat of government continued unchanged in the family mansion:—a Dutch-built house, with a front, or rather gable-end of yellow brick, tapering to a point, with the customary iron weathercock at the top. Everything about the building bore the air of long-settled ease and security. Flights of martins peopled the little coops nailed against its walls, and swallows built their nests under the eaves; and every one knows that these house-loving birds bring good luck to the dwelling where they take up their abode. In a bright sunny morning in early summer, it was delectable to hear their cheerful notes, as they sported about in the pure sweet air, chirping forth, as it were, the greatness and prosperity of the Webbers.

Thus quietly and comfortably did this excellent family vegetate under the shade of a mighty buttonwood tree, which by little and little grew so great as entirely to overshadow their palace. The city gradually spread its suburbs round their domain. Houses sprang up to interrupt their prospects. The rural lanes in the vicinity began to grow into the bustle and populousness of streets; in short, with all the habits of rustic life they began to find themselves the inhabitants of a city. Still, however, they maintained their hereditary character, and hereditary possessions, with all the tenacity of petty German princes in the midst of the empire. Wolfert was the last of the line, and succeeded to the patriarchal bench at the door, under the family tree, and swayed the sceptre of his fathers, a kind of rural potentate in the midst of a metropolis.

To share the cares and sweets of sovereignty, he had taken unto himself a helpmate, one of that excellent kind, called stirring women; that is to say, she was one of those notable little housewives who are always busy when there is nothing to do. Her activity, however, took one particular direction; her whole life seemed devoted to intense knitting; whether at home or abroad, walking or sitting, her needles were continually in motion, and it is even affirmed that by her unwearied industry she very nearly supplied her household with stockings throughout the year. This worthy couple were blessed with one daughter, who was brought up with great tenderness and care; uncommon pains had been taken with her education, so that she could stitch in every variety of way; make all kinds of pickles and preserves, and mark her own name on a sampler. The influence of her taste was seen also in the family garden, where the ornamental began to mingle with the useful; whole rows of fiery marigolds and splendid hollyhocks bordered the cabbage beds; and gigantic sunflowers lolled their broad jolly faces over the fences, seeming to ogle most affectionately the passers-by.

Thus reigned and vegetated Wolfert Webber over his paternal acres, peacefully and contentedly. Not but that, like all other sovereigns, he had his occasional cares and vexations. The growth of his native city sometimes caused him annoyance. His little territory gradually became hemmed in by streets and houses, which intercepted air and sunshine. He was now and then subjected to the irruptions of the border population that infest the streets of a metropolis; who would make midnight forays into his dominions, and carry off captive whole platoons of his noblest subjects. Vagrant swine would make a descent, too, now and then, when the gate was left open, and lay all waste before them; and mischievous urchins would decapitate the illustrious sunflowers, the glory of the garden, as they lolled their heads so fondly over the walls. Still all these were petty grievances, which might now and then ruffle the surface of his mind, as a summer breeze will ruffle the surface of a mill-pond; but they could not disturb the deep-seated quiet of his soul. He would but seize a trusty staff, that stood behind the door, issue suddenly out, and anoint the back of the aggressor, whether pig or urchin, and then return within doors, marvellously refreshed and tranquillized.

The chief cause of anxiety to honest Wolfert, however, was the growing prosperity of the city. The expenses of living doubled and trebled; but he could not double and treble the magnitude of his cabbages; and the number of competitors prevented the increase of price; thus, therefore, while every one around him grew richer, Wolfert grew poorer, and he could not, for the life of him, perceive how the evil was to be remedied.

This growing care, which increased from day to day, had its gradual effect upon our worthy burgher; insomuch, that it at length implanted two or three wrinkles in his brow; things unknown before in the family of the Webbers; and it seemed to pinch up the corners of his cocked hat into an expression of anxiety, totally opposite to the tranquil, broad-brimmed, low-crowned beavers of his illustrious progenitors.

Perhaps even this would not have materially disturbed the serenity of his mind, had he had only himself and his wife to care for; but there was his daughter gradually growing to maturity; and all the world knows that when daughters begin to ripen no fruit nor flower requires so much looking after. I have no talent at describing female charms, else fain would I depict the progress of this little Dutch beauty. How her blue eyes grew deeper and deeper, and her cherry lips redder and redder; and how she ripened and ripened, and rounded and rounded in the opening breath of sixteen summers, until, in her seventeenth spring, she seemed ready to burst out of her bodice, like a half-blown rosebud.

Ah, well-a-day! could I but show her as she was then, tricked out on a Sunday morning, in the hereditary finery of the old Dutch clothes-press, of which her mother had confided to her the key. The wedding-dress of her grandmother, modernized for use, with sundry ornaments, handed down as heirlooms in the family. Her pale brown hair smoothed with buttermilk in flat waving lines on each side of her fair forehead. The chain of yellow virgin gold, that encircled her neck; the little cross, that just rested at the entrance of a soft valley of happiness, as if it would sanctify the place. The—but, pooh!—it is not for an old man like me to be prosing about female beauty; suffice it to say, Amy had attained her seventeenth year. Long since had her sampler exhibited hearts in couples desperately transfixed with arrows, and true lovers'knots worked in deep-blue silk; and it was evident she began to languish for some more interesting occupation than the rearing of sunflowers or pickling of cucumbers.

From *Bracebridge Hall**

DOLPH HEYLIGER.

> "I take the town of Concord, where I dwell,
> All Kilborn be my witness, if I were not
> Begot in bashfulness, brought up in shamefacedness.
> Let 'un bring a dog but to my vace that can
> Zay I have beat 'un, and without a vault;
> Or but a cat will swear upon a book,
> I have as much as zet a vire her tail,
> And I'll give him or her a crown for 'mends."
>
> —*Tale of a Tub.*

In the early time of the province of New York, while it groaned under the tyranny of the English governor, Lord Cornbury, who carried his cruelties towards the Dutch inhabitants so far as to allow no Dominie, or schoolmaster, to officiate in their language, without his special license; about this time, there lived in the jolly little old city of the Manhattoes, a kind motherly dame, known by the name of Dame Heyliger. She was the widow of a Dutch sea-captain, who died suddenly of a fever, in consequence of working too hard, and eating too heartily, at the time when all the inhabitants turned out in a panic, to fortify the place

The Works of Washington Irving, Fulton Edition (New York: Century Company, 1909).

"Sunnyside—Home of Washington Irving," from a watercolor by J. Henry Hill, 1878. Courtesy of Historic Hudson Valley.

against the invasion of a small French privateer.* He left her with very little money, and one infant son, the only survivor of several children. The good woman had need of much management, to make both ends meet, and keep up a decent appearance. However, as her husband had fallen a victim to his zeal for the public safety, it was universally agreed that "something ought to be done for the widow;" and on the hopes of this "something" she lived tolerably for some years; in the mean time, everybody pitied and spoke well of her; and that helped along.

She lived in a small house, in a small street, called Garden Street, very probably from a garden which may have flourished there some time or other. As her necessities every year grew greater, and the talk of the public about doing "something for her" grew less, she had to cast about for some mode of doing something for herself, by way of helping out her slender means, and maintaining her independence, of which she was somewhat tenacious.

Living in a mercantile town, she had caught something of the spirit, and determined to venture a little in the great lottery of commerce. On a sudden, therefore, to the great surprise of the street, there appeared at her window a grand array of gingerbread kings and queens, with their arms stuck a-kimbo, after the invariable royal manner. There were also several broken tumblers, some filled with sugar-plums, some with marbles; there were, moreover, cakes of various kinds, and barley sugar, and Holland dolls, and wooden horses, with here and there gilt-covered picture-books, and now and then a skein of thread, or a dangling pound of candles. At the door of the house sat the good old dame's cat, a decent demure-looking personage, who seemed to scan everybody that passed, to criticise their dress, and now and then to stretch her neck, and look out with sudden curiosity, to see what was going on at the other end of the street; but if by chance any idle vagabond dog came by, and offered to be uncivil—hoity-toity!—how she would bristle up, and growl, and spit, and strike out her paws! she was as indignant as ever was an ancient and ugly spinster, on the approach of some graceless profligate.

But though the good woman had to come down to those humble means of subsistence, yet she still kept up a feeling of family pride, being descended from the Vanderspiegels, of Amsterdam; and she had the family arms painted and framed, and hung over her mantel-piece. She was, in truth, much respected by all the poorer people of the place; her house was quite a resort of the old wives of the neighborhood; they would drop in there of a winter's afternoon, as she sat knitting on one side of her fireplace, her cat purring on the other, and the tea-kettle singing before it; and they would gossip with her until late in the evening. There was always an arm-chair for Peter de Groodt, sometimes called Long Peter, and sometimes Peter Longlegs, the clerk and sexton of the little Lutheran church, who was her great crony, and indeed the oracle of her fireside.

*In 1705.

Nay, the Dominie himself did not disdain, now and then, to step in, converse about the state of her mind, and take a glass of her special good cherry-brandy. Indeed, he never failed to call on new-year's day, and wish her a happy new year; and the good dame, who was a little vain on some points, always piqued herself on giving him as large a cake as any one in town.

I have said that she had one son. He was the child of her old age; but could hardly be called the comfort—for, of all unlucky urchins, Dolph Heyliger was the most mischievous. Not that the whipster was really vicious; he was only full of fun and frolic, and had that daring, gamesome spirit, which is extolled in a rich man's child, but execrated in a poor man's. He was continually getting into scrapes: his mother was incessantly harassed with complaints of some waggish pranks which he had played off; bills were sent in for windows that he had broken; in a word, he had not reached his fourteenth year before he was pronounced, by all the neighborhood, to be a "wicked dog, the wickedest dog in the street!" Nay, one old gentleman, in a claret-colored coat, with a thin red face, and ferret eyes, went so far as to assure Dame Heyliger, that her son would, one day or other, come to the gallows!

Yet, notwithstanding all this, the poor old soul loved her boy. It seemed as though she loved him the better, the worse he behaved; and that he grew more in her favor, the more he grew out of favor with the world. Mothers are foolish, fond-hearted beings; there's no reasoning them out of their dotage; and, indeed, this poor woman's child was all that was left to love her in this world;—so we must not think it hard that she turned a deaf ear to her good friends, who sought to prove to her that Dolph would come to a halter.

To do the varlet justice, too, he was strongly attached to his parent. He would not willingly have given her pain on any account; and when he had been doing wrong, it was but for him to catch his poor mother's eye fixed wistfully and sorrowfully upon him, to fill his heart with bitterness and contrition. But he was a heedless youngster, and could not, for the life of him, resist any new temptation to fun and mischief. Though quick at his learning, whenever he could be brought to apply himself, he was always prone to be led away by idle company, and would play truant to hunt after birds'-nests, to rob orchards, or to swim in the Hudson.

In this way he grew up, a tall, lubberly boy; and his mother began to be greatly perplexed what to do with him, or how to put him in a way to do for himself; for he had acquired such an unlucky reputation, that no one seemed willing to employ him.

Many were the consultations that she held with Peter de Groodt, the clerk and sexton, who was her prime counsellor. Peter was as much perplexed as herself, for he had no great opinion of the boy, and thought he would never come to good. He at one time advised her to send him to sea—a piece of advice only given in the most desperate cases; but Dame Heyliger would not listen to such an idea; she could not think of letting Dolph go out of her sight. She was sitting one day knitting by her fireside, in great perplexity, when the sexton entered with an air of unusual vivacity and briskness. He had just come from a funeral. It had been that of a boy of Dolph's years, who had been apprentice to a famous German doctor, and had died of a consumption. It is true, there had been a whisper that the deceased had been brought to his end by being made the subject of the doctor's experiments, on which he was apt to try the effects of a new compound, or a quieting draught. This, however, it is likely, was a mere scandal; at any rate, Peter de Groodt did not think it worth mentioning; though, had we time to philosophize, it would be a curious matter for speculation, why a doctor's family is apt to be so lean and cadaverous, and a butcher's so jolly and rubicund.

Peter de Groodt, as I said before, entered the house of Dame Heyliger with unusual alacrity. A bright idea had popped into his head at the funeral, over which he had chuckled as he shovelled the earth into the grave of the doctor's disciple. It had occurred to him, that, as the situation of the deceased was vacant at the doctor's, it would be the very place for Dolph. The boy had parts, and could pound a pestle and run an errand with any boy in the town—and what more was wanted in a student?

The suggestion of the sage Peter was a vision of glory to the mother. She already saw Dolph, in her mind's eye, with a cane at his nose, a knocker at his door, and an M.D. at the end of his name—one of the established dignitaries of the town.

The matter, once undertaken, was soon effected; the sexton had some influence with the doctor, they having had much dealing together in the way of their separate professions; and the very next morning he called and conducted the urchin, clad in his Sunday clothes, to undergo the inspection of Dr. Karl Lodovick Knipperhausen.

They found the doctor seated in an elbow-chair, in one corner of his study, or laboratory, with a large volume, in German print, before him. He was a short, fat man, with a dark, square face, rendered more dark by a black velvet cap. He had a little, knobbed nose, not unlike the ace of spades, with a pair of spectacles gleaming on each side of his dusky countenance, like a couple of bow-windows.

Dolph felt struck with awe, on entering into the presence of this learned man; and gazed about him with boyish wonder at the furniture of this chamber of knowledge, which appeared to him almost as the den of a magician. In the centre stood a claw-footed table, with pestle and mortar, phials and gallipots, and a pair of small, burnished scales. At one end was a heavy clothes-press, turned into a receptacle for drugs and compounds; against which hung the doctor's hat and cloak, and gold-headed cane, and on the top grinned a human skull. Along the mantel-piece were glass vessels, in which were snakes and lizards, and a human fœtus preserved in spirits. A closet, the doors of which were taken off, contained three whole shelves of books, and some, too, of mighty folio dimensions—a collection, the like of which Dolph had never before beheld. As, however, the library did not take up the whole of the closet, the doctor's thrifty housekeeper had occupied the rest with pots of pickles and preserves; and had hung about the room, among awful implements of the healing art, strings of red pepper and corpulent cucumbers, carefully preserved for seed.

Peter de Groodt, and his *protégé*, were received with great gravity and stateliness by the doctor, who was a very wise, dignified little man, and never smiled. He surveyed Dolph from head to foot, above, and under, and through his spectacles; and the poor lad's heart quailed as these great glasses glared on him like two full moons. The doctor heard all that Peter de Groodt had to say in favor of the youthful candidate; and then, wetting his thumb with the end of his tongue, he began deliberately to turn over page after page of the great black volume before him. At length, after many hums and haws, and strokings of the chin, and all that hesitation and deliberation with which a wise man proceeds to do what he intended to do from the very first, the doctor agreed to take the lad as a disciple; to give him bed, board, and clothing, and to instruct him in the healing art; in return for which, he was to have his services until his twenty-first year.

Behold, then, our hero, all at once transformed from an unlucky urchin, running wild about the streets, to a student of medicine, diligently pounding a pestle, under the auspices of the learned Doctor Karl Lodovick Knipperhausen. It was a happy transition for his fond old mother. She was delighted with the idea of her boy's being brought up worthy of his ancestors; and anticipated the day when he would be able to hold up his head with the lawyer, that lived in the large house opposite; or, peradventure, with the Dominie himself.

Doctor Knipperhausen was a native of the Palatinate of Germany; whence, in company with many of his countrymen, he had taken refuge in England, on account of religious persecution. He was one of nearly three thousand Palatines, who came over from England in 1710, under the protection of Governor Hunter. Where the doctor had studied, how he had acquired his medical knowledge, and where he had received his diploma, it is hard at present to say, for nobody knew at the time; yet it is certain that his profound skill and abstruse knowledge were the talk and wonder of the common people, far and near.

His practice was totally different from that of any other physician; consisting in mysterious compounds, known only to himself, in the preparing and administering of which, it was said, he always consulted the stars. So high an opinion was entertained of his skill, particularly by the German and Dutch inhabitants, that they always resorted to him in desperate cases. He was one of those infallible doctors, that are always effecting sudden and surprising cures, when the patient has been given up by all the regular physicians; unless, as is shrewdly observed, the case has been left too long before it was put into their hands. The doctor's library was the talk and marvel of the neighborhood, I might almost say of the entire burgh. The good people looked with reverence at a man who had read three whole shelves full of books, and some of them, too, as large as a family Bible. There were many disputes among the members of the little Lutheran church, as to which was the wiser man, the doctor or the Dominie. Some of his admirers even went so far as to say, that he knew more than the governor himself—in a word, it was thought that there was no end to his knowledge!

No sooner was Dolph received into the doctor's family, than he was put in possession of the lodging of his predecessor. It was a garret-room of a steep-roofed Dutch house, where the rain pattered on the shingles, and the lightning gleamed, and the wind piped through the crannies in stormy weather; and where whole troops of hungry rats, like Don Cossacks, galloped about in defiance of traps and ratsbane.

He was soon up to his ears in medical studies, being employed, morning, noon, and night, in rolling pills, filtering tinctures, or pounding the pestle and mortar, in one corner of the laboratory; while the doctor would take his seat in another corner, when he had nothing else to do, or expected visitors, and, arrayed in his morning-gown and velvet cap, would pore over the contents of some folio volume. It is true, that the regular thumping of Dolph's pestle, or, perhaps, the drowsy buzzing of the summer flies, would now and then lull the little man into a slumber; but then his spectacles were always wide awake, and studiously regarding the book.

There was another personage in the house, however, to whom Dolph was obliged to pay allegiance. Though a bachelor, and a man of such great dignity and importance, the doctor was, like many other wise men, subject to petticoat government. He was completely under the sway of his housekeeper; a spare, busy, fretting housewife, in a little, round, quilted, German cap, with a huge bunch of keys jingling at the girdle of an exceedingly long waist. Frau Ilsé (or Frow Ilsy, as it was pronounced) had accompanied him in his various migrations from Germany to England, and from England to the province; managing his establishment and himself too: ruling him, it is true, with a gentle hand, but carrying a high hand with all the world beside. How she had acquired such ascendency, I do not pretend to say. People, it is true, did talk—but have not people been prone to talk ever since the world began? Who can tell how women generally contrive to get the upper hand? A husband, it is true, may now and then be master in his own house; but who ever knew a bachelor that was not managed by his housekeeper?

Indeed, Frau Ilsy's power was not confined to the doctor's household. She was one of those prying gossips who know every one's business better than they do themselves; and whose all-seeing eyes, and all-telling tongues, are terrors throughout a neighborhood.

Nothing of any moment transpired in the world of scandal of this little burgh, but it was known to Frau Ilsy. She had her crew of cronies, that were perpetually hurrying to her little parlor, with some precious bit of news; nay, she would sometimes discuss a whole volume of secret history, as she held the street-door ajar, and gossiped with one of these garrulous cronies in the very teeth of a December blast.

Between the doctor and the housekeeper, it may easily be supposed that Dolph had a busy life of it. As Frau Ilsy kept the keys, and literally ruled the roast, it was starvation to offend her, though he found the study of her temper more perplexing even than that of medicine. When not busy in the laboratory, she kept him running hither and thither on her errands; and on Sundays he was obliged to accompany her to and from church, and carry her Bible. Many a time has the poor varlet stood shivering and blowing his fingers, or holding his frost-bitten nose, in the church-yard, while Ilsy and her cronies were huddled together, wagging their heads, and tearing some unlucky character to pieces.

With all his advantages, however, Dolph made very slow progress in his art. This was no fault of the doctor's, certainly, for he took unwearied pains with the lad, keeping him close to the pestle and mortar, or on the trot about town with phials and pill-boxes; and if he ever flagged in his industry, which he was rather apt to do, the doctor would fly into a passion, and ask him if he ever expected to learn his profession, unless he applied himself closer to the study. The fact is, he still retained the fondness for sport and mischief that had marked his childhood; the habit, indeed, had strengthened with his years, and gained force from being thwarted and constrained. He daily grew more and more untractable, and lost favor in the eyes both of the doctor and the housekeeper.

In the mean time the doctor went on, waxing wealthy and renowned. He was famous for his skill in managing cases not laid down in the books. He had cured several old women and young girls of witchcraft; a terrible complaint, nearly as prevalent in the province in those days as hydrophobia is at present. He had even restored one strapping country girl to perfect health, who had gone so far as to vomit crooked pins and needles; which is considered a desperate stage of the malady. It was whispered, also, that he was possessed of the art of preparing love-powders; and many applications had he in consequence from love-sick patients of both sexes. But all these cases formed the mysterious part of his practice, in which, according to the cant phrase, "secrecy and honor might be depended on." Dolph, therefore, was obliged to turn out of the study whenever such consultations occurred, though it is said he learnt more of the secrets of the art at the key-hole, than by all the rest of his studies put together.

As the doctor increased in wealth, he began to extend his possessions, and to look forward, like other great men, to the time when he should retire to the repose of a country-seat. For this purpose he had purchased a farm, or, as the Dutch settlers called it, a *bowerie*, a few miles from town. It had been the residence of a wealthy family, that had returned some time since to Holland. A large mansion-house stood in the centre of it, very much out of repair, and which, in consequence of certain reports, had received the appellation of the Haunted House.

Either from these reports, or from its actual dreariness, the doctor found it impossible to get a tenant; and, that the place might not fall to ruin before he could reside in it himself, he placed a country boor, with his family, in one wing, with the privilege of cultivating the farm on shares.

The doctor now felt all the dignity of a landholder rising within him. He had a little of the German pride of territory in his composition, and almost looked upon himself as owner of a principality. He began to complain of the fatigue of business; and was fond of riding out "to look at his estate." His little expeditions to his lands were attended with a bustle and parade that created a sensation throughout the neighborhood. His wall-eyed horse stood, stamping and whisking off the flies, for a full hour before the house. Then the doctor's saddle-bags would be brought out and adjusted; then, after a little while, his cloak would be rolled up and strapped to the saddle; then his umbrella would be buckled to the cloak; while, in the mean time, a group of ragged boys, that observant class of beings, would gather before the door. At length, the doctor would issue forth, in a pair of jack-boots that reached above his knees, and a cocked hat flapped down in front. As he was a short, fat man, he took some time to mount into the saddle; and when there, he took some time to have the saddle and stirrups properly adjusted, enjoying the wonder and admiration of the urchin crowd. Even after he had set off, he would pause in the middle of the street, or trot back two or three times to give some parting orders; which were answered by the housekeeper from the door, or Dolph from the study, or the black cook from the cellar, or the chambermaid from the garret-window; and there were generally some last words bawled after him, just as he was turning the corner.

The whole neighborhood would be aroused by this pomp and circumstance. The cobbler would leave his last; the barber would thrust out his frizzed head, with a comb sticking in it; a knot would collect at the grocer's door, and the word would be buzzed from one end of the street to the other, "The doctor's riding out to his country-seat!"

These were golden moments for Dolph. No sooner was the doctor out of sight, than pestle and mortar were abandoned; the laboratory was left to take care of itself, and the student was off on some madcap frolic.

Indeed, it must be confessed, the youngster, as he grew up, seemed in a fair way to fulfill the prediction of the old claret-colored gentleman. He was the ringleader of all holiday sports, and midnight gambols; ready for all kinds of mischievous pranks, and harebrained adventures.

There is nothing so troublesome as a hero on a small scale, or, rather, a hero in a small town. Dolph soon became the abhorrence of all drowsy, housekeeping old citizens, who hated noise, and had no relish for waggery. The good dames, too, considered him as little better than a reprobate, gathered their daughters under their wings whenever he approached, and pointed him out as a warning to their sons. No one seemed to hold him in much regard, excepting the wild striplings of the place, who were captivated by his open-hearted, daring manners, and the negroes, who always look upon every idle, do-nothing youngster as a kind of gentleman. Even the good Peter de Groodt, who had considered himself a kind of patron of the lad, began to despair of him; and would shake his head dubiously, as he listened to a long complaint from the housekeeper, and sipped a glass of her raspberry brandy.

Still his mother was not to be wearied out of her affection, by all the waywardness of her boy; nor disheartened by the stories of his misdeeds, with which her good friends were continually regaling her. She had, it is true, very little of the pleasure which rich people enjoy, in always hearing their children praised; but she considered all this ill-will as a kind of persecution which he suffered, and she liked him the better on that account. She saw him growing up, a fine, tall, good-looking youngster, and she looked at him with the secret pride of a mother's heart. It was her great desire that Dolph should appear like a gentleman, and all the money she could save went towards helping out his pocket and his wardrobe. She would look out of the window after him, as he sallied forth in his best array, and her heart would yearn with delight; and once, when Peter de Groodt, struck with the youngster's gallant appearance on a bright Sunday morning, observed, "Well, after all, Dolph does grow a comely fellow!" the tear of pride started into the mother's eye: "Ah, neighbor! neighbor!" exclaimed she, "they may say what they please; poor Dolph will yet hold up his head with the best of them."

Dolph Heyliger had now nearly attained his one-and-twentieth-year, and the term of his medical studies was just expiring; yet it must be confessed that he knew little more of the profession than when he first entered the doctor's doors. This, however, could not be from any want of quickness of parts, for he showed amazing aptness in mastering other branches of knowledge, which he could only have studied at intervals. He was, for instance, a sure marksman, and won all the geese and turkeys at Christmas holidays. He was a bold rider; he was famous for leaping and wrestling; he played tolerably on the fiddle; could swim like a fish; and was the best hand in the whole place at fives or nine-pins.

All these accomplishments, however, procured him no favor in the eyes of the doctor, who grew more and more crabbed and intolerant, the nearer the term of apprenticeship approached. Frau Ilsy, too, was forever finding some occasion to raise a windy tempest about his ears; and seldom encountered him about the house, without a clatter of the tongue; so that at length the jingling of her keys, as she approached, was to Dolph like the ringing of the prompter's bell, that gives notice of a theatrical thunder-storm. Nothing but the infinite good-humor of the heedless youngster, enabled him to bear all this domestic tyranny without open rebellion. It was evident that the doctor and his housekeeper were preparing to beat the poor youth out of the nest, the moment his term should have expired; a shorthand mode which the doctor had of providing for useless disciples.

Indeed, the little man had been rendered more than usually irritable lately, in consequence of various cares and vexations which his country estate had brought upon him. The doctor had been repeatedly annoyed by the rumors and tales which prevailed concerning the old mansion; and found it difficult to prevail even upon the countryman and his family to remain there rent-free. Every time he rode out to the farm, he was teased by some fresh complaint of strange noises and fearful sights, with which the tenants were disturbed at night; and the doctor would come home fretting and fuming, and vent his spleen upon the whole household. It was indeed a sore grievance, that affected him both in pride and purse. He was threatened with an absolute loss of the profits of his property; and then, what a blow to his territorial consequence, to be the landlord of a haunted house!

It was observed, however, that with all his vexation, the doctor never proposed to sleep in the house himself; nay, he could never be prevailed upon to remain on the premises after dark, but made the best of his way for town, as soon as the bats began to flit about in the twilight. The fact was, the doctor had a secret belief in ghosts, having passed the early part of his life in a country where they particularly abound; and indeed the story went, that, when a boy, he had once seen the devil upon the Hartz mountains in Germany.

At length, the doctor's vexations on this head were brought to a crisis. One morning, as he sat dozing over a volume in his study, he was suddenly started from his slumbers by the bustling in of the housekeeper.

"Here's a fine to do!" cried she, as she entered the room. "Here's Claus Hopper come in, bag and baggage, from the farm, and swears he'll have nothing more to do with it. The whole family have been frightened out of their wits; for there's such racketing and rummaging about the old house, that they can't sleep quiet in their beds!"

"Donner und blitzen!" cried the doctor, impatiently; "will they never have done chattering about that house? What a pack of fools, to let a few rats and mice frighten them out of good quarters!"

"Nay, nay," said the housekeeper, wagging her head knowingly, and piqued at having a good ghost story doubted, "there's more in it than rats and mice. All the neighborhood talks about the house; and then such sights have been seen in it! Peter de Groodt tells me, that the family that sold you the house and went to Holland, dropped several strange hints about it, and said, 'they wished you joy of your bargain;' and you know yourself there's no getting any family to live in it."

"Peter de Groodt's a ninny—an old woman," said the doctor, peevishly; "I'll warrant he's been filling these people's heads full of stories. It's just like his nonsense about the ghost that haunted the church belfry, as an excuse for not ringing the bell that cold night when Harmanus Brinkerhoff's house was on fire. Send Claus to me."

Claus Hopper now made his appearance: a simple country lout, full of awe at finding himself in the very study of Dr. Knipperhausen, and too much embarrassed to enter in much detail of the matters that had caused his alarm. He stood twirling his hat in one hand, resting sometimes on one leg, sometimes on the other, looking occasionally at the doctor, and now and then stealing a fearful glance at the death's-head that seemed ogling him from the top of the clothespress.

The doctor tried every means to persuade him to return to the farm, but all in vain; he maintained a dogged determination on the subject; and at the close of every argument or solicitation, would make the same brief, inflexible reply, "Ich kan nicht, mynheer." The doctor was a "little pot, and soon hot;" his patience was exhausted by these continual vexations about his estate. The subborn refusal of Claus Hopper seemed to him like flat rebellion; his temper suddenly boiled over, and Claus was glad to make a rapid retreat to escape scalding.

When the bumpkin got to the housekeeper's room, he found Peter de Groodt, and several other true believers, ready to receive him. Here he indemnified himself for the restraint he had suffered in the study, and opened a budget of stories about the haunted house that astonished all his hearers. The housekeeper believed them all, if it was only to spite the doctor for having received her intelligence so uncourteously. Peter de Groodt matched them with many a wonderful legend of the times of the Dutch dynasty, and of the Devil's Stepping-stones; and of the pirate hanged at Gibbet Island, that continued to swing there at night long after the gallows was taken down; and of the ghost of the unfortunate Governor Leisler, hanged for treason, which haunted the old fort and the government house. The gossiping knot dispersed, each charged with direful intelligence. The sexton disburdened himself at a vestry meeting that was held that very day, and the black cook forsook her kitchen, and spent half the day at the street pump, that gossiping place of servants, dealing forth the news to all that came for water. In a little time, the whole town was in a buzz with tales about the haunted house. Some said that Claus Hopper had seen the devil, while others hinted that the house was haunted by the ghosts of some of the patients whom the doctor had physicked out of the world, and that was the reason why he did not venture to live in it himself.

All this put the little doctor in a terrible fume. He threatened vengeance on any one who should affect the value of his property by exciting popular prejudices. He complained loudly of thus being in a manner dispossessed of his territories by mere bugbears; but he secretly determined to have the house exorcised by the Dominie. Great was his relief, therefore, when, in the midst of his perplexities, Dolph stepped forward and undertook to garrison the haunted house. The youngster had been listening to all the stories of Claus Hopper and Peter de Groodt: he was fond of adventure, he loved the marvellous, and his imagination had become quite excited by these tales of wonder. Besides, he had led such an uncomfortable life at the doctor's, being subjected to the intolerable thraldom of early hours, that he was delighted at the prospect of having a house to himself, even though it should be a haunted one. His offer was eagerly accepted, and it was determined that he should mount guard that very night. His only stipulation was, that thé enterprise should be kept secret from his mother; for he knew the poor soul would not sleep a wink, if she knew her son was waging war with the powers of darkness.

When night came on, he set out on this perilous expedition. The old black cook, his only friend in the household, had provided him with a little mess for supper, and a rushlight; and she tied round his neck an amulet, given her by an African conjurer, as a charm against evil spirits. Dolph was escorted on his way by the doctor and Peter de Groodt, who had agreed to accompany him to the house, and to see him safe lodged. The night was overcast, and it was very dark when they arrived at the grounds which surrounded the mansion. The sexton led the way with a lantern. As they walked along the avenue of acacias, the fitful light, catching from bush to bush, and tree to tree, often startled the doughty Peter, and made him fall back upon his followers; and the doctor grappled still closer hold of Dolph's arm, observing that the ground was very slippery and uneven. At one time they were nearly put to total rout by a bat, which came flitting about the lantern; and the notes of the insects from the trees, and the frogs from a neighboring pond, formed a most drowsy and doleful concert.

The front door of the mansion opened with a grating sound, that made the doctor turn pale. They entered a tolerably large hall, such as is common in American country-houses, and which serves for a sitting-room in warm weather. From this they went up a wide staircase, that groaned and creaked as they trod, every step making its particular note, like the key of a harpsichord. This led to another hall on the second story, whence they entered the room where Dolph was to sleep. It was large, and scantily furnished; the shutters were closed; but as they were broken, there was no want of a circulation of air. It appeared to have been that sacred chamber, known among Dutch housewives by the name of "the best bed-room;" which is the best furnished room in the house, but in which scarce anybody is ever permitted to sleep. Its splendor, however, was all at an end. There were a few broken articles of furniture about the room, and in the centre stood a heavy deal table and a large arm-chair, both of which had the look of being coeval with the mansion. The fireplace was wide, and had been faced with Dutch tiles, representing Scripture stories; but some of them had fallen out of their places, and lay shattered about the hearth. The sexton lit the rushlight; and the doctor, looking fearfully about the room, was just exhorting Dolph to be of good cheer, and to pluck up a stout heart, when a noise in the chimney, like voices and struggling, struck a sudden panic into the sexton. He took to his heels with the lantern; the doctor followed hard after him; the stairs groaned and creaked as they hurried down, increasing their agitation and speed by its noises. The front door slammed after them; and Dolph heard them scrabbling down the avenue, till the sound of their feet was lost in the distance. That he did not join in this precipitate retreat, might have been owing to his possessing a little more courage than his companions, or perhaps that he had caught a glimpse of the cause of their dismay, in a nest of chimney swallows, that came tumbling down into the fireplace.

Being now left to himself, he secured the front door by a strong bolt and bar; and having seen that the other entrances were fastened, returned to his desolate chamber. Having made his supper from the basket which the good old cook had provided, he locked the chamber door, and retired to rest on a mattress in one corner. The night was calm and still; and nothing broke upon the profound quiet but the lonely chirping of a cricket from the chimney of a distant chamber. The rushlight, which stood in the centre of the deal table, shed a feeble yellow ray, dimly illumining the chamber, and making uncouth shapes and shadows on the walls, from the clothes which Dolph had thrown over a chair.

With all his boldness of heart, there was something subduing in this desolate scene; and he felt his spirits flag within him, as he lay on his hard bed and gazed about the room. He was turning over in his mind his idle habits, his doubtful prospects, and now and then heaving a heavy sigh, as he thought on his poor old mother; for there is nothing like the silence and loneliness of night to bring dark shadows over the brightest mind. By and by, he thought he heard a sound as of some one walking below stairs. He listened, and distinctly heard a step on the great staircase. It approached solemnly and slowly, tramp—tramp—tramp! It was evidently the tread of some heavy personage; and yet how could he have got into the house without making a noise? He had examined all the fastenings, and was certain that every entrance was secure. Still the steps advanced, tramp—tramp—tramp! It was evident that the person approaching could not be a robber—the step was too loud and deliberate; a robber would either be stealthy or precipitate. And now the footsteps had ascended the staircase; they were slowly advancing along the passage, resounding through the silent and empty apartments. The very cricket had ceased its melancholy note, and nothing interrupted their awful distinctness. The door, which had been locked on the inside, slowly swung open, as if self-moved. The footsteps entered the room; but no one was to be seen. They passed slowly and audibly across it, tramp—tramp—tramp! but whatever made the sound was invisible. Dolph rubbed his eyes, and stared about him; he could see to every part of the dimly-lighted chamber; all was vacant; yet still he heard those mysterious footsteps, solemnly walking about the chamber. They ceased, and all was dead silence. There was something more appalling in this invisible visitation, than there would have been in any thing that addressed itself to the eyesight. It was awfully vague and indefinite. He felt his heart beat against his ribs; a cold sweat broke out upon his forehead; he lay for some time in a state of violent agitation; nothing, however, occurred to increase his alarm. His light gradually burnt down into the socket, and he fell asleep. When he awoke it was broad daylight; the sun was peering through the cracks of the window-shutters, and the birds were merrily singing about the house. The bright, cheery day soon put to flight all the terrors of the preceding night. Dolph laughed, or rather tried to laugh, at all that had passed, and endeavored to persuade himself that it was a mere freak of the imagination, conjured up by the stories he had heard; but he was a little puzzled to find the door of his room locked on the inside, notwithstanding that he had positively seen it swing open as the footsteps had entered. He returned to town in a state of considerable perplexity; but he determined to say nothing on the subject, until his doubts were either confirmed or removed by another night's watching. His silence was a grievous disappointment to the gossips who had gathered at the doctor's mansion. They had prepared their minds to hear direful tales, and were almost in a rage at being assured he had nothing to relate.

The next night, then, Dolph repeated his vigil. He now entered the house with some trepidation. He was particular in examining the fastenings of all the doors, and securing them well. He locked the door of his chamber and placed a chair against it; then, having despatched his supper, he threw himself on his mattress and endeavored to sleep. It was all in vain—a thousand crowding fancies kept him waking. The time slowly dragged on, as if minutes were spinning themselves out into hours. As the night advanced, he grew more and more nervous; and he almost started from his couch, when he heard the mysterious footstep again on the staircase. Up it came, as before, solemnly and slowly, tramp—tramp—tramp! It approached along the passage; the door again swung open, as if there had been neither lock nor impediment, and a strange-looking figure stalked into the room. It was an elderly man, large and robust, clothed in the old Flemish fashion. He had on a kind of short cloak, with a garment under it, belted round the waist; trunk hose, with great bunches or bows at the knees; and a pair of russet boots, very large at top, and standing widely from his legs. His hat was broad and slouched, with a feather trailing over one side. His iron-gray hair hung in thick masses on his neck; and he had a short grizzled beard. He walked slowly round the room, as if examining that all was safe; then, hanging his hat on a peg beside the door, he sat down in the elbow-chair, and, leaning his elbow on the table, fixed his eyes on Dolph with an unmoving and deadening stare.

Dolph was not naturally a coward; but he had been brought up in an implicit belief in ghosts and goblins. A thousand stories came swarming to his mind, that he had heard about this building; and as he looked at this strange personage, with his uncouth garb, his pale visage, his grizzly beard, and his fixed, staring, fish-like eye, his teeth began to chatter, his hair to rise on his head, and a cold sweat to break out all over his body. How long he remained in this situation he could not tell, for he was like one fascinated. He could not take his gaze off from the spectre; but lay staring at him with his whole intellect absorbed in the contemplation. The old man remained seated behind the table, without stirring or turning an eye, always keeping a dead steady glare upon Dolph. At length the household cock from a neighboring farm clapped his wings, and gave a loud cheerful crow that rung over the fields. At the sound, the old man slowly rose and took down his hat from the peg; the door opened and closed after him; he was heard to go slowly down the staircase—tramp—tramp—tramp!—and when he had got to the bottom, all was again silent. Dolph lay and listened earnestly; counted every footfall; listened and listened if the steps should return—until, exhausted by watching and agitation, he fell into a troubled sleep.

Daylight again brought fresh courage and assurance. He would fain have considered all that had passed as a mere dream; yet there stood the chair in which the unknown had seated himself; there was the table on which he had leaned; there was the peg on which he had hung his hat; and there was the door locked precisely as he himself had locked it, with the chair placed against it. He hastened down-stairs and examined the doors and windows; all were exactly in the same state in which he had left them, and there was no apparent way by which any being could have entered and left the house without leaving some trace behind. "Pooh!" said Dolph to himself, "it was all a dream;"—but it would not do; the more he endeavored to shake the scene off from his mind, the more it haunted him.

Though he persisted in a strict silence as to all that he had seen or heard, yet his looks betrayed the uncomfortable night that he had passed. It was evident that there was something wonderful hidden under this mysterious reserve. The doctor took him into the study, locked the door, and sought to have a full and confidential communication; but he could get nothing out of him. Frau Ilsy took him aside into the pantry, but to as little purpose; and Peter de Groodt held him by the button for a full hour in the church-yard, the very place to get at the bottom of a ghost story, but came off not a whit wiser than the rest. It is always the case, however, that one truth concealed makes a dozen current lies. It is like a guinea locked up in a bank, that has a dozen paper representatives. Before the day was over, the neighborhood was full of reports. Some said that Dolph Heyliger watched in the haunted house with pistols loaded with silver bullets; others, that he had a long talk with the spectre without a head; others, that Dr. Knipperhausen and the sexton had been hunted down the Bowery lane, and quite into town, by a legion of ghosts of their customers. Some shook their heads, and thought it a shame the doctor should put Dolph to pass the night alone in that dismal house, where he might be spirited away, no one knew whither; while others observed, with a shrug, that if the devil did carry off the youngster, it would be but taking his own.

These rumors at length reached the ears of the good Dame Heyliger, and, as may be supposed, threw her into a terrible alarm. For her son to have opposed himself to danger from living foes, would have been nothing so dreadful in her eyes as to dare alone the terrors of the haunted house. She hastened to the doctor's, and passed a great part of the day in attempting to dissuade Dolph from repeating his vigil; she told him a score of tales, which her gossiping friends had just related to her, of persons who had been carried off when watching alone in old ruinous houses. It was all to no effect. Dolph's pride, as well as curiosity, was piqued. He endeavored to calm the apprehensions of his mother, and to assure her that there was no truth in all the rumors she had heard; she looked at him dubiously, and shook her head; but finding his determination was not to be shaken, she brought him a little thick Dutch Bible, with brass clasps, to take with him, as a sword wherewith to fight the powers of darkness; and, lest that might not be sufficient, the housekeeper gave him the Heidelberg catechism by way of dagger.

The next night, therefore, Dolph took up his quarters for the third time in the old mansion. Whether dream or not, the same thing was repeated. Towards midnight, when every thing was still, the same sound echoed through the empty halls—tramp—tramp—tramp! The stairs were again ascended; the door again swung open; the old man entered, walked round the room, hung up his hat, and seated himself by the table. The same fear and trembling came over poor Dolph, though not in so violent a degree. He lay in the same way, motionless and fascinated, staring at the figure, which regarded him, as before, with a dead, fixed, chilling gaze. In this way they remained for a long time, till, by degrees, Dolph's courage began gradually to revive. Whether alive or dead, this being had certainly some object in his visitation; and he recollected to have heard it said, spirits have no power to speak until spoken to. Summoning up resolution, therefore, and making two to three attempts before he could get his parched tongue in motion, he addressed the unknown in the most solemn form of adjuration, and demanded to know what was the motive of his visit.

No sooner had he finished, than the old man rose, took down his hat, the door opened, and he went out, looking back upon Dolph just as he crossed the threshold, as if expecting him to follow. The youngster did not hesitate an instant. He took the candle in his hand, and the Bible under his arm, and obeyed the tacit invitation. The candle emitted a feeble, uncertain ray; but still he could see the figure before him, slowly descend the stairs. He followed, trembling. When it had reached the bottom of the stairs, it turned through the hall towards the back door of the mansion. Dolph held the light over the balustrades; but, in his eagerness to catch a sight of the unknown, he flared his feeble taper so suddenly, that it went out. Still there was sufficient light from the pale moonbeams, that fell through a narrow window, to give him an indistinct view of the figure, near the door. He followed, therefore, down-stairs, and turned towards the place; but when he arrived there, the unknown had disappeared. The door remained fast barred and bolted; there was no other mode of exit; yet the being, whatever he might be, was gone. He unfastened the door, and looked out into the fields. It was a hazy, moonlight night, so that the eye could distinguish objects at some distance. He thought he saw the unknown in a footpath which led from the door. He was not mistaken; but how had he got out of the house? He did not pause to think, but followed on. The old man proceeded at a measured pace, without looking about him, his footsteps sounding on the hard ground. He passed through the orchard of apple-trees, always keeping the footpath. It led to a well, situated in a little hollow, which had supplied the farm with water. Just at this well, Dolph lost sight of him. He rubbed his eyes, and looked again; but nothing was to be seen of the unknown. He reached the well, but nobody was there. All the surrounding ground was open and clear; there was no bush nor hiding-place. He looked down the well, and saw, at a great depth, the reflection of the sky in the still water. After remaining here for some time, without seeing or hearing any thing more of his mysterious conductor, he returned to the house, full of awe and wonder. He bolted the door, groped his way back to bed, and it was long before he could compose himself to sleep.

His dreams were strange and troubled. He thought he was following the old man along the side of a great river, until they came to a vessel on the point of sailing; and that his conductor led him on board and vanished. He remembered the commander of the vessel, a short swarthy man, with crisped black hair, blind of one eye, and lame of one leg; but the rest of his dream was very confused. Sometimes he was sailing; sometimes on shore; now amidst storms and tempests, and now wandering quietly in unknown streets. The figure of the old man was strangely mingled up with the incidents of the dream; and the whole distinctly wound up by his finding himself on board of the vessel again, returning home, with a great bag of money!

When he woke, the gray, cool light of dawn was streaking the horizon, and the cocks passing the *reveille* from farm to farm throughout the country. He rose more harassed and perplexed than ever. He was singularly confounded by all that he had seen and dreamt, and began to doubt whether his mind was not affected, and whether all that was passing in his thoughts might not be mere feverish fantasy. In his present state of mind, he did not feel disposed to return immediately to the doctor's, and undergo the cross-questioning of the household. He made a scanty breakfast, therefore, on the remains of the last night's provisions, and then wandered out into the fields to meditate on all that had befallen him. Lost in thought, he rambled about, gradually approaching the town, until the morning was far advanced, when he was roused by a hurry and bustle around him. He found himself near the water's edge, in a throng of people, hurrying to a pier, where was a vessel ready to make sail. He was unconsciously carried along by the impulse of the crowd, and found that it was a sloop, on the point of sailing up the Hudson to Albany. There was much leave-taking and kissing of old women and children, and great activity in carrying on board baskets of bread and cakes, and provisions of all kinds, notwithstanding the mighty joints of meat that dangled over the stern; for a voyage to Albany was an expedition of great moment in those days. The commander of the sloop was hurrying about, and giving a world of orders, which were not very strictly attended to; one man being busy in lighting his pipe, and another in sharpening his snicker-snee.

The appearance of the commander suddenly caught Dolph's attention. He was short and swarthy, with crisped black hair; blind of one eye, and lame of one leg—the very commander that he had seen in his dream! Surprised and aroused, he considered the scene more attentively, and recalled still further traces of his dream: the appearance of the vessel, of the river, and of a variety of other objects, accorded with the imperfect images vaguely rising to recollection.

As he stood musing on these circumstances, the captain suddenly called out to him in Dutch, "Step on board, young man, or you'll be left behind!" He was startled by the summons; he saw that the sloop was cast loose, and was actually moving from the pier; it seemed as if he was actuated by some irresistible impulse; he sprang upon the deck, and the next moment the sloop was hurried off by the wind and tide. Dolph's thoughts and feelings were all in tumult and confusion. He had been strongly worked upon by the events that had recently befallen him, and could not but think there was some connection between his present situation and his last night's dream. He felt as if under supernatural influence; and tried to assure himself with an old and favorite maxim of his, that "one way or other, all would turn out for the best." For a moment, the indignation of the doctor at his departure without leave, passed across his mind—but that was matter of little moment. Then he thought of the distress of his mother at his strange disappearance, and the idea gave him a sudden pang; he would have entreated to be put on shore; but he knew with such wind and tide the entreaty would have been in vain. Then, the inspiring love of novelty and adventure came rushing in full tide through his bosom; he felt himself launched strangely and suddenly on the world, and under full way to explore the regions of wonder that lay up this mighty river, and beyond those blue mountains which had bounded his horizon since childhood. While he was lost in this whirl of thought, the sails strained to the breeze; the shores seemed to hurry away behind him; and, before he perfectly recovered his self-possession, the sloop was ploughing her way past Spiking-devil and Yonkers, and the tallest chimney of the Manhattoes had faded from his sight.

I have said, that a voyage up the Hudson in those days was an undertaking of some moment; indeed, it was as much thought of as a voyage to Europe is at present. The sloops were often many days on the way; the cautious navigators taking in sail when it blew fresh, and coming to anchor at night; and stopping to send the boat ashore for milk or tea, without which it was impossible for the worthy old lady passengers to subsist. And there were the much-talked-of perils of the Tappan Zee, and the Highlands. In short, a prudent Dutch burgher would talk of such a voyage for months, and even years, beforehand; and never undertook it without putting his affairs in order, making his will, and having prayers said for him in the Low Dutch churches.

In the course of such a voyage, therefore, Dolph was satisfied he would have time enough to reflect, and to make up his mind as to what he should do when he arrived at Albany. The captain, with his blind eye and lame leg, would, it is true, bring his strange dream to mind, and perplex him sadly for a few moments; but, of late, his life had been made up so much of dreams and realities, his nights and days had been so jumbled together, that he seemed to be moving continually in a delusion. There is always, however, a kind of vagabond consolation in a man's having nothing in this world to lose; with this Dolph comforted his heart, and determined to make the most of the present enjoyment.

In the second day of the voyage they came to the Highlands. It was the latter part of a calm, sultry day, that they floated gently with the tide between these stern mountains. There was that perfect quiet which prevails over nature in the languor of summer heat; the turning of a plank, or the accidental falling of an oar on deck, was echoed from the mountain side and reverberated along the shores; and if by chance the captain gave a shout of command, there were airy tongues which mocked it from every cliff.

Dolph gazed about him in mute delight and wonder, at these scenes of nature's magnificence. To the left the Dunderberg reared its woody precipices, height over height, forest over forest, away into the deep summer sky. To the right strutted forth the bold promontory of Antony's Nose, with a solitary eagle wheeling about it; while beyond, mountain succeeded to mountain, until they seemed to lock their arms together, and confine this mighty river in their embraces. There was a feeling of quiet luxury in gazing at the broad, green bosoms here and there scooped out among the precipices; or at woodlands high in air, nodding over the edge of some beetling bluff, and their foliage all transparent in the yellow sunshine.

In the midst of his admiration, Dolph remarked a pile of bright, snowy clouds peering above the western heights. It was succeeded by another, and another, each seemingly pushing onwards its predecessor, and towering, with dazzling brilliancy, in the deep-blue atmosphere: and now muttering peals of thunder were faintly heard rolling behind the mountains. The river, hitherto still and glassy, reflecting pictures of the sky and land, now showed a dark ripple at a distance, as the breeze came creeping up it. The fish-hawks wheeled and screamed, and sought their nests on the high dry trees; the crows flew clamorously to the crevices of the rocks, and all nature seemed conscious of the approaching thunder-gust.

The clouds now rolled in volumes over the mountain tops; their summits still bright and snowy, but the lower parts of an inky blackness. The rain began to patter down in broad and scattered drops; the wind freshened, and curled up the waves; at length it seemed as if the bellying clouds were torn open by the mountain tops, and complete torrents of rain came rattling down. The lightning leaped from cloud to cloud, and streamed quivering against the rocks, splitting and rending the stoutest forest trees. The thunder burst in tremendous explosions; the peals were echoed from mountain to mountain; they crashed upon Dunder-berg, and rolled up the long defile of the Highlands, each headland making a new echo, until old Bull Hill seemed to bellow back the storm.

For a time the scudding rack and mist, and the sheeted rain, almost hid the landscape from the sight. There was a fearful gloom, illumined still more fearfully by the streams of lightning which glittered among the rain-drops. Never had Dolph beheld such an absolute warring of the elements: it seemed as if the storm was tearing and rending its way through this mountain defile, and had brought all the artillery of heaven into action.

The vessel was hurried on by the increasing wind, until she came to where the river makes a sudden bend, the only one in the whole course of its majestic career.[1] Just as they turned the point, a violent flaw of wind came sweeping down a mountain gully, bending the forest before it, and, in a moment, lashing up the river into white froth and foam. The captain saw the danger, and cried out to lower the sail. Before the order could be obeyed, the flaw struck the sloop, and threw her on her beam-ends. Every thing now was fright and confusion: the flapping of the sails, the whistling and rushing of the wind, the bawling of the captain and crew, the shrieking of the passengers, all mingled with the rolling and bellowing of the thunder. In the midst of the uproar, the sloop righted; at the same time the mainsail shifted, the boom came sweeping the quarter-deck, and Dolph, who was gazing unguardedly at the clouds, found himself, in a moment, floundering in the river.

For once in his life, one of his idle accomplishments was of use to him. The many truant hours he had devoted to sporting in the Hudson, had made him an expert swimmer; yet, with all his strength and skill, he found great difficulty in reaching the shore. His disappearance from the deck had not been noticed by the crew, who were all occupied by their own danger. The sloop was driven along with inconceivable rapidity. She had hard work to weather a long promontory on the eastern shore, round which the river turned, and which completely shut her from Dolph's view.

It was on a point of the western shore that he landed, and, scrambling up the rocks, threw himself, faint and exhausted, at the foot of a tree. By degrees, the thunder-gust passed over. The clouds rolled away to the east, where they lay piled in feathery masses, tinted with the last rosy rays of the sun. The distant play of the lightning might be seen about the dark bases, and now and then might be heard the faint muttering of the thunder. Dolph rose, and sought about to see if any path led from the shore; but all was savage and trackless. The rocks were piled upon each other; great trunks of trees lay shattered about, as they had been blown down by the strong winds which draw through these mountains, or had fallen through age. The rocks, too, were overhung with wild vines and briars, which completely matted themselves together, and opposed a barrier to all ingress; every movement that he made, shook down a shower from the dripping foliage. He attempted to scale one of these almost perpendicular heights; but, though strong and agile, he found it an Herculean undertaking. Often he was

---

[1] This must have been the bend at West-Point.

supported merely by crumbling projections of the rock, and sometimes he clung to roots and branches of trees, and hung almost suspended in the air. The wood-pigeon came cleaving his whistling flight by him, and the eagle screamed from the brow of the impending cliff. As he was thus clambering, he was on the point of seizing hold of a shrub to aid his ascent, when something rustled among the leaves, and he saw a snake quivering along like lightning, almost from under his hand. It coiled itself up immediately, in an attitude of defiance, with flattened head, distended jaws, and quickly-vibrating tongue, that played like a little flame about its mouth. Dolph's heart turned faint within him, and he had well-nigh let go his hold, and tumbled down the precipice. The serpent stood on the defensive but for an instant; and finding there was no attack, it glided away into a cleft of the rock. Dolph's eye followed with fearful intensity, and saw a nest of adders, knotted, and writhing, and hissing in the chasm. He hastened with all speed to escape from so frightful a neighborhood. His imagination full of this new horror, saw an adder in every curling vine, and heard the tail of a rattlesnake in every dry leaf that rustled.

At length he succeeded in scrambling to the summit of a precipice; but it was covered by a dense forest. Wherever he could gain a look-out between the trees, he beheld heights and cliffs, one rising beyond another, until huge mountains overtopped the whole. There were no signs of cultivation, no smoke curling among the trees, to indicate a human residence. Every thing was wild and solitary. As he was standing on the edge of a precipice overlooking a deep ravine fringed with trees, his feet detached a great fragment of rock; it fell, crashing its way through the tree tops, down into the chasm. A loud whoop, or rather yell, issued from the bottom of the glen; the moment after, there was the report of a gun; and a ball came whistling over his head, cutting the twigs and leaves, and burying itself deep in the bark of a chestnut-tree.

Dolph did not wait for a second shot, but made a precipitate retreat; fearing every moment to hear the enemy in pursuit. He succeeded, however, in returning unmolested to the shore, and determined to penetrate no farther into a country so beset with savage perils.

He sat himself down, dripping, disconsolately, on a wet stone. What was to be done? Where was he to shelter himself? The hour of repose was approaching; the birds were seeking their nests, the bat began to flit about in the twilight, and the nighthawk soaring high in the heaven, seemed to be calling out the stars. Night gradually closed in, and wrapped every thing in gloom; and though it was the latter part of summer, the breeze, stealing along the river, and among these dripping forests, was chilly and penetrating, especially to a half-drowned man.

As he sat drooping and despondent in this comfortless condition, he perceived a light gleaming through the trees near the shore, where the winding of the river made a deep bay. It cheered him with the hope of a human habitation, where he might get something to appease the clamorous cravings of his stomach, and, what was equally necessary in his shipwrecked condition, a comfortable shelter for the night. With extreme difficulty he made his way towards the light, along ledges of rocks down which he was in danger of sliding into the river, and over great trunks of fallen trees; some of which had been blown down in the late storm, and lay so thickly together, that he had to struggle through their branches. At length he came to the brow of a rock overhanging a small dell, whence the light proceeded. It was from a fire at the foot of a great tree, in the midst of a grassy interval, or plat, among the rocks. The fire cast up a red glare among the gray crags and impending trees; leaving chasms of deep gloom, that resembled entrances to caverns. A small brook rippled close by, betrayed by the quivering reflection of the flame. There were two figures moving about the fire, and others squatted before it. As they were between him and the light, they were in complete shadow; but one of them happening to move round to the opposite side, Dolph was startled at perceiving, by the glare falling on painted features, and glittering on silver ornaments, that he was an Indian. He now looked more narrowly, and saw guns leaning against a tree, and a dead body lying on the ground.

Here was the very foe that had fired at him from the glen. He endeavored to retreat quietly, not caring to entrust himself to these half-human beings in so savage and lonely a place. It was too late: the Indian, with that eagle quickness of eye so remarkable in his race, perceived something stirring among the bushes on the rock: he seized one of the guns that leaned against the tree; one moment more, and Dolph might have had his passion for adventure cured by a bullet. He hallooed loudly, with the Indian salutation of friendship: the whole party sprang upon their feet; the salutation was returned, and the straggler was invited to join them at the fire.

On approaching, he found, to his consolation, the party was composed of white men as well as Indians. One, evidently the principal personage, or commander, was seated on a trunk of a tree before the fire. He was a large, stout man, somewhat advanced in life, but hale and hearty. His face was bronzed almost to the color of an Indian's; he had strong but rather jovial features, an aquiline nose, and a mouth shaped like a mastiff's. His face was half thrown in shade by a broad hat, with a buck's-tail in it. His gray hair hung short in his neck. He wore a hunting-frock, with Indian leggings, and moccasons, and a tomahawk in the broad wampum belt round his waist. As Dolph caught a distinct view of his person and features, something reminded him of the old man of the haunted house. The man before him, however, was different in dress and age; he was more cheery, too, in aspect, and it was hard to define where the vague resemblance lay—but a resemblance there certainly was. Dolph felt some degree of awe in approaching him; but was assured by a frank, hearty welcome. He was still further encouraged, by perceiving that the dead body, which had caused him some alarm, was that of a deer; and his satisfaction was complete, in discerning, by savory steams from a kettle suspended by a hooked stick over the fire, that there was a part cooking for the evening's repast.

He had in fact fallen in with a rambling hunting party, such as often took place in those days among the settlers along the river. The hunter is always hospitable; and nothing makes men more social and uncermonious, than meeting in the wilderness. The commander of the party poured out a dram of cheering liquor, which he gave him with a merry leer, to warm his heart; and ordered one of his followers to fetch some garments from a pinnace, moored in a cove close by, while those in which our hero was dripping might be dried before the fire.

Dolph found, as he had suspected, that the shot from the glen, which had come so near giving him his quietus when on the precipice, was from the party before him. He had nearly crushed one of them by the fragments of rock which he had detached; and the jovial old hunter, in the broad hat and buck-tail, had fired at the place where he saw the bushes move, supposing it to be some wild animal. He laughed heartily at the blunder; it being what is considered an exceeding good joke among hunters; "but faith, my lad," said he, "if I had but caught a glimpse of you to take sight at, you would have followed the rock. Antony Vander Heyden is seldom known to miss his aim." These last words were at once a clew to Dolph's curiosity; and a few questions let him completely into the character of the man before him, and of his band of woodland rangers. The commander in the broad hat and hunting-frock was no less a personage than the Heer Antony Vander Heyden, of Albany, of whom Dolph had many a time heard. He was, in fact, the hero of many a story; his singular humors and whimsical habits, being matters of wonder to his quiet Dutch neighbors. As he was a man of property, having had a father before him, from whom he inherited large tracts of wild land, and whole barrels full of wampum, he could indulge his humors without control. Instead of staying quietly at home, eating and drinking at regular meal times; amusing himself by smoking his pipe on the bench before the door, and then turning into a comfortable bed at night; he delighted in all kinds of rough, wild expeditions. Never so happy as when on a hunting party in the wilderness, sleeping under trees or bark sheds, or cruising down the river, or on some woodland lake, fishing and fowling, and living the Lord knows how.

He was a great friend to Indians, and to an Indian mode of life; which he considered true natural liberty and manly enjoyment. When at home, he had always several Indian hangers-on, who loitered about his house, sleeping like hounds in the sunshine, or preparing hunting and fishing-tackle for some new expedition, or shooting at marks with bows and arrows.

Over these vagrant beings, Heer Antony had as perfect command as a hunts-man over his pack; though they were great nuisances to the regular people of his neighborhood. As he was a rich man, no one ventured to thwart his humors; indeed, his hearty, joyous manner made him universally popular. He would troll a Dutch song, as he tramped along the street; hail every one a mile off; and when he entered a house, would slap the good man familiarly on the back, shake him by the hand till he roared, and kiss his wife and daughter before his face—in short, there was no pride nor ill-humor about Heer Antony.

Besides his Indian hangers-on, he had three or four humble friends among the white men, who looked up to him as a patron, and had the run of his kitchen, and the favor of being taken with him occasionally on his expeditions. With a medley of such retainers he was at present on a cruise along the shores of the Hudson, in a pinnace kept for his own recreation. There were two white men with him, dressed partly in the Indian style, with moccasons and hunting-shirts; the rest of his crew consisted of four favorite Indians. They had been prowling about the river, without any definite object, until they found themselves in the Highlands; where they had passed two or three days, hunting the deer which still lingered among these mountains.

"It is lucky for you, young man," said Antony Vander Heyden, "that you happened to be knocked overboard to-day, as to-morrow morning we start early on our return homewards, and you might then have looked in vain for a meal among the mountains—but come, lads, stir about! stir about! Let's see what prog we have for supper; the kettle has boiled long enough; my stomach cries cupboard; and I'll warrant our guest is in no mood to dally with his trencher."

There was a bustle now in the little encampment. One took off the kettle, and turned a part of the contents into a huge wooden bowl; another prepared a flat rock for a table; while a third brought various utensils from the pinnace; Heer Antony himself brought a flask or two of precious liquor from his own private locker—knowing his boon companions too well to trust any of them with the key.

A rude but hearty repast was soon spread; consisting of venison smoking from the kettle, with cold bacon, boiled Indian corn, and mighty loaves of good brown household bread. Never had Dolph made a more delicious repast; and when he had washed it down with two or three draughts from the Heer Antony's flask, and felt the jolly liquor sending its warmth through his veins, and glowing round his very heart, he would not have changed his situation, no, not with the governor of the province.

The Heer Antony, too, grew chirping and joyous; told half-a-dozen fat stories, at which his white followers laughed immoderately, though the Indians, as usual, maintained an invincible gravity.

"This is your true life, my boy!" said he, slapping Dolph on the shoulder; "a man is never a man till he can defy wind and weather, range woods and wilds, sleep under a tree, and live on bass-wood leaves!"

And then would he sing a stave or two of a Dutch drinking song, swaying a short squat Dutch bottle in his hand, while his myrmidons would join in the chorus, until the woods echoed again;—as the good old song has it:

> "They all with a shout made the elements ring,
>   So soon as the office was o'er;
> To feasting they went with true merriment,
>   And tippled strong liquor gillore."

In the midst of his joviality, however, Heer Antony did not lose sight of discretion. Though he pushed the bottle without reserve to Dolph, he always took care to help his followers himself, knowing the beings he had to deal with; and was particular in granting but a moderate allowance to the Indians. The repast being ended, the Indians having drunk their liquor and smoked their pipes, now wrapped themselves in their blankets, stretched themselves on the ground with their feet to the fire, and soon fell sleep, like so many tired hounds. The rest of the party remained chatting before the fire, which the gloom of the forest, and the dampness of the air from the late storm, rendered extremely grateful and comforting. The conversation gradually moderated from the hilarity of supper-time, and turned upon hunting adventures, and exploits and perils in the wilderness; many of which were so strange and improbable, that I will not venture to repeat them, lest the veracity of Antony Vander Heyden and his comrades should be brought into question. There were many legendary tales told, also, about the river, and the settlements on its borders; in which valuable kind of lore, the Heer Antony seemed deeply versed. As the sturdy bush-beater sat in a twisted root of a tree, that served him for an arm-chair, dealing forth these wild stories, with the fire gleaming on his strongly-marked visage, Dolph was again repeatedly perplexed by something that reminded him of the phantom of the haunted house; some vague resemblance, not to be fixed upon any precise feature or lineament, but pervading the general air of his countenance and figure.

The circumstance of Dolph's falling overboard led to the relation of divers disasters and singular mishaps that had befallen voyagers on this great river, particularly in the earlier periods of colonial history; most of which the Heer deliberately attributed to supernatural causes. Dolph stared at this suggestion; but the old gentleman assured him it was very currently believed by the settlers along the river, that these highlands were under the dominion of supernatural and mischievous beings, which seemed to have taken some pique against the Dutch colonists in the early time of the settlement. In consequence of this, they have ever taken particular delight in venting their spleen, and indulging their humors, upon the Dutch skippers; bothering them with flaws, head winds, counter currents, and all kinds of impediments; insomuch, that a Dutch navigator was always obliged to be exceedingly wary and deliberate in his proceedings; to come to anchor at dusk; to drop his peak, or take in sail, whenever he saw a swag-bellied cloud rolling over the mountains; in short, to take so many precautions, that he was often apt to be an incredible time in toiling up the river.

Some, he said, believed these mischievous powers of the air to be evil spirits conjured up by the Indian wizards, in the early times of the province, to revenge themselves on the strangers who had dispossessed them of their country. They even attributed to their incantations the misadventure which befell the renowned Hendrick Hudson, when he sailed so gallantly up this river in quest of a north-west passage, and, as he thought, run his ship aground; which they affirm was nothing more nor less than a spell of these same wizards, to prevent his getting to China in this direction.

The greater part, however, Heer Antony observed, accounted for all the extraordinary circumstances attending this river, and the perplexities of the skippers who navigated it, by the old legend of the Storm-ship, which haunted Point-no-point. On finding Dolph to be utterly ignorant of this tradition, the Heer stared at him for a moment with surprise, and wondered where he had passed his life, to be uninformed on so important a point of history. To pass away the remainder of the evening, therefore, he undertook the tale, as far as his memory would serve, in the very words in which it had been written out by Mynheer Selyne, an early poet of the New Nederlandts. Giving, then, a stir to the fire, that sent up its sparks among the trees like a little volcano, he adjusted himself comfortably in his root of a tree; and throwing back his head, and closing his eyes for a few moments, to summon up his recollection, he related the following legend . . . [of the storm ship].

From *A History of New York-From The Beginning Of The World To The End Of The Dutch Dynasty, By Diedrich Knickerbocker**

KNICKERBOCKER HISTORY OF NEW YORK

"About this time the testy little governor of the New Netherlands appears to have had his hands full, and with one annoyance and the other to have been kept continually on the bounce. He was on the very point of following up the expedition of Jan Jansen Alpendam by some belligerent measures against the marauders of Merryland, when his attention was suddenly called away by belligerent troubles springing up in another quarter, the seeds of which had been sown in the tranquil days of Walter the Doubter.

The reader will recollect the deep doubt into which the most pacific governor was thrown on Killian Van Rensellaer's taking possession of Bearn Island by wapen recht. While the governor doubted and did nothing, the lordly Killian went on to complete his sturdy little castellum of Rensellaerstein, and to garrison it with a number of his tenants from the Helderberg, a mountain region famous for the hardest heads and the hardest fists in the province. Nicholas Koorn, a faithful squire of the patroon, accustomed to strut at his heels, wear his cast-off clothes, and imitate his lofty bearing, was established in this post as wacht-meester. His duty it was to keep an eye on the river, and oblige every vessel that passed, unless on the service of their High Mightinesses, to strike its flag, lower its peak, and pay toll to the lord of Rensellaerstein.

This assumption of sovereign authority within the territories of the Lords

*The Works of Washington Irving, The Kinderhook Edition (New York: G. P. Putnam's Sons, 1880).

States General, however, it might have been tolerated by Walter the Doubter, had been sharply contested by William the Testy on coming into office; and many written remonstrances had been addressed by him to Killian Van Rensellaer, to which the latter never deigned reply. Thus, by degrees, a sore place, or, in Hibernian parlance, a raw, had been established in the irritable soul of the little governor, insomuch that he winced at the very name of Rensellaerstein.

Now it came to pass that, on a fine sunny day, the Company's yacht, the Half-Moon, having been on one of its stated visits to Fort Aurania, was quietly tiding it down the Hudson. The commander, Govert Lockerman, a veteran Dutch skipper of few words but great bottom, was seated on the high poop, quietly smoking his pipe under the shadow of the proud flag of Orange, when, on arriving abreast of Bearn Island, he was saluted by a stentorian voice from the shore, "Lower they flag, and be d——d to thee!"

Govert Lockerman, without taking his pipe out of his mouth, turned up his eye from under his broad-brimmed hat to see who had hailed him thus discourteously. There, on the ramparts of the fort, stood Nicholas Koorn, armed to the teeth, flourishing a brass-hilted sword, while a steeple-crowned hat and cocks tail-feather, formerly worn by Killian Van Rensellaer himself, gave an inexpressible loftiness to his demeanor.

Govert Lockerman eyed the warrior from top to toe, but was not to be dismayed. Taking the pipe slowly out of his mouth, "To whom should I lower my flag?" demanded he. "To the high and mighty Killian Van Rensellaer, the lord of Rensellaerstein!" was the reply. "I lower it to none but the Prince of Orange and my masters the Lords States General." So saying, he resumed his pipe and smoked with an air of dogged determination.

Bang! went a gun from the fortress; the ball cut both sail and rigging. Govert Lockerman said nothing, but smoked the more doggedly.

Bang! went another gun; the shot whistled close astern.

"Fire, and be d——d," cried Govert Lockerman, cramming a new charge of tobacco into his pipe, and smoking with still increasing vehemence.

"Bang!" went a third gun. The shot passed over his head, tearing a hole in the "princely flag of Orange."

This was the hardest trial of all for the pride and patience of Govert Lockerman. He maintained a stubborn, though swelling silence; but his smothered rage might be perceived by the short vehement puffs of smoke emitted from his pipe, by which he might be tracked for miles, as he slowly floated out of shot and out of sight of Bearn Island. In fact, he never gave vent to his passion until he got fairly among the Highlands of the Hudson; when he let fly whole volleys of Dutch oaths, which are said to linger to this very day among the echoes of the Dunderberg, and to give particular effect to the thunder-storms in that neighborhood.

It was the sudden apparition of Govert Lockerman at Dog's Misery, bearing in his hand the tattered flag of Orange, that arrested the attention of William the Testy, just as he was devising a new expedition against the marauders of Merryland. I will not pretend to describe the passion of the little man when he heard of the outrage of Rensellaerstein. Suffice it to say, in the first transports of his fury, he turned Dog's Misery topsy-turvy; kicked every cur out of doors, and threw the cats out of the window; after which, his spleen being in some measure relieved, he went into a council of war with Govert Lockerman, the skipper, assisted by Antony Van Corlear, the Trumpeter.

The eyes of all New Amsterdam were now turned to see what would be the end of this direful feud between William the Testy and the patron of Rensellaerwick; and some, observing the consultations of the governor with the skipper and the trumpeter, predicted warlike measures by sea and land. The wrath of William Kieft, however, though quick to rise, was quick to evaporate. He was a perfect brush-heap in a blaze, snapping and crackling for a time, and then ending in smoke. Like many other valiant potentates, his first thoughts were all for war, his sober second thoughts of diplomacy.

Accordingly, Govert Lockerman was once more despatched up the river in the Company's yacht, the Gold Hoop, bearing Antony the Trumpeter as ambassador, to treat with the beligerent powers of Rensellaerstein. In the fullness of time the yacht arrived before Bearn Island, and Antony the Trumpeter, mounting the poop, sounded a parley to the fortress. In a little while the steeple-crowned hat of Nicholas Koor, the wacht-meester, rose above the battlements, followed by his iron visage, and ultimately his whole person armed as before, to the very teeth; while, one by one, a whole row of Helderbergers reared their round burly heads above the wall, and beside each pumpkin-head peered the end of a rusty musket. Nothing daunted by this formidable array, Antony Van Corlear drew forth and read with audible voice a missive from William the Testy, protesting against the usurpation of Bearn Island, and ordering the garrison to quit the premises, bag and baggage, on pain of the vengeance of the potentate of the Manhattoes.

In reply, the wacht-meester applied the thumb of his right hand to the end of his nose, and the thumb of his left hand to the little finger of the right, and spreading each hand like a fan, made an aerial flourish with his fingers. Antony Van Corlear was sorely perplexed to understand this sign, which seemed to him something mysterious and masonic. Not liking to betray his ignorance, he again read with a loud voice the missive of William the Testy, and again Nicholas Koorn applied the thumb of his right hand to the end of his nose, and the thumb of his left hand to the little finger of the right, and repeated this kind of nasal weather-cock. Antony Van Corlear now persuaded himself that his was some short-hand sign or symbol, current in diplomacy, which, though unintelligible to a new diplomat, like himself, would speak volumes to the experienced intellect of William the Testy; considering his embassy therefore at an end, he sounded his trumpet with great complacency, and set sail on his return down the river, every now and then practicing this mysterious sign of the wacht-meester, to keep it accurately in mind.

Arrived at New Amsterdam he made a faithful report of his embassy to the governor, accompanied by a manual exhibition of the response of Nicholas Koorn. The governor was equally perplexed with his embassy. He was deeply versed in the mysteries of freemasonry; but they threw no light on the matter. He knew every variety of windmill and weather-cock, but was not a whit the wiser as to the aerial sign in question. He had even dabbled in Egyptian hieroglyphics and the mystic symbols of the obelisks, but none furnished a key to the reply of Nicholas Koorn. He called a meeting of his council. Antony Van Corlear stood forth in the midst, and putting the thumb of his right hand to his nose, and the thumb of his left hand to the finger of the right he gave a faithful facsimile of the portentous sign. Having a nose of unusual dimensions, it was as if the reply had been put in capitals; but all in vain: the worthy burgomasters were equally perplexed with the governor. Each one put his thumb to the end of his nose, spread his fingers like a fan, imitated the motion of Antony Van Corlear, and then smoked in dubious silence. Several times was Antony obliged to stand forth like a fugleman and repeat the sign, and each time a circle of nasal weather-cocks might be seen in the council-chamber.

Perplexed in the extreme, William the Testy sent for all the soothsayers, and fortune-tellers and wise men of the Manhattoes, but none could interpret the mysterious reply of Nicholas Koorn. The council broke up in sore perplexity. The matter got abroad, and Antony Van Corlear was stopped at every corner to repeat the signal to a knot of anxious newsmongers, each of whom departed with his thumb to his nose and his fingers in the air, to carry the story home to his family. For several days all business was neglected in New Amsterdam; nothing was talked of but the diplomatic mission of Antony Van Corlear the Trumpeter,—nothing was to be seen but knots of politicians with their thumbs to their noses. In the mean time the fierce feud between William the Testy and Killian Van Rensellaer, which at first had menaced deadly warfare, gradually cooled off, like many other war-questions, in the prolonged delays of diplomacy.

Still to this early affair of Rensellaerstein may be traced the remote origin of those windy wars in modern days which rage in the bowels of the Helderberg, and have wellnigh shaken the great patroonship of the Van Rensellaers to its foundation; for we are told that the bully boys of the Helderberg, who served under Nicholas Koorn the wacht-meester, carried back to their mountains the hieroglyphic sign which had so sorely puzzled Antony Van Corlear and the sages of the Manhattoes, so that to the present day the thumb to the nose and the fingers in the air is apt to be the reply of the Helderbergers whenever called upon for any long arrears in rent."

"Antony Van Corlear drowning in Spuyten Duyvil Creek while blowing his trumpet." Anonymous woodcut. Editor's collection.

Portrait of Joseph Rodman Drake from the frontispiece of the first edition of *The Culprit Fay and Other Poems* by Joseph Rodman Drake. Painted by Rodgers and engraved by T. Kelly. New York: Dearborn, 1835.

Joseph Rodman Drake

Joseph Rodman Drake (1795-1820) was born in New York City and became a practicing physician. He and Fitz-Greene Halleck wrote a series of light satiric verses for the New York Evening Post in 1819, later collected in *The Croakers* in 1840. His best-known and greatest work is the epic-lyric *tour-de-force*, "The Culprit Fay." It is set amidst the Hudson Highlands and is in the manner of Christoph Martin Wieland's (1733-1813) poem "Oberon" of 1780, which was translated into English in 1798 by John Quincy Adams. "The Culprit Fay" deals with elves, ouphes, and similar sylvan creations of European imagination set amidst Americn scenery. The work also shows influences of Shakespeare's *Midsummer Night's Dream* and *The Tempest*.

The "Culprit Fay" is a work of great lyric beauty. Other popular poems by Drake are "To A Friend," "Niagara," "Lines on Leaving New Rochelle," "Bronx," and "The American Flag." After his premature death in 1820 at the age of twenty-five, his works were collected and published by his daughter in 1835.

Fitz-Greene Halleck (1790-1867) was born at Guilford, Connecticut, but came to New York in his youth. For many years he served as personal secretary to John Jacob Astor. His first literary activity was writing *The Croakers* in conjunction with Joseph Rodman Drake in 1819. His major work is "Fanny" (1819), a long satire in the style of Byron, which Nathaniel Parker Willis quotes appropriately in his essay entitled "View of New York, from Weehawken," included in this volume. Other well-known shorter poems are "Marco Bozzaris" and his elegy upon the death of Drake, beginning "Green be the turf above thee. . . ."

To a Friend.*

Stanza III

Are there no scenes to touch the poet's soul?
No deeds of arms to wake the lordly strain?
Shall Hudson's billows unregarded roll?
Has Warren, has Montgomery died in vain?
Shame! that while every mountain stream and plain
Hath theme for truth's proud voice or fancy's wand,
No native bard the patriot harp hath ta'en,
But left to minstrels of a foreign strand
To sing the beauteous scenes of nature's loveliest land.

*Joseph Rodman Drake, *The Culprit Fay and Other Poems* (New York: George Dearborn, 1835). 1st Edition.

THE CULPRIT FAY.*

"My visual orbs are purged from film, and lo!
  "Instead of Anster's turnip-bearing vales
"I see old fairy land's miraculous show!
  "Her trees of tinsel kissed by freakish gales,
"Her Ouphs that, cloaked in leaf-gold, skim the breeze,
  "And fairies, swarming————"
                    TENNANT'S ANSTER FAIR.

I.

'Tis the middle watch of a summer's night—
The earth is dark, but the heavens are bright;
Naught is seen in the vault on high
But the moon, and the stars, and the cloudless sky,
And the flood which rolls its milky hue,
A river of light on the welkin blue.
The moon looks down on old Cronest,
She mellows the shades on his shaggy breast,
And seems his huge grey form to throw
In a silver cone on the wave below;
His sides are broken by spots of shade,
By the walnut bough and the cedar made,
And through their clustering branches dark
Glimmers and dies the fire-fly's spark—
Like starry twinkles that momently break
Through the rifts of the gathering tempest's rack.

II.

The stars are on the moving stream,
  And fling, as its ripples gently flow,
A burnished length of wavy beam
  In an eel-like, spiral line below;
The winds are whist, and the owl is still,
  The bat in the shelvy rock is hid,
And naught is heard on the lonely hill
But the cricket's chirp and the answer shrill
  Of the gauze-winged katy-did;
And the plaint of the wailing whip-poor-will
  Who mourns unseen, and ceaseless sings,

*The Culprit Fay and Other Poems (New York: George Dearborn, 1835). 1st Edition.

"The Maiden and the Fay." Drawing by Arthur Lumley, engraved by John P. Davis, from *The Culprit Fay. A Poem* by Joseph Rodman Drake (New York: Carleton, 1867).

"Cronest—'Tis the middle watch of a summer's night." Drawing by Arthur Lumley, engraved by John P. Davis, from *The Culprit Fay. A Poem* by Joseph Rodman Drake (New York: Carleton, 1867).

Ever a note of wail and wo,
 Till morning spreads her rosy wings,
And earth and sky in her glances glow.

III.

'Tis the hour of fairy ban and spell:
The wood-tick has kept the minutes well;
He has counted them all with click and stroke,
Deep in the heart of the mountain oak,
And he has awakened the sentry elve
 Who sleeps with him in the haunted tree,
To bid him ring the hour of twelve,
 And call the fays to their revelry;
Twelve small strokes on his tinkling bell—
('Twas made of the white snail's pearly shell:—)
"Midnight comes, and all is well!
Hither, hither, wing your way!
'Tis the dawn of the fairy day."

IV.

They come from beds of lichen green,
They creep from the mullen's velvet screen;
 Some on the backs of beetles fly
From the silver tops of moon-touched trees,
 Where they swung in their cobweb hammocks high,
And rock'd about in the evening breeze;
 Some from the hum-bird's downy nest—
They had driven him out by elfin power,
 And pillowed on plumes of his rainbow breast,
Had slumbered there till the charmed hour;
 Some had lain in the scoop of the rock,
With glittering ising-stars inlaid;
 And some had opened the four-o'clock,
And stole within its purple shade.
 And now they throng the moonlight glade,
Above—below—on every side,
 Their little minim forms arrayed
In the tricksy pomp of fairy pride!

V.

They come not now to print the lea,
In freak and dance around the tree,

Or at the mushroom board to sup,
And drink the dew from the buttercup;—
A scene of sorrow waits them now,
For an Ouphe has broken his vestal vow;
He has loved an earthly maid,
And left for her his woodland shade;
He has lain upon her lip of dew,
And sunned him in her eye of blue,
Fann'd her cheek with his wing of air,
Played with the ringlets of her hair,
And, nestling on her snowy breast,
Forgot the lily-king's behest.
For this the shadowy tribes of air
    To the elfin court must haste away:—
And now they stand expectant there,
    To hear the doom of the Culprit Fay.

VI.

The throne was reared upon the grass
Of spice-wood and of sassafras;
On pillars of mottled tortoise-shell
    Hung the burnished canopy—
And o'er it gorgeous curtains fell
    Of the tulip's crimson drapery.
The monarch sat on his judgment-seat,
    On his brow the crown imperial shone,
The prisoner Fay was at his feet,
    And his peers were ranged around the throne.
He waved his sceptre in the air,
    He looked around and calmy spoke;
His brow was grave and his eye severe,
    But his voice in a softened accent broke:

VII.

"Fairy! Fairy! list and mark,
    Thou hast broke thine elfin chain,
Thy flame-wood lamp is quenched and dark,
    And thy wings are dyed with a deadly stain—
Thou hast sullied thine elfin purity
    In the glance of a mortal maiden's eye,
Thou hast scorned our dread decree,
And thou shouldst pay the forfeit high,

But well I know her sinless mind
Is pure as the angel forms above,
Gentle and meek, and chaste and kind,
Such as a spirit well might love,
Fairy! had she spot or taint,
Bitter had been thy punishment.
Tied to the hornet's shardy wings;
Tossed on the pricks of nettles' stings;
Or seven long ages doomed to dwell
With the lazy worm in the walnut-shell;
Or every night to writhe and bleed
Beneath the tread of the centipede;
Or bound in a cobweb dungeon dim,
Your jailer a spider huge and grim,
Amid the carrion bodies to lie,
Of the worm, and the bug, and the murdered fly:
These it had been your lot to bear,
Had a stain been found on the earthly fair.
Now list, and mark our mild decree—
Fairy, this your doom must be:

VIII.

"Thou shalt seek the beach of sand
Where the water bounds the elfin land,
Thou shalt watch the oozy brine
Till the sturgeon leaps in the bright moonshine,
Then dart the glistening arch below,
And catch a drop from his silver bow.
The water-spirits will wield their arms
    And dash around, with roar and rave,
And vain are the woodland spirits' charms,
    They are the imps that rule the wave.
Yet trust thee in thy single might,
If thy heart be pure and they spirit right,
Thou shalt win the warlock fight.

IX.

"If the spray-bead gem be won,
    The stain of thy wing is washed away,
But another errand must be done
    Ere thy crime be lost for aye;
Thy flame-wood lamp is quenched and dark,

Thou must re-illume its spark.
Mount thy steed and spur him high
To the heaven's blue canopy;
And when thou seest a shooting star,
Follow it fast, and follow it far—
The last faint spark of its burning train
Shall light the elfin lamp again.
Thou hast heard our sentence, Fay;
Hence! to the water-side, away!"

X.

The goblin marked his monarch well;
   He spake not, but he bowed him low,
Then plucked a crimson colen-bell,
   And turned him round in act to go.
The way is long, he cannot fly,
   His soiled wing has lost its power,
And he winds adown the mountain high,
   For many a sore and weary hour.
Through dreary beds of tangled fern,
Through groves of nightshade dark and dern,
Over the grass and through the brake,
Where toils the ant and sleeps the snake;
   Now o'er the violet's azure flush
He skips along in lightsome mood;
   And now he thrids the bramble bush,
Till its points are dyed in fairy blood.
He has leapt the bog, he has pierced the briar,
He has swum the brook, and waded the mire,
Till his spirits sank, and his limbs grew weak,
And the red waxed fainter in his cheek.
He had fallen to the ground outright,
   For rugged and dim was his onward track,
But there came a spotted toad in sight,
   And he laughed as he jumped upon her back
He bridled her mouth with a silk-weed twist;
   He lashed her sides with an osier thong;
And now through evening's dewy mist,
   With leap and spring they bound along,
Till the mountain's magic verge is past,
And the beach of sand is reached at last.

XI.

Soft and pale is the moony beam,
Moveless still the glassy stream,
The wave is clear, the beach is bright
  With snowy shells and sparkling stones;
The shore-surge comes in ripples light,
  In murmurings faint and distant moans;
And ever afar in the silence deep
Is heard the splash of the sturgeon's leap,
And the bend of his graceful bow is seen—
A glittering arch of silver sheen,
Spanning the wave of burnished blue,
And dripping with gems of the river dew.

XII.

The elfin cast a glance around,
  As he lighted down from his courser toad,
Then round his breast his wings he wound,
  And close to the river's brink he stood,
He sprang on a rock, he breathed a prayer,
  Above his head his arms he threw,
Then tossed a tiny curve in air,
  And headlong plunged in the waters blue.

XIII.

Up sprung the spirits of the waves,
From sea-silk beds in their coral caves,
With snail-plate armour snatched in haste,
They speed their way through the liquid waste,
Some are rapidly borne along
On the mailed shrimp or the prickly prong,
Some on the blood-red leeches glide,
Some on the stony star-fish ride,
Some on the back of the lancing squab,
Some on the sideling soldier-crab;
And some on the jellied quarl, that flings
At once a thousand streamy strings—
They cut the wave with the living oar
And hurry on to the moonlight shore,
To guard their realms and chase away
The footsteps of the invading Fay.

XIV.

Fearlessly he skims along,
His hope is high, and his limbs are strong,
He spreads his arms like the swallow's wing,
And throws his feet with a frog-like fling;
His locks of gold on the waters shine,
　　At his breast the puny foam-beads rise,
His back gleams bright above the brine,
　　And the wake-line foam behind him lies.
But the water-sprites are gathering near
　　To check his course along the tide;
Their warriors come in swift career
　　And hem him round on every side;
On his thigh the leech has fixed his hold,
The quarl's long arms are round him roll'd,
The prickly prong has pierced his skin,
And the squab has thrown his javelin,
The gritty star has rubbed him raw,
And the crab has struck with his giant claw;
He howls with rage, and he shrieks with pain,
He strikes around, but his blows are vain;
Hopeless is the unequal fight,
Fairy! naught is left but flight.

XV.

He turned him round and fled amain
With hurry and dash to the beach again;
He twisted over from side to side,
And laid his cheek to the cleaving tide.
The strokes of his plunging arms are fleet,
And with all his might he flings his feet,
But the water-sprites are round him still,
To cross his path and work him ill.
They bade the wave before him rise;
They flung the sea-fire in his eyes,
And they stunned his ears with the scallop stroke,
With the porpoise heave and the drum-fish croak.
Oh! but a weary wight was he
When he reached the foot of the dog-wood tree;
—Gashed and wounded, and stiff and sore,
He laid him down on the sandy shore;

He blessed the force of the charmed line,
  And he banned the water-goblins' spite,
For he saw around in the sweet moonshine,
Their little wee faces above the brine,
Giggling and laughing with all their might
At the piteous hap of the Fairy wight.

XVI.

Soon he gathered the balsam dew
  From the sorrel leaf and the henbane bud;
Over each wound the balm he drew,
  And with cobweb lint he staunched the blood.
The mild west wind was soft and low,
It cooled the heat of his burning brow,
And he felt new life in his sinews shoot,
As he drank the juice of the cal'mus root;
And now he treads the fatal shore,
As fresh and vigorous as before.

XVII.

Wrapped in musing stands the sprite:
'Tis the middle wane of night,
  His task is hard, his way is far,
But he must do his errand right
  Ere dawning mounts her beamy car,
And rolls her chariot wheels of light;
And vain are the spells of fairy-land,
He must work with a human hand.

XVIII.

He cast a saddened look around
  But he felt new joy his bosom swell,
When, glittering on the shadowed ground,
  He saw a purple muscle shell;
Thither he ran, and he bent him low,
He heaved at the stern and he heaved at the bow,
And he pushed her over the yielding sand,
Till he came to the verge of the haunted land.
She was as lovely a pleasure boat
  As ever fairy had paddled in,

For she glowed with purple paint without,
   And shone with silvery pearl within;
A sculler's notch in the stern he made,
An oar he shaped of the bootle blade;
Then sprung to his seat with a lightsome leap,
And launched afar on the calm blue deep.

XIX.

The imps of the river yell and rave;
They had no power above the wave,
But they heaved the billow before the prow,
   And they dashed the surge against her side,
And they struck her keel with jerk and blow,
   Till the gunwale bent to the rocking tide.
She wimpled about in the pale moonbeam,
Like a feather that floats on a wind-tossed strea
And momently athwart her track
The quarl upreared his island back,
And the fluttering scallop behind would float,
And spatter the water about the boat;
But he bailed her out with his colen-bell,
   And he kept her trimmed with a wary tread,
While on every side like lightning fell
   The heavy strokes of his bottle-blade.

XX.

Onward still he held his way,
Till he came where the column of moonshine la
And saw beneath the suface dim
The brown-backed sturgeon slowly swim:
Around him were the goblin train—
But he skulled with all his might and main,
And followed wherever the sturgeon led,
Till he saw him upward point his head;
Then he dropped his paddle blade,
And held his colen goblet up
To catch the drop in its crimson cup.

XXI.

With sweeping tail and quivering fin,
   Through the wave the sturgeon flew,

And, like the heaven-shot javelin,
  He sprung above the waters blue.
Instant as the star-fall light,
  He plunged him in the deep again,
But left an arch of silver bright
  The rainbow of the moony main.
It was a strange and lovely sight
  To see the puny goblin there;
He seemed an angel form of light,
  With azure wing and sunny hair,
Throned on a cloud of purple fair,
Circled with blue and edged with white,
And sitting at the fall of even
Beneath the bow of summer heaven.

XXII.

A moment and its lustre fell,
  But ere it met the billow blue,
He caught within his crimson bell,
  A droplet of its sparkling dew—
Joy to thee, Fay! thy task is done,
Thy wings are pure, for the gem is won—
Cheerly ply thy dripping oar
And haste away to the elfin shore.

XXIII.

He turns, and lo! on either side
The ripples on his path divide;
And the track o'er which his boat must pass
Is smooth as a sheet of polished glass.
Around, their limbs the sea-nymphs lave,
  With snowy arms half swelling out,
While on the glossed and gleamy wave
  Their sea-green ringlets loosely float;
They swim around with smile and song;
  They press the bark with pearly hand,
And gently urge her course along,
  Toward the beach of speckled sand;
  And, as he lightly leapt to land,
They bade adieu with nod and bow,
Then gayly kissed each little hand,
And dropped in the chrystal deep below.

XXIV.

A moment staied the fairy there;
He kissed the beach and breathed a prayer,
Then spread his wings of gilded blue,
And on to the elfin court he flew;
As ever ye saw a bubble rise,
And shine with a thousand changing dyes,
Till lessening far through ether driven,
It mingles with the hues of heaven:
As, at the glimpse of morning pale,
The lance-fly spreads his silken sail,
And gleams with blendings soft and bright,
Till lost in the shades of fading night;
So rose from earth the lovely Fay—
So vanished, far in heaven away!

    *   *   *   *   *   *   *   *

Up, Fairy! quit thy chick-weed bower,
The cricket has called the second hour,
Twice again, and the lark will rise
To kiss the streaking of the skies—
Up! thy charmed armour don,
Thou'lt need it ere the night be gone.

XXV.

He put his acorn helmet on;
It was plumed of the silk of the thistle down:
The corslet plate that guarded his breast
Was once the wild bee's golden vest;
His cloak, of a thousand mingled dyes,
Was formed of the wings of butterflies;
His shield was the shell of a lady-bug queen,
Studs of gold on a ground of green;
And the quivering lance which he brandished bright,
Was the sting of a wasp he had slain in fight.
  Swift he bestrode his fire-fly steed;
He bared his blade of the bent grass blue;
He drove his spurs of the cockle seed,
  And away like a glance of thought he flew,
To skim the heavens and follow far
The fiery trail of the rocket-star.

XXVI.

The moth-fly, as he shot in air,
Crept under the leaf, and hid her there;

"He caught within his crimson bell a droplet of its sparkling dew—" Drawing by Arthur Lumley, engraved by John P. Davis, from *The Culprit Fay. A Poem* by Joseph Rodman Drake (New York: Carleton, 1867).

"Flame-shot tongues around him played, and near him many a fiendish eye
glared with fell malignity." Drawing by Arthur Lumley, engraved by John P.
Davis, from *The Culprit Fay. A Poem* by Joseph Rodman Drake (New York:
Carleton, 1867).

The katy-did forgot its lay,
The prowling gnat fled fast away,
The fell mosqueto checked his drone
And folded his wings till the Fay was gone,
And the wily beetle dropped his head,
And fell on the ground as if he were dead;
They crouched them close in the darksome shade,
   They quaked all o'er with awe and fear,
For they had felt the blue-bent blade,
   And writhed at the prick of the elfin spear;
Many a time on a summer's night,
When the sky was clear and the moon was bright,
They had been roused from the haunted ground,
By the yelp and bay of the fairy hound;
They had heard the tiny bugle horn,
They had heard the twang of the maize-silk string,
When the vine-twig bows were tightly drawn,
And the nettle shaft through air was borne,
Feathered with down of the hum-bird's wing.
And now they deemed the courier ouphe,
   Some hunter sprite of the elfin ground;
And they watched till they saw him mount the roof
   That canopies the world around;
Then glad they left their covert lair,
And freaked about in the midnight air.

XXVII.

Up to the vaulted firmament
His path the fire-fly courser bent,
And at every gallop on the wind,
He flung a glittering spark behind;
He flies like a feather in the blast
Till the first light cloud in heaven is past,
   But the shapes of air have begun their work,
And a drizzly mist is round him cast,
   He cannot see through the mantle murk,
He shivers with cold, but he urges fast,
   Through storm and darkness, sleet and shade,
He lashes his steed and spurs amain,
For shadowy hands have twitched the rein,
   And flame-shot tongues around him played,
And near him many a fiendish eye
Glared with a fell malignity,

And yells of rage, and shrieks of fear,
Came screaming on his startled ear.

XXVIII.

His wings are wet around his breast,
The plume hangs dripping from his crest,
His eyes are blur'd with the lightning's glare,
And his ears are stunned with the thunder's blare,
But he gave a shout, and his blade he drew,
   He thrust before and he struck behind,
Till he pierced their cloudy bodies through,
   And gashed their shadowy limbs of wind,
Howling the misty spectres flew,
   They rend the air with frightful cries,
For he has gained the welkin blue,
   And the land of clouds beneath him lies.

XXIX.

Up to the cope careering swift
   In breathless motion fast,
Fleet as the swallow cuts the drift,
   Or the sea-roc rides the blast,
The sapphire sheet of eve is shot,
   The sphered moon is past,
The earth but seems a tiny blot
   On a sheet of azure cast.
O! it was sweet in the clear moonlight,
   To tread the starry plain of even,
To meet the thousand eyes of night,
   And feel the cooling breath of heaven!
But the Elfin made no stop or stay
Till he came to the bank of the milky-way,
Then he checked his courser's foot
And watched for the glimpse of the planet-shoot.

XXX.

Sudden along the snowy tide
   That swelled to meet their footsteps' fall,
The sylphs of heaven were seen to glide,
   Attired in sunset's crimson pall;
Around the Fay they weave the dance,
   They skip before him on the plain,

And one has taken his wasp-sting lance,
    And one upholds his bridle rein;
With warblings wild they lead him on
    To where through clouds of amber seen,
Studded with stars, resplendent shone
    The palace of the sylphid queen.
Its spiral columns gleaming bright
Were streamers of the northern light;
Its curtain's light and lovely flush
Was of the morning's rosy blush,
And the ceiling fair that rose aboon
The white and feathery fleece of noon.

XXXI.

But oh! how fair the shape that lay
    Beneath a rainbow bending bright,
She seemed to the entranced Fay
    The loveliest of the forms of light;
Her mantle was the purple rolled
    At twilight in the west afar;
'Twas tied with threads of dawning gold,
    And buttoned with a sparkling star.
Her face was like the lily roon
    That veils the vestal planet's hue;
Her eyes, two beamlets from the moon,
    Set floating in the welkin blue.
Her hair is like the sunny beam,
And the diamond gems which round it gleam
Are the pure drops of dewy even
That ne'er have left their native heaven.

XXXII.

She raised her eyes to the wondering sprite,
    And they leapt with smiles, for well I ween
Never before in the bowers of light
    Had the form of an earthly Fay been seen.
Long she looked on his tiny face;
    Long with his butterfly cloak she played;
She smoothed his wings of azure lace,
    And handled the tassel of his blade;
And as he told in accents low
The story of his love and wo,

She felt new pains in her bosom rise,
And the tear-drop started in her eyes.
And 'O sweet spirit of earth,' she cried,
'Return no more to your woodland height,
But ever here with me abide
In the land of everlasting light!
Within the fleecy drift we'll lie,
We'll hang upon the rainbow's rim;
And all the jewels of the sky
Around thy brow shall brightly beam!
And thou shalt bathe thee in the stream
That rolls its whitening foam aboon,
And ride upon the lightning's gleam,
And dance upon the orbed moon!
We'll sit within the Pleiad ring,
We'll rest on Orion's starry belt,
And I will bid my sylphs to sing
The song that makes the dew-mist melt;
Their harps are of the umber shade,
That hides the blush of waking day,
And every gleamy string is made
Of silvery moonshine's lengthened ray;
And thou shalt pillow on my breast,
While heavenly breathings float around,
And, with sylphs of ether blest,
Forget the joys of fairy ground.'

XXXIII.

She was lovely and fair to see
And the elfin's heart bent fitfully;
But lovelier far, and still more fair,
The earthly form imprinted there,
Nought he saw in the heavens above
Was half so dear as his mortal love,
For he thought upon her looks so meek,
And he thought of the light flush on her cheek;
Never again might he bask and lie
On that sweet cheek and moonlight eye,
But in his dreams her form to see,
To clasp her in his reverie,
To think upon his virgin bride,
Was worth all heaven and earth beside.

XXXIV.

'Lady,' he cried, 'I have sworn to-night,
On the word of a fairy knight,
To do my sentence-task aright;
My honour scarce is free from stain,
I may not soil its snows again;
Betide me weal, betide me wo,
Its mandate must be answered now.'
Her bosom heaved with many a sigh,
The tear was in her drooping eye;
But she led him to the palace gate,
And called the sylphs who hovered there,
And bade them fly and bring him straight
Of clouds condensed a sable car.
With charm and spell she blessed it there,
From all the fiends of upper air;
Then round him cast the shadowy shroud,
And tied his steed behind the cloud;
And presssed his hand as she bade him fly
Far to the verge of the northern sky,
For by its wane and wavering light
There was a star would fall to-night.

XXXV.

Borne afar on the wings of the blast,
Northward away, he speeds him fast,
And his courser follows the cloudy wain
Till the hoof-strokes fall like pattering rain.
The clouds roll backward as he flies,
Each flickering star behind him lies,
And he has reached the northern plain
And backed his fire-fly steed again,
Ready to follow in its flight
The streaming of the rocket-light.

XXXVI.

The star is yet in the vault of heaven,
But it rocks in the summer gale;
And now 'tis fitful and uneven,
And now 'tis deadly pale;
And now 'tis wrapp'd in sulphur smoke,
And quenched is its rayless beam,

And now with a rattling thunder-stroke
  It bursts in flash and flame.
As swift as the glance of the arrowy lance
  That the storm-spirit flings from high,
The star-shot flew o'er the welkin blue,
  As it fell from the sheeted sky.
As swift as the wind in its trail behind
  The elfin gallops along,
The fiends of the clouds are bellowing loud,
  But the sylphid charm is strong;
He gallops unhurt in the shower of fire,
  While the cloud-fiends fly from the blaze;
He watches each flake till its sparks expire,
  And rides in the light of its rays.
But he drove his steed to the lightning's speed,
  And caught a glimmering spark;
Then wheeled around to the fairy ground,
  And sped through the midnight dark.
       *   *   *   *   *   *   *   *

Ouphe and goblin! imp and sprite!
  Elf of eve! and starry Fay!
Ye that love the moon's soft light,
  Hither—hither wend your way;
Twine ye in a jocund ring,
  Sing and trip it merrily,
Hand to hand, and wing to wing,
  Round the wild witch-hazel tree.

Hail the wanderer again,
  With dance and song, and lute and lyre,
Pure his wing and strong his chain,
  And doubly bright his fairy fire.
Twine ye in an airy round,
  Brush the dew and print the lea;
Skip and gambol, hop and bound,
  Round the wild witch-hazel tree.

The beetle guards our holy ground,
  He flies about the haunted place,
And if mortal there be found,
  He hums in his ears and flaps his face;

The leaf-harp sounds our roundelay,
    The owlet's eyes our lanterns be;
Thus we sing, and dance, and play,
Round the wild witch-hazel tree.

But hark! from tower on tree-top high,
    The sentry elf his call has made,
A streak is in the eastern sky,
    Shapes of moonlight! flit and fade!
The hill-tops gleam in morning's spring,
The sky-lark shakes his dappled wing,
The day-glimpse glimmers on the lawn,
The cock has crowed and the Fays are gone.

PART III

The Post-Knickerbockers

James Fenimore Cooper. Anonymous portrait. Editor's collection.

Perhaps the most important writer to describe the Hudson region is James Fenimore Cooper (1789-1851). In 1790, William Cooper, the founder of Cooperstown, brought his family there from their former home in Burlington, New Jersey, when his son James Fenimore was only one year old. William Cooper was the leading citizen of the new town, and was later made a judge. In 1802, at the age of thirteen, James Fenimore matriculated at Yale, but he was expelled in 1805. He returned to his father's home, Otsego Hall, for two months and then went to sea as a merchant sailor.

After a few years, he entered the Navy, in which he remained until 1811. Shortly thereafter, he married Susan DeLancey, of a prominent old Tory family, and settled in Scarsdale, in Westchester County, where he lived the life of a country gentleman.

About 1815, he moved to Cooperstown and built a small home for himself which he called The Chalet. In 1817, he moved back to Westchester and began a period of extensive European travel and residence—and a writing career. Beginning first with some rather commonplace Gothic tales such as *The Heidenmauer,* Jane Austin-like social comedy such as *Precaution,* and Byronesque adventure tales such as *The Bravo,* he soon turned to writing sea stories such as *Wing and Wing,* which was published in 1842. He was not at home, however, as a follower of Walpole, Lewis, and Radcliffe. His earlier nautical career provided him material for the sea stories, *The Pilot* in 1823 and *Red Rover* in 1828.

While residing in Paris, he became famous for his buckwheat pancake breakfasts (in the world's culinary capital!) and for the witty conversation at his table. Cooper acquired aristocratic prejudices while abroad, and these caused him to become personally unpopular upon his return home. His books *Homeward Bound,* and *Home As Found* (1838) make unfavorable comparisons between American and European manners and society. Many Americans thought that his marriage into a Tory family and his sympathetic treatment of the character Mr. Wharton, in *The Spy* (1821) were not quite appropriate for an American author.

Upon his final return home to Cooperstown in 1834, he converted his father's home, Otsego Hall, into a pseudo-Gothic castle such as Sir Walter Scott's home Abbotsford and Horace Walpole's Strawberry Hill, with crenelations and ogee windows. He forbade the townsfolk to continue their usual practice of picnicking on Threemile Point, on Otsego Lake, which he owned. This action outraged the townspeople, causing much ill feeling. They contested their right of entry but lost the case. Thus Cooper's popularity with his neighbors declined. Cooper's father, "old Judge Cooper," had suffered a similar decline in esteem after an unpopular prosecution of Jedediah Peak under the Alien and Sedition Law. Cooper attempted to justify his attitude in *Home As Found,* which is a veiled account of the episode, that still rankles in the ancestral memory of the townsfolk.

Cooper's eye for topography and interest in the events of New York and American history brought him to his most successful mature style. *The Spy* (1821) deals with events during the Revolution in Westchester and Dutchess Counties. *Lionel Lincoln* is a similar tale. His knowledge of oldtime manor life in New York led to the Littlepage Papers, a trilogy of novels consisting of *Satanstoe* (1845), *The Chainbearer* (1845), and *The Redskins* (1846).

Cooper found his greatest success with the Leatherstocking Tales. The character of Leatherstocking, alias Natty Bumppo, alias La Longue Carabine, alias Hawkeye, alias Pathfinder, is based upon an old Cooperstown huntsman named Shipman, who wore leather leggings. The five novels were written in a different order than the chronology of the loosely connected action. *The Deerslayer* which takes place around Otsego Lake about 1740 was published in 1841. *The Pathfinder,* which takes place in the Oswego area and on the waters and shores of Lake Ontario in 1756, was published in 1840. *The Last of the Mohicans,* which takes place at and around Glens Falls, Lake George, and the Adirondack Mountains in 1757, was published in 1826. *The Pioneers,* which takes place around Cooperstown in 1793, was published in 1823. *The Prairie,* which takes place on the western plains in 1804, was published in 1827.

In 1839 Cooper completed his monumental *History of the Navy of the United States.* He died in 1851 and is buried in the cemetery of Christ Episcopal Church. Otsego Hall burned down in 1853.

From *Water Witch**

PREFACE.

It was a bold attempt to lay the scene of a work like this, on the coast of America. We have had our buccaneers on the water, and our witches on the land, but we believe this is the first occasion on which the rule has been reversed. After an experience that has now lasted more than twenty years, the result has shown that the public prefer the original order of things. In other words, the book has proved a comparative failure.

The facts of this country are all so recent, and so familiar, that every innovation on them, by means of the imagination, is coldly received, if it be not absolutely frowned upon. Perhaps it would have been safer to have written a work of this

*All the following extracts from the novels of James Fenimore Cooper are from *The Complete Works of J. Fenimore Cooper,* Leather-Stocking Edition in Thirty-two Volumes (New York: G. P. Putnam Sons, undated. The compiler owns No. 733 of a limited number of 1,000 copies that appear to date from the late nineteenth century.)

character without a reference to any particular locality. The few local allusions that are introduced are not essential to the plot, and might have been dispensed with without lessening the interest of the tale.

Nevertheless, this is probably the most imaginative book ever written by the author. Its fault is in blending too much of the real with the purely ideal. Half-way measures will not do in matters of this sort; and it is always safer to preserve the identity of a book by a fixed and determinate character, than to make the effort to steer between the true and the false.

Several liberties have been taken with the usages of the colony, with a view to give zest to the descriptions. If the Dutch of this country ever resorted to the common practice of Holland, in giving such names as the "Lust in Rust" to their villas, it has not only passed out of sight, but out of mind. In the other country, as one moves along the canals, he sees names of this character painted on different objects, every mile he advances, and admires the contentment which is satisfied with a summer-house, a pipe, a canal, a meadow that is almost under water, and, indeed, with a country that is what seamen term "awash." But nothing of this sort was ever seen here. The fine natural scenery forbade it; and a villa on the banks of the Hudson was a residence that possessed in itself advantages to set at naught such small contrivances of luxury.

Some persons may object to the manner in which we have sketched the conduct and character of Cornbury. We believe, however, that the truth is not exceeded in anything said of this individual, who would seem to have had neither dignity, self-respect, nor principles. The fact that he remained in this country a prisoner for debt, is historical, his creditors most probably hoping to extort from Anne further concessions in behalf of her worthless relative.

As for the Patroon of Kinderhook, the genus seems about to expire among us. Not only are we to have no more patroons, but the decree has gone forth from the virtuous and infallible voters that there are to be no more estates.

"All the realm shall be in common, and in Cheapside shall my palfrey go to grass."

The collected wisdom of the State has decided that it is true policy to prevent the affluent from investing their money in land! The curse of mediocrity weighs upon us, and its blunders can be repaired only through the hard lessons of experience.

This book was written in Italy, and first printed (in English) in Germany. To the last circumstance is probably owing the great number of typographical errors that are to be found in it. The American compositor, however, quite likely conceiving that he had a right to correct the blunders of a foreigner, has taken the law into his own hands, and exercised a sovereign power over our labors. That our good old-fashioned mode of spelling should receive the modern improvements, was, perhaps, unavoidable; but surely, we never spelt "coamings" (of a hatch), "combings"; "rullock," "oar-lock," or "row-lock"; or made many other similar "long-shore" blunders that are to be found in the original editions of this book.

Care has been had to do ourselves justice in these particulars, and we think that the book is more improved, in all these respects, in the present edition, than any other work that has passed through our hands.

CHAPTER I. NEW YORK BAY

> "What, shall this speech be spoke for our excuse,
> Or shall we on without apology?"
> *Romeo and Juliet.*

The fine estuary which penetrates the American coast between the fortieth and forty-first degrees of latitude, is formed by the confluence of the Hudson, the Hackensack, the Passaic, the Raritan, and a multitude of smaller streams; all of which pour their tribute into the ocean within the space named. The islands of Nassau and Staten are happily placed to exclude the tempests of the open sea, while the deep and broad arms of the latter offer every desirable facility for foreign trade and internal intercourse. To this fortunate disposition of land and water, with a temperate climate, a central position, and an immense interior that is now penetrated in every direction either by artificial or by natural streams, the city of New York is indebted for its extraordinary prosperity. Though not wanting in beauty, there are many bays that surpass this in the charms of scenery; but it may be questioned if the world possesses another site that unites so many natural advantages for the growth and support of a widely extended commerce. As if never wearied with her kindness, Nature has placed the Island of Manhattan at the precise point that is most desirable for the position of a town. Millions might inhabit the spot, and yet a ship could load near every door; and while the surface of the land just possesses the inequalities that are required for health and cleanliness, its bosom is filled with the material most needed in construction.

The consequences of so unusual a concurrence of favorable circumstances are well known. A vigorous, healthful, and continued growth, that has no parallel even in the history of this extraordinary and fortunate country, has already raised the insignificant provincial town of the last century to the level of the second-rate cities of the other hemisphere. The New Amsterdam of this continent already rivals its parent of the other; and, so far as human powers may pretend to predict, a few fleeting years will place her on a level with the proudest capitals of Europe.

It would seem that, as Nature has given its periods to the stages of animal life, it has also set limits to all moral and political ascendency. While the city of the Medici is receding from its crumbling walls, like the human form shrinking into "the lean and slippered pantaloon," the Queen of the Adriatic sleeping on her muddy isles, and Rome itself is only to be traced by fallen temples and buried columns, the youthful vigor of America is fast covering the wilds of the West with the happiest fruits of human industry.

By the Manhattanese who is familiar with the forest of masts, the miles of wharves, the countless villas, the hundred churches, the castles, the smoking and busy vessels that crowd his bay, the daily increase and the general movement of his native town, the picture we are about to sketch will scarcely be recognized. He who shall come a generation later will probably smile, that subject of admiration should have been found in the existing condition of the city; and yet we shall attempt to carry the recollections of the reader but a century back in the brief history of his country.

As the sun rose on the morning of the 3rd of June, 171–, the report of a cannon was heard rolling along the waters of the Hudson. Smoke issued from an embrasure of a small fortress, that stood on the point of land where the river and the bay mingle their waters. The explosion was followed by the appearance of a flag, which, as it rose to the summit of its staff and unfolded itself heavily in the light current of air, showed the blue field and red cross of the English ensign. At the distance of several miles, the dark masts of a ship were to be seen, faintly relieved by the verdant background of the heights of Staten Island. A little cloud floated over this object, and then an answering signal came dull and rumbling to the town. The flag that the cruiser set was not visible in the distance. . . .

CHAPTER II. CANAL STREET

In this manner he proceeded in his walk for several minutes longer, shortly quitting the lower streets, to enter one that ran along the ridge which crowned the land in that quarter of the island. Here he soon stopped before the door of a house which, in that provincial town, had altogether the air of a patrician dwelling.

Two false gables, each of which was surmounted by an iron weathercock, intersected the roof of this building, and the high and narrow stoop was built of the red freestone of the country. The material of the edifice itself was, as usual, the small, hard brick of Holland, painted a delicate cream color.

A single blow of the massive glittering knocker brought a servant to the door. . . . .

A deep, narrow creek penetrated the island at this point, for the distance of a quarter of a mile. Each of its banks had a row of buildings, as the houses line a canal in the cities of Holland. As the natural course of the inlet was necessarily respected, the street had taken a curvature not unlike that of a new moon. The houses were ultra-Dutch, being low, angular, fastidiously neat, and all erected with gables to the street. Each had its ugly and inconvenient entrance, termed a stoop, its vane or weathercock, its dormer-windows, and its graduated battlement-walls. Near the apex of one of the latter, a little iron crane projected into the street. A small boat, of the same metal, swung from its end,—a sign that the building to which it was appended was the ferry-house.

An inherent love of artificial and confined navigation had probably induced the burghers to select this spot as the place whence so many craft departed from the town: since it is certain that the two rivers could have furnished divers points more favorable for such an object, inasmuch as they possess the advantage of wide and unobstructed channels.

Fifty blacks were already in the street, dipping their brooms into the creek, and flourishing water over the sidewalks, and on the fronts of the low edifices. This light, but daily duty was relieved by clamorous collisions of wit, and by shouts of merriment, in which the whole street would join, as with one joyous and reckless movement of the spirit.

The language of this light-hearted and noisy race was Dutch, already corrupted by English idioms, and occasionally by English words; a system of change that has probably given rise to an opinion, among some of the descendants of the earlier colonists, that the latter tongue is merely a *patois* of the former. This opinion which so much resembles that which certain well-read English scholars entertained of the plagiarisms of the continental writers, when they first began to dip into their works, is not strictly true; since the language of England has probably bestowed as much on the dialect of which we speak, as it has ever received from the purer sources of the school of Holland. Here and there a grave burgher, still in his night-cap, might be seen with a head thrust out of an upper window, listening to these barbarisms of speech, and taking note of all the merry jibes that flew from mouth to mouth, with an indomitable gravity that no levity of those beneath could undermine.

As the movement of the ferry-boat was necessarily slow, the alderman and his companion were enabled to step into it before the fasts were thrown aboard. The periagua, as the craft was called, partook of a European and an American character. It possessed the length, narrowness, and clean bow of the canoe, from which its name was derived, with the flat bottom and lee-boards of a boat constructed for the shallow waters of the Low Countries. Twenty years ago vessels of this description abounded in our rivers, and even now their two long and unsupported masts, and high, narrow-headed sails, are daily seen bending like reeds to the breeze, and dancing lightly over the billows of the bay. There is a variety of the class of a size and pretension altogether superior to that just mentioned, which deserves a place among the most picturesque and striking boats that float. He who has had occasion to navigate the southern shore of the Sound must have often seen the vessel to which we allude. It is distinguished by its great length, and masts which, naked of cordage, rise from the hull like two tall and faultless trees. When the eye runs over the daring height of canvas, the noble confidence of the rig, and sees the comparatively vast machine handled with ease and grace by the dexterity of two fearless and expert mariners, it excites some such admiration as that which springs from the view of a severe temple of antiquity. The nakedness and simplicity of the construction, coupled with the boldness and rapidity of its movements, impart to the craft an air of grandeur that its ordinary uses would not give reason to expect.

Though, in some respects, of singularly aquatic habits, the original colonists of New York were far less adventurous, as mariners, than their present descendants. A passage across the bay did not often occur in the tranquil lives of the burghers; and it is still within the memory of man, that a voyage between the two principal towns of the State was an event to excite the solicitude of friends, and the anxiety of the traveller. The perils of the Tappan Zee, as one of the wider reaches of the Hudson is still termed, were often dealt with by the good wives of the colony, in their relations of marvels; and she who had oftenest encountered them unharmed, was deemed a sort of marine Amazon.

CHAPTER V. STATEN ISLAND

If we say that Alida de Barbérie did not cast a glance behind her as the party quitted the wharf, in order to see whether the boat that contained the commander of the cruiser followed the example of the others, we shall probably portray the maiden as one that was less subject to the influence of coquetry than the truth would justify. To the great discontent of the alderman, whatever might have been the feelings of his niece on the occasion, the barge continued to approach the shore, in a manner which showed that the young seaman betrayed no visible interest in the result of the chase.

The heights of Staten Island, a century ago, were covered, as much as they are at present, with a growth of dwarf-trees. Footpaths led among this meagre vegetation in divers directions; and as the hamlet at the quarantine-ground was the point whence they all diverged, it required a practised guide to thread their mazes without a loss of both time and distance. It would seem, however, that the worthy burgher was fully equal to the office; for, moving with more than his usual agility, he soon led his companions into the wood, and, by frequently altering his course, so completely confounded their sense of the relative bearings of places, that it is not probable one of them all could very readily have extricated himself from the labyrinth. . . .

CHAPTER VII. SANDY HOOK

> "I am no pilot; yet, wert thou as far
> As that vast shore washed with the furthest sea,
> I would adventure for such merchandise."
> *Romeo and Juliet.*

A happy mixture of land and water, seen by a bright moon, and beneath the sky of the fortieth degree of latitude, cannot fail to make a pleasing picture. Such was the landscape which the reader must now endeavor to present to his mind.

The wide estuary of Raritan is shut in from the winds and billows of the open sea by a long, low, and narrow cape, or point, which, by a medley of the Dutch and English languages, that is by no means rare in the names of places that lie within the former territories of the United Provinces of Holland, is known by the name of Sandy Hook. This tongue of land appears to have been made by the unremitting and opposing actions of the waves on one side, and of the currents of the different rivers, that empty their waters into the bay, on the other. It is commonly connected with the low coast of New Jersey, to the south; but there are periods of many years in succession, during which there exists an inlet from the sea, between what may be termed the inner end of the cape and the mainland. During these periods, Sandy Hook of course becomes an island. Such was the fact at the time of which it is our business to write.

The outer or ocean side of this low and narrow bank of sand is a smooth and regular beach, like that seen on most of the Jersey coast, while the inner is indented, in a manner to form several convenient anchoring-grounds, for ships that seek a shelter from easterly gales. One of the latter is a circular and pretty cove, in which vessels of light draught are completely embayed, and where they may in safety ride secure from any winds that blow. The harbor—or, as it is always called, the Cove—lies at the point where the cape joins the main, and the inlet just named communicates directly with its waters whenever the passage is open. The Shrewsbury, a river of the fourth or fifth class, or, in other words, a stream of a few hundred feet in width, and of no great length, comes from the south, running nearly parallel with the coast, and becomes a tributary of the bay, also, at a point near the Cove. Between the Shrewsbury and the sea, the land resembles that on the cape, being low and sandy, though not entirely without fertility. It is covered with a modest growth of pines and oaks, where it is not either subject to the labors of the husbandman, or in natural meadow. But the western bank of the river is an abrupt and high acclivity, which rises to the elevation of a mountain. It was near the base of the latter that Alderman Van Beverout, for reasons that may be more fully developed as we proceed in our tale, had seen fit to erect his villa, which, agreeably to a usage of Holland, he had called the Lust in Rust; an appellation that the merchant, who had read a few of the classics in his boyhood, was wont to say meant nothing more nor less than "otium cum dignitate."

If a love of retirement and a pure air had its influence in determining the selection of the burgher of Manhattan, he could not have made a better choice. The adjoining lands had been occupied, early in the previous century, by a respectable family of the name of Hartshorne, which continues seated at the place to the present hour. The extent of their possessions served, at that day, to keep others at a distance. If to this fact be added the formation and quality of the ground, which was, at so early a period, of trifling value for agricultural purposes, it will be seen there was as little motive as there was opportunity for strangers to intrude. As to the air, it was refreshed by the breezes of the ocean, which was scarcely a mile distant; while it had nothing to render it unhealthy or impure. With this sketch of the general features of the scene where so many of our incidents occurred, we shall proceed to describe the habitation of the alderman a little more in detail. . . .

The existence of the inlet which united the ocean with the waters of the Cove was but little known, except to the few whose avocations kept them near the spot. The pass being much more than half the time closed, its varying character, and the little use that could be made of it under any circumstances, prevented the place from being a subject of general interest with the coasters. Even when open, the depth of its water was uncertain, since a week or two of calms, or of westerly winds, would permit the tides to clean its channel, while a single easterly gale was sufficient to choke the entire inlet with sand. No wonder, then, that Alida felt an amazement which was not quite free from superstitious alarm, when, at that hour and in such a scene, she saw a vessel gliding, as it were, unaided by sails or sweeps, out of the thicket that fringed the ocean side of the Cove, into its very centre.

The strange and mysterious craft was a brigantine of that mixed construction, which is much used even in the most ancient and classical seas of the other hemisphere, and which is supposed to unite the advantages of both a square and of a fore-and-aft rigged vessel, but which is nowhere seen to display the same beauty of form, and symmetry of equipment, as on the coasts of this Union. The first and smallest of its masts had all the complicated machinery of a ship, with its superior and inferior spars, its wider reaching though light and manageable yards, and its various sails, shaped and arranged to meet every vicissitude and caprice of the winds; while the latter, or larger of the two, rose like the straight trunk of a pine from the hull, simple in its cordage, and speading a single sheet of canvas, that in itself was sufficient to drive the fabric with vast velocity through the water. The hull was low, graceful in its outlines, dark as the raven's wing, and so modelled as to float on its element like a sea-gull riding the billows. There were many delicate and attenuated lines among its spars, which were intended to spread broader folds of canvas to the light airs when necessary; but these additions to the tracery of the machine, which added so much to its beauty by day, were now, seen as it was by the dimmer and more treacherous rays of the moon, scarcely visible. In short, as the vessel had entered the Cove floating with the tide, it was so singularly graceful and fairy-like in form, that Alida at first was fain to discredit her senses, and to believe it no more than some illusion of the fancy. Like most others, she was ignorant of the temporary inlet, and, under the circumstances, it was not difficult to lend a momentary credence to so pleasing an idea.

But the delusion was only momentary. The brigantine turned in its course, and, gliding into the part of the Cove where the curvature of the shores offered most protection from the winds and waves, and perhaps from curious eyes, its motion ceased. A heavy plunge in the water was audible even at the villa, and Alida then knew that an anchor had fallen into the bay.

Although the coast of North America offered little to invite lawless depredation, and it was in general believed to be so safe, yet the possibility that cupidity might be invited by the retired situation of her uncle's villa did not fail to suggest itself to the mind of the young heiress. Both she and her guardian were reputed to be wealthy; and disappointment on the open sea might drive desperate men to the commission of crimes that in more prosperous moments would not suggest themselves. The freebooters were said to have formerly visited the coast of the neighboring island, and men were just then commencing those excavations for hidden treasures and secreted booty which have been, at distant intervals, continued to our own time. . . .

That baneful influence which necessarily exerts itself near an irresponsible power, coupled with the natural indifference with which the principal regards the dependant, had caused the English ministry to fill too many of their posts of honor and profit in their colonies with needy and dissolute men of rank, or of high political connections at home. The province of New York had, in this respect, been particularly unfortunate. The gift of it by Charles to his brother and successor, had left it without the protection of those charters and other privileges that had been granted to most of the governments of America. The connection with the crown was direct, and for a long period, the majority of the inhabitants were considered as of a different race, and of course as of one less to be considered than that of their conquerors. Such was the laxity of the times on the subject of injustice to the people of this hemisphere, that the predatory expeditions of Drake and others against the wealthy occupants of the more southern countries, seem to have left no spots on their escutcheons; and the honors and favors of Queen Elizabeth had been liberally extended to men who would now be deemed freebooters. In short, that system of violence and specious morality which commenced with the gifts of Ferdinand and Isabella, and the bulls of the Popes, was continued with more or less of modification, until the descendants of those single-minded and virtuous men who peopled the Union took the powers of government into their own hands, and proclaimed political ethics that were previously as little practised as understood.

Alida knew that both the Earl of Bellamont and the unprincipled nobleman who has been introduced in the earlier pages of this tale, had not escaped the imputation of conniving at acts on the sea far more flagrant than any of an unlawful trade. . . .

"Some from this country are fond of believing that our own bay, these summer skies, and the climate in general, should have a strict resemblance to those of a region which lies precisely in our own latitude," observed Alida, so hastily, as to betray a desire to preserve the peace between her guests.

"That your Manhattan and Raritan waters are broad and pleasant, none can deny, and that lovely beings dwell on their banks, lady," returned Seadrift, gallantly lifting his cap, "my own senses have witnessed. But 't were wiser to select some other point of your excellence, for comparison, than a competition with the glorious waters, the fantastic and mountain isles, and the sunny hill-sides of modern Napoli! 'Tis certain the latitude is even in your favor, and that a beneficent sun does not fail of its office in one region more than in the other. But the forests of America are still too pregnant of vapors and exhalations, not to impair the purity of the native air. If I have seen much of the Mediterranean, neither am I a stranger to these coasts. While there are so many points of resemblance in their climates, there are also many and marked causes of differ-ence."

"Teach us, then, what forms these distinctions, that, in speaking of our bay and skies, we may not be led into error."

"You do me honor, lady; I am of no great schooling, and of humble powers of speech. Still, the little that observation may have taught me, shall not be churlishly withheld. Your Italian atmosphere, taking the humidity of the seas, is sometimes hazy. Still water in large bodies, other than in the two seas, is little known in those distant countries. Few objects in nature are dryer than an Italian river, during those months when the sun has most influence. The effect is visible in the air, which is in general elastic, dry, and obedient to the general laws of the climate. There floats less exhalation, in the form of fine and nearly invisible vapor, than in these wooded regions. At least, so he of whom I spoke, as one who guided my youth, was wont to say."

"You hesitate to tell us of our skies, our evening light, and of our bay?"

"It shall be said, and said sincerely. Of the bays, each seems to have been appropriated to that for which nature most intended it—the one is poetic, indolent, and full of graceful but glorious beauty; more pregnant of enjoyment than of usefulness. The other will, one day, be the mart of the world!"

"You still shrink from pronouncing on their beauty," said Alida, disappointed in spite of an affected indifference to the subject.

"It is ever the common fault of old communities to overvalue themselves, and to undervalue new actors in the great drama of nations, as men long successful disregard the efforts of new aspirants for favor," said Seadrift, while he looked with amazement at the pettish eye of the frowning beauty. "In this instance, however, Europe has not so greatly erred. They who see much resemblance between the bay of Naples and this of Manhattan, have fertile brains; since it rests altogether on the circumstance that there is much water in both, and a passage between an island and the mainland, in one, to resemble a passage between two islands, in the other. This is an estuary, that a gulf; and while the former has the green and turbid water of a shelving shore and of tributary rivers, the latter has the blue and limpid element of a deep sea. In these distinctions, I take no account of ragged and rocky mountains, with the indescribable play of golden and rosy light upon their broken surfaces, nor of a coast that teems with the recollections of three thousand years!"

"I fear to question more. But surely our skies may be mentioned, even by the side of those you vaunt?"

"Of the skies truly, you have more reason to be confident. I remember that standing on the Capo di Monte, which overlooks the little, picturesque, and crowded beach of the Marina Grande, and Sorrento, a spot that teems with all that is poetic in the fisherman's life, he of whom I have spoken, once pointed to the transparent vault above, and said, 'There is the moon of America!' The colors of the rocket were not more vivid than the stars that night, for a Tramontana had swept every impurity from the air, far upon the neighboring sea. But nights like that are rare, indeed, in any clime! The inhabitants of low latitudes enjoy them occasionally; those of higher, never."

"Then our flattering belief, that these western sunsets rival those of Italy, is delusion?"

"Not so, lady. They rival without resembling. The color of the étui, on which so fair a hand is resting, is not softer than the hues one sees in the heavens of Italy. But if your evening sky wants the pearly light, the rosy clouds, and the soft tints which, at that hour, melt into each other, across the entire vault of Napoli, it far excels in the vividness of the glow, in the depth of the transitions, and in the richness of colors. Those are only more delicate, while these are more gorgeous! When there shall be less exhalation from your forests, the same causes may produce the same effects. Until then America must be content to pride herself on an exhibition of nature's beauty in a new, though scarcely in a less pleasing, form."

"Then they who come among us from Europe are but half right when they deride the pretensions of our bay and heavens?"

"Which is much nearer the truth than they are wont to be, on the subject of this continent. Speak of the many rivers, the double outlets, the numberless basins, and the unequalled facilities of your Manhattan harbor; for in time they will come to render all the beauties of the unrivalled Bay of Naples vain; but tempt not the stranger to push the comparison beyond. Be grateful for your skies, lady, for few live under fairer or more beneficent. But I tire you with these opinions, when here are colors that have more charms for a young and lively imagination then even the tints of nature!"

La belle Barbérie smiled on the dealer in contraband with an interest that sickened Ludlow; and she was about to reply, in better humor, when the voice of her uncle announced his near approach.

From *Afloat and Ashore*

New York, in that day, and on the Hudson side of the town, commenced a short distance above Duane Street. Between Greenwich, as the little hamlet around the State prison was called, and the town proper, was an interval of a mile and a half of open fields, dotted here and there with country-houses. Much of this space was in broken hills, and a few piles of lumber lay along the shores. St. John's Church had no existence, and most of the ground in its vicinity was in a low swamp. As we glided along the wharves, we caught sight of the first market I had ever seen—such proofs of an advanced civilization not having yet made their way into the villages of the interior. It was called "The Bear," from the circumstance that the first meat ever exposed for sale in it was of that animal; but the appellation has disappeared before the intellectual refinement of these later times—the name of the soldier and statesman, Washington, having fairly supplanted that of the bear! Whether this great moral improvement was brought about by the Philosophical Society, or the Historical Society, or "The Merchants," or the Aldermen of New York, I have never ascertained. If the latter, one cannot but admire their disinterested modesty in conferring this notable honor on the Father of his Country, inasmuch as all can see that there never has been a period when their own board has not possessed distinguished members, every way qualified to act as godfathers to the most illustrious markets of the republic. But Manhattan, in the way of taste, has never had justice done it. So profound is its admiration for all the higher qualities, that Franklin and Fulton have each a market to himself, in addition to this bestowed on Washington. Doubtless there would have been Newton Market, and Socrates Market, and Solomon Market, but for the patriotism of the town, which has forbidden it from going out of the hemisphere in quest of names to illustrate. Bacon Market would doubtless have been too equivocal to be tolerated, under any circumstances. Then Bacon was a rogue, though a philosopher, and markets are always appropriated to honest people. At all events, I am rejoiced the reproach of having a market called "The Bear" has been taken away, as it was tacitly admitting our living near, if not absolutely in, the woods.

We passed the Albany basin, a large receptacle for North River craft, that is now in the bosom of the town and built on, and recognized in it the masthead of the Wallingford. Neb was shown the place, for he was to bring the boat round to it, and join the sloop, in readiness to return in her. We rounded the Battery, then a circular strip of grass, with an earthen and wooden breastwork running along the margin of the water, leaving a narrow promenade on the exterior. This brought us to Whitehall, since so celebrated for its oarsmen, where we put in for a haven. . . .

From *Satanstoe*, Chapter VI

"Nay, be brief:
I see into thy end, and am almost
A man already."

Cymbeline.

As Dirck accompanied Miss Mordaunt to her father's house in Crown Street,[1] I took an occasion to give Jason the slip, being in no humor to listen to his lectures on the proprieties of life, and left the Pinkster field as fast as I could. Notwithstanding the size and importance of New York, a holiday like this could not fail to draw great crowds of persons to witness the sports. In 1757, James De Lancey was at the head of the government of the province, as indeed he had been, in effect, for much of his life; and I remember to have met his chariot, carrying the younger children of the family to the field, on my way into the town. As the day advanced, carriages of one sort and another made their appearance in Broadway, principally conveying the children of their different owners. All these belonged to people of the first mark; and I saw the ship that denotes the arms of Livingston, the lance of the De Lanceys, the burning castle of the Morrises, and other armorial bearings that were well known in the province. Carriages, certainly, were not as common in 1757 as they have since become; but most of our distinguished people rode in their coaches, chariots, or phaetons, or conveyances of some sort or other, when there was occasion to go so far out of town as the common, which is the site of the present "Park." The roads on the island of Manhattan were very pretty and picturesque, winding among rocks and through valleys, being lined with groves and copses in a way to render all the drives rural and retired. Here and there, one came to a country-house, the residence of some person of importance, which by its comfort and snugness, gave all the indications of wealth and of a prudent taste. Mr. Speaker Nicoll[2] had occupied a

[1]Now Liberty Street.
[2]The person meant here was William Nicoll, Esquire, Patentee of Islip, a large estate on Long Island, that is still in the family, under a patent granted in 1683. This gentleman was a son of Mr. Secretary Nicoll, who is supposed to have been a relative of Colonel Nicoll, the first English governor. Mr. Speaker Nicoll, as the son was called, in consequence of having filled that office for nearly a generation, was the direct ancestor of the Nicolls of Islip and Shelter Island, as well as of a branch long settled at Stratford, Connecticut. The house alluded to by Mr. Littlepage, as a relic of antiquity in his day, —American antiquity, be it remembered, —was standing a few years since, if it be not still standing, at the point of junction between the Old Boston Road and the New Road, and nearly opposite to the termination of the long avenue that led to Rosehill, originally a seat of the Wattses. The house stood a short distance above the present Union Square, and not far from that of the present Gramercy. It was, or is, a brick house of one story, with a small court-yard in front; the House of Refuge being at a little distance on its right. If still standing, it must now be one of the oldest buildings of any sort, in a town of 400,000 souls! As Mr. Speaker Nicoll resigned the chair in 1718, this house must be at least a hundred and thirty or forty years old; and it may be questioned if a dozen as old, public or private, can be found on the whole island.

dwelling of this sort for a long series of years, that was about a league from town, and which is still standing, as I pass it constantly travelling between Satanstoe and York. I never saw the patentee myself, as he died long before my birth; but his house near town still stands, as I have said, a memorial of past ages!

The whole town seemed alive, and everybody had a desire to get a glance at the sports of the Pinkster field. . . .

I dare say there were fifty young ladies promenading the church-walk when I reached it, and nearly as many young men in attendance on them; no small portion of the last being scarlet-coats, though the mohairs had their representatives there too. A few blue-jackets were among us also, there being two or three king's cruisers in port. As no one presumed to promenade the Mall who was not of a certain stamp of respectability, the company were all gayly dressed; and I will confess that I was much struck with the air of the place, the first time I showed myself among the gay idlers. The impression made on me that morning was so vivid that I will endeavor to describe the scene as it now presents itself to my mind.

In the first place there was the noble street, quite eighty feet in width in its narrowest part, and gradually expanding as you looked towards the bay, until it opened into an area of more than twice that width, at the place called the Bowling Green.¹ Then came the fort, crowning a sharp eminence, and overlooking everything in that quarter of the town. In the rear of the fort, or in its front, taking a water view, lay the batteries that had been built on the rocks which form the southwestern termination of the island. Over these rocks, which were black and picturesque, and over the batteries they supported, was obtained a view of the noble bay, dotted here and there with some speck of a sail, or possibly with some vessel anchored on its placid bosom. Of the two rows of elegant houses, most of them brick, and, with very few exceptions, principally of two stories in height, it is scarcely necessary to speak, as there are few who have not heard of, and formed some notion of Broadway; a street that all agree is one day to be the pride of the western world.

In the other direction, I will admit that the view was not so remarkable, the houses being principally of wood, and of a somewhat ignoble appearance. Nevertheless, the army were said to frequent those habitations quite as much as they did any other in the place. After reaching the Common, or present Park, where the great Boston road led off into the country, the view was just the reverse of that which was seen in the opposite quarter. Here all was inland, and rural. It is

As the regular family residence of the Nicolls was in Suffolk, or on their estates, it is probable that the above mentioned was, in a measure, owing to an intermarriage with the Wattses, as much as to the necessity of the Speaker's passing so much time at the seat of government.—EDITOR.

¹Mr. Cornelius Littlepage betrays not a little of provincial admiration, as the reader will see. I have not thought it necessary to prune these passages, their causes being too familiar to leave any danger of their insertion's being misunderstood. Admiration of Broadway, certainly not more than a third-class street, as streets go in the old world, is so very common among us as to need no apology.—EDITOR.

true the new Bridewell had been erected in that quarter, and there was also a new jail, both facing the Common; and the king's troops had barracks in their rear; but high, abrupt, conical hills, with low marshy lands, orchards and meadows, gave to all that portion of the island a peculiarly novel and somewhat picturesque character. Many of the hills in that quarter, and indeed all over the widest part of the island, are now surmounted by country-houses, as some were then, including Petersfield, the ancient abode of the Stuyvesants, or that farm which, by being called after the old Dutch governor's retreat, has given the name of Bowery, or Bouerie, to the road that led to it; as well as the Bowery House, as it was called, the country abode of the then lieutenant-governor, James De Lancey; Mount Bayard, a place belonging to that respectable family; Mount Pitt, another that was the property of Mrs. Jones, the wife of Mr. Justice Jones, a daughter of James De Lancey, and various other mounts, houses, hills, and places, that are familiar to the gentry and people of New York.

But the reader can imagine for himself the effect produced by such a street as Broadway, reaching very nearly half a mile in length, terminating at one end in an elevated, commanding fort, with its background of batteries, rocks, and bay, and at the other with the Common, on which troops were now constantly parading, the Bridewell and jail, and the novel scene I have just mentioned. Nor is Trinity itself to be forgotten. This edifice, one of the noblest, if not the most noble of its kind in all the colonies, with its Gothic architecture, statues in carved stone, and flanking walls, was a close accessory of the view, giving to the whole grandeur, and a moral.[1]

As has been said, I found the Mall crowded with young persons of fashion and respectability. This Mall was near a hundred yards in length; and it follows that there must have been a goodly show of youth and beauty. The fine weather had commenced; spring had fairly opened; Pink-ster blossoms (the wild honeysuckle) had been seen in abundance throughout the week; and every thing and person appeared gay and happy. . . .

CHAPTER IX.

A very tolerable road conducted us through some woods, to the heights, and we soon found ourselves on an eminence, that overlooked a long reach of the Hudson, extending from Haverstraw to the north, as far as Staten Island to the south; a distance of near forty miles. On the opposite shore, rose the wall-like barrier of the Palisadoes, lifting the table-land on their summits to an elevation of

[1]The provincial admiration of Mr. Cornelius Littlepage was not quite as much in fault as respects the church, as the superciliousness of our more modern tastes and opinions may lead us to suspect. The church that was burned in 1776 was a larger edifice than that just pulled down, and in many respects was its superior.—EDITOR.

several hundred feet. The noble river itself, fully three quarters of a mile in width, was unruffled by a breath of air, lying in one single, extended, placid sheet, under the rays of a bright sun, resembling molten silver. I scare remember a lovelier morning; everything appeared to harmonize with the glorious but tranquil grandeur of the view, and the rich promises of a bountiful nature. The trees were mostly covered with the beautiful clothing of a young verdure; the birds had mated, and were building in nearly every tree; the wild-flowers started up beneath the hoofs of our horses; and every object, far and near, seemed, to my young eyes, to be attuned to harmony and love.

"This is a favorite ride of mine, in which Anneke often accompanies me," said Herman Mordaunt. . . .

Herman Mordaunt rode in advance, with Jason; and he led the party by pretty bridle-paths, along the heights for nearly two miles, occasionally opening a gate, without dismounting, until he reached a point that overlooked Lilacsbush, which was soon seen, distant from us less than half a mile.

"Here we are, on my own domain," he said, as he pulled up to let us join him, "that last gate separating me from my nearest neighbor south. These hills are of no great use, except as early pastures, though they afford many beautiful views.

"I have heard it predicted," I remarked, "that the time would come, some day, when the banks of the Hudson would contain many such seats as that of the Philipses, at Yonkers, and one or two more like it, that I am told are now standing above the Highlands."

"Quite possibly; it is not easy to foretell what may come to pass in such a country. I dare say, that in time, both towns and seats will be seen on the banks of the Hudson, and a powerful and numerous nobility to occupy the last. By the way, Mr. Littlepage, your father and my friend Colonel Follock have been making a valuable acquisition in lands, I hear; having obtained a patent for an extensive estate, somewhere in the neighborhood of Albany?"

"It is not so very extensive, sir, there being only some forty thousand acres of it, altogether; nor is it very near Albany, by what I can learn, since it must lie at a distance of some forty miles, or more, from that town. Next winter, however, Dirck and myself are to go in search of the land, when we shall learn all about it."

"Then we may meet in that quarter of the country. I have affairs of importance at Albany, which have been too long neglected; and it has been my intention to pass some months at the north, next season, and early in the season, too. We may possibly meet in the woods."

"You have been at Albany, I suppose, Mr. Mordaunt?"

"Quite often, sir; the distance is so great, that one has not much inducement to go there unless carried by affairs, however, as has been my case. I was at Albany before my marriage, and have had various occasions to visit it since."

"My father was there when a soldier; and he tells me it is a part of the province well worth seeing. At all events, I shall encounter the risk and fatigue next season; for it is useful to young persons to see the world. Dirck and myself may make the campaign, should there be one in that direction."

I fancied Anneke manifested some interest in this conversation; but we rode on, and soon alighted at the door of Lilacsbush. . . .

CHAPTER X.

Albany

We passed our third night at a small hamlet called Rhinebeck, in a settlement in which many German names were to be found. Here we were travelling through the vast estates of the Livingstons, a name well known in our colonial history. We breakfasted at Claverack, and passed through a place called Kinderhook—a village of Low Dutch origin and some antiquity. That night we succeeded in coming near Albany, by making a very hard day's drive of it. There was no village at the place where we slept; but the house was a comfortable and exceedingly neat Dutch tavern. After quitting Fishkill we had seen more or less of the river, until we passed Claverack, where we took our leave of it. It was covered with ice, and sleighs were moving about it, with great apparent security; but we did not like to try it. Our whole party preferred a solid highway, in which there was no danger of the bottom dropping out.

As we were now about to enter Albany, the second largest town in the colony, and one of the largest inland towns in the whole country, if such a word can properly be given to a place that lies on a navigable river, it was thought necessary to make some few arrangements in order to do it decently. Instead of quitting the tavern at daylight, therefore, as had been our practice previously, we remained until after breakfast, having recourse to our trunks in the meantime. Dirck, Jason, and myself, had provided ourselves with fur caps for the journey, with earlaps and other contrivances for keeping one's self warm. The cap of Dirck, and my own, were of very fine martens' skin, and as they were round and high, and each was surmounted with a handsome tail that fell down behind, they had both a smart and military air. I thought I had never seen Dirck look so nobly and well, as he did in his cap, and I got a few compliments on my own air in mine, though they were only from my mother, who, I think, would feel disposed to praise me, even if I looked wretchedly. The cap of Jason was better suited to his purse, being lower, and of foxskins, though it had a tail also. Mr. Worden had declined travelling in a cap, as unsuited to his holy office. Accordingly he wore his clerical beaver, which differed a little from the ordinary cocked hats that we all wore, as a matter of course, though not so much as to be very striking.

All of us had overcoats well trimmed with furs, mine and Dirck's being really handsome, with trimmings of marten, while those of our companions were less showy and expensive. On a consultation, Dirck and I decided that it was better taste to enter the town in travellers' dresses, than to enter it in any other, and we merely smartened up a little, in order to appear as gentlemen. The case was very different with Jason. According to his idea, a man should wear his best clothes on a journey, and I was surprised to see him appear at breakfast in black breeches, striped woollen stockings, large plated buckles in his shoes, and a coat that I well knew he religiously reserved for high-days and holidays. This coat was of a light pea-green color, and but little adapted to the season; but Jason had not much notion of the fitness of things, in general, in matters of taste. Dirck and myself wore our ordinary snuff-colored coats, under our furs; but Jason threw aside all the overcoats, when we came near Albany, in order to enter the place in his best. Fortunately for him, the day was mild, and there was a bright sun to send its warm rays through the pea-green covering, to keep his blood from chilling. As for Mr. Worden, he wore a cloak of black cloth, laying aside all the furs but a tippet and muff, both of which he used habitually in cold weather.

In this guise, then, we left the tavern, about nine in the morning, expecting to reach the banks of the river about ten. Nor were we disappointed; the roads being excellent, a light fall of snow having occurred in the night, to freshen the track. It was an interesting moment to us all, when the spires and roofs of that ancient town, Albany, first appeared in view! We had journeyed from near the southern boundary of the colony to a place that stood at no great distance from its frontier settlements on the north. The town itself formed a pleasing object, as we approached it, on the opposite side of the Hudson. There it lay, stretching along the low land on the margin of the stream, and on its western bank, sheltered by high hills, up the side of which the principal street extended, for the distance of fully a quarter of a mile. Near the head of this street stood the fort, and we saw a brigade paraded in the open ground near it, wheeling and marching about. The spires of two churches were visible, one, the oldest, being seated on the low land, in the heart of the place, and the other on the height at no great distance from the fort,—or about half-way up the acclivity, which forms the barrier to the inner country, on the side of the river. Both these buildings were of stone, of course, shingle tenements being of very rare occurrence in the colony of New York, though common enough farther east.[1]

[1] In nothing was the difference of character between the people of New England and those of the middle colonies more apparent than in the nature of the dwellings. In New York, for instance, men worth thousands dwelt in humble, low (usually one story) dwellings of stone, having window-shutters, frequently within as well as without, and the other appliances of comfort; whereas the farmer farther east was seldom satisfied, though his means were limited, unless he lived in a house as good as his neighbor's; and the strife dotted the whole of their colonies with wooden buildings, of great pretensions for the age, that rarely had even exterior shutters, and which frequently stood for generations unfinished. The difference was not of Dutch origin, for it was just as apparent in New

I will own that not one of our party liked the idea of crossing the Hudson, in a loaded sleigh on the ice, and that in the month of March. There were no streams about us to be crossed in this mode, nor was the cold exactly sufficient to render such a transit safe, and we felt as the inexperienced would be apt to feel in circumstances so unpleasant. I must do Jason the credit to admit that he showed more plain, practical good sense than any of us, determining our course in the end by his view of the matter. As for Mr. Worden, however, nothing could induce him to venture on the ice in a sleigh, or near a sleigh, though Jason remonstrated in the following terms:

"Now, look here, Rev. Mr. Worden"—Jason seldom omitted anybody's title—"you've only to turn your eyes on the river to see it is dotted with sleighs, far and near. There are highways north and south, and if that be the place where the crossing is at the town, it is more like a thoroughfare than a spot that is risky. In my judgment, these people who live hereabouts ought to know whether there is any danger or not."

Obvious as was this truth, "Rev. Mr. Worden" made us stop on *terra firma*, and permit him to quit the sleigh, that he might cross the river on foot. Jason ventured a hint or two about faith and its virtues, as he stripped himself to the pea-green, in order to enter the town in proper guise, throwing aside everything that concealed his finery. As for Dirck and myself, we kept our seats manfully, and trotted on the river at the point where we saw sleighs and foot-passengers going and coming in some numbers. The Rev. Mr. Worden, however, was not content to take the beaten path, for he knew there was no more security in being out on the ice, near a sleigh, than there was in being in it, so he diverged from the road, which crossed at the ferry, striking diagonally athwart the river toward the wharves of the place.

It seemed to me to be a sort of holiday among the young and idle, one sleigh passing us after another, filled with young men and maidens, all sparkling with the excitement of the moment, and gay with youth and spirits. We passed no less than four of these sleighs on the river, the jingling of the bells, the quick movement, the laughter and gayety, and the animation of the whole scene, far exceeding anything of the sort I had ever before witnessed. We were nearly across the river, when a sleigh more handsomely equipped than any we had yet seen dashed down the bank, and came whirling past us like a comet. It was full of ladies, with the exception of one gentleman, who stood erect in front, driving. I recognized Bulstrode, in furs like all of us, capped and tailed, if not plumed; while among the half-dozen pairs of brilliant eyes that were turned with their owners' smiling faces on us, I saw one which never could be forgotten by me,

Jersey or Pennsylvania as in New York; and I think it may be attributed to a very obvious consequence of a general equality of condition, a state of society in which no one is content to wear even the semblance of poverty, but those who cannot by any means prevent it; but in which all strive to get as high as possible, in appearances at least.—EDITOR.

that belonged to Anneke Mordaunt. I question if we were recognized, for the passage was like that of a meteor; but I could not avoid turning to gaze after the gay party. This change of position enabled me to be a witness of a very amusing consequence of Mr. Worden's experiment. A sleigh was coming in our direction, and the party in it seeing one who was known for a clergyman walking on the ice, turned aside and approached him on a gallop, in order to offer the courtesy of a seat to a man of his sacred profession. Our divine heard the bells, and fearful of having a sleigh so near him, he commenced a downright flight, pursued by the people in the sleigh as fast as their horses could follow. Everybody on the ice pulled up to gaze in wonder at this strange spectacle, until the whole party reached the shore, the Rev. Mr. Worden pretty well blown, as the reader may suppose.

CHAPTER XI.

. . . [A]way they drove at a furious rate, startling all the echoes of Albany with their bells. By this time Mr. Worden was seated, and we followed more moderately, our team having none of the Dutch courage of a pair of horses fresh from the stable. Such were the circumstances under which we made our entrance into the ancient city of Albany. We were all in hopes the little affair of the chase would soon be forgotten, for no one likes to be associated with a ridiculous circumstance, but we counted without our host. Guert Ten Eyck was not of a temperament to let such an affair sleep, but, as I afterward ascertained, he told it with the laughing embellishments that belonged to his reckless character, until, in turn, the Rev. Mr. Worden came to be known, throughout all that region, by the nickname of the "Loping Dominie."

The reader may be assured our eyes were about us, as we drove through the streets of the second town in the colony. We were not accustomed to houses constructed in the Dutch style, in New York, though the English mode of building had been most in vogue there for half a century. It was not so with Albany, which remained, essentially, a Dutch town in 1758.¹ We heard little beside Dutch, as we passed along. The women scolded their children in Low Dutch, a use, by the way, for which the language appears singularly well adapted; the negroes sang Dutch songs; the men called to each other in Dutch, and Dutch rang in our ears, as we walked our horses through the streets toward the tavern. There were many soldiers about, and other proofs of the presence of a

¹The population of Albany could not have reached four thousand in 1758. Its Dutch character remained down to the close of this century, with gradual changes. The writer can remember when quite as much Dutch as English was heard in the streets of Albany, though it has now nearly disappeared. The present population must be near forty thousand.

Mr. Littlepage's description was doubtless correct at the time he wrote; but Albany would now be considered a first-class country town in Europe. It has much better claims to compare with the towns of the old world, in this character, than New York has to compare with their capitals.—EDITOR.

considerable military force were not wanting; still the place struck me as very provincial and peculiar, after New York. Nearly all the houses were built with their gables to the streets, and each had heavy wooden Dutch stoops, with seats, at its door. A few had small court-yards in front, and here and there was a building of somewhat more pretension than usual. I do not think, however, there were fifty houses in the place that were built with their gables off the line of the streets.

We were no sooner housed than Dirck and I sallied forth to look at the place. Here we were, in one of the oldest towns of America,—a place that could boast of much more than a century's existence,—and it was natural to feel curious to look about one. Our inn was in the principal street—that which led up the hill toward the fort. This street was a wide avenue, that quite put Broadway out of countenance, so far as mere width was concerned. The streets that led out of it, however, were principally little better than lanes, as if the space that had been given to two or three of the main streets had been taken off of the remainder. The High Street, as we English would call it, was occupied by sleds, filled with wood for sale; sleds loaded with geese, turkeys, tame and wild, and poultry of all sorts; sleds with venison, still in the skin, piled up in heaps, etc.—all these eatables being collected, in unusual quantities as we were told, to meet the extraordinary demand created by the different military messes. Deer were no strangers to us, for Long Island was full of all sorts of game, as were the upper counties of New Jersey. Even Westchester, old and well settled as it had become, was not yet altogether clear of deer, and nothing was easier than to knock over a buck in the Highlands. Nevertheless, I had never seen venison, wild turkeys, and sturgeons in such quantities as they were to be seen that day in the principal street of Albany.

The crowd collected in this street, the sleighs that were whirling past, filled with young men and maidens, the incessant jingling of bells, the spluttering and jawing in Low Dutch, the hearty English oaths of sergeants and sutlers'-men and cooks of messes, the loud laughs of the blacks, and the beauty of the cold, clear day, altogether produced some such effects on me as I had experienced when I went to the theatre. Not the least striking picture of the scene was Jason, in the middle of the street, gaping about him, in the cocked-hat, the pea-green coat, and the striped woollen stockings.

Dirck and myself naturally examined the churches. These were two, as has been said already—one for the Dutch, and the other for the English. The first was the oldest. It stood at the point where the two principal streets crossed each other, and in the centre of the street, leaving sufficient passages all round it. The building was square, with a high, pointed roof, having a belfry and weathercock on its apex; windows, with diamond panes and painted glass, and a porch that was well suited both to the climate and to appearances. . . .¹

¹There were two churches of this character built on this spot. The second, much larger than the first, but of the same form, was built round the other, in which service was held to the last, when it was

Here, Guert shook us both by the hand again, most cordially, and left us. Dirck and I next strolled up the hill, going as high as the English church, which stood also in the centre of the principal street, an imposing and massive edifice in stone. With the exception of Mother Trinity in New York, this was the largest, and altogether the most important edifice devoted to the worship of my own church I had ever seen. In Westchester there were several of Queen Anne's churches, but none on a scale to compare with this. Our small edifices were usually without galleries, steeples, towers, or bells; while St. Peter's, Albany, if not actually St. Peter's, Rome, was a building of which a man might be proud. A little to our surprise, we found the Reverend Mr. Worden and Mr. Jason Newcome had met at the door of this edifice, having sent a boy to the sexton in quest of the key. In a minute or two, the urchin returned, bringing not only the key of the church, but the excuses of the sexton for not coming himself. The door was opened, and we went in.

I have always admired the decorous and spiritual manner in which the Rev. Mr. Worden entered a building that had been consecrated to the services of the Deity. I know not how to describe it; but it proved how completely he had been drilled in the decencies of his profession. Off came his hat, of course; and his manner, however facetious and easy it may have been the moment before, changed on the instant to gravity and decorum. Not so with Jason. He entered St. Peter's, Albany, with exactly the same indifferent and cynical air with which he had seemed to regard everything but money, since he entered "York colony." Usually he wore his cocked-hat on the back of his head, thereby lending himself a lolloping, negligent, and, at the same time, defying air; but I observed that, as we all uncovered, he brought his own beaver up over his eyebrows, in a species of military bravado. To uncover to a church, in his view of the matter, was a sort of idolatry; there might be images about, for anything he knew; "and a man could never be enough on his guard ag'n being carried away by such evil deceptions," as he had once before answered to a remonstrance of mine, for wearing his hat in our own parish church.

I found the interior of St. Peter's quite as imposing as its exterior. Three of the pews were canopied, having coats-of-arms on their canopies. These, the boy told us, belonged to the Van Rensselaer and Schuyler families. All these were covered with black cloth, in mourning for some death in those ancient families, which were closely allied. I was very much struck with the dignified air that these patrician seats gave the house of God.[1] There were also several hatchments suspended against the walls; some being placed there in commemoration of

literally thrown out of the windows of its successor. The last edifice disappeared about forty years since.—EDITOR.

[1] I cannot recollect one of these canopied pews that is now standing, in this part of the Union. The last, of my knowledge, were in St. Mark's, New York, and, I believe, belonged to the Stuyvesants, the patron family of that church. They were taken down when that building was repaired, a few years since. This is one of the most innocent of all our innovations of this character. Distinctions in the house of God are opposed to the very spirit of the Christian religion; and it were far more fitting that

officers of rank, from home, who had died in the king's service in the colony; and others to mark the deaths of some of the more distinguished of our own people.

Mr. Worden expressed himself well pleased with appearances of things, in and about this building; though Jason regarded all with ill-concealed disgust.

"What is the meaning of them pews with tops to them, Corny?" the pedagogue whispered me, afraid to encounter the parson's remarks by his own criticism.

"They are the pews of families of distinction in this place, Mr. Newcome; and the canopies, or tops, as you call them, are honorable signs of their owners' conditions."

"Do you think their owners will sit under such coverings in paradise, Corny?" continued Jason, with a sneer.

"It is impossible for me to say, sir; it is probable, however, the just will not require any such mark to distinguish them from the unjust."

"Let me see," said Jason, looking round and affecting to count; "there are just three—bishop, priest, and deacon, I suppose. Waal, there's a seat for each, and they can be comfortable here, whatever may turn up herea'ter."

I turned away, unwilling to dispute the point, for I knew it was as hopeless to expect that a Danbury man would feel like a New Yorker, on such a subject, as it was to expect that a New Yorker could be made to adopt Danbury sentiments. As for the argument, however, I have heard others of pretty much the same calibre often urged against the three orders of the ministry.

On quitting St. Peter's, I communicated the invitation of Guert Ten Eyck to Mr. Worden, and urged him to be of the party. I could see that the notion of a pleasant supper was anything but unpleasant to the missionary. Still he had his scruples, inasmuch as he had not yet seen his reverend brother who had the charge of St. Peter's, did not know exactly the temper of his mind, and was particularly desirous of officiating for him, in the presence of the principal personages of the place, on the approaching Sunday. He had written a note to the chaplain; for the person who had the cure of the Episcopalians held that rank in the army, St. Peter's being as much of an official chapel as a parish church; and he must have an interview with that individual before he could decide. Fortunately, as we descended the street, toward our inn, we saw the very person in question. . . .

---

pews should be altogether done away with, the true mode of assembling under the sacred roof, than that men should be classed even at the foot of the altar.

It may be questioned if a hatchment is now hung up, either on the dwelling or in a church, in any part of America. They were to be seen, however, in the early part of the present century. Whenever any such traces of ancient usages are met with among us, by the traveller from the old world, he is apt to mistake them for the shadows "that coming events cast before" instead of those of the past.— EDITOR.

CHAPTER XV.

"When lo! the voice of loud alarm
His inmost soul appalls:
What ho! Lord William, rise in haste!
The water saps thy walls!"
Lord William.

The visit to Madam Schuyler occurred of a Saturday evening; and the matter of our adventure in company with Jack and Moses, was to be decided on the following Monday. When I rose and looked out of my window on the Sunday morning, however, there appeared but very little prospect of its being effected that spring, inasmuch as it rained heavily, and there was a fresh south wind. We had reached the twenty-first of March, a period of the year when a decided thaw was not only ominous to the sleighing, but when it actually predicted a permanent breaking up of the winter. The season had been late, and it was thought the change could not be distant.

The rain and south wind continued all that day, and torrents of water came rushing down the short, steep streets, effectually washing away everything like snow. Mr. Worden preached, notwithstanding, and to a very respectable congregation. Dirck and myself attended; but Jason preferred sitting out a double half-hour-glass sermon in the Dutch church, delivered in a language of which he understood very little, to lending his countenance to the rites of the English service. Both Anneke and Mary Wallace found their way up the hill, going in a carriage; though I observed that Herman Mordaunt was absent. Guert was in the gallery, in which we also sat; but I could not avoid remarking that neither of the young ladies raised her eyes once, during the whole service, as high as our pews. Guert whispered something about this, as he hastened down stairs to hand them to their carriage, when the congregation was dismissed, begging me at the same time, to be punctual to the appointment for the next day. What he meant by this last remembrancer I did not understand; for the hills were beginning to exhibit their bare breast, and it was somewhat surprising with what rapidity a rather unusual amount of snow had disappeared. I had no opportunity to ask an explanation, as Guert was too busy in placing the ladies in the carriage, and the weather was not such as to admit of my remaining a moment longer in the street than was indispensably necessary.

A change occurred in the weather during the night, the rain having ceased, though the atmosphere continued mild, and the wind was still from the south. It was the commencement of the spring; and, as I walked round to Guert Ten Eyck's house, to meet him at breakfast, I observed that several vehicles with wheels were already in motion in the streets, and that divers persons appeared to be

177

putting away their sleighs and sleds, as things of no further use, until the next winter. Our springs do not certainly come upon us as suddenly as some of which I have read, in the old world; but when the snow and winter endure as far into March as had been the case with that of the year 1758, the change is often nearly magical.

"Here, then, is the spring opening," I said to Dirck, as we walked along the well-washed streets; "and, in a few weeks, we must be off to the bush. Our business on the patent must be got along with before the troops are put in motion, or we may lose the opportunity of seeing a campaign."

With such expectations and feelings I entered Guert's bachelor abode; and the first words I uttered, were to sympathize in his supposed disappointment.

"It is a great pity you did not propose the drive to the ladies for Saturday," I began; "for that was not only a mild day, but the sleighing was excellent. As it is, you will have to postpone your triumph until next winter."

"I do not understand you!" cried Guert; "Jack and Moses were never in better heart, or in better condition. I think they are equal to going to Kinderhook in two hours!"

"But who will furnish the roads with snow? By looking out of the window, you will see that the streets are nearly bare."

"Streets and roads! Who cares for either, while we have the river? We often use the river here, weeks at a time, when the snow has left us. The ice has been remarkably even the whole of this winter, and, now the snow is off it, there will be no danger from the air-holes."

I confess I did not much like the notion of travelling twenty miles on the ice, but was far too much of a man to offer any objections.

We breakfasted, and proceeded in a body to the residence of Herman Mordaunt. When the ladies first heard that we had come to claim the redemption of the half-promise given at Madam Schuyler's their surprise was not less than mine had been, half an hour before, while their uneasiness was probably greater.

"Surely, Jack and Moses cannot exhibit all their noble qualities without snow!" exclaimed Anneke, laughing, "Ten Eycks though they be?"

"We Albanians have the advantage of travelling on the ice, when the snow fails us," answered Guert. "Here is the river, near by, and never was the sleighing on it better than at this moment."

"But it has been many times safer, I should think. This looks very much like the breaking up of winter!"

"That is probable enough, and so much greater the reason why we should not delay, if you and Miss Mary ever intend to learn what the blacks can do. It is for the honor of Holland that I desire it, else would I not presume so far. I feel every condescension of this sort, that I receive from you two ladies, in a way I cannot express; for no one knows, better than myself, how unworthy I am of your smallest notice."

This brought the signs of yielding, at once, into the mild countenance of Mary Wallace. Guert's self-humiliation never failed to do this. There was so much obvious truth in his admission, so sincere a disposition to place himself, where nature and education, or a *want* of education had placed him, and most of all so profound a deference for the mental superiority of Mary herself, that the female heart found it impossible to resist. To my surprise, Guert's mistress, contrary to her habit in such things, was the first to join him, and to second his proposal. Herman Mordaunt entering the room at this instant, the whole thing was referred to him, as in reason it ought to have been.

"I remember to have travelled on the Hudson, a few years since," returned Herman Mordaunt, "the entire distance between Albany and Sing-Sing, and a very good time we had of it; much better than had we gone by land, for there was little or no snow."

"Just our case now, Miss Anneke!" cried Guert. "Good sleighing on the river, but none on the land."

"Was that near the end of March, dear Papa?" asked Anneke, a little inquiringly.

"No, certainly not, for it was early in February. But the ice, at this moment, must be near eighteen inches thick, and strong enough to bear a load of hay."

"Yes, Massa Herman," observed Cato, a gray-headed black, who never called his master by any other name, having known him from an infant; "yes, Massa Herman, a load do come over dis minute."

It appeared unreasonable to distrust the strength of the ice, after this proof to the contrary, and Anneke submitted. The party was arranged forthwith, and in the following manner: the two ladies, Guert and myself, were to be drawn by the blacks, while Herman Mordaunt, Dirck, and any one else they could enlist, were to follow in the New York sleigh. It was hoped that an elderly female connection, Mrs. Bogart, who resided at Albany, would consent to be of the party, as the plan was to visit and dine with another, and a mutual connection of the Mordaunts, at Kinderhook. While the sleighs were getting ready, Herman Mordaunt walked round to the house of Mrs. Bogart, made his request, and was successful.

The clock in the tower of the English church struck ten, as both sleighs drove from Herman Mordaunt's door. There was literally no snow in the middle of the streets; but enough of it, mingled with ice, was still to be found nearer the houses, to enable us to get down to the ferry, the point where sleighs usually went upon the river. Here Herman Mordaunt, who was in advance, checked his horses, and turned to speak to Guert on the propriety of proceeding. The ice near the shore had evidently been moved, the river having risen a foot or two, in consequence of the wind and thaw, and there was a sort of icy wave cast up near the land, over which it was indispensable to pass in order to get fairly on the river. As the top of this ridge or wave was broken, it exposed a fissure that enabled us to see the thickness of the ice, and this Guert pointed out in proof of its strength. There was nothing unusual in a small movement of the covering of the river, which the current often produces; but unless the vast fields below got in movement, it was impossible for those above materially to change their positions. Sleighs were passing too, still bringing to town hay from the flats on the eastern bank, and there was no longer any hesitation. Herman Mordaunt's sleigh passed slowly over the ridge, having a care to the legs of the horses, and ours followed in the same cautious manner, though the blacks jumped across the fissures in spite of their master's exertions.

Once on the river, however, Guert gave the blacks the whip and rein, and away we went like the wind. The smooth, icy surface of the Hudson was our road, the thaw having left very few traces of any track. The water had all passed beneath the ice, through cracks and fissures of one sort and another, leaving us an even, dry surface to trot on. The wind was still southerly, though scarcely warm, while a bright sun contributed to render our excursion as gay to the eye as it certainly was to our feelings. In a few minutes every trace of uneasiness had vanished. Away we went, the blacks doing full credit to their owner's boasts, seeming scarcely to touch the ice, from which their feet appeared to rebound with a sort of elastic force. Herman Mordaunt's bays followed on our heels, and the sleighs had passed over the well-known shoal of the Overslaugh, within the first twenty minutes after they touched the river.

Every northern American is familiar with the effect that the motion of a sleigh produces on the spirits, under favorable circumstances. Had our party been altogether composed of Albanians, there would probably have been no drawback on the enjoyment, for use would have prevented apprehension; but it required the few minutes I have mentioned to give Anneke and Mary Wallace full confidence in the ice. By the time we reached the Overslaugh, however, their fears had vanished; and Guert confirmed their sense of security, by telling them to listen to the sounds produced by his horses' hoofs, which certainly conveyed the impression of moving on a solid foundation.

Mary Wallace had never before been so gay in my presence, as she appeared to be that morning. Once or twice, I fancied her eyes almost as bright as those of Anneke's, and certainly her laugh was as sweet and musical. Both the girls were full of spirits, and some little things occurred that gave me hopes Bulstrode had no reason to fancy himself as secure as he sometimes seemed to be. A casual remark of Guert's had the effect to bring out some of Anneke's private sentiments on the subject; or at least, so they appeared to be to me.

"I am surprised that Mr. Mordaunt forgot to invite Mr. Bulstrode to be one of our party, to-day," cried Guert, when we were below the Overslaugh. "The major loves sleighing, and he would have filled the fourth seat in the other sleigh very agreeably. As for coming into this, that would be refused him, were he even a general!"

"Mr. Bulstrode is English," answered Anneke with spirit, "and fancies American amusements beneath the tastes of one who has been presented at the court of St. James."

"Well, Miss Anneke, I cannot say that I agree with you at all, in this opinion of Mr. Bulstrode," Guert returned innocently. "It is true, he is English; that he fancies an advantage, as does Corny Littlepage, here; but we must make proper allowances for home-love and foreign dislike."

"'Corny Littlepage, here,' is only *half* English, and that half is colony-born and colony-bred," answered the laughing girl, "and he has loved a sleigh from the time when he first slid down hill—"

"Ah! Miss Anneke—let me entreat—"

"Oh! no allusion is intended to the Dutch church and its neighborhood;—but the sports of childhood are always dear to us, as are sometimes the discomforts. Habit and prejudice are sister handmaidens; and I never see one of these gentlemen from home taking extraordinary interest in any of our peculiarly colony usages, but I distrust an extra amount of complaisance, or a sort of enjoyment in which we do not strictly share."

"Is this altogether liberal to Bulstrode, Miss Anneke," I ventured to put in; "he seems to like us, and I am sure he has good reason so to do. That he likes *some* of us, is too apparent to be concealed or denied."

"Mr. Bulstrode is a skilful actor, as all who saw his Cato must be aware," retorted the charming girl, compressing her pouting lips in a way that seemed to me to be inexpressibly pleasing; "and those who saw his Scrub must be equally convinced of the versatility of his talents. No, no; Major Bulstrode is better where he is, or will be to-day, at four o'clock—at the head of the mess of the —th, instead of dining in a snug Dutch parlor, with my cousin, worthy Mrs. Van der Heyden, at a dinner got up with colony hospitality, and colony good-will, and colony plainness. The entertainment we shall receive to-day, sweetened, as it will be, by the welcome which will come from the heart, can have no competitor in countries where a messenger must be sent two days before the visit, to ask permission to come, in order to escape cold looks and artificial surprise. I would prefer surprising my friends from the heart, instead of from the head."

Guert expressed his astonishment that any one should not always be glad and willing to receive his friends; and insisted on it, that no such inhospitable customs *could* exist. I knew, however, that society could not exist on the same terms in old and in new countries—among a people that was pressed upon by numbers, and a people that had not yet felt the evils of a superabundant population. Americans are like dwellers in the country, who are always glad to see their friends; and I ventured to say something of the causes of these differences in habits.

Nothing occurred worthy of being dwelt on, in our ride to Kinderhook. Mrs.

Van der Heyden resided at a short distance from the river, and the blacks and the bays had some little difficulty in dragging us through the mud to her door. Once there, however, our welcome fully verified the theory of the colony habits, which had been talked over in our drive down. Anneke's worthy connection was not only glad to see her, as anybody might have been, but she would have been glad to receive as many as her house would hold. Few excuses were necessary, for we were all welcome. The visit would retard her dinner an hour, as she frankly admitted—but that was nothing; and cakes and wine were set before us in the interval, did we feel hungry in consequence of a two hours' ride. Guert was desired to make free, and go to the stables to give his own orders. In a word, our reception was just that which every colonist has experienced, when he has gone unexpectedly to visit a friend, or a friend's friend. Our dinner was excellent, though not accompanied by much form. The wine was good; Mrs. Van der Heyden's deceased husband having been a judge of what was desirable in that respect. Everybody was in good-humor; and our hostess insisted on giving us coffee before we took our departure.

"There will be a moon, cousin Herman," she said, "and the night will be both light and pleasant. Guert knows the road, which cannot well be missed, as it is the river; and if you quit me at eight, you will reach home in good season to go to rest. It is so seldom I see you, that I have a right to claim every minute you can spare. There remains much to be told concerning our old friends and mutual relatives."

When such words are accompanied by looks and acts that prove their sincerity, it is not easy to tear ourselves away from a pleasant house. We chatted on, laughed, listened to stories and colony anecdotes that carried us back to the last war, and heard a great many eulogiums on beaux and belles, that we young people had, all our lives, considered as respectable, elderly, common-place sort of persons.

At length the hour arrived when even Mrs. Bogart herself admitted we ought to part. Anneke and Mary were kissed, enveloped in their furs, and kissed again, and then we took our leave. As we left the house, I remarked that a clock in the passage struck eight. In a few minutes every one was placed, and the runners were striking fire from the flints of the bare ground. We had less difficulty in descending than in ascending the bank of the river, though there was no snow. It did not absolutely freeze, nor had it actually frozen since the commencement of the thaw, but the earth had stiffened since the disappearance of the sun. I was much rejoiced when the blacks sprang upon the ice, and whirled us away, on our return road at a rate even exceeding the speed with which they had come down it in the morning. I thought it high time we should be in motion on our return; and in motion we were, if flying at the rate of eleven miles in the hour could thus be termed.

The light of the moon was not clear and bright, for there was a haze in the atmosphere, as is apt to occur in the mild weather of March; but there was enough to enable Guert to dash ahead with as great a velocity as was at all desirable. We were all in high spirits; us two young men so much the more, because each of us fancied he had seen that day evidence of a tender interest existing in the heart of his mistress toward himself. Mary Wallace had managed, with a woman's tact, to make her suitor appear even respectable in female society, and had brought out in him many sentiments that denoted a generous disposition and a manly heart, if not a cultivated intellect; and Guert was getting confidence, and with it the means of giving his capacity fairer play. As for Anneke, she now knew my aim, and I had some right to construe several little symptoms of feeling, that escaped her in the course of the day, favorably. I fancied that, gentle as it always was, her voice grew softer, and her smile sweeter and more winning, as she addressed herself to, or smiled on me; and she did just enough of both not to appear distant, and just little enough to appear conscious; at least such were the conjectures of one who I do not think could be properly accused of too much confidence, and whose natural diffidence was much increased by the self-distrust of the purest love.

Away we went, Guert's complicated chimes of bells jingling their merry tones in a manner to be heard half a mile, the horses bearing hard on the bits, for they knew that their own stables lay at the end of their journey, and Herman Mordaunt's bays keeping so near us that, notwithstanding the noise we made with our own bells, the sounds of his were constantly in our ears. An hour went swiftly by, and we had already passed Coejeman's, and had a hamlet that stretched along the strand, and which lay quite beneath the high bank of the river, in dim distant view. This place has since been known by the name of Monkey Town, and is a little remarkable as being the first cluster of houses on the shores of the Hudson after quitting Albany. I dare say it has another name in law, but Guert gave it the appellation I have mentioned.

I have said that the night had a sombre, misty light, the moon wading across the heavens through a deep but thin ocean of vapor. We saw the shores plainly enough, and we saw the houses and trees, but it was difficult to distinguish smaller objects at any distance. In the course of the day twenty sleighs had been met or passed, but at that hour everybody but ourselves appeared to have deserted the river. It was getting late for the simple habits of those who dwelt on its shores. When about half way between the islands opposite Coejeman's and the hamlet just named, Guert, who stood erect to drive, told us that some one who was out late, like ourselves, was coming down. The horses of the strangers were in a very fast trot, and the sleigh was evidently inclining toward the west shore, as if those it held intended to land at no great distance. As it passed, quite swiftly, a man's voice called out something on a high key, but our bells made so much noise that it was not easy to understand him. He spoke in Dutch, too, and none of our ears, those of Guert excepted, were sufficiently expert in that language to be particularly quick in comprehending what he said. The call passed unheeded then, such things being quite frequent among the Dutch, who seldom passed each other on the highway without a greeting of some sort or other. I was thinking of this practice, and of the points that distinguished our own habits from those of the people of this part of the colony, when sleigh-bells sounded quite near me, and turning my head I saw Herman Mordaunt's bays galloping close to us, as if wishing to get alongside. At the next moment the object was affected, and Guert pulled up.

"Did you understand the man who passed down, Guert?" demanded Herman Mordaunt, as soon as all noises ceased. "He called out to us, at the top of his voice, and would hardly do that without an object."

"These men seldom go home, after a visit to Albany, without filling their jugs," answered Guert, dryly; "what could he have to say, more than to wish us good-night!"

"I cannot tell, but Mrs. Bogart thought she understood something about 'Albany,' and 'the river.'"

"The ladies always fancy Albany is to sink into the river after a great thaw," answered Guert, good-humoredly; "but I can show either of them that the ice is sixteen inches thick, here where we stand."

Guert then gave me the reins, stepped out of the sleigh, went a short distance to a large crack that he had seen while speaking, and returned with a thumb placed on the handle of the whip, as a measure to show that his statement was true. The ice at that spot was certainly nearer eighteen than sixteen inches thick. Herman Mordaunt showed the measure to Mrs. Bogart, whose alarm was pacified by this positive proof. Neither Anneke nor Mary exhibited any fear; but, on the contrary, as the sleighs separated again, each had something pleasant, but feminine, to say at the expense of poor Mrs. Bogart's imagination.

I believe I was the only person in our own sleigh who felt any alarm after the occurrence of this little incident. Why uneasiness beset me, I cannot precisely say. It must have been altogether on Anneke's account, and not in the least on my own. Such accidents as sleighs breaking through, on our New York lakes and rivers, happened almost every winter, and horses were often drowned; though it was seldom the consequences proved so serious to their owners. I recalled to mind the fragile nature of ice, the necessary effects of the great thaw and the heavy rains, remembering that frozen water might still retain most of its apparent thickness, after its consistency was greatly impaired. But I could do nothing! If we landed, the roads were impassable for runners, almost for wheels, and another hour might carry the ladies, by means of the river, to their comfortable homes. That day, however, which, down to the moment of meeting the unknown sleigh, had been the very happiest of my life, was entirely changed in its aspect, and I no longer regarded it with any satisfaction. Had Anneke been at home, I could gladly have entered into a contract to pass a week on the river myself, as the condition of her safety. I thought but little of the others, to my shame be it said, though I cannot do myself the injustice to imagine, had Anneke been away, that I would have deserted even a horse, while there was a hope of saving him.

Away we went! Guert drove rapidly, but he drove with judgment, and it seemed as if his blacks knew what was expected of them. It was not long before we were trotting past the hamlet I have mentioned. It would seem that the bells of the two sleighs attracted the attention of the people on the shore, all of whom had not yet gone to bed; for the door of the house opened, and two men issued out of it, gazing at us as we trotted past at a pace that defied pursuit. These men also hallooed to us, in Dutch, and again Herman Mordaunt galloped up alongside, to speak to us.

"Did you understand these men?" he called out, for this time Guert did not see fit to stop the horses; "they, too, had something to tell us."

"These people always have something to tell an Albany sleigh, Mr. Mordaunt," answered Guert; "though it is not often that which it would do any good to hear."

"But Mrs. Bogart thinks they also had something to say about 'Albany,' and the 'river.'"

"I understand Dutch as well as excellent Mrs. Bogart," said Guert, a little dryly; "and I heard nothing; while I fancy I understand the river better. This ice would bear a dozen loads of hay, in a close line."

This again satisfied Herman Mordaunt and the ladies, but it did not satisfy me. Our own bells made four times the noise of those of Herman Mordaunt; and it was very possible that one, who understood Dutch perfectly, might comprehend a call in that language, while seated in his own sleigh, when the same call could not be comprehended by the same person, while seated in Guert's. There was no pause, however; on we trotted; and another mile was passed, before any new occurrence attracted attention.

The laugh was again heard among us, for Mary Wallace consented to sing an air, that was rendered somewhat ludicrous by the accompaniment of the bells. This song, or verse or two, for the singer got no further on account of the interruption, had drawn Guert's and my attention behind us, or away from the horses, when a whirling sound was heard, followed immediately by a loud shout. A sleigh passed within ten yards of us, going down, and the whirling sound was caused by its runners, while the shout came from the solitary man, who stood erect, waving his whip and calling to us in a loud voice, as long as he could be heard. This was but for a moment, however, as his horses were on the run; and the last we could see of the man, through the misty moonlight, he had turned his whip on his team, to urge it ahead still faster. In an instant, Herman Mordaunt was at our side, for the third time that night, and he called out to us somewhat authoritatively to stop.

"What can all this mean, Guert?" he asked. "Three times have we had warnings about 'Albany' and the 'river.' I heard this man myself utter those two words, and cannot be mistaken."

"I dare say, sir, that you may have heard something of the sort," answered the still incredulous Guert; "for these chaps have generally some impertinence to utter, when they pass a team that is better than their own. These blacks of mine, Herman Mordaunt, awaken a good deal of envy, whenever I go out with them; and a Dutchman will forgive you any other superiority, sooner than he will overlook your having the best team. That last man had a spur in his head, moreover, and is driving his cattle, at this moment, more like a spook than like a humane and rational being. I dare say he asked if we owned Albany and the river."

Guert's allusion to his horses occasioned a general laugh; and laughter is little favorable to cool reflection. We all looked out on the solemn and silent night, cast our eyes along the wide and long reach of the river, in which we happened to be, and saw nothing but the calm of nature, rendered imposing by solitude and the stillness of the hour. Guert smilingly renewed his assurances that all was right, and moved on. Away we went. Guert evidently pressed his horses, as if desirous of being placed beyond this anxiety as soon as possible. The blacks flew, rather than trotted; and we were all beginning to submit to the exhilaration of so rapid and easy a motion, when a sound which resembled that which one might suppose the simultaneous explosion of a thousand rifles would produce, was heard, and caused both drivers to pull up; the sleighs stopping quite near each other, and at the same instant! A slight exclamation escaped old Mrs. Bogart; but Anneke and Mary remained still as death.

"What means that sound, Guert?" inquired Herman Mordaunt; the concern he felt being betrayed by the very tone of his voice. "Something seems wrong!"

"Something *is* wrong," answered Guert, coolly, but very decidedly; "and it is something that must be seen to."

As this was said, Guert stepped out on the ice, which he struck a hard blow with the heel of his boot, as if to make certain of its solidity. A second report was heard, and it evidently came from behind us. Guert gazed intently down the river; then he laid his head close to the surface of the ice, and looked again. At the same time, three or four more of these startling reports followed each other in quick succession. Guert instantly rose to his feet.

"I understand it, now," he said, "and find I have been rather too confident. The ice, however, is safe and strong, and we have nothing to fear from its weakness. Perhaps it would be better to quit the river notwithstanding, though I am far from certain the better course will not be to push on."

"Let us know the danger at once, Mr. Ten Eyck," said Herman Mordaunt, "that we may decide for the best."

"Why, sir, I am afraid that the rains and the thaw together, have thrown so much water into the river, all at once, as it might be, as to have raised the ice and broken it loose, in spots, from the shores. When this happens above, before the ice has disappeared below, it sometimes causes dams to form, which heap up such a weight as to break the whole plain of ice far below it, and thus thrown cakes over cakes until walls twenty or thirty feet high are formed. This has not happened yet, therefore there is no immediate danger; but by bending your heads low, you can see that such a break has just taken place about half a mile below us."

We did as Guert directed, and saw that a mound had arisen across the river nearer than the distance named by our companion, completely cutting off retreat by the way we had come. The bank on the west side of the Hudson was high at the point where we were, and looking intently at it, I saw the manner in which the trees disappeared, the more distant behind those that were nearer, that we were actually in motion! An involuntary exclamation caused the whole party to comprehend this startling fact at the same instant. We were certainly in motion, though very slowly, on the ice of that swollen river, in the quiet and solitude of a night in which the moon rather aided in making danger apparent than in assisting us to avoid it! What was to be done? It was necessary to decide, and that promptly and intelligently.

We waited for Herman Mordaunt to advise us, but he referred the matter at once to Guert's greater experience.

"We cannot land here," answered the young man, "so long as the ice is in motion, and I think it better to push on. Every foot will bring us so much nearer to Albany, and we shall get among the islands a mile or two higher, where the chances of landing will be greatly increased. Besides, I have often crossed the river on a cake, for they frequently stop, and I have known even loaded sleighs profit by them to get over the river. As yet there is nothing very alarming;—let us push on, and get nearer to the islands."

This, then, was done, though there was no longer heard the laugh or the song among us. I could see that Herman Mordaunt was uneasy about Anneke, though he could not bring her into his own sleigh, leaving Mary Wallace alone; neither could he abandon his respectable connection, Mrs. Bogart. Before we re-entered the sleighs, I took an occasion to assure him that Anneke should be my especial care.

"God bless you, Corny, my dear boy," Herman Mordaunt answered, squeezing my hand with fervor. "God bless you, and enable you to protect her. I was about to ask you to change seats with me; but, on the whole, I think my child will be safer with you than she could be with me. We will await God's pleasure as accident has placed us."

"I will desert her only with life, Mr. Mordaunt. Be at ease on that subject."

"I know you will not—I am sure you will not, Littlepage; that affair of the lion is a pledge that you will not. Had Bulstrode come, we should have been strong enough to—but Guert is impatient to be off. God bless you, boy—God bless you. Do not neglect my child."

Guert was impatient, and no sooner was I in the sleigh than we were once more in rapid motion. I said a few words to encourage the girls, and then no sound of a human voice mingled with the gloomy scene.

CHAPTER XVI.

> "He started up, each limb convulsed
> With agonizing fear,
> He only heard the storm of night—
> 'T was music to his ear."
> *Lord William.*

Away we went! Guert's aim was the islands, which carried him nearer home, while it offered a place of retreat, in the event of the danger's becoming more serious. The fierce rapidity with which we now moved prevented all conversation, or even much reflection. The reports of the rending ice, however, became more and more frequent, first coming from above, and then from below. More than once it seemed as if the immense mass of weight that had evidently collected somewhere near the town of Albany, was about to pour down upon us in a flood—when the river would have been swept for miles, by a resistless torrent. Nevertheless, Guert held on his way; firstly, because he knew it would be impossible to get on either of the main shores, anywhere near the point where we happened to be; and secondly, because having often seen similar dammings of the waters, he fancied we were still safe. That the distant reader may understand the precise character of the danger we ran, it may be well to give him some notion of the localities.

The banks of the Hudson are generally high and precipitous, and in some places they are mountainous. No flats worthy of being mentioned, occur, until Albany is approached; nor are those which lie south of that town of any great extent, compared with the size of the stream. In this particular the Mohawk is a very different river, having extensive flats that, I have been told, resemble those of the Rhine, in miniature. As for the Hudson, it is generally esteemed in the colony as a very pleasing river; and I remember to have heard intelligent people from home admit, that even the majestic Thames itself is scarcely more worthy to be visited, or that it better rewards the trouble and curiosity of the enlightened traveller.[1]

---

[1]This remark of Mr. Cornelius Littlepage's may induce a smile in the reader. But few persons of fifty can be found, who cannot recall the time, when it was a rare thing to imagine anything American as good as its English counterpart. The American who could write a book—a real, live book—forty years since, was a sort of prodigy. It was the same with him who could paint any picture beyond a common portrait. The very fruits and natural productions of the country were esteemed doubtingly; and he was a bold man who dared to extol even canvas-back ducks, in the year 1800! At the present day, the feeling is fast undergoing an organic change. It is now the fashion to extol everything American, and from submitting to a degree that was almost abject, to the feeling of colonial dependency, the country is filled, to-day, with the most profound provincial self-admiration. It is to be hoped that the next change will bring us to something like the truth.—EDITOR.

While there are flats on the shores of the Hudson, and of some extent, in the vicinity of Albany, the general formation of the adjacent country is preserved—being high, bold, and in some quarters, more particularly to the northward and eastward, mountainous. Among these hills the stream meanders for sixty or eighty miles north of the town, receiving tributaries as it comes rushing down toward the sea. The character of the river changes entirely, a short distance above Albany; the tides flowing to that point, rendering it navigable, and easy of ascent in summer, all the way from the sea. Of the tributaries, the principal is the Mohawk, which runs a long distance toward the west—they tell me, for I have never visited those remote parts of the colony—among fertile plains, that are bounded north and south by precipitous highlands. Now, in the spring, when the vast quantities of snow, that frequently lie four feet deep in the forests, and among the mountains and valleys of the interior, are suddenly melted by the south winds and rains, freshets necessarily succeed, which have been known to do great injury. The flats of the Mohawk, they tell me, are annually overflowed, and a moderate freshet is deemed a blessing; but occasionally a union of the causes I have mentioned, produces a species of deluge that has a very opposite character. Thus it is, that houses are swept away; and bridges from the smaller mountain streams have been known to come floating past the wharves of Albany, holding their way toward the ocean. At such times the tides produce no counter-current; for it is a usual thing, in the early months of the spring, to have the stream pour downward for weeks, the whole length of the river, and to find the water fresh even as low as New York.

Such was the general nature of the calamity we had been so unexpectedly made to encounter. The winter had been severe, and the snows unusually deep; and, as we drove furiously onward, I remembered to have heard my grandfather predict extraordinary freshets in the spring, from the character of the winter, as we had found it, even previously to my quitting home. The great thaw, and the heavy rains of the late storms, had produced the usual effect; and the waters thus let loose among the distant as well as the nearer hills, were now pouring down upon us in their collected might. In such cases, the first effect is, to loosen the ice from the shores; and local causes forcing it to give way at particular points, a breaking up of its surface occurs and dams are formed, that set the stream back in floods upon all the adjacent low land, such as the flats in the vicinity of Albany.

We did not then know it, but, at the very moment Guert was thus urging his blacks to supernatural efforts—actually running them as if on a race-course— there was a long reach of the Hudson, opposite to, for a short distance below, and for a considerable distance above the town, which was quite clear of stationary ice. Vast cakes continued to come down, it is true, passing on to increase the dam that had formed below, near and on the Overslaugh, where it was buttressed by the islands, and rested on the bottom; but the whole of that firm field, on which we had first driven forth that morning, had disappeared! This we did not know at the time, or it might have changed the direction of Guert's movements; but I learned it afterward, when placed in a situation to inquire into the causes of what had occurred.

Herman Mordaunt's bells, and the rumbling sound of his runners, were heard close behind us, as our own sleigh flew along the river at a rate that I firmly believe could not have been much less than that of twenty miles in the hour. As we were whirled northward, the reports made by the rending of the ice increased in frequency and force. They really became appalling! Still the girls continued silent, maintaining their self-command in a most admirable manner; though I doubt not that they felt, in the fullest extent, the true character of the awful circumstances in which we were placed. Such was the state of things, as Guert's blacks began sensibly to relax in their speed, for want of wind. They still galloped on, but it was no longer with the swiftness of the wind; and their master became sensible of the folly of hoping to reach the town ere the catastrophe should arrive. He reined in his panting horses, therefore, and was just falling into a trot, as a violent report was heard directly in our front. At the next instant the ice rose, positively beneath our horses' hoofs, to the height of several feet, taking the form of the roof of a house. It was too late to retreat, and Guert shouting out "Jack"—"Moses," applied the whip, and the spirited animals actually went over the mound, leaping a crack three feet in width, and reaching the level ice beyond. All this was done, as it might be, in the twinkling of an eye. While the sleigh flew over this ridge, it was with difficulty I held the girls in their seats; though Guert stood nobly erect, like the pine that is too firmly rooted to yield to the tempest. No sooner was the danger passed, however, than he pulled up, and came to a dead halt.

We heard the bells of Herman Mordaunt's sleigh on the other side of the barrier, but could see nothing. The broken cakes, pressed upon by millions of tons' weight above, had risen fully ten feet, into an inclination that was nearly perpendicular; rendering crossing it next to impossible, even to one afoot. Then came Herman Mordaunt's voice, filled with paternal agony and human grief, to increase the awe of that dreadful moment!

"Shore!—shore!"—he shouted, or rather yelled—"In the name of a righteous Providence, to the shore, Guert!"

The bells passed off toward the western bank, and the rumbling of the runners accompanied their sound. That was a breathless moment to us four. We heard the rending and grinding of the ice, on all sides of us; saw the broken barriers behind and in front; heard the jingling of Herman Mordaunt's bells, as it became more and more distant, and finally ceased; and felt as if we were cut off from the rest of our species. I do not think either of us felt any apprehension of breaking through; for use had so accustomed us to the field of the river, while the more appalling grounds of alarm were so evident, that no one thought of such a source of danger. Nor was there much, in truth, to apprehend from that cause. The thaw had not lasted long enough materially to diminish either the thickness or the tenacity of the common river ice; though it was found unequal to resisting the enormous pressure that bore upon it from above. It is probable that a cake of an acre's size would have upheld, not only ourselves, but our sleigh and horses, and carried us, like a raft, down the stream; had there been such a cake free from stationary impediments. Even the girls now comprehended the danger, which was in a manner suspended over us—as the impending wreath of snow menaces the fall of the *avalanche*. But it was no moment for indecision or inaction.

Cut off, as we were, by an impassable barrier of ice, from the route taken by Herman Mordaunt, it was necessary to come to some resolution on our own course. We had the choice of endeavoring to pass to the western shore, on the upper side of the barrier, or of proceeding toward the nearest of several low islands which lay in the opposite direction. Guert determined on the last, walking his horses to the point of land, there being no apparent necessity for haste, while the animals greatly needed breath. As we went along, he explained to us that the fissure below cut us off from the only point where landing on the western shore could be practicable. At the same time, he put in practice a pious fraud, which had an excellent effect on the feelings and conduct of both the girls, throughout the remainder of the trying scenes of that fearful night; more especially on those of Anneke. He dwelt on the good fortune of Herman Mordaunt, in being on the right side of the barrier that separated the sleighs, in a way to induce those who did not penetrate his motive, to fancy the rest of the party were in a place of security, as the consequence of this accident. Thus did Anneke believe her father safe, and thus was she relieved from much agonizing doubt.

As soon as the sleigh came near the point of the island, Guert gave me the reins, and went ahead to examine whether it were possible to land. He was absent fifteen minutes; returning to us only after he had made a thorough search into the condition of the island, as well as that of the ice in its eastern channel. These were fifteen fearful minutes; the rending of the masses above, and the grinding of cake on cake, sounding like the roar of the ocean in a tempest. Notwithstanding all the awful accessories of this dreadful night, I could not but admire Guert's coolness of manner, and his admirable conduct. He was more than resolute; for he was cool, collected, and retained the use of all his faculties in perfection. As plausible as it might seem, to one less observant and clear-headed, to attempt escaping to the western shore, Guert had decided right in moving toward the island. The grinding of the ice, in another quarter, had apprised him that the water was forcing its way through, near the mainland; and that escape would be nearly hopeless on that side of the river. When he rejoined us, he called me to the heads of the horses, for a conference; first solemnly assuring our precious companions that there were no grounds for immediate apprehension. Mary Wallace anxiously asked him to repeat this to her, on the faith due from man to woman; and he did it; when I was permitted to join him without further opposition.

"Corny," said Guert, in a low tone, "Providence has punished me for my wicked wish of seeing Mary Wallace in the claws of lions; for all the savage beasts of the old world could hardly make our case more desperate than it now is. We must be cool, however, and preserve the girls, or die like men."

"Our fates are, and must be the same. Do you devote yourself to Mary, and leave Anneke to me. But why this language; surely our case is by no means so desperate?"

"It might not be so difficult for two active, vigorous young men to get ashore; but it would be different with females. The ice is in motion all around us; and the cakes are piling and grinding on each other in a most fearful manner. Were it light enough to see, we should do much better; but, as it is, I dare not trust Mary Wallace any distance from this island, at present. We may be compelled to pass the night here, and must make provision accordingly. You hear the ice grinding on the shore; a sign that everything is going down stream. God send that the waters break through ere long; though they may sweep all before them, when they do come. I fear me, Corny, that Herman Mordaunt and his party are lost!"

"Merciful Providence!—can it be as bad as that!—I rather hope they have reached the land."

"That is impossible, on the course they took. Even a man would be bewildered and swept away, in the torrent that is driving down under the west shore. It is that vent to the water which saves us. But, no more words. You now understand the extent of the danger, and will know what you are about. We must get our precious charge on the island, if possible, without further delay. Half an hour—nay, half a minute may bring down the torrent."

Guert took the direction of everything. Even while we had been talking, the ice moved materially; and we found ourselves fifty feet further from the island than we had been. By causing the horses to advance, this distance was soon recovered; but it was found impossible to lead or drive them over the broken cakes with which the shore of the island now began to be lined. After one or two spirited and determined efforts, Guert gave the matter up, and asked me to help the ladies from the sleigh.

Never did women behave better than did these delicate and lovely girls, on an occasion so awfully trying. Without remonstrances, tears, exclamations, or questions, both did as desired; and I cannot express the feeling of security I felt, when I had helped each over the broken and grinding border of white ice that separated us from the shore. The night was far from cold; but the ground was now frozen sufficiently to prevent any unpleasant consequences from walking on what would otherwise have been a slimy, muddy alluvion; for the island was so very low as often to be under water, when the river was particularly high. This, indeed, formed our danger, after we had reached it.

When I returned to Guert, I found him already drifted down some little distance; and this time we moved the sleigh so much above the point, as to be in less danger of getting out of sight of our precious wards. To my surprise, Guert was busy in stripping the harness from the horses, and Jack already stood only in his blinkers. Moses was soon reduced to the same state. I was wondering what was to be done next, when Guert drew each bridle from its animal, and gave a smart crack of his whip. The liberated horses started back with affright—snorted, reared, and turning away, they went down the river, free as air, and almost as swift; the incessant and loud snapping of their master's whip in no degree tending to diminish their speed. I asked the meaning of this.

"It would be cruel not to let the poor beasts make use of the strength and sagacity nature has given them to save their lives," answered Guert, straining his eyes after Moses, the horse that was behind, so long as his dark form could be distinguished, and leaning forward to listen to the blows of their hoofs, while the noises around us permitted them to be heard. "To us they would only be an incumbrance, since they could never be forced over the cracks and caked ice in harness; nor would it be at all safe to follow them, if they could. The sleigh is light, and we are strong enough to shove it to land, when there is an opportunity; or, it may be left on the island."

Nothing could have served more effectually to convince me of the manner in which Guert regarded our situation, than to see him turn loose beasts which I knew he so highly prized. I mentioned this; and he answered me with a melancholy seriousness, that made the impression so much the stronger—

"It is possible they may get ashore, for nature has given a horse a keen instinct. They can swim, too, where you and I would drown. At all events, they are not fettered with harness, but have every chance it is in my power to give them. Should they land, any farmer would put them in his stable, and I should soon hear where they were to be found; if, indeed, I am living in the morning to make the inquiry."

"What is next to be done, Guert?" I asked, understanding at once both his feelings and his manner of reasoning.

"We must now run the sleigh on the island; after which it will be time to look about us, and to examine if it be possible to get the ladies on the mainland."

Accordingly, Guert and I applied ourselves to the task, and had no great difficulty in dragging the sleigh over the cakes, grinding and in motion as they were. We pulled it as far as the tree beneath which Anneke and Mary stood; when the ladies got into it and took their seats, enveloped in the skins. The night was not cold for the season, and our companions were thickly clad, having tippets and muffs; still, the wolves' skins of Guert contributed to render them more comfortable. All apprehension of immediate danger now ceased for a short time; nor do I think either of the females fancied they could run any more risk, beyond that of exposure to the night air, so long as they remained on *terra firma*. Such was not the case, however, as a very simple explanation will render apparent to the reader.

All the islands in this part of the Hudson are low, being rich alluvial meadows bordered by trees and bushes; most of the first being willows, sycamores, or nuts.

The fertility of the soil had given to these trees rapid growths, and they were generally of some stature; though not one among them had that great size which ought to mark the body and branches of a venerable tenant of the forest. This fact, of itself, proved that no one tree of them all was very old; a circumstance that was certainly owing to the ravages of the annual freshets. I say annual; for though the freshet which now encompassed us was far more serious than usual, each year brought something of the sort; and the islands were constantly increasing or diminishing under their action. To prevent the last, a thicket of trees was left at the head of each island, to form a sort of barricade against the inroads of the ice in spring. So low was the face of the land, or meadow, however, that a rise of a very few feet in the river would be certain to bring it entirely under water. All this will be made more apparent by our own proceedings, after we had placed the ladies in the sleigh; and more especially by the passing remarks of Guert while employed in his subsequent efforts.

No sooner did Guert Ten Eyck believe the ladies to be temporarily safe, than he proposed to me that we should take a closer look at the state of the river, in order to ascertain the most feasible means of getting on the mainland. This was said aloud, and in a cheerful way, as if he no longer felt any apprehension, and evidently to me, to encourage our companions. Anneke desired us to go, declaring that now she knew herself to be on dry land all her own fears had vanished. We went accordingly, taking our first direction toward the head of the island.

A very few minutes sufficed to reach the limits of our narrow domain; and as we approached them Guert pointed out to me the mound of ice that was piling up behind it, as a most fearful symptom.

"There is our danger," he said, with emphasis, "and we must not trust to these trees. This freshet goes beyond any I ever saw on the river; and not a spring passes that we have not more or less of them. Do you not see, Corny, what saves us now?"

We are on an island, and cannot be in much danger from the river while we stay here."

"Not so, my dear friend, not at all so. But come with me, and look for yourself."

I followed Guert, and did look for myself. We sprang upon the cakes of ice, which were piled quite thirty feet in height, on the head of the island, extending right and left, as far as our eyes could see, by that misty light. It was by no means difficult moving about on this massive pile, the movement in the cakes being slow, and frequently interrupted; but there was no concealing the true character of the danger. Had not the island and the adjacent main interposed their obstacles, the ice would have continued to move bodily down the stream, cake shoving over cake until the whole found vent in the wider space below, and floated off toward the ocean. Not only was our island there, however, but other islands lay near us, straitening the different channels or passages in such a way as to compel the formation of an icy dam; and on the strength of this dam rested all our security. Were it to be ruptured anywhere near us, we should inevitably be swept off in a body. Guert thought, however, as has been said already, that the waters had found narrow issues under the mainland, both east and west of us; and should this prove to be true, there was a hope that the great calamity might be averted. In other words, if these floodgates sufficed, we might escape; otherwise the catastrophe was certain.

"I cannot excuse it to myself to remain here, without endeavoring to see what is the state of things nearer to the shore," said Guert, after we had viewed the fast accumulating mass of broken ice above us, as well as the light permitted, and we had talked over together the chances of safety, and the character of the danger. "Do you return to the ladies, Corny, and endeavor to keep up their spirits, while I cross this channel on our right, to the next island, and see what offers in that direction."

"I do not like the idea of your running all the risk alone; besides, something may occur to require the strength of two, instead of that of one, to overcome it."

"You can go with me as far as the next island, if you will, where we shall be able to ascertain at once whether it be ice or water that separates us from the eastern shore. If the first, you can return as fast as possible for the ladies, while I look for a place to cross. I do not like the appearance of this dam, to be honest with you; and have great fears for those who are now in the sleigh."

We were in the very act of moving away, when a loud cracking noise, that arose within a few yards, alarmed us both; and running to the spot whence it proceeded, we saw that a large willow had snapped in two, like a pipestem, and that the whole barrier of ice was marching, slowly but grandly, over the stump, crushing the fallen trunk and branches beneath its weight, as the slow-moving wheel of the loaded cart crushes the twig. Guert grasped my arm, and his fingers nearly entered the flesh, under his iron pressure.

"We must quit this spot," he said firmly, "and at once. Let us go back to the sleigh."

I did not know Guert's intentions, but I saw it was time to act with decision. We moved swiftly down to the spot where we had left the sleigh; and the reader will judge of our horror, when we found it gone! The whole of the low point of the island where we had left it, was already covered with cakes of ice that were in motion, and which had doubtless swept off the sleigh during the few minutes that we had been absent! Looking around us, however, we saw an object on the river, a little distance below, that I fancied was the sleigh, and was about to rush after it, when a voice, filled with alarm, took us in another direction. Mary Wallace came out from behind a tree, to which she had fled for safety, and seizing Guert's arm, implored him not to quit her again.

"Whither has Anneke gone?" I demanded in an agony I cannot describe—"I see nothing of Anneke!"

"She would not quit the sleigh," answered Mary Wallace, almost panting for breath—"I implored—entreated her to follow me—said you must soon return; but she refused to quit the sleigh. Anneke is in the sleigh, if that can now be found."

I heard no more; but springing on the still moving cakes of ice, went leaping from cake to cake, until my sight showed me that, sure enough, the sleigh was on the bed of the river, over which it was now in slow motion; forced downward before the new coating of ice that was fast covering the original surface. At first I could see no one in the sleigh; but, on reaching it, I found Anneke buried in the skins. She was on her knees; the precious creature was asking succor from God!

I had a wild but sweet consolation in thus finding myself, as it might be, cut off from all the rest of my kind, in the midst of that scene of gloom and desolation, alone with Anneke Mordaunt. The moment I could make her conscious of my presence, she inquired after Mary Wallace, and was much relieved on learning that she was with Guert, and would not be left by him, for a single instant, again that night. Indeed, I saw their figures dimly, as they moved swiftly across the channel that divided the two islands, and disappeared in that direction, among the bushes that lined the place to which they had gone.

"Let us follow," I said eagerly. "The crossing is yet easy, and we, too, may escape to the shore."

"Go you!" said Anneke, over whom a momentary physical torpor appeared to have passed. "Go you, Corny," she said; "a man may easily save himself; and you are an only child, the sole hope of your parents."

"Dearest, beloved Anneke! why this indifference, this apathy on your own behalf? Are you not an only child, the sole hope of a widowed father?—do you forget him?"

"No, no, no!" exclaimed the dear girl, hurriedly. "Help me out of the sleigh, Corny; there, I will go with you anywhere—anyhow—to the end of the world, to save my father from such anguish!"

From that moment the temporary imbecility of Anneke vanished, and I found her for the remainder of the time we remained in jeopardy, quick to apprehend, and ready to second all my efforts. It was this passing submission to an imaginary doom, on the one hand, and the headlong effect of sudden fright on the other, which had separated the two girls, and which had been the means of dividing the whole party as described.

I scarcely know how to describe what followed. So intense was my apprehension on behalf of Anneke, that I can safely say, I did not think of my own fate in the slightest degree as disconnected from hers. The self-devoted reliance with which the dear girl seemed to place all her dependence on me, would of itself have produced this effect, had she not possessed my whole heart, as I was now so fully aware. Moments like those make one alive to all the affections, and strip off every covering that habit, or the dissembling of our manners, is so apt to throw over the feelings. I believe I both spoke and acted toward Anneke, as one would cling to, or address the being dearest to him in the world, for the next few minutes; but I can suppose the reader will naturally prefer learning what we did, under such circumstances, rather than what we said, or how we felt.

I repeat, it is not easy for me to describe what followed. I know we first rather ran than walked, across the channel on which I had last seen the dim forms of Guert and Mary, and even crossed the island to its eastern side, in the hope of being able to reach the shore in that quarter. The attempt was useless, for we found the water running down over the ice like a race-way. Nothing could be seen of our late companions; and my loud and repeated calls to them were unanswered.

"Our case is hopeless, Cornelius," said Anneke; speaking with a forced calmness, when she found retreat impossible in that direction. "Let us return to the sleigh, and submit to the will of God!"

"Beloved Anneke!—Think of your father, and summon your whole strength. The bed of the river is yet firm; we will cross it, and try the opposite shore."

Cross it we did, my delicate companion being as much sustained by my supporting arm as by her own resolution; but we found the same obstacle to retreat interposing there also. The island above had turned the waters aside, until they found an outlet under each bank—shooting along their willowy shores, with the velocity of arrows. By this time, owing to our hurried movement, I found Anneke so far exhausted, that it was absolutely necessary to pause a minute to take breath. This pause was also necessary, in order to look about us, and to decide understandingly as to the course it was necessary now to pursue. This pause, brief as it was, moreover contributed largely to the apparent horrors of our situation.

The grating or grinding of the ice above us, cake upon cake, now sounded like the rushing of heavy winds, or the incessant roaring of a surf upon the sea-shore. The piles were becoming visible, by their height and their proximity, as the ragged barriers set slowly but steadily down upon us; and the whole river seemed to me to be in motion downward. At this awful instant, when I began to think it was the will of Providence that Anneke and I were to perish together, a strange sound interrupted the fearful natural accessories of that frightful scene. I certainly heard the bells of a sleigh; at first they seemed distant and broken—then nearer and incessant, attended by the rumbling of runners on the ice. I took off my cap and pressed my head, for I feared my brain was unsettled. There it came, however, more and more distinctly, until the trampling of horses' hoofs mingled in the noise.

"Can there be others as unhappy as ourselves!" exclaimed Anneke, forgetting her own fears in generous sympathy. "See, Littlepage!—see, *dear* Cornelius— yonder surely comes another sleigh!"

Come it did, like the tempest, or the whirlwinds; passing within fifty feet of us. I knew it at a glance. It was the sleigh of Herman Mordaunt, empty; with the horses, maddened by terror, running wherever their fears impelled. As the sleigh passed, it was thrown on one side; then it was once more whirled up again; and it went out of sight, with the rumbling sound of the runners mingling with the jingling of bells and the stamp of hoofs.

At this instant a loud, distant cry from a human voice was certainly heard. It seemed to me, as if some one called my name; and Anneke said, she so understood it, too. The call, if call it was, came from the south, and from under the western shore. At the next moment, awful reports proceeded from the barrier above; and, passing an arm around the slender waist of my lovely companion, to support her, I began a rapid movement in the direction of that call. While attempting to reach the western shore, I had observed a high mound of broken ice, that was floating down; or rather, was pressed down on the smooth surface of the frozen river, in advance of the smaller cakes that came by in the current. It was increasing in size by accession from these floating cakes, and threatened to form a new dam at some narrow pass below, as soon as of sufficient size. It occurred to me we should be temporarily safe could we reach that mound, for it rose so high as to be above danger from the water. Thither, then, I ran, almost carrying Anneke on my arm; our speed increased by the terrific sounds from the dam above us.

We reached the mound, and found the cakes so piled, as to be able to ascend them; though not without an effort. After getting up a layer or two, the broken mass became so irregular and ragged, as to render it necessary for me to mount first, and then to drag Anneke up after me. This I did, until exhausted; and we both seated ourselves on the edge of a cake, in order to recover our breath. While there, it struck me, that new sounds arose from the river; and, bending forward to examine, I saw that the water had forced its way through the dam above and was coming down upon us in a torrent.

CHAPTER XVII.

> "My heart leaps up when I behold
>   A rainbow in the sky:
> So was it when my life began;
> So is it now I am a man;
> So be it when I shall grow old,
>   Or let me die!
>
> "The child is father of the man;
>   And I could wish my days to be
>   Bound each to each by natural piety."
>   WORDSWORTH.

Five minutes longer on the ice of the main channel, and we should have been swept away. Even as we still sat looking at the frightful force of the swift current, as well as the dim light of that clouded night would permit, I saw Guert Ten Eyck's sleigh whirl past us; and, only a minute later, Herman Mordaunt's followed; the poor exhasted beasts struggling in the harness for freedom, that they might swim for their lives. Anneke heard the snorting of those wretched horses; but her unpractised eyes did not detect them, immersed, as they were, in the current; nor had she recognized the sleigh that whirled past us, as her father's. A little later, a fearful shriek came from one of the fettered beasts; such a heart-piercing cry as it is known the horse often gives. I said nothing on the subject, knowing that love for her father was one of the great incentives which had aroused my companion to exertion; and being unwilling to excite fears that were now latent.

Two or three minutes of rest were all that circumstances permitted. I could see that everything visible on the river was in motion downward; the piles of ice on which we were placed, as well as the cakes that glanced by us in their quicker descent. Our own motion was slow, on account of the mass which doubtless pressed on the shoals of the west side of the river, as well as on account of the friction against the lateral fields of ice, and occasionally against the shore. Still we were in motion; and I felt the necessity, on every account, of getting as soon as possible on the western verge of our floating island, in order to profit by any favorable occurrence that might offer.

Dear Anneke! How admirably did she behave that fearful night! From the moment she regained her entire consciousness, after I found her praying in the bottom of the sleigh, down to that instant, she had been as little of an incumbrance to my own efforts, as was at all possible. Reasonable, resolute, compliant, and totally without any ill-timed exhibition of womanly apprehension, she had done all she was desired to do unhesitatingly, and with intelligence. In ascending that pile of ice, by no means an easy task under any circumstances, we had acted in perfect concert, every effort of mine being aided by one of her own, directed by my advice and greater experience.

"God has not deserted us, dearest Anneke," I said, now that my companion's strength appeared to have returned, "and we may yet hope to escape. I can anticipate the joy we shall bring to your father's heart, when he again takes you to his arms, safe and uninjured."

"Dear, *dear* father! What agony he must now be suffering on my account. Come, Corny, let us go to him at once, if it be possible."

As this was said, the precious girl arose, and adjusted her tippet in a way that should cause her no incumbrance; like one ready to set about the execution of a serious task with all her energies. The muff had been dropped on the river; for neither of us had any sensibility to cold. The night, however, was quite mild, for the season; and we probably should not have suffered, had our exertions been less violent. Anneke declared herself ready to proceed, and I commenced the difficult and delicate task of aiding her across an island composed of icy fragments, in order to reach its western margin. We were quite thirty feet in the air; and a fall into any of the numerous caverns among which we had to proceed, might have been fatal, certainly would have crippled the sufferer. Then the surface of the ice was so smooth as to render walking on it an exceedingly delicate operation; more especially as the cakes lay at all manner of inclinations to the plane of the horizon. Fortunately, I wore buckskin moccasins over my boots; and their rough leather aided me greatly in maintaining my footing. Anneke, too, had socks of cloth; without which I do not think she could have possibly moved. By these aids, however, and by proceeding with the utmost caution, we had actually succeeded in attaining our object, when the floating mass shot into an eddy, and turning slowly around under this new influence, placed us on the outer side of the island again! Not a murmur escaped Anneke, at this disappointment; but, with a sweetness of temper that spoke volumes in favor of her natural disposition, and a regisnation that told her training, she professed a readiness to renew her efforts. To this I would not consent, however; for I saw that the eddy was still whirling us about; and I thought it best to escape from its influence altogether, before we threw away our strength fruitlessly. Instead of recrossing the pile, therefore, I told my fair companion that we would descend to a cake that lay level on the water, and which projected from the mass to such a distance as to be close to the shore, should we again get near it. This descent was made, after some trouble, though I was compelled to receive Anneke entirely into my arms, in order to effect it. Effect it I did; placing the sweet girl safely at my side, on the outermost and lowest of all the cakes in our confused pile.

In some respects this change was for the better, while it did not improve our situation in others. It placed both Anneke and myself behind a shelter, as respected the wind; which, though neither very strong nor very cold, had enough of March about it to render the change acceptable. It took my companion, too, from a position where motion was difficult, and often dangerous; leaving her on a level, even spot, where she could walk with ease and security, and keep the blood in motion by exercise. Then it put us both in the best possible situation to profit by any contact with that shore, along and near which our island was now slowly moving.

There could not longer be any doubt of the state of the river in general. It had broken up; spring had come like a thief in the night; and the ice below having given way, while the mass above had acquired too much power to be resisted, everything was set in motion; and like the death of the strong man, the disruption of fields in themselves so thick and adhesive, had produced an agony surpassing the usual struggle of the seasons. Nevertheless, the downward motion had begun in earnest, and the centre of the river was running like a sluice, carrying away in its current those masses which had just before formed so menacing an obstacle above.

Luckily, our own pile was a little aside from the great downward rush. I have since thought that it touched the bottom, which caused it to turn, as well as retarded its movement. Be this as it might, we still remained in a little bay slowly turning in a circle; and glad was I to see our low cake coming round again, in sight of the western shore. The moment now demanded decision; and I prepared Anneke to meet it. A large, low, level cake had driven up on the shore, and extended out so far as to promise that our own cake would touch it, in its evolutions. I knew that the ice in general had not broken in consequence of any weakness of its own, but purely under the weight of the enormous pressure from above, and the mighty force of the current; and that we ran little, or no risk, in trusting our persons on the uttermost limits of any considerable fragment. A station was taken, accordingly, near a projection of the cake we were on; when we waited for the expected contact. At such moments the slightest disappointment carries with it the force of the greatest circumstances. Several times did it appear to us that our island was on the point of touching the fastened cake, and as often did it incline aside; at no time coming nearer than within six or eight feet. This distance it would have been easy enough for *me* to leap across, but to Anneke it was a barrier as impassable as the illimitable void. The sweet girl saw this; and she acted like herself under the circumstances. She took my hand, pressed it, and said earnestly, and with patient sweetness:

"You see how it is, Corny; I am not permitted to escape; but you can easily reach the shore. Go, then, and leave me in the hands of Providence. Go; I never can forget what you have already done; but it is useless to perish together!"

I have never doubted that Anneke was perfectly sincere in her wish that I should, at least, save my own life. The feeling with which she spoke; the despair that was coming over her; and the movement of our island, which at that moment gave signs of shooting away from the shore altogether, roused me to a sudden, and certainly, to a very bold attempt. I tremble, even at this distance of time, as I write the particulars. A small cake of ice was floating in between us and that which lay firmly fastened to the shore. Its size was such as to allow it to pass between the two; though not without coming nearly, if not absolutely, in contact with one, if not with both. I observed all this; and saying one word of encouragement to Anneke, I passed an arm around her waist, waited the proper moment, and sprang forward. It was necessary to make a short leap, with my precious burden on my arm, in order to gain this floating bridge; but it was done, and successfully. Scarcely permitting Anneke's foot to touch this frail support, which was already sinking under our joint weight, I crossed it at two or three steps, and threw all my power into a last and desperate effort. I succeeded here, also; and fell upon the firmer cake with a heart filled with gratitude to God. The touch told me that we were safe; and in the next instant we reached the solid ground. Under such circumstances, one usually looks back to examine the danger he has just gone through. I did so; and saw that the floating cake of ice had already passed down, and was out of reach; while the mass that had been the means of saving us, was slowly following, under some new impulse received from the furious currents of the river. But we were saved; and most devoutly did I thank my God, who had mercifully aided our escape from perils so imminent.

I was compelled to wait for Anneke, who fell upon her knees, and remained there quite a minute, before I could aid her in ascending the steep acclivity which formed the western bank of the Hudson, at this particular point. We reached the top, however, after a little delay, and pausing once or twice to take breath: when we first became really sensible of the true character of the scene from which we had been delivered. Dim as was the light, there was enough to enable us to overlook a considerable reach of the river, from that elevated stand. The Hudson resembled chaos rushing headlong between the banks. As for the cakes of ice—some darting past singly, and others piled as high as houses—of course the stream was filled with such; but a large, dark object was seen coming through that very channel over which Anneke and I had stood less than an hour before, sailing down the current with fearful rapidity. It was a house; of no great size, it is true, but large enough to present a singular object on the river. A bridge, of some size, followed; and a sloop, that had been borne away from the wharves of Albany, soon appeared in the strange assemblage, that was thus suddenly collected on this great artery of the colony.

But the hour was late; Anneke was yet to care for; it was necessary to seek a shelter. Still supporting my lovely companion, who now began to express her uneasiness on account of her father and her other friends, I held the way inland; knowing that there was a high road parallel to the river, and at no great distance from it. We reached the highway in the course of ten minutes, and turned our faces northward, as the direction which led toward Albany. We had not advanced far before I heard the voices of men, who were coming toward us; and glad was I to recognize that of Dirck Follock among the number. I called aloud, and was answered by a shout of exultation, which, as I afterward discovered, spontaneously broke out of his mouth, when he recognized the form of Anneke. Dirck was powerfully agitated when we joined him; I had never, previously, seen anything like such a burst of feeling from him; and it was some time before I could address him.

"Of course your whole party is safe?" I asked, a little doubtingly; for I had actually given up all who had been in Herman Mordaunt's sleigh for lost.

"Yes, thank God! all but the sleigh and horses. But where are Guert Ten Eyck and Miss Wallace?"

"Gone ashore on the other side of the river; we parted, and they took that direction, while we came hither." I said this to quiet Anneke's fears; but I had misgivings about their having got off the river at all. "But let me know the manner of your own escape."

Dirck then gave us a history of what had passed; the whole party turning back to accompany us as soon as I told them that their errand—a search for the horses—was useless. The substance of what we heard was as follows: In the first effort to reach the western shore, Herman Mordaunt had been met by the very obstacle which Guert had foreseen, and he turned south, hoping to find some spot at which to land, by going farther from the dam that had formed above. After repeated efforts, and having nearly lost his sleigh and the whole party, a point was reached at which Herman Mordaunt determined to get his female companion on shore, at every hazard. This was to be done only by crossing floating cakes of ice, in a current that was already running at the rate of four or five miles in the hour. Dirck was left in charge of the horses while the experiment was made; but seeing the adventurers in great danger, he flew to their assistance—when the whole party were immersed, though not in deep water. Left to themselves, and alarmed with the floundering in the river and the grinding of the cakes, Herman Mordaunt's bays went off in the confusion. Mrs. Bogart was assisted to the land, and was helped to reach the nearest dwelling—a comfortable farm-house, about a quarter of a mile beyond the point where we had met the party. There Mrs. Bogart had been placed in a warm bed, and the gentlemen were supplied with such dry clothes as the rustic wardrobe of these simple people could furnish. The change made, Dirck was on his way to ascertain what had become of the sleigh and horses, as has been mentioned.

On inquiry, I found that the spot where Anneke and myself had landed, was quite three miles below the island on which Guert and I had drawn the sleigh. Nearly the whole of this distance had we floated with the pile of broken ice, in the short time we were on it; a proof of the furious rate at which the current was setting downward. No one had heard anything of Guert and Mary, but I encouraged my companion to believe that they were necessarily safe on the other shore. I certainly deemed this to be very questionable, but there was no use in anticipating evil.

On reaching the farm-house, Herman Mordaunt's delight and gratitude may more easily be imagined than described. He folded Anneke to his heart, and she wept like an infant on his bosom. Nor was I forgotten in this touching scene, but came in for a full share of notice.

"I want no details, noble young man"—I am professing to write the truth, and must be excused for relating such things as these, but—"I want no details, noble young man," said Herman Mordaunt, squeezing my hand, "to feel certain that, under God, I owe my child's life, for the second time, to you. I wish to heaven!—but, no matter—it is now too late—some other way may and must offer. I scarce know what I say, Littlepage; but what I mean is, to express faintly, some small portion of the gratitude I feel, and to let you know how sensibly and deeply your services are felt and appreciated."

The reader may think it odd, that this incoherent, but pregnant speech, made little impression on me at the time, beyond the grateful conviction of having fully rendered the greatest of all services to Anneke and her father; though I had better occasion to remember it afterward.

It is unnecessary to dwell more particularly on the occurrences at the farmhouse. The worthy people did what they could to make us comfortable, and we were all warm in bed in the course of the next half hour.

On the following morning a wagon was harnessed, and we left these simple countrymen and women—who refused everything like compensation, as a matter of course—and proceeded homeward. I have heard it said that we Americans are mercenary; it may be so, but not a man, probably, exists in the colonies, who would accept money for such assistance. We were two hours in reaching Albany, on wheels; and entered the place about ten, in a very different style from that in which we had quitted it the day before. As we drove along, the highway frequently led us to points that commanded views of the river, and we had so many opportunities of noting the effects of the freshet. Of ice, very little remained. Here and there a cake or a pile was seen still adhering to the shore, and occasionally fragments floated downward; but, as a rule, the torrent had swept all before it. I particularly took notice of the island on which we had sought refuge. It was entirely under water, but its outlines were to be traced by the bushes which lined its low banks. Most of the trees on its upper end were cut down, and all that grew on it would unquestionably have gone, had not the dam given way as early as it did. A great number of trees had been broken down on all the islands; and large tops and heavy trunks were still floating in the current, that were lately tenants of the forest, and had been violently torn from their places.

We found all the lower part of Albany, too, under water. Boats were actually moving through the streets, a considerable portion of its inhabitants having no other means of communicating with their neighbors. A sloop of some size lay up on one of the lowest spots; and, as the water was already subsiding, it was said she would remain there until removed by the shipwrights. Nobody was drowned in the place; for it is not usual for the people of these colonies to remain in their beds, at such times, to await the appearance of the enemy in at their windows. We often read of such accidents destroying hundreds in the Old World; but in the New, human life is of too much account to be unnecessarily thrown away, and so we make some efforts to preserve it.

As we drove into the street in which Herman Mordaunt lived, we heard a shout, and turning our heads, we saw Guert Ten Eyck waving his cap to us, with joy delineated in every feature of his handsome face. At the next moment he was at our side.

"Herman Mordaunt," he cried, shaking that gentleman most cordially by the hand, "I look upon you as one raised from the dead; you and my excellent neighbor, Mrs. Bogart, and Mr. Follock, here! How you got off the river is a mystery to me, for I well know that the water commonly breaks through first under the west shore. Corny and Miss Anneke—God bless you both! Mary Wallace is in terror lest ill news come from some of you; but I will run ahead and let her know the glad tidings. It is but five minutes since I left her, starting at every sound, lest it prove the foot of some ill-omened messenger."

Guert stopped to say no more. In a minute he was inside of Herman Mordaunt's house; in another Anneke and Mary Wallace were locked in each other's arms. After exchanging salutes, Mrs. Bogart was conveyed to her own residence and there was a termination to that memorable expedition.

Guert had less to communicate, in the way of dangers and marvels, than I had anticipated. It seemed, that when he and Miss Wallace reached the inner margin of the last island, a large cake of ice had entered the strait, and got jammed; or rather, that it went through, forced by the tremendous pressure above; though not without losing large masses, as it came in contact with the shores, and grinding much of its material into powder, by the attrition. Guert's presence of mind and decision did him excellent service here. Without delaying an instant, the moment it was in his power, he led Mary on that cake, and crossed the narrow branch of the river, which alone separated him from the mainland, on it, dry-shod. The water was beginning to find its way over this cake, as it usually did on all those that lay low, and which even stopped in their progress; but this did not offer any serious obstacles to persons who were so prompt. Safe themselves, our friends remained to see if we could not be induced to join them; and the call we heard, was from Guert, who had actually recrossed to the island, in the hope of meeting us, and directing us to a place of safety. Guert never said anything to me on the subject, himself; but I subsequently gathered from Mary Wallace's accounts, that the young man did not rejoin her without a good deal of hazard and difficulty, and after a long and fruitless search for his companions. Finding it useless to remain any longer on the river-side, Guert and his companion held their way toward Albany. About midnight they reached the ferry opposite to the town; having walked quite six miles, filled with uneasiness on account of those who had been left behind. Guert was a man of decision, and he wisely determined it would be better to proceed, than to attempt waking up the inmates of any of the houses he passed. The river was now substantially free from ice, though running with great velocity. But Guert was an expert oarsman; and finding a skiff, he persuaded Mary Wallace to enter it; actually succeeding, by means of the eddies, in landing her within ten feet of the very spot where the hand-sled had deposited himself and myself, only a few days before. From this point, there was no difficulty in walking home; and Miss Wallace actually slept in her own bed, that eventful night, if indeed she *could* sleep.

Such was the termination of this adventure; one that I have rightly termed memorable. In the end, Jack and Moses came in safe and sound; having probably swum ashore. They were found in the public road, only a short distance from the town, and were brought in to their master the same day. Every one who took any interest in horses—and what Dutchman does not?—knew Jack and Moses, and there was no difficulty in ascertaining to whom they belonged. What is singular, however, both sleighs were recovered, though at long intervals of time, and under very different circumstances. That of Guert, wolves' skins and all, actually went down the whole length of the river on the ice; passing out to sea through the

Narrows. It must have gone by New York in the night, or doubtless it would have been picked up; while the difficulty of reaching it, was its protector on the descent, above the town. Once outside of the Narrows, it was thrown by the tide and winds upon the shore of Staten Island; where it was hauled to land, housed, and being properly advertised in our New York paper, Guert actually got tiding of it in time to receive it, skins and all, by one of the first sloops that ascended the Hudson that year; which was within a fortnight after the river had opened. The year 1758 was one of great activity, on account of the movements of the army, and no time was then unnecessarily lost.

The history of Herman Mordaunt's sleigh was very different. The poor bays must have drowned soon after we saw them floating past us in the torrent. Of course, life had no sooner left them, than they sank to the bottom of the river, carrying with them the sleigh to which they were still attached. In a few days the animals rose to the surface, as is usual with all swollen bodies, bringing up the sleigh again. In this condition, the wreck was overtaken by a downward-bound sloop, the men of which saved the sleigh, harness, skins, foot-stoves, and such other articles as would not float away.

Our adventure made a good deal of noise in the circle of Albany; and I have reason to think that my own conduct was approved by those who heard it. Bulstrode paid me an especial visit of thanks, the very day of my return, when the following conversation took place between us:

"You seem fated, my dear Corny," the major observed, after he had paid the usual compliments, "to be always serving me in the most material way, and I scarcely know how to express all I feel on the occasion. First, the lion, and now this affair of the river—but that Guert will drown or make away with the whole family, before the summer is over, unless Mr. Mordaunt puts a stop to his interference."

"This accident was one that might have overtaken the oldest and most prudent man in Albany. The river seemed as solid as the street when we went on it; and another hour, even as it was, would have brought us all home in entire safety."

"Ay, but that hour came near bringing death and desolation into the most charming family in the colony; and you have been the means of averting the heaviest part of the blow. I wish to heaven, Littlepage, that you would consent to come into the army! Join us as a volunteer, the moment we move, and I will write to Sir Harry to obtain a pair of colors for you. As soon as he hears that we are indebted to your coolness and courage for the life of Miss Mordaunt, he will move heaven and earth to manifest his gratitude. The instant this good parent made up his mind to accept Miss Mordaunt as a daughter, he began to consider her as a child of his own."

"And Anneke—Miss Mordaunt herself, Mr. Bulstrode—does she regard Sir Harry as a father?"

"Why, that must be coming by slow degrees, as a matter of course, you know. Women are slower than us men to admit such totally novel impressions; and I dare say Anneke fancies one father enough for her, just at this moment; though she sends very pleasant messages to Sir Harry, I can assure you, when in the humor! But what makes you so grave, my good Corny?"

"Mr. Bulstrode, I conceive it no more than fair, to be as honest as yourself in this matter. You have told me that you are a suitor for Miss Mordaunt's hand; I will now own to you that I am your rival."

My companion heard this declaration with a quiet smile and the most perfect good-nature.

"So you actually wish to become the husband of Anneke Mordaunt, yourself, my dear Corny, do you?" he said, so coolly, that I was at a loss to know of what sort of materials the man could be made.

"I do, Major Bulstrode—it is the first and last wish of my heart."

"Since you seem disposed to reciprocate my confidence you will not take offence if I ask you a question or two?"

"Certainly not, sir; your own frankness shall be a rule for my government."

"Have you ever let Miss Mordaunt know that such are your wishes?"

"I have, sir; and that in the plainest terms—such as cannot well be misunderstood."

"What! last night? On that infernal ice? While she thought her life was in your hands!"

"Nothing was said on the subject last night, for we had other thoughts to occupy our minds."

"It would have been a most ungenerous thing to take advantage of a lady's fears—"

"Major Bulstrode!—I cannot submit—"

"Hush, my dear Corny," interrupted the other, holding out a hand in a most quiet and friendly manner; "there must be no misunderstanding between you and me. Men are never greater simpletons than when they let the secret consciousness of their love of life push them into swaggering about their honor; when their honor has, in fact, nothing to do with the matter in hand. I shall not quarrel with you; and must beg you, in advance, to receive my apologies for any little indecorum into which I may be betrayed by surprise; as for great pieces of indecorum, I shall endeavor to avoid them."

"Enough has been said, Mr. Bulstrode; I am no wrangler, to quarrel with a shadow; and, I trust, not in the least that most contemptible of all human beings, a social bully, to be on all occasions menacing the sword or the pistol. Such men usually do nothing when matters come to a crisis. Even when they fight, they fight bunglingly and innocently."

"You are right, Littlepage, and I honor your sentiments. I have remarked that the most expert swordsman with his tongue, and the deadest shot at a shingle, are commonly as innocent as lambs of the shedding of blood on the ground. They can sometimes screw themselves up to meet an adversary, but it exceeds their powers to use their weapons properly, when it comes to serious work. The swaggerer is ever a coward at heart, however well he may wear a mask for a time. But enough of this. We understand each other, and are to remain friends under all circumstances. May I question further?"

"Ask what you please, Bulstrode—I shall answer, or not, at my own discretion."

"Then permit me to inquire, if Major Littlepage has authorized you to offer proper settlements?"

"I am authorized to offer nothing. Nor is it usual for the husband to make settlements on his wife, in these colonies, further than what the law does for her, in favor of her own. The father sometimes has a care for the third generation. I should expect Herman Mordaunt to settle his estate on his daughter, and her rightful heirs, let her marry whom she may."

"Ay, that is a very American notion; and one on which Herman Mordaunt, who remembers his extraction, will be little likely to act. Well, Corny, we are rivals, as it would seem; but that is no reason we should not remain friends. We understand each other—though, perhaps, I ought to tell you all."

"I should be glad to know all, Mr. Bulstrode; and can meet any fate, I hope like a man. Whatever it may cost me, if Anneke prefer another, her happiness will be dearer to me than my own."

"Yes, my dear fellow, we all say and think so at one-and-twenty; which is about your age, I believe. At two-and-twenty, we begin to see that our own happiness has an equal claim on us; and at three-and-twenty we even give it the preference. However, I will be just if I am selfish. I have no reason to believe Anne Mordaunt does prefer me; though my perhaps is not altogether without a meaning, either."

"In which case I may possibly be permitted to know to what it refers?"

"It refers to the father; and I can tell you, my fine fellow, that fathers are of some account in the arrangement of marriages between parties of any standing. Had not Sir Harry authorized my own proposals, where should I have been? Not a farthing of settlement could I have offered, while he remained Sir Harry; notwithstanding I had the prodigious advantage of the entail. I can tell you what it is, Corny, the existing power is always an important power, since we all think more of the present time than of the future. That is the reason so few of us get to heaven. As for Herman Mordaunt, I deem it no more than fair to tell you he is on my side, heart and hand. He likes my offers of settlement; he likes my family; he likes my rank, civil and military; and I am not altogether without the hope that he likes me."

I made no direct answer, and the conversation soon changed. Bulstrode's declaration, however, caused me to remember both the speech and manner of Herman Mordaunt, when he thanked me for saving his daughter's life. I now began to reflect on it; and reflected on it much during the next few months. In the end the reader will learn the effect it had on my happiness.

From *The Last of the Mohicans*

The river was confined between high and cragged rocks, one of which impended above the spot where the canoe rested. As these, again, were surmounted by tall trees, which appeared to totter on the brows of the precipice, it gave the stream the appearance of running through a deep and narrow dell. All beneath the fantastic limbs and ragged tree-tops, which were, here and there, dimly painted against the starry zenith, lay alike in shadowed obscurity. Behind them, the curvature of the banks soon bounded the view, by the same dark and wooded outline; but in front, and apparently at no great distance, the water seemed piled against the heavens, whence it tumbled into caverns, out of which issued those sullen sounds that had loaded the evening atmosphere. It seemed, in truth, to be a spot devoted to seclusion, and the sisters imbibed a soothing impression of security, as they gazed upon its romantic, though not unappalling beauties. A general movement among their conductors, however, soon recalled them from a contemplation of the wild charms that night had assisted to lend the place, to a painful sense of their real peril.

The horses had been secured to some scattered shrubs that grew in the fissures of the rocks, where, standing in the water, they were left to pass the night. The scout directed Heyward and his disconsolate fellow-travellers to seat themselves in the forward end of the canoe, and took possession of the other himself, as erect and steady as if he floated in a vessel of much firmer materials. The Indians warily retraced their steps towards the place they had left, when the scout, placing his pole against a rock, by a powerful shove, sent his frail bark directly into the centre of the turbulent stream. For many minutes the struggle between the light bubble in which they floated, and the swift current, was severe and doubtful. Forbidden to stir even a hand, and almost afraid to breathe, lest they should expose the frail fabric to the fury of the stream, the passengers watched the glancing waters in feverish suspense. Twenty times they thought the whirling eddies were sweeping them to destruction, when the master-hand of their pilot would bring the bows of the canoe to stem the rapid. A long, a vigorous, and, as it appeared to the females, a desperate effort, closed the struggle. Just as Alice veiled her eyes in horror, under the impression that they were about to be swept within the vortex at the foot of the cataract, the canoe floated, stationary, at the side of a flat rock, that lay on a level with the water.

"Where are we? and what is next to be done?" demanded Heyward, perceiving that the exertions of the scout had ceased.

"You are at the foot of Glenn's," returned the other, speaking aloud, without fear of consequences, within the roar of the cataract; "and the next thing is to make a steady landing, lest the canoe upset, and you should go down again the hard road we have travelled, faster than you came up; 't is a hard rift to stem, when the river is a little swelled; and five is an unnatural number to keep dry, in the hurry-skurry, with a little birchen bark and gum. There, go you all on the rock, and I will bring up the Mohicans with the venison. A man had better sleep without his scalp, than famish in the midst of plenty."

His passengers gladly complied with these directions. As the last foot touched the rock, the canoe whirled from its station, when the tall form of the scout was seen, for an instant, gliding above the waters, before it disappeared in the impenetrable darkness that rested on the bed of the river. Left by their guide, the travellers remained a few minutes in helpless ignorance, afraid even to move along the broken rocks, lest a false step should precipitate them down some one of the many deep and roaring caverns, into which the water seemed to tumble, on every side of them. Their suspense, however, was soon relieved; for aided by the skill of the natives, the canoe shot back into the eddy, and floated again at the side of the low rock before they thought the scout had even time to rejoin his companions.

"We are now fortified, garrisoned, and provisioned," cried Heyward, cheerfully, "and may set Montcalm and his allies at defiance. . . ."

CHAPTER VI.

"Those strains that once did sweet in Zion glide;
He wales a portion with judicious care;
And 'Let us worship God,' he says, with solemn air."
                                                    BURNS.

Heyward, and his female companions, witnessed this mysterious movement with secret uneasiness; for, though the conduct of the white man had hitherto been above reproach, his rude equipments, blunt address, and strong antipathies, together with the character of his silent associates, were all causes for exciting distrust in minds that had been so recently alarmed by Indian treachery.

The stranger alone disregarded the passing incidents. He seated himself on a projection of the rocks, whence he gave no other signs of consciousness than by the struggles of his spirit, as manifested in frequent and heavy sighs. Smothered voices were next heard, as though men called to each other in the bowels of the earth, when a sudden light flashed upon those without, and laid bare the much-prized secret of the place.

At the farther extremity of a narrow, deep cavern in the rock, whose length appeared much extended by the perspective and the nature of the light by which it was seen, was seated the scout, holding a blazing knot of pine. The strong glare of the fire fell full upon his sturdy, weather-beaten countenance and forest attire, lending an air of romantic wildness to the aspect of an individual, who, seen by the sober light of day, would have exhibited the peculiarities of a man remarkable for the strangeness of his dress, the iron-like inflexibility of his frame, and the singular compound of quick, vigilant sagacity, and of exquisite simplicity, that by turns usurped the possession of his muscular features. At a little distance in advance stood Uncas, his whole person thrown powerfully into view. The travellers anxiously regarded the upright, flexible figure of the young Mohican, graceful and unrestrained in the attitudes and movements of nature. Though his person was more than usually screened by a green and fringed hunting-shirt, like that of the white man, there was no concealment to his dark, glancing, fearless eye, alike terrible and calm; the bold outline of his high, haughty features, pure in their native red; or to the dignified elevation of his receding forehead, together with all the finest proportions of a noble head, bared to the generous scalping tuft. It was the first opportunity possessed by Duncan and his companions, to view the marked lineaments of either of their Indian attendants, and each individual of the party felt relieved from a burden of doubt, as the proud and determined, though wild expression of the features of the young warrior forced itself on their notice. They felt it might be a being partially benighted in the vale of ignorance, but it could not be one who would willingly devote his rich natural gifts to the purposes of wanton treachery. The ingenuous Alice gazed at his free air and proud carriage, as she would have looked upon some precious relic of the Grecian chisel, to which life had been imparted by the intervention of a miracle; while Heyward, though accustomed to see the perfection of form which abounds among the uncorrupted natives, openly expressed his admiration at such an unblemished specimen of the noblest proportions of man.

"I could sleep in peace," whispered Alice, in reply, "with such a fearless and generous looking youth for my sentinel. Surely, Duncan, those cruel murders, those terrific scenes of torture, of which we read and hear so much, are never acted in the presence of such as he!"

"This, certainly, is a rare and brilliant instance of those natural qualities, in which these peculiar people are said to excel," he answered. "I agree with you, Alice, in thinking that such a front and eye were formed rather to intimidate than to deceive; but let us not practise a deception upon ourselves, by expecting any other exhibition of what we esteem virtue than according to the fashion of a savage. As bright examples of great qualities are but too uncommon among Christians, so are they singular and solitary with the Indians; though, for the honor of our common nature, neither are incapable of producing them. Let us then hope that this Mohican may not disappoint our wishes, but prove, what his looks assert him to be, a brave and constant friend."

"Now Major Heyward speaks as Major Heyward should," said Cora; "who, that looks at this creature of nature, remembers the shade of his skin!"

A short, and apparently an embarrassed silence succeeded this remark, which was interrupted by the scout calling to them, aloud, to enter.

"This fire begins to show too bright a flame," he continued, as they complied, "and might light the Mingos to our undoing. Uncas, drop the blanket, and show the knaves its dark side. This is not such a supper as a major of the Royal

Americans has a right to expect, but I've known stout detachments of the corps glad to eat their venison raw, and without a relish too.[1] Here, you see, we have plenty of salt, and can make a quick broil. There's fresh sassafras boughs for the ladies to sit on, which may not be as proud as their my-hog-guinea chairs, but which sends up a sweeter flavor than the skin of any hog can do, be it of Guinea, or be it of any other land. Come, friend, don't be mournful for the colt; 't was an innocent thing, and had not seen much hardship. Its death will save the creature many a sore back and weary foot!"

Uncas did as the other had directed, and when the voice of Hawkeye ceased, the roar of the cataract sounded like the rumbling of distant thunder.

"Are we quite safe in this cavern?" demanded Heyward. "Is there no danger of surprise? A single armed man, at its entrance, would hold us at his mercy."

A spectral-looking figure stalked from out the darkness behind the scout, and seizing a blazing brand, held it towards the farther extremity of their place of retreat. Alice uttered a faint shriek, and even Cora rose to her feet, as this appalling object moved into the light; but a single word from Heyward calmed them, with the assurance it was only their attendant, Chingachgook, who, lifting another blanket, discovered that the cavern had two outlets. Then, holding the brand, he crossed a deep, narrow chasm in the rocks, which ran at right angles with the passage they were in, but which, unlike that, was open to the heavens, and entered another cave, answering to the description of the first, in every essential particular.

"Such old foxes as Chingachgook and myself are not often caught in a burrow with one hole," said Hawkeye, laughing; "you can easily see the cunning of the place—the rock is black limestone, which everybody knows is soft; it makes no uncomfortable pillow, where brush and pine wood is scarce; well, the fall was once a few yards below us, and I dare to say was, in its time, as regular and as handsome a sheet of water as any along the Hudson. But old age is a great injury to good looks, as these sweet young ladies have yet to l'arn! The place is sadly changed! These rocks are full of cracks, and in some places they are softer than at othersome, and the water has worked out deep hollows for itself, until it has fallen back, ay, some hundred feet, breaking here and wearing there, until the falls have neither shape nor consistency."

"In what part of them are we?" asked Heyward.

"Why, we are nigh the spot that Providence first placed them at, but where, it seems, they were too rebellious to stay. The rock proved softer on each side of us, and so they left the centre of the river bare and dry, first working out these two little holes for us to hide in."

[1]In vulgar parlance the condiments of a repast are called by the American "a relish," substituting the thing for its effect. These provincial terms are frequently put in the mouths of the speakers, according to their several conditions in life. Most of them are of local use, and others quite peculiar to the particular class of men to which the character belongs. In the present instance, the scout uses the word with immediate reference to the salt, with which his own party was so fortunate as to be provided.

"We are then on an island?"

"Ay! there are the falls on two sides of us, and the river above and below. If you had daylight, it would be worth the trouble to step up on the height of this rock, and look at the perversity of the water. It falls by no rule at all; sometimes it leaps, sometimes it tumbles; there, it skips; here, it shoots; in one place 't is white as snow, and in another 't is green as grass; hereabouts, it pitches into deep hollows, that rumble and quake the 'arth; and hereaway, it ripples and sings like a brook, fashioning whirlpools and gulleys in the old stone, as if 't was no harder than trodden clay. The whole design of the river seems disconcerted. First it runs smoothly, as if meaning to go down the descent as things were ordered; then it angles about and faces the shores; nor are there places wanting where it looks backward, as if unwilling to leave the wilderness, to mingle with the salt! Ay, lady, the fine cobweb-looking cloth you wear at your throat, is coarse, and like a fish-net, to little spots I can show you, where the river fabricates all sorts of images, as if, having broke loose from order, it would try its hand at everything. And yet what does it amount to! After the water has been suffered to have its will, for a time, like a headstrong man, it is gathered together by the hand that made it, and a few rods below you may see it all, flowing on steadily towards the sea, as was foreordained from the first foundation of the 'arth!"

While his auditors received a cheering assurance of the security of their place of concealment, from this untutored description of Glenn's,[1] they were much inclined to judge differently from Hawkeye, of its wild beauties. But they were not in a situation to suffer their thoughts to dwell on the charms of natural objects; and, as the scout had not found it necessary to cease his culinary labors while he spoke, unless to point out, with a broken fork, the direction of some particularly obnoxious point in the rebellious stream, they now suffered their attention to be drawn to the necessary, though more vulgar consideration of their supper. . . .

"First let us examine into the security of your fortress," he answered, "and then we will speak of rest."

He approached the farther end of the cavern, to an outlet, which, like the others, was concealed by blankets, and removing the thick screen, breathed the fresh and reviving air from the cataract. One arm of the river flowed through a deep, narrow ravine, which its current had worn in the soft rock, directly beneath his feet, forming an effectual defence, as he believed, against any danger from

[1] Glenn's Falls are on the Hudson, some forty or fifty miles above the head of tide, or the place where that river becomes navigable for sloops. The description of this picturesque and remarkable little cataract, as given by the scout, is sufficiently correct, though the application of the water to the uses of civilized life has materially injured its beauties. The rocky island and the two caverns are well known to every traveller, since the former sustains a pier of a bridge, which is now thrown across the river, immediately above the fall. In explanation of the taste of Hawkeye, it should be remembered that men always prize that most which is least enjoyed. Thus, in a new country, the woods and other objects, which in an old country would be maintained at great cost, are got rid of, simply with a view of "improving," as it is called.

that quarter; the water, a few rods above them, plunging, glancing, and sweeping along, in its most violent and broken manner.

"Nature has made an impenetrable barrier on this side," he continued, pointing down the perpendicular declivity into the dark current, before he dropped the blanket; "and as you know that good men and true are on guard in front, I see no reason why the advice of our honest host should be disregarded. I am certain Cora will join me in saying that sleep is necessary to you both. . . ."

The Indians silently repaired to their appointed stations, which were fissures in the rocks, whence they could command the approaches to the foot of the falls. In the centre of the little island, a few short and stunted pines had found root, forming a thicket, into which Hawkeye darted with the swiftness of a deer, followed by the active Duncan. Here they secured themselves, as well as circumstances would permit, among the shrubs and fragments of stone that were scattered about the place. Above them was a bare, rounded rock, on each side of which the water played its gambols, and plunged into the abysses beneath, in the manner already described. As the day had now dawned, the opposite shores no longer presented a confused outline, but they were able to look into the woods, and distinguish objects beneath the canopy of gloomy pines.

The river had worn away the edge of the soft rock in such a manner, as to render its first pitch less abrupt and perpendicular than is usual at waterfalls. With no other guide than the ripple of the stream where it met the head of the island, a party of their insatiable foes had ventured into the current, and swam down upon this point, knowing the ready access it would give, if successful, to their intended victims. As Hawkeye ceased speaking, four human heads could be seen peering above a few logs of drift-wood that had lodged on these naked rocks, and which had probably suggested the idea of the practicability of the hazardous undertaking. At the next moment, a fifth form was seen floating over the green edge of the fall, a little from the line of the island. The savage struggled powerfully to gain the point of safety, and, favored by the glancing water, he was already stretching forth an arm to meet the grasp of his companions, when he shot away again with the whirling current, appeared to rise into the air, with uplifted arms and starting eyeballs, and fell, with a sullen plunge, into that deep and yawning abyss over which he hovered. A single, wild, despairing shriek rose from the cavern, and all was hushed again, as the grave.

From *The Spy*, Chapter XVI. COLD SPRING.

> "And let me the canakin clink, clink,
> And let me the canakin clink.
> A soldier's a man:
> A life's but a span;
> Why then, let a soldier drink."
> *Othello.*

The position held by the corps of dragoons, we have already said, was a favorite place of halting with their commander. A cluster of some half-dozen small and dilapidated buildings formed what, from the circumstance of two roads intersecting each other at right angles, was called the village of the Four Corners. As usual, one of the most imposing of these edifices had been termed, in the language of the day, "a house of entertainment for man and beast." On a rough board suspended from the gallows-looking post that had supported the ancient sign, was, however, written in red chalk, "Elizabeth Flanagan, her hotel," an ebullition of the wit of some of the idle wags of the corps. The matron, whose name had thus been exalted to an office of such unexpected dignity, ordinarily discharged the duties of a female sutler, washerwoman, and, to use the language of Katy Haynes, petticoat-doctor to the troops. She was the widow of a soldier who had been killed in the service, and who, like herself, was a native of a distant island, and had early tried his fortune in the colonies of North America. She constantly migrated with the troops; and it was seldom that they became stationary for two days at a time but the little cart of the bustling woman was seen driving into the encampment, loaded with such articles as she conceived would make her presence most welcome. With a celerity that seemed almost supernatural, Betty took up her ground and commenced her occupation. Sometimes the cart itself was her shop; at others the soldiers made her a rude shelter of such materials as offered; but on the present occasion she had seized on a vacant building, and, by dint of stuffing the dirty breeches and half-dried linen of the troopers into the broken windows, to exclude the cold, which had now become severe, she formed what she herself had pronounced to be "most illigant lodgings." The men were quartered in the adjacent barns, and the officers collected in the "Hotel Flanagan," as they facetiously called headquarters. Betty was well known to every trooper in the corps, could call each by his Christian or nickname, as best suited her fancy; and, although absolutely intolerable to all whom habit had not made familiar with her virtues, was a general favorite with these partisan warriors. Her faults were, a trifling love of liquor, excessive filthiness, and a total disregard of all the decencies of language; her virtues, an unbounded love for her adopted country, perfect honesty when dealing on certain known principles with the soldiery, and great good-nature. Added to these, Betty had the merit of being the inventor of that beverage which is so well known, at the present hour, to all the patriots who make a winter's march between the commercial and political capitals of this great State, and which is distinguished by the name of "cock-tail." Elizabeth Flanagan was peculiarly well qualified, by education and circumstances, to perfect this improvement in liquors, having been literally brought up on its principal ingredient, and having acquired from her Virginian customers the use of mint, from its flavor in a julep to its height of renown in the article in question. Such, then, was the mistress of the mansion, who, reckless of the cold northern blasts, showed her blooming face from the door of the building to welcome the arrival of her favorite, Captain Lawton, and his companion, her master in matters of surgery. . . .

Chapter XXX. Mt. Beacon

Clouds were gathering more gloomily in the rear of the hill, until its form could no longer be discerned. Frances threw back her rich curls with both hands on her temples, in order to possess her senses in their utmost keenness; but the towering hill was entirely lost to the eye. At length she discovered a faint and twinkling blaze in the direction in which she thought the building stood, that, by its reviving and receding lustre, might be taken for the glimmering of a fire. But the delusion vanished, as the horizon again cleared, and the star of the evening shone forth from a cloud, after struggling hard, as if for existence. She now saw the mountain to the left of the place where the planet was shining, and suddenly a streak of mellow light burst upon the fantastic oaks that were thinly scattered over its summit, and gradually moved down its side, until the whole pile became distinct under the rays of the rising moon. Although it would have been physically impossible for our heroine to advance without the aid of the friendly light, which now gleamed on the long line of level land before her, yet she was not encouraged to proceed. If she could see the goal of her wishes, she could also perceive the difficulties that must attend her reaching it.

While deliberating in distressing incertitude, now shrinking with the timidity of her sex and years from the enterprise, and now resolving to rescue her brother at every hazard, Frances turned her looks towards the east, in earnest gaze at the clouds which constantly threatened to involve her again in comparative darkness. Had an adder stung her, she could not have sprung with greater celerity than she recoiled from the object against which she was leaning, and which she for the first time noticed. The two upright posts, with a cross-beam on their tops, and a rude platform beneath, told but too plainly the nature of the structure; even the cord was suspended from an iron staple, and was swinging to and fro, in the night air. Frances hesitated no longer, but rather flew than ran across the meadow, and was soon at the base of the rock, where she hoped to find something like a path to the summit of the mountain. Here she was compelled to pause for breath, and she improved the leisure by surveying the ground about her. The ascent was quite abrupt, but she soon found a sheep-path that wound among the shelving rocks and through the trees, so as to render her labor much less tiresome than it otherwise would have been. Throwing a fearful glance behind, the determined girl commenced her journey upward. Young, active, and impelled by her generous motive, she moved up the hill with elastic steps, and very soon emerged from the cover of the woods, into an open space of more level ground, that had evidently been cleared of its timber, for the purpose of cultivation. But either the war or the sterility of the soil had compelled the adventurer to abandon the advantages that he had obtained over the wilderness, and already the bushes and briers were springing up afresh, as if the plough had never traced its furrows through the mould which nourished them.

Frances felt her spirits invigorated by these faint vestiges of the labor of man, and she walked up the gentle acclivity with renewed hopes of success. The path now diverged in so many different directions, that she soon saw it would be useless to follow their windings, and abandoning it, at the first turn, she labored forward towards what she thought was the nearest point of the summit. The cleared ground was soon passed, and woods and rocks, clinging to the precipitous sides of the mountain, again opposed themselves to her progress. Occasionally, the path was to be seen running along the verge of the clearing, and then striking off into the scattering patches of grass and herbage, but in no instance could she trace it upward. Tufts of wool, hanging to the briers, sufficiently denoted the origin of these tracks, and Frances rightly conjectured that whoever descended the mountain, would avail himself of their existence, to lighten the labor. Seating herself on a stone, the wearied girl again paused to rest and to reflect; the clouds were rising before the moon, and the whole scene at her feet lay pictured in the softest colors.

The white tents of the militia were stretched in regular lines, immediately beneath her. The light was shining in the window of her aunt, who, Frances easily fancied, was watching the mountain, racked with all the anxiety she might be supposed to feel for her niece. Lanterns were playing about in the stable-yard, where she knew the horses of the dragoons were kept, and believing them to be preparing for their night march, she again sprang upon her feet, and renewed her toil.

Our heroine had to ascend more than a quarter of a mile farther, although she had already conquered two thirds of the height of the mountain. But she was now without a path, or any guide to direct her in her course. Fortunately, the hill was conical, like most of the mountains in that range, and, by advancing upwards, she was certain of at length reaching the desired hut, which hung, as it were, on the very pinnacle. Nearly an hour did she struggle with the numerous difficulties that she was obliged to overcome, when, having been repeatedly exhausted with her efforts, and, in several instances, in great danger from falls, she succeeded in gaining the small piece of table-land on the summit. . . .

CHAPTER XXXII. MT. BEACON

A steep and laborious ascent brought them from the level of the tide-waters to the high lands that form, in this part of the river, the eastern banks of the Hudson. Retiring a little from the highway, under the shelter of a thicket of cedars, the pedler threw his form on a flat rock, and announced to his companion that the hour for rest and refreshment was at length arrived. The day was now opened, and objects could be seen in the distance, with distinctness. Beneath them lay the Hudson, stretching to the south in a straight line, as far as the eye could reach. To the north, the broken fragments of the Highlands threw upwards their lofty heads, above masses of fog that hung over the water, and by which the course of the river could be traced into the bosom of hills whose conical summits were grouped together, one behind another, in that disorder which might be supposed to have succeeded their gigantic, but fruitless, efforts to stop the progress of the flood. Emerging from these confused piles, the river, as if rejoicing at its release from the struggle, expanded into a wide bay, which was ornamented by a few fertile and low points that jutted humbly into its broad basin. On the opposite, or western shore, the rocks of Jersey were gathered into an array that has obtained for them the name of the "Palisades," elevating themselves for many hundred feet, as if to protect the rich country in their rear from the inroads of the conqueror; but, disdaining such an enemy, the river swept proudly by their feet, and held its undeviating way to the ocean. A ray of the rising sun darted upon the slight cloud that hung over the placid river, and at once the whole scene was in motion, changing and assuming new forms, and exhibiting fresh objects in each successive moment. At the daily rising of this great curtain of nature, at the present time, scores of white sails and sluggish vessles are seen thickening on the water, with that air of life which denotes the neighborhood to the metropolis of a great and flourishing empire; but to Henry and the pedler it displayed only the square yards and lofty masts of a vessel of war, riding a few miles below them. Before the fog had begun to move, the tall spars were seen above it, and from one of them a long pennant was feebly borne abroad in the current of night air that still quivered along the river; but as the smoke arose, the black hull, the crowded and complicated mass of rigging, and the heavy yards and booms, spreading their arms afar, were successfully brought into view.

William Cullen Bryant

William Cullen Bryant (1794-1878) was born in the Berkshires, but spent most of his life in and around New York City. He attended Williams College for a year and studied law privately, being admitted to the bar in 1815. He practiced law in Great Barrington until 1825, when he moved to New York City. By this time he was already known as a poet. His "Thanatopsis " was written in 1811 and published in the *North American Review* in 1817. He had already written his "To A Waterfowl" and "Inscription for the Entrance to a Wood."

Upon arriving in New York in 1826, he became associate editor of the New York *Evening Post*. From 1829 until his death he was editor-in-chief

William Cullen Bryant in his Library at Roslyn, Long Island. Engraving attributed to Asher B. Durand, ca. 1870. Editor's collection.

"Early Morning at Cold Spring," by Asher B. Durand. 1850. Oil on canvas. Courtesy of Montclair Art Museum, Montclair, New Jersey, Lang Acquisition Fund. This scene was the inspiration for Bryant's "A Scene on the Bank of the Hudson."

and a part owner. He also travelled extensively, lectured, and wrote prolifically. Aside from his lyrics, he translated Homer's *Iliad* (1870) and *Odyssey* (1872) into blank verse.

One of America's finest nature poets, he rarely localized his poems. He frequently visited the Catskills with his friends, Asher B. Durand and Thomas Cole, leaders of the Hudson River School of landscape painting. His poem "Catterskill Falls" soon became famous and in turn brought attention and fame to the falls themselves. These falls, usually spelled Kaaterskill Falls, are inland from Catskill Landing, in the Kaaterskill Clove. They are the highest in New York State, with a combined fall of 260 feet, in two leaps of 175 feet and 85 feet, and are extremely picturesque. Bryant was one of the few people to visit the falls in winter, and he chose to stress this beautiful and unfamiliar aspect in his poem.

Bryant wrote the text for some of, and edited the entire text for, *Picturesque America,* which came out in 1872 and had engravings by Harry Fenn and other notable scenic artists.

A Scene on the Banks of the Hudson.*

Cool shades and dews are round my way,
And silence of the early day;
Mid the dark rocks that watch his bed,
Glitters the mighty Hudson spread,
Unrippled, save by drops that fall
From shrubs that fringe his mountain wall;
And o'er the clear still water swells
The music of the Sabbath bells.
All, save this little nook of land,
Circled with trees, on which I stand;
All, save that line of hills which lie
Suspended in the mimic sky—
Seems a blue void, above, below,
Through which the white clouds come and go;
And from the green world's farthest steep
I gaze into the airy deep.
Loveliest of lovely things are they,
On earth, that soonest pass away.
The rose that lives its little hour
Is prized beyond the sculptured flower.
Even love, long tried and cherished long,
Becomes more tender and more strong
At thought of that insatiate grave

The Poems of William Cullen Bryant (New York: The Heritage Press, 1947).

From which its yearnings cannot save.
River! in this still hour thou hast
Too much of heaven on earth to last;
Nor long may thy still waters lie,
An image of the glorious sky.
Thy fate and mine are not repose,
And ere another evening close,
Thou to thy tides shalt turn again,
And I to seek the crowd of men.

CATTERSKILL FALLS.*

Midst greens and shades the Catterskill leaps,
    From cliffs where the wood-flower clings;
All summer he moistens his verdant steeps,
    With the sweet light spray of the mountain-springs,
And he shakes the woods on the mountain-side,
When they drip with the rains of autumn-tide.

But when, in the forest bare and old,
    The blast of December calls,
He builds, in the starlight clear and cold,
    A palace of ice where his torrent falls,
With turret, and arch, and fretwork fair,
And pillars blue as the summer air.

For whom are those glorious chambers wrought,
    In the cold and cloudless night?
Is there neither spirit nor motion of thought
    In forms so lovely, and hues so bright?
Hear what the gray-haired woodmen tell
Of this wild stream and its rocky dell.

'Twas hither a youth of dreamy mood,
    A hundred winters ago,
Had wandered over the mighty wood,
    When the panther's track was fresh on the snow,
And keen were the winds that came to stir
The long dark boughs of the hemlock-fir.

*The Poems of William Cullen Bryant (New York: The Heritage Press, 1947).

Catterskill Falls, photo by Arthur G. Adams, 1970.

Too gentle of mien he seemed and fair,
    For a child of those rugged steeps;
His home lay low in the valley where
    The kingly Hudson rolls to the deeps;
But he wore the hunter's frock that day,
And a slender gun on his shoulder lay.

And here he paused, and against the trunk
    Of a tall gray linden leant,
When the broad clear orb of the sun had sunk,
    From his path in the frosty firmament,
And over the round dark edge of the hill
A cold green light was quivering still.

And the crescent moon, high over the green,
    From a sky of crimson shone,
On that icy palace, whose towers were seen
    To sparkle as if with stars of their own,
While the water fell with a hollow sound,
'Twixt the glistening pillars ranged around.

Is that a being of life, that moves
    Where the crystal battlements rise?
A maiden watching the moon she loves,
    At the twilight hour, with pensive eyes?
Was that a garment which seemed to gleam
Betwixt the eye and the falling stream?

'Tis only the torrent tumbling o'er,
    In the midst of those glassy walls,
Gushing, and plunging, and beating the floor
    Of the rocky basin in which it falls.
'Tis only the torrent—but why that start?
Why gazes the youth with a throbbing heart?

He thinks no more of his home afar,
    Where his sire and sister wait.
He heeds no longer how star after star
    Looks forth on the night as the hour grows late.
He heeds not the snow-wreaths, lifted and cast
From a thousand boughs, by the rising blast.

His thoughts are alone of those who dwell
  In the halls of frost and snow,
Who pass where the crystal domes upswell
  From the alabaster floors below,
Where the frost-trees shoot with leaf and spray,
And frost-gems scatter a silvery day.

"And oh that those glorious haunts were mine!"
  He speaks, and throughout the glen
Thin shadows swim in the faint moonshine,
  And take a ghastly likeness of men,
As if the slain by the wintry storms
Came forth to the air in their earthly forms.

There pass the chasers of seal and whale,
  With their weapons quaint and grim,
And bands of warriors in glittering mail,
  And herdsmen and hunters huge of limb;
There are naked arms, with bow and spear,
And furry gauntlets the carbine rear.

There are mothers—and oh how sadly their eyes
  On their children's white brows rest!
There are youthful lovers—the maiden lies,
  In a seeming sleep, on the chosen breast;
There are fair wan women with moonstruck air,
The snow-stars flecking their long loose hair.

They eye him not as they pass along,
  But his hair stands up with dread,
When he feels that he moves with that phantom throng,
  Till those icy turrets are over his head,
And the torrent's roar as they enter seems
Like a drowsy murmur heard in dreams.

The glittering threshold is scarcely passed,
  When there gathers and wraps him round
A thick white twilight, sullen and vast,
  In which there is neither form nor sound;
The phantoms, the glory, vanish all,
With the drying voice of the waterfall.

"Catterskill Falls," drawing by William Bartlett, from *American Scenery* (London: Virtue, 1836).

Portrait Bust of Thomas Cole by Horatio Greenough (1805–1852). Courtesy of Wadsworth Athenaeum, Hartford, Connecticut.

Slow passes the darkness of that trance,
    And the youth now faintly sees
Huge shadows and gushes of light that dance
    On a rugged ceiling of unhewn trees,
And walls where the skins of beasts are hung,
And rifles glitter on antlers strung.

On a couch of shaggy skins he lies;
    As he strives to raise his head,
Hard-featured woodmen, with kindly eyes,
    Come round him and smooth his furry bed,
And bid him rest, for the evening star
Is scarcely set and the day is far.

They had found at eve the dreaming one
    By the base of that icy steep,
When over his stiffening limbs begun
    The deadly slumber of frost to creep,
And they cherished the pale and breathless form,
Till the stagnant blood ran free and warm.

Thomas Cole

The English-born painter Thomas Cole (1801-48), founder of the Hudson
River School of landscape painting, and a native of Catskill, was also a poet. He
was particularly impressed with the view from atop the Great Wall of Manitou, or
first escarpment of the Catskill Mountains inland from the Village of Catskill.

THE WILD*

Friends of my heart, lovers of Nature's works,
Let me transport you to those wild blue mountains
That rear their summits near the Hudson's wave
Though not the loftiest that begirt the land,
They yet sublimely rise, and on their heights
Your souls may have a sweet foretaste of heaven,
And traverse wide the boundless.

*By Thomas Cole in *Picturesque Catskills—Greene County,* by R. Lionel De Lisser (Northampton, Mass.: Picturesque Publishing Co., 1894).

From this rock,
The nearest to the sky, let us look out
Upon the earth, as the first swell of day
Is bearing back the duskiness of night.
But lo! a sea of mist o'er all beneath;
An ocean, shoreless, motionless and mute,
No rolling swell is there, no sounding surf;
Silent and solemn all; the stormy main
To stillness frozen, while the crested waves
Leaped in the whirlwind, and the loosened foam
Flew o'er the angry deep.

See! Now ascends
The Lord of Day, waking with pearly fire
The dormant depths, See how his glowing breath
The rising surges kindles; lo! they heave
Like golden sands upon Sahara's gales.
Those airy forms disporting from the mass,
Like winged ships, sail o'er the wondrous plain.
Beautiful vision! Now the veil is rent,
And the coy earth her virgin bosom bares,
Slowly unfolding to the enraptured gaze
Her thousand charms.

George Pope Morris

George Pope Morris (1802-64) is still remembered for his popular poem "The Oak," which is better known for its first line, "Woodman, spare that tree!" He was born in Philadelphia and, as a young man, worked as a printer. In 1823 he established the *New York Mirror*, a literary weekly. After his initial success with the *Mirror*, he established the *National Press* in 1846. Less than a year later, N. P. Willis joined him as a partner, and the name of the paper was changed to the *Home Journal*, a literary weekly. He and Willis remained in partnership in this highly successful paper until his death in 1864.

Morris had a home, which he called Undercliff, at the foot of Mt. Taurus near Cold Spring. Besides his poems and prose writings, Morris wrote a successful play entitled *Briar Cliff*, and the libretto for an opera, *The Maid of Saxony*, and also edited a book entitled *Prose and Poetry of Europe and America* with Willis. His collected poems were published in 1853 by Charles Scribner. Of local

George Pope Morris. Anonymous portrait
from Hudson–Fulton Souvenir Magazine,
Brooklyn, 1909.

Grave of Janet McRae, Union Cemetery, Hudson Falls, New York. Photo by Alfred H. Marks, 1978. She was killed in 1777, and her body was moved here in 1852.

interest is his "Croton Ode," written at the request of the Corporation of the City of New York, and sung near the Park Fountain, by members of the New York Sacred Music Society, on the completion of the Croton Aqueduct, October 14, 1842. Other shorter poems of Hudson River interest are "Janet McRea," "The Dog Star Rages," "Ida," and "The Oak." The famous tree described in the poem actually stood in a little woodland pass not far from the village of Bloomingdale on Manhattan Island, approximately on the site of Lincoln Center.

JANET McREA.*

I.

She heard the fight was over,
   And won the wreath of fame!
When tidings from her lover,
   With his good war-steed came:
To guard her safely to his tent,
The red-men of the woods were sent.
   They led her where sweet waters gush
Under the pine-tree bough!
   The tomahawk is raised to crush—
'Tis buried in her brow!
She sleeps beneath that pine-tree now!

II.

Her broken-hearted lover
   In hopeless conflict died!
The forest-leaves now cover
   That soldier and his bride!
The frown of the Great Spirit fell
Upon the red-men like a spell!
   No more those waters slake their thirst,
Shadeless to them that tree!
   O'er land and lake they roam accurst,
And in the clouds they see
Thy spirit, unavenged, McRea!

THE DOG-STAR RAGES.†

I.

Unseal the city fountains,
   And let the waters flow

Poems By George P. Morris (New York: Charles Scribner, 1853).
†*Poems By George P. Morris* (New York: Charles Scribner, 1853).

In coolness from the mountains
  Unto the plains below.
My brain is parched and erring,
  The pavement hot and dry,
And not a breath is stirring
  Beneath the burning sky.

II.

The belles have all departed—
  There does not linger one!
Of course the mart's deserted
  By every mother's son,
Except the street musician,
  And men of lesser note,
Whose only earthly mission
  Is but to toil and vote.

III.

A woman—blessings on her!—
  Beneath my window see;
She's singing—what an honour!—
  "Oh! Woodman, spare that tree!"
Her "man" the air is killing—
  His organ's out of tune—
They're gone, with my last shilling,
  To Florence's saloon.

IV.

New-York is most compactly
  Of brick and mortar made—
Thermometer exactly
  One hundred in the shade!
A furnace would be safer
  Than this my letter-room,
Where gleams the sun, a wafer
  About to seal my doom.

V.

The town looks like an ogre,
  The country like a bride;
Wealth hies to Saratoga,
  And Worth to Sunny-side.

While Fashion seeks the islands
  Encircled by the sea,
Taste finds the Hudson highlands
  More beautiful and free.

VI.

The omnibuses rumble
  Along their cobbled way—
The "twelve inside" more humble
  Than he who takes the pay:
From morn till midnight stealing,
  His horses come and go—
The only creatures feeling
  The "luxury of wo!"

VII.

We editors of papers,
  Who coin our brains for bread
By solitary tapers
  While others doze in bed,
Have tasks as sad and lonely,
  However wrong or right,
But with this difference only,
  The horses rest at night.

VIII.

From twelve to nearly fifty
  I've toiled and idled not,
And, though accounted thrifty,
  I'm scarcely worth a groat;
However, I inherit
  What few have ever gained—
A bright and cheerful spirit
  That never has complained.

IX.

A stillness and a sadness
  Pervade the City Hall,
And speculating madness
  Has left the street of Wall;
The Union Square looks really
  Both desolate and dark,

And that's the case, or nearly,
From Battery to Park.

X.

Had I a yacht, like Miller,
That skimmer of the seas—
A wheel rigged on a tiller,
And a fresh gunwale breeze,
A crew of friends well chosen,
And all a-taunto, I
Would sail for regions frozen—
I'd rather freeze than fry.

XI.

Oh, this confounded weather!
(As some one sung or said,)
My pen, though but a feather,
Is heavier than lead;
At every pore I'm oozing—
(I'm "caving in" to-day)—
My plumptitude I'm losing,
And dripping fast away.

XII.

I'm weeping like the willow
That droops in leaf and bough—
Let Croton's sparkling billow
Flow through the city now;
And, as becomes her station,
The muse will close her prayer:
God save the Corporation!
Long live the valiant Mayor!

IDA* OR WHERE HUDSON'S WAVE.

I.

Where Hudson's wave o'er silvery sands
Winds through the hills afar,
Old Cronest like a monarch stands,
Crowned with a single star!

Poems By George P. Morris (New York: Charles Scribner, 1853).

228

Villa on the Hudson, print by Currier & Ives. Internal evidence from the site and architecture indicates that this was probably "Undercliff," the home of George Pope Morris at Cold Spring.

And there, amid the billowy swells
    Of rock-ribbed, cloud-capped earth,
My fair and gentle Ida dwells,
    A nymph of mountain-birth.

II.

The snow-flake that the cliff receives,
    The diamonds of the showers,
Spring's tender blossoms, buds and leaves,
    The sisterhood of flowers,
Morn's early beam, eve's balmy breeze,
    Her purity define;
Yet Ida's dearer far than these
    To this fond breast of mine.

III.

My heart is on the hills. The shades
    Of night are on my brow:
Ye pleasant haunts and quiet glades,
    My soul is with you now!
I bless the star-crowned highlands where
    My Ida's footsteps roam:
O for a falcon's wing to bear
    Me onward to my home!

THE OAK.*

I

Woodman, spare that tree!
    Touch not a single bough!
In Youth it sheltered me,
    And I'll protect it now.
'Twas my forefather's hand
    That placed it near his cot;
There, woodman, let it stand,
    Thy axe shall harm it not.

II

That old familiar tree,
    Whose glory and renown

Poems By George P. Morris (New York: Charles Scribner, 1853).

Are spread o'er land and sea—
And wouldst thou hew it down?
Woodman, forbear thy stroke!
Cut not its earth-bound ties;
Oh, spare that aged oak,
Now towering to the skies!

III

When but an idle boy,
I sought its grateful shade;
In all their gushing joy
Here, too, my sisters played.
My mother kissed me here;
My father pressed my hand—
Forgive this foolish tear,
But let that old oak stand!

IV

My heart-strings round thee cling,
Close as thy bark, old friend!
Here shall the wild-bird sing,
And still thy branches bend.
Old tree! the storm still brave!
And, woodman, leave the spot;
While I've a hand to save,
Thy axe shall harm it not!

Charles Fenno Hoffman

Charles Fenno Hoffman (1806-84) was born in New York City. He came from a prominent family, and his father, Josiah Ogden Hoffmann, served three terms as member of the New York Assembly, and also as Attorney General of the State of New York. He attended the Dutchess County Academy at Poughkeepsie, but ran away because of cruel treatment. Also as a child, he had an accident on a pier which resulted in the loss of his right leg above the knee. Nonetheless he remained active and even athletic throughout life. He attended Columbia University, from which he graduated with an M.A. degree in 1837. He had previously been admitted to the bar in 1827. He first moved to Albany and took up the practice of law and then to New York, where he practiced law unsuccessfully

Nathaniel Parker Willis. Anonymous engraving from *Poems, Sacred, Passionate and Humorous* of Nathaniel Parker Willis (New York: Clark & Maynard, 1879).

until 1830. At this time he began writing articles and stories for magazines. In the early 1830s, he became co-editor of the *American Magazine.* In 1833, he established the *Knickerbocker,* a literary journal. Hoffman edited the *Mirror* for a short time beginning in 1837 and later he moved on to Horace Greeley's *New Yorker.* He joined the staff of the *Evening Gazette* in 1847 and became editor of *Literary World* in 1847.

In 1835, he wrote a travel book on Michigan and Illinois entitled *A Winter in the West.* He wrote a regional novel entitled *Greyslaer: A Romance of the Mohawk* in 1840 and, in 1838, an essay entitled "Scenes and Sources of the Hudson." This and other tales which had appeared in the *Mirror* were later published in *Wild Scenes in the Forest and Prairie.* Poetic works include "Kachesco: A Legend of the Sources of the Hudson," "Lays of the Hudson" (1846), "Rhymes on West Point," " To the Hudson River," "Moonlight Upon the Hudson." His manuscript " Red Spur of the Ramapo" was burned by a chambermaid who used it to kindle a fire and was consequently never published.

In the late 1840s, his health began to fail, and it became apparent he suffered severe manic-depressive psychosis. He was placed under the care of a specialist in 1849 and was pronounced cured within a year. Six months later he had a relapse and was hospitalized. In 1854, he had a second relapse and was committed to the State Hospital in Harrisburg, Pennsylvania, where he died thirty years later in 1884.

Nathaniel Parker Willis

Nathaniel Parker Willis (1806-67) was one of the best known and most popular writers of his time. He was born in Portland, Maine, but grew up in Boston. His father, Nathaniel Willis, had founded the *Boston Reformer,* a religious newspaper, in 1816. He attended the Boston Latin School and Yale, where he graduated in 1827. Previously he had written and published anonymously some religious poems and had won a substantial cash prize for them. He embarked upon a literary career, editing two annuals, the *Token,* and the *Legendary,* a series of volumes of tales published by S. G. Goodrich. In 1829, he founded the *American Monthly Magazine* in Boston and, in 1831, merged his magazine with George Pope Morris's *New York Mirror.* His column, entitled the "Editor's Table," treated current literary topics, art, books, and personal experience.

Willis went abroad in 1831 and communicated his impressions to the *Mirror* in essays on such famous personages as Thomas Moore, Lady Blessington, Disraeli, Bulwer, and d'Orsay. While residing in England, he married Mary Leighton Stace in 1835. She was the daughter of Commissary General William

Stace, commander of the Royal Arsenal at Woolwich, and an officer who had seen much service and greatly distinguished himself at Waterloo. His European travels are described in *Pencillings by the Way* (1835) and *Inklings of Adventure* (1836).

Upon return to America, Willis purchased an estate, Glenmary, in the Susquehanna Valley near Owego. Here he hoped to pass the remainder of his days in rural and literary employment. His *Letters from Under a Bridge* give graphic and charming descriptions of the life of the region. The idyll was not to last because his wife's father died and his publishers failed. He was forced to sell Glenmary and return to New York to earn a living. Meanwhile, a daughter, Imogen, had been born.

In the period 1838-39, Willis had three plays produced. His *Bianca Visconti* won a prize, and Edgar Allan Poe praised his *Tortesa the Usurer*. While in New York, he established a literary journal called *Corsair,* in cooperation with a Dr. Porter. He took another short trip to Europe, engaging William Makepeace Thackeray as a contributor for the *Corsair*. While in London, he published a volume of poetry and prose entitled *Loiterings of Travel*. He also wrote the text for two illustrated works published by George Virtue, descriptive of the scenery of Ireland and the United States, the latter entitled *American Scenery*. About this same period in 1851, he wrote a small travel guidebook entitled *Trenton Falls; Picturesque and Descriptive*.

Returning home, Willis found that Dr. Porter had become discouraged with the *Corsair* and had abandoned it. Willis thus joined his former associate George Pope Morris in a daily newspaper called the *Evening Mirror*. The intense strain of publishing told upon his health, and the shock of the death of his wife, Mary, prostrated him. He again went abroad in the hope of regaining his health. While there, he had an attack of "brain fever," but this trip also provided material for the essays entitled *Invalid Rambles in Germany*.

Upon returning to America he married Cornelia, only daughter of the Honorable Joseph Grinnell, of New Bedford, Massachusetts, in 1846. In later life he became very attached to his father-in-law. Willis and his second wife established themselves at his country house called Idlewild near Cornwall. This location was recommended to him by his physician for the dry climate, which was even then recognized as beneficial in cases of tuberculosis. The air north of the Hudson Highlands is considerably more dry than along the Atlantic seaboard, and the fast communication afforded by such boats as the *Alida* and the new Erie Railroad put his literary offices in the City within easy reach. Also, George Pope Morris had his country home just across the river at Undercliff.

Publication of the daily *Evening Mirror* was proving too difficult for both Willis and Morris, and they sold the paper and established instead a literary weekly called the *National Press* in 1846. Less than a year later they changed its name to the *Home Journal*. This paper was a great popular success and was published until the time of Morris's death in 1864.

Willis greatly enjoyed the rural life at Idlewild and spent much time on landscaping the grounds. He took an interest in the local place names and instigated changing the names of Butter Hill to Storm King Mountain and of Murderer's Creek to Moodna Creek. His time at Idlewild was described in a series of articles for the *Home Journal,* later collected as *Out-doors at Idlewild* (1855) and *The Convalescent*. These books give many charming descriptions of pastoral and river life and are valuable documents of regional history. Other works by Willis include *Dashes at Life with a Free Pencil* (1845), *Open Air Musings in the City,* and *Letters from Watering-Places*. Willis died at Idlewild on January 20, 1867.

The Four Rivers.*

THE HUDSON—THE MOHAWK—THE CHENANGO—THE SUSQUEHANNAH.

Some observer of Nature offered a considerable reward for two blades of striped grass exactly similar. The infinite diversity, of which this is one instance, exists in a thousand other features of Nature, but in none more strikingly than in the scenery of rivers. What two in the world are alike? How often does the attempt fail to compare the Hudson with the Rhine—the two, perhaps, among celebrated rivers, which are the nearest to a resemblance? Yet looking at the first determination of a river's course, and the natural operation of its search for the sea, one would suppose that, in a thousand features, their valleys would scarce be distinguishable.

I think, of all excitements in the world, that of the first discovery and exploration of a noble river, must be the most eager and enjoyable. Fancy "the bold Englishman," as the Dutch called Hendrich Hudson, steering his little yacht, the Halve-Mane, for the first time through the Highlands! Imagine his anxiety for the channel, forgotten as he gazed up at the towering rocks, and round the green shores, and onward, past point and opening bend, miles away into the heart of the country; yet with no lessening of the glorious stream beneath him, and no decrease of promise in the bold and luxuriant shores! Picture him lying at anchor below Newburgh, with the dark pass of the "Wey-Gat" frowning behind him, the lofty and blue Cattskills beyond, and the hillsides around covered with the red lords of the soil, exhibiting only less wonder than friendliness. And how beautifully was the assurance of welcome expressed, when the "very kind old man" brought a bunch of arrows, and broke them before the stranger, to induce him to partake fearlessly of his hospitality!

---

*It was on the excursion here described, that the author first saw the spot which he afterwards made a residence, and where the foregoing letters were written.

Nathaniel Parker Willis, from *Letters from Under a Bridge,* included in *Rural Letters, and Other Records of Thought at Leisure, Written in the Intervals of More Hurried Literary Labor* (Auburn, New York: Alden, Beardsley & Co., 1853).

The qualities of the Hudson are those most likely to impress a stranger. It chances felicitously that the traveller's first entrance beyond the sea-board is usually made by the steamer to Albany. The grand and imposing outlines of rock and horizon answer to his anticipations of the magnificence of a new world; and if he finds smaller rivers and softer scenery beyond, it strikes him but as a slighter lineament of a more enlarged design. To the great majority of tastes, this, too, is the scenery to live among. The stronger lines of natural beauty affect most tastes; and there are few who would select country residence by beauty at all, who would not sacrifice something to their preference for the neighborhood of sublime scenery. The quiet, the merely rural—a thread of a rivulet instead of a broad river—a small and secluded valley, rather than a wide extent of view, bounded by bold mountains, is the choice of but few. The Hudson, therefore, stands usually foremost in men's aspirations for escape from the turmoil of cities, but, to my taste, though there are none more desirable to see, there are sweeter rivers to live upon.

I made one of a party, very lately, bound upon a rambling excursion up and down some of the river-courses of New York. We had anticipated empty boats, and absence of all the gay company usually found radiating from the city in June, and had made up our minds for once to be contented with the study of inanimate nature. Never were wiseheads more mistaken. Our kind friend, Captain Dean, of the Stevens, stood by his plank when we arrived, doing his best to save the lives of the female portion of the crowd rushing on board; and never, in the most palmy days of the prosperity of our country, have we seen a greater number of people on board a boat, nor a stronger expression of that busy and thriving haste, which is thought to be an exponent of national industry. How those varlets of newsboys contrive to escape in time, or escape at all, from being crushed or carried off; how everybody's baggage gets on board, and everybody's wife and child; how the hawsers are slipped, and the boat got under way, in such a crowd and such a crush, are matters understood, I suppose, by Providence and the captain of the Stevens—but they are beyond the comprehension of the passenger.

Having got out of hearing of "Here's the Star!" "Buy the old Major's paper, sir!" "Here's the Express!" "Buy the New-Ery!" "Would *you* like a New-Era, sir?" "Take a Sun, miss?" and a hundred such deafening cries, to which New York has of late years become subject, we drew breath and comparative silence off the green shore of Hoboken, thanking Heaven for even the repose of a steamboat, after the babel of a metropolis. Stillness, like all other things, is relative.

The passage of the Hudson is doomed to be be-written, and we will not again swell its great multitude of describers. Bound onward, we but gave a glance, in passing, to romantic Undercliff and Cro'-Nest, hallowed by the most imaginative poetry our country has yet committed to immortality;* gave our malison to the

*Drake's "Culprit Fay."

black smoke of iron-works defacing the green mantle of Nature, and our benison to every dweller on the shore who has painted his fence white, and smoothed his lawn to the river; and, sooner than we used to do by some five or six hours, (ere railroads had supplanted the ploughing and crawling coaches to Schenectady,) we fed our eyes on the slumbering and broad valley of the Mohawk.

How startled must be the Naiad of this lovely river to find her willowy form embraced between railroad and canal—one intruder on either side of the bed so sacredly overshaded! Pity but there were a new knight of La Mancha to avenge the hamadryads and water-nymphs of their wrongs from wood-cutters and contractors! Where sleep Pan and vengeful Oread, when a Yankee settler hews me down twenty wood-nymphs of a morning? There lie their bodies, limbless trunks, on the banks of the Mohawk, yet no Dutchman stands sprouting into leaves near by, nor woollen jacket turning into bark, as in the retributive olden time! We are abandoned of these gods of Arcady! They like not the smoke of steam funnels!

WHARVES ON SUNDAY.*

I am inclined to think it is not peculiar to myself to have a Sabbath taste for the water-side. There is an affinity, felt I think by man and boy, between the stillness of the day and the audible hush of boundaries to water. Premising that it was at first with the turned-up nose of conscious travestie, I have to confess the finding of a Sabbath solitude, to my mind, along the river-side in New-York—the first mile toward Albany on the bank of the Hudson. Indeed, if quiet be the object, the nearer the water the less jostled the walk on Sunday. You would think, to cross the city anywhere from river to river, that there was a general hydrophobia—the entire population crowding to the high ridge of Broadway, and hardly a soul to be seen on either the East River or the Hudson. But, with a little thoughtful frequenting, those deserted river-sides become contemplative and pleasant rambling-places; and, if some whim of fashion do not make the bank of the Hudson like the Marina of Smyrna, a fashionable resort, I have my Sunday afternoons provided for, during the pigritude of city durance.

Yesterday (Sunday) it blew one of those unfolding west winds, chartered expressly to pull the kinks out of the belated leaves—a breeze it was delightful to set the face to—strong, genial, and inspiriting, and smelling (in New-York) of the snubbed twigs of Hoboken. The Battery looked very delightful, with the grass laying its cheek to the ground, and the trees all astir and trinkling; but on Sunday this lovely resort is full of smokers of bad cigars—unpleasant gentlemen to take the wind of. I turned the corner with a look through the fence, and was in comparative solitude the next moment.

*Nathaniel Parker Willis, from *Open-air Musings in the City*, included in *Rural Letters and Other Records of Thought at Leisure, Written in The Intervals of More Hurried Literary Labor* (Auburn, New York: Alden, Beardsley & Co., 1853).

The monarch of our deep water-streams, the gigantic "Massachusetts," lay at her wharf, washed by the waving hands of the waters taking leave of the Hudson. The river ends under the prow—or, as we might say with a poetic license, joins on, at this point, to Stonington—so easy is the transit from wharf to wharf in that magnificent conveyance. From this point up, extends a line of ships, rubbing against the pier the fearless noses that have nudged the poles and the tropics, and been breathed on by spice-islands and icebergs—an array of nobly-built merchantmen, that, with the association of their triumphant and richly-freighted comings and goings, grows upon my eye with a certain majesty. It is a broad street here, of made land, and the sidewalks in front of the new stores are lumbered with pitch and molasses, flour and red ochre, bales, bags, and barrels, in unsightly confusion—but the wharf-side, with its long line of carved figure-heads, and bowsprits projecting over the street, is an unobstructed walk—on Sundays at least—and more suggestive than many a gallery of marble statues. The vessels that trade to the North Sea harbor here, unloading their hemp and iron; and the superb French packet-ships, with their gilded prows; and, leaning over the gangways and taffrails, the Swedish and Norwegian sailors jabber away their Sunday's idle time; and the negro-cooks lie and look into the puddles; and, altogether, it is a strangely-mixed picture—Power reposing, and Fret and Business gone from the six-days' whip and chain. I sat down on a short hawser-post, and conjured the spirits of ships around me. They were as communicative as would naturally be expected in a *tête-à-tête* when quite at leisure. Things they had seen and got wind of in the Indian seas, strange fishes that had tried the metal of their copper bottoms, porpoises they had run over asleep, wrecks and skeletons they had thrown a shadow across when under prosperous headway—these and particulars of the fortunes they had brought home, and the passengers coming to look through one more country to find happiness, and the terrors and dangers, heartaches and dreams, that had come and gone with each bill of lading—the talkative old bowsprits told me all. I sat and watched the sun setting between two outlandish-looking vessels, and, at twilight, turned to go home, leaving the spars and lines drawn in clear tracery, on a sky as rosy and fading as a poet's prospects at seventeen.

FROM OPEN-AIR MUSINGS*

We had a June May, and a May June, and the brick world of Manhattan has not, as yet, become too hot to hold us. This is to be our first experiment at passing the entire summer in the city, and we had laid up a few alleviations which have as yet kept the shelf, with our white hat, uncalled for by any great rise in the thermometer. There is no knowing, however, when we shall hear from Texas and

*Nathaniel Parker Willis, *Open-Air Musings in the City* (Auburn, N.Y.: Alden, Beardsley & Co., 1853).

Sloop seen from sidewheel steamboat, with Dunderberg Mountain in the Highlands in the background. A view familiar to Nathaniel P. Willis. Photo taken from steamer *Alexander Hamilton* of sloop *Clearwater*, by Arthur G. Adams, 1969.

the warm "girdle round the earth," (the equator—no reference to English dominion,) and our advice to the stayers in town may be called for by a south wind before it is fairly printed. First—*our substitute for a private yacht.* Not having twenty thousand dollars to defray our aquatic tendencies—having, on the contrary, an occasional spare shilling—we take our moonlight trip on the river— dividing the cool breezes, 'twixt shore and shore—*in the Jersey ferry-boat.* Smile those who have private yachts! We know no pleasanter trip, after the dusk of the evening, than to stroll down to the ferry, haul a bench to the bow of the ferry-boat, and "open up" the evening breeze for two miles and back, for a shilling! After eight o'clock, there are, on an average, ten people in the boat, and you have the cool shoulder under the railing, as nearly as possible, to yourself. The long line of lamps on either shore makes a gold flounce to the "starry skirt of heaven"—the air is as pure as the rich man has it in his grounds, and all the money in the world could not mend the outside of your head, as far as the horizon. (And the horizon, at such a place and hour, becomes a substitute for the small hoop you have stepped out of.) No man is richer than we, or could be better off—till we reach the Jersey shore—and we are as rich going back. Try this of a hot evening, all who prefer coolness and have a mind that is good company. . . .

Excerpts from Letters from Idlewild.*

LETTER I.

The Highland Terrace.

[The following description, written for Mr. Putnam's very splendid work, the "Book of the Picturesque," was published immediately before the commencement of the Letters from Idlewild, and while the author was deciding upon the spot for his future residence.]

West Point is Nature's Northern Gate to New York City. As soon as our rail-trains shall equal those of England, and travel fifty or sixty miles an hour, the Hudson, as far as West Point, will be but a fifty-mile extension of Broadway. The river banks will have become a suburban avenue—a long street of villas, whose busiest resident will be content that the City Hall is within an hour of his door. From this metropolitan avenue into the agricultural and rural region, the outlet will be at the city's Northern Gate, of West Point—a gate whose threshold divides Sea-board from In-land, and whose mountain pillars were heaved up with the changeless masonry of creation.

The passage through the Mountain-Gate of West Point is a three-mile Labyrinth, whose clue-thread is the channel of the river—a complex wilderness, of

Out-Doors at Idlewild; or, The Shaping of a Home on the Banks of the Hudson (New York: Charles Scribner, 1855).

romantic picturesqueness and beauty, which will yet be the teeming Switzerland of our country's Poetry pencil—and, at the upper and northern outlet of this labyrinthine portal of the city, there is a formation of hills which has an expression of most apt significance. *It looks like a gesture of welcome from Nature, and an invitation to look around you!* From the shoulder-like bluff upon the river, an outspreading range of Highlands extends back, *like the curve of a waving arm*—the single mountain of SHAWANGUNK (connected with the range by a valley like the bend of a graceful wrist), *forming the hand at the extremity*. It is of the area within the curve of this bended arm—a HIGHLAND TERRACE of ten or twelve miles square, on the west bank of the river—that we propose to define the capabilities, and probable destiny.

The HIGHLAND TERRACE we speak of—ten miles square, and lying within the curve of this outstretched arm of mountains—has an average level of about one hundred and twenty feet above the river. It was early settled; and, the rawness of first clearings having long ago disappeared, the well-distributed *second woods* are full grown, and stand, undisfigured by stumps, in park-like roundness and maturity. The entire area of the Terrace contains several villages, and is divided up into cultivated farms, and walls and fences in good condition, the roads lined with trees, the orchards full, the houses and barns sufficiently hidden with foliage to be picturesque—the whole neighborhood, in fact, within any driving distance, quite rid of the angularity and well-known ungracefulness of a newly-settled country.

Though the Terrace is a ten-mile plain, however, its roads are remarkably varied and beautiful, from the *curious multiplicity of deep glens*. These are formed by the many streams which descend from the half-bowl of mountains inclosing the plain, and—their descent being rapid and sudden, and the river into which they empty being one or two hundred feet below the level of the country around—they have gradually worn beds much deeper than ordinary streams, and are, from this and the character of the soil, unusually picturesque. At every mile or so, in driving which way you will, you come to a sudden descent into a richly wooded vale—a bright, winding brook at bottom, and romantic recesses constantly tempting to loiter. In a long summer, and with perpetual driving over these ten-mile interlacings of wooded roads and glens, we daily found new scenery, and heard of beautiful spots, within reach and still unseen. From every little rise of the road, it must be remembered, the broad bosom of the Hudson is visible, with foreground variously combined and broken; and the lofty mountains (encircling just about as much scenery as the eye can compass for enjoyment), form an *ascending background and a near horizon* which are hardly surpassed in the world for boldness and beauty. To what degree sunsets and sunrises, clouds, moonlight, and storms, are aggrandized and embellished by this peculiar formation of country, any student and lover of nature will at once understand. Life may be, outwardly, as much more beautiful, amid such scenery, as action amid the scenery of a stage is more dramatic than in an unfurnished room.

The *accessibilities* from Highland Terrace are very desirable. West Point is perhaps a couple of miles below, by the river bank; and, though mountain-bluffs and precipices now cut off the following of this line by land, a road has been surveyed and commenced along the base of Cro'-nest, which, when completed, will be one of the most picturesque drives in the world. A part of it is to be blown out from the face of the rock; and, as the lofty eminences will almost completely overhang it, nearly the whole road will be in shade in the afternoon. To pass along this romantic way for an excursion to the superb military grounds of West Point, and to have the parades and music within an easy drive, will be certainly an unusual luxury for a country neighborhood. The communication is already open for vehicles, by means of a steam ferry, which runs between Cornwall Landing (at the foot of the Terrace), and Cold Spring and the Military Wharf—bringing these three beautiful spots within a few minutes' reach of each other—Morris the song-writer's triple-view site of "Undercliff," by the way, overlooking the central of these Highland-Ferry Landings.

It may be a greater or less attraction to the locality of the Terrace, but it is no disadvantage, at least, that three of the best frequented summer resorts are within an afternoon drive of any part of it—the WEST POINT HOTEL, COZZEN'S, which is a mile below, and POWELTON HOUSE, which is five or six miles above the Point, at Newburgh. For accessibility to these fashionable haunts of strangers and travellers, and the gaieties and hospitalities for which they give opportunity—for enjoyment of military shows and music—for all manner of pleasure excursions by land and water, to glens and mountain-tops, fishing, hunting, and studying of the picturesque—Highland Terrace will probably be a centre of attraction quite unequalled.

The river-side length of the Terrace is about five miles—CORNWALL at one end and NEWBURGH at the other. At both these places there are landings for the steamers, and from both these are steam ferries to the opposite side of the river, bringing the fine neighborhood of FISHKILL and COLD SPRING within easy reach. NEWBURGH is the metropolis of the Terrace—with its city-like markets, hotels, stores, trades and mechanic arts—an epitome of New York convenience within the distance of an errand. Downing, one of our most eminent horticulturists, once resided here, and Powell, one of the most enterprising of our men of wealth, lives here still; and, along one of the high acclivities of the Terrace, are the beautiful country seats of Durand, our first landscape painter, Miller, who has presented the neighborhood with a costly and beautiful church of stone, Verplanck, Sands, and many others, whose tastes in ground and improvements add beauty to the river drive.

To the class of seekers for sites of rural residences, for whom we are drawing this picture, the fact that the Terrace is *beyond suburban distance from New York,* will be one of its chief recommendations. What may be understood as "Cockney annoyances" will not reach it. But it will still be sufficiently and variously accessible from the city. On its own side of the river there is a rail-route from

Newburgh to Jersey city, whose first station is in the centre of the Terrace, at "Vail's Gate," and by which New York will eventually be brought within two hours or less. By the two ferries to the opposite side of the river, the stations of the Hudson Railroad are also accessible, bringing the city within equal time on another route. The many boats upon the river, touching at the two landings at all hours of day and night, enable you to vary the journey to and fro, with sleeping, reading, or tranquil enjoyment of the scenery. Friends may come to you with positive luxury of locomotion, and without fatigue; and the monotony of access to a place of residence, by any one conveyance—an evil very commonly complained of—is delightfully removed.

There is a very important advantage of the Highland Terrace, which we have not yet named. It is *the spot on the Hudson where the two greatest thoroughfares of the North are to cross each other*. The intended route from Boston to Lake Erie here intersects the rail and river routes between New York and Albany. Coming by Plainfield and Hartford to Fishkill, it here takes ferry to Newburgh, and traverses the Terrace by the connecting link already completed to the Erie Railroad—thus *bringing Boston within six or eight hours* of this portion of the river. Western and Eastern travel will then be direct from this spot, like Southern and Northern; and Albany and New York, Boston and Buffalo, will be four points all within reach of an easy excursion.

To many, the most essential charm of Highland Terrace, however (as a rural residence in connection with life in New York), will be the fact that it is the *nearest accessible point of complete inland climate*. Medical science tells us that nothing is more salutary than change from the seaboard to the interior, or from the interior to the seaboard; and between these two climates the ridge of mountains at West Point is the first effectual separation.

The raw east winds of the coast, so unfavorable to some constitutions, are stopped by this wall of cloud-touching peaks, and, with the rapid facilities of communication between salt and fresh air, the balance can be adjusted without trouble or inconvenience, and as much taken of either as is found healthful or pleasant. The trail of climate which the writer has made, for a long summer, in the neighborhood of these mountainous hiding-places of electricity, the improvement of health in his own family, and the testimony of many friends who have made the same experiment, warrant him in commending it as a peculiarly salutary and invigorating air.

We take pains to specify, once more, that it is to a certain class, in view of a certain new phase in the philosophy of life, that these remarks are addressed. For those who must be in the city late and early, on any and every day, the distance will be inconvenient, unless with unforeseen advances in the rate of locomotion. For those who require the night and day dissipations of New York, and who have no resources of their own, a nearer residence might also be more desirable. For mere seekers of seclusion and economy it is too near the city, and the neighborhood would be too luxurious. But for those who have their time in some degree at their own disposal—who have competent means for luxurious independence—who have rural tastes and metropolitan refinements rationally blended—who have families which they wish to surround with the healthful and elegant belongings of a home, while, at the same time they wish to keep pace with the world, and enjoy what is properly and only enjoyable in the stir of cities—for this class—the class, as we said before, made up of Leisure, Refinement, and Luxury—modern and recent changes are preparing a new theory of what is enjoyable in life. It is a mixture of city and country, *with the home in the country.* And the spot with the most advantages for the first American trial of this new combination, is, we venture confidently to record, the HIGHLAND TERRACE, ENCIRCLED IN THE EXTENDED ARM OF THE MOUNTAINS ABOVE WEST POINT.

LETTER XXXIV.

Mellow Middle in a November day—Ascent to Storm-King—Road from Newburgh to West Point—Chances for Human Eyries—Difference of Climate between the two Mountain-sides—Home-like familiarity of a Brook, &c., &c.
November 19, 1854.

The scoop of the rich yellow centre from a slice of nutmeg melon, leaving a respectable depth of the colder-tinted unripeness at either end, is very like the cut of warm and fruity sunshine which lies mellow in the middle of a November day—say from ten o'clock till three—and by confining oneself to these delicious mouthfuls of noon, the summer feast of out-doors need scarce be perceptibly lessened. An artist might reasonably miss the long shadows of morning and evening, it is true. But the renewed overflowingness and sparkle of the water-courses, at this season, redeem any tameness of the landscape; and, with exercise in such elastic sunshine, one looks, somehow, through different eyes. What would be glare in summer, is joyous illumination now.

We started after breakfast yesterday (Nov. 5th), to ascend to the cloud-piled shoulder of old Storm-King, and look over upon the parade-ground of West Point—the young "sodgers" being near neighbors of ours by straight line, though the mountain between is a mile or two thick through its un-tunnelled bottom, and divides us as effectually as the Appenines cut off Florence from Bologna. With the work made by the water-spout of a few weeks ago, it promised to be something like the cat's walk over the house-tops, for any smoothness of road. We should properly have been mounted on mules. Nothing ever happens to a lady on horseback, however; and my neighbor's daughter, and my own daughter and niece, were young travellers enough to rather wish for an adventure, while my neighbor and I were old travellers enough to make the best of one. Besides, we were out for the idleness of an autumn day. We could let people in Broadway see a month's sight in a morning—we could let electricity travel its 300,000 miles a second—and be happy, ourselves, for that day, with neither the fashionable indigestion of event nor the popular distancing of thought and observation.

The principal road across the mountains, from Newburgh to West Point, is a fork or two farther west than the pass for which we pointed our horses' heads; and, after leaving the Highland level upon which Idlewild stands, we had little to follow except the track of the woodsman and such gullies as had been ploughed by the floods. The ascent of this range is by no means the gradual acclivity that it looks to be, from below. It is a labyrinth of knolls and hollows, over which one travels like an ant through a basket of eggs, coming continually upon small mountain farms, islanded among irreclaimable rocks, and so hidden behind and among them as to seem contrived by hermits for inextricable privacy. Oh what eyries, for such human eagles as wish to live alone, and yet have the world within pouncing reach! The bright springs make miniature meadows, just large enough for the rear window of a mountain hut to look out upon, and the crags and slopes are the models of walls for grasses. Sheep and cows are charmingly at home there—fences unnecessary—wood plenty—land eight to ten dollars the acre—West Point music gratis with every South wind—and society and other epidemics wholly unknown. These attractions prove sufficient for one very cultivated man, by the way. He tried city-life for a while, after leaving college, and then expended a small competency in a farm on this ridge. After getting his cottage built, he sought out a beautiful and poor girl, wholly uneducated, married her, and commenced cultivating a virgin mind and a virgin farm. Both succeeded to his entire contentment. His wife grew a lady of uncommon dignity and intelligence; and, while they passed their evenings with books, their farm and dairy were models by daylight. The story was told me by one of my working neighbors who knew them well.

Somewhere about noon we came upon brooks running the other way, and began to smell (we thought) a little of the salt air of the seaboard—the ridge we had mounted being an effectual Panama between this and an inland air much more Pacific for the lungs. In the cannon of the military post at the foot of the descent on one side and the rolls of Orange County butter at the foot of the descent on the other, my chronic cough-memory found a very correct exponent of the two climates which the mountain divides. To my eminent friend Doctor Gray, who prescribed the velvet side of this Isthmus so near New York (instead of the Trip to the Tropics which I took in spite of him, and found so ineffectual), I owe what gratitude my present better health is worth; and I mention it here for the benefit of the large public of consumptive given-over-dom of which I have now ceased to be one. To the pulmonary patients who abound in our harsh seaboard atmosphere, this Highland Terrace is a far better Malvern than the Antilles—the poor, at least, should know.

Descending through a silence-bound, tree-riven, wilderness (a place that feels, as you ride through it, like a chaos, with an eternity or two still on hand), we came suddenly to a breathless little mountain lake, sprinkled with rock islands, and lovely enough for a poem or a dream. Its outlet is a water-slide, overhung by a romantic crag, and, just now, a flood dashes brilliantly down the slanting precipice; though, in summer, I believe, when most resorted to by riding parties from West Point and Cozzens's, the cascade is perversely dry. Hereabouts terminates the military road commenced by the Government as a Simplon between West Point and Newburgh; and into the proposed route of this we now struck to return to Idlewild. Our neighbor, who with his fair daughter had accompanied us, has a family of yeomen sons—manly fellows at the perfection of the first American remove from English stock—and the stone house of one of them stands not far from the lake, in the centre of a mountain farm. The rosy wife soon spread an excellent dinner for us. General Washington, who often earned an appetite by the same ride (for, it was the only road between Fort Putnam and his head-quarters at Newburgh), would have felt his patriotism improved, many a time, I doubt not, by as good a dinner on the same spot.

Idlewild brook takes its rise hereabouts; and, as the road down the mountain follows its course for three miles, till it brings us to our gate (the stream here leaving the highway, and plunging into a deep gorge of our own grounds, quite hidden from public view)—it was like being accompanied home by a member of the family accidentally found astray among the hills. How domesticated a brook gets to be, to be sure! We praise its beauty—we blame its violence—we have a good-bye for it when we leave home, and a feeling of how-d'ye-do when we see it again—take pride in it when the stranger sees its loveliness, and confide to it (when we are alone together) many a thought elsewhere untold, many a wild dream, many a sadness. For moods which could not bear solitude, the running brook is often company enough. It was reasonable in the ancients to recognize them as nymphs. They grow to seem conscious and friendly, as the motionless rocks never could do. And we frequent them, open heart and mind to them, let their murmur dispel melancholy, and let them wile away discontent with their music without words—believing in them irresistibly, or with the same instinctive and vague credence with which we believe it forever to be the same brook, though the same water is never seen in it twice.

LETTER XLVI.

Hudson Frozen Solid—Boats on Runners—Water-lilies—Indian Legend, and Poem on it by a Friend—Philosophy of naming Streams hereabouts—Angola and its Epidemic—Story of Smart Boy, &c., &c.

February 11, 1854.

The Hudson is frozen solid, from the Storm-King's foot to Danskammer, but the ice seems rather to accelerate than hinder *navigation*. A sail-boat upon three runners—the hinder on rigged upon a piviot, and operating as a most effectual rudder—has been flying over the ice to-day with a velocity quite marvellous, and tacking and rounding-to so gracefully and instantaneously that it is a pity it can only be done when the swallows are at the South—their preëminence at a short turn being a nose out of joint, just now, for this neighborhood. From the distance of the shore, the runners are invisible, and the flying craft looks like an ordinary boat; while its unnatural speed and the tangle of horses and sleighs through which it zigzags, in the thoroughfare between Fishkill and Newburgh, makes a strange confusion of sails and trotting horses, to an unaccustomed eye. With locomotives passing continually on both sides of the river, and the multitudes of skaters in every direction, velocity of all kinds seems easy enough. . . .

LETTER XLVIII.

Living in the Country all the Year round—Trips to the City—Hindrances by Snow on the Track—Chat in the hindered Cars—Mr. Irving—Bad Ventilation—Late Arrival, &c., &c.

March 11, 1854.

Living in the country all the year round, has its occasional misgivings of worth while. There are "spells of weather," as the country people call them, which, for a day or two at a time, in this northern climate, make all out-doors intolerable. The "sloshy going" is discouraging enough—when the snow is just so much melted with a raw east wind as to hold water six or eight inches deep on a side hill—but this, though it makes an island of the house, imprisons only those vintager snails,* the women and children. There is a worse stage of winter which imprisons also man and horse—the cold after a thaw, when the roads are an impassable slough of false mud, and the animal that you ride plants one foot safely on the surface, but can scarcely extricate the other from the stiffening mud in which he "slumps" to the knee. There is no exercise to be got by riding, and walking is out of the question. The lungs pine for expansion. Blood runs slow. Sidewalks and omnibuses begin to loom up with a forgotten glory.

In watching the railway trains from my library window, I find I have no feeling of *being-left-behind*, except in the un-get-about-able weather. Happily at rest

---

*Nature seems to have distinctly endowed some of her creatures with the instinct and faculty of doing without open air for long periods. Of the peculiar snail that lives upon the grape, Berneaud says:—"On the approach of winter, the vintager snails, several together, retire into holes in the earth, shutting the openings of their shells with a *calcareous operculum*, and not making their appearance again till the following spring. Our ladies certainly have this "calcareous operculum," or some other compound of in-door resignation, unknown to the ruder sex.

while others are wearily urged onward—or tiresomely on a shelf while others have liberty to change the scene—are two impressions receivable from the same smoke of a flying locomotive in the distance. I should often start for a week in the city, with the latter feeling, if it were not for the horse in the stable, and the chance of out-doors freedom to-morrow; but, last week, the winter's "protracted agony" got the upper hand, and, with my "7,000,000 pores" voting for a change of air, I gave in. And, of some of my experiences in getting to the city, I may as well make a passing chronicle—adding, as it will, to an understanding of the *life hereabouts* which it is the object of these sketches to illustrate.

We usually speak of the city as about two hours distant; and, though a snow-storm came on in the night, after my preparations to go, I thought it would be such a ploughing as I had frequently seen to offer little or no impediment to the trains during the winter, and started from home at daylight to meet the cars, in full faith of a noon in the city. As I did not reach my hotel till the following midnight, and did not get my baggage for still eighteen hours more, the reader will see what slovenly service it is, after all, spoken of so grandly by the philosopher:—"Man is a world, and hath another world to attend on him." A pocket full of crackers may be a very comfortable addition to such a couple of worlds.

Missing the Newburgh-and-Erie train, which goes down upon our side of the Hudson, and then driving four miles in an open wagon against a snow-storm of powdered needles, and crossing the river to Fishkill by a ferry made doubtful by the ice, I got seated in the cars somewhere between nine and ten o'clock, thinking, that, for this trip of pleasure, the Compensation Office must have taken the payment in advance. We started well enough out of the village. The rails had been cleared by the brakemen. A little farther on, among the rocks, however, the drifts began to look formidable, and I soon saw that we had been reached, in the Highlands, by only a thin skirt of the storm of the night before. The drifts grew deeper and deeper—our headway slower and slower—and finally, in a rocky gorge, just opposite Cozzen's Summer Hotel, we came to a stand still for the day—a tall snow-bank on each side (neither of them "a bank whereon the *wile-time* grows") our only prospect from the windows. We found afterwards that the stop was partly from a dread of meeting an up-train and running the noses of the two locomotives together under the snow; and that the delay of the up-train was owing to the break down of an engine—but our several halts chanced to be in spots where the demand for "pies and coffee" had not been anticipated, and the cause of the delay was less thought of than the famishing consequences. At one place, I believe, a passenger or two waded back a long distance to a country grocery of which they had got a glimmer in passing, and found biscuits and gingerbread; but the remaining stomachs of our own train, and those which kept accumulating behind us from the West, "bore on" with unassisted resignation till midnight.

We Americans are a patient and merry people under difficulties. I do not think travellers have sufficiently given us credit for this national quality of *jolly indomitableness*. The successive additions to our long line of trains stretched to very near a mile, by sundown, and a mile of more gay and cheerful people— hungry as they all were—could not be found on a French holiday. A footpath was soon tracked through the snow, along one side of the cars, at each stopping-place, and merriment resounded under all the windows—everybody apparently acquainted with everybody, and no sign of the fretful grumbler that would have abounded in such a disappointed multitude in Europe. Yet most of those five hundred jokers were business men, to whom the delay was a serious inconvenience.

One of our long halts was under "Sunny Side," Irving's residence. It was long after dark, and the car was double-filled—the passengers had been condensed into the forward trains, to detach as many cars as possible, and so save weight. As many persons were standing up as sitting down. Conversation was general, and whoever "had the floor" was heard by all. One man announced that we were but a stone's-throw from Washington Irving's. "Well," said a rough-looking fellow from the corner, "I would rather lay eyes on *that man* than any man in the world." "I've seen him," said another; "he looks like a gentleman, I tell you!" And then they went into a discussion of his various works—two "strong-minded" ladies who were on the front seat taking a lively and very audible part in it. [Chancing to meet Mr. Irving, two days after, at the Astor Library, and finding he was at home at the time, I inquired whether his ears had burned, about eight o'clock on a certain evening; but, as he said "no," there is less magnetism in a car-full of compliments than would be set down, for that quantity of electric influence, probably, by the Misses Fox.]

The only ill temper that I discovered, during the fourteen hours of unfed delay, was between those who cared for fresh air, and those who preferred the allowance of about the ventilation they would get in a coffin. With the standing and sitting passengers, and the cars motionless, the atmospheric vitality within was exhaustible in five minutes at furthest; and, strangely enough, most of those sitting at the windows after dark refused to open them. I suffered painfully myself from the foulness of the atmosphere, all day. Then the stove was kept almost red-hot, and with the snow brought in by the feet of the passers to and fro, the bottom of the car was a pool of water. Like others, probably, who had not foreseen this, I was not provided with India rubbers, and of course sat with damp feet all the way—a dangerous addition to an empty stomach and a pestilent atmosphere. Ah, Messrs. Presidents and Directors of railways, is it not possible to have the ventilation of cars independent of those who do not know the meaning of fresh air.

We arrived at Thirty-first street in the neighborhood of eleven o'clock; but, as no announcement was made of that happy fact, we sat fifteen or twenty minutes in the cars, wasting our resignation on a supposed snow-bank. With the discovery that the snow in the streets would prevent the cars from going farther, and that the baggage had so accumulated with the numerous trains that it could not be delivered till morning, the next query was how to travel the three miles to our various homes and hotels in the city. There was one four-horse sleigh in waiting, and probably between five and eight hundred passengers. Not sorry, myself, to stir my blood with a walk for that distance before taking my lungs to bed, I gave my check to an Express agent (who brought my trunk to me at seven the next evening), and, with hundreds of men, women and children, started down-town-wards. With a long stumble over the unshovelled sidewalks of slumbering and ill-lighted suburbs, I found myself, towards midnight, in the neighborhood of Union Square, and, over a venison steak which I found smoking on the supper-table at the Clarendon, vowed never again to make even a two-hours' pilgrimage in a rail-car without provision against accident—say a cracker or two and some shape of fluid consolation.

LETTER L.

Breaking up of the River-ice—Dates of previous Resumings of Navigation—Companionship in the distant Views of Travel—Nature's Illnesses—Hillsides, &c., &c.
March 25, 1854.

The most stirring bit of news, probably, in the whole year, for this neighbor-hood, is the breaking up of the ice at the mountain-lock, at West Point, and the passing of the first steamer through. "A boat up yesterday" (March 9) is this morning's announcement of suspended life re-begun. Our dock is once more noisy and lively, like returning voice and color to the Highland lip; and the wagons begin to come and go on the branching roads, like blood that has again found circulation in the veins. The trance is over. We shake hands with the city again, and resume our suburban interchanges and daily commerce, to and fro.

But, from a solid valley to a flowing river, the change is large. The rippled surface of the Hudson flows, *now,* where I was watching a trotting race of eight or ten sleighs but *a few days ago.* The manly boys of my neighbor Roe's school-family skated to Newburgh, it hardly seems further off than yesterday, and, to-day, the sloop-prows are ploughing on the track of their skate-irons. We could take a walk where now we must take a boat. The hills opposite were apparently across a two-mile *meadow*—they are now across a two-mile *river.* For the familiar landscape seen from the window of one's home, this is a startling variation.

The river has been closed this year for sixty-two days. It may be interesting to record the length of a few previous shuttings-up, as given in a little table by the Albany *Argus*—the dates of the closing of the river and the number of days navigation was suspended:

1842, November 29	....	closed	136	days.
1843, December 9	....	do.	95	do.
1844, do. 11	....	do.	74	do.
1845, do. 4	....	do.	100	do.
1846, do. 15	....	do.	112	do.
1847, do. 24	....	do.	89	do.
1848, do. 27	....	do.	82	do.
1849, do. 25	....	do.	73	do.
1850, do. 17	....	do.	70	do.
1851, do. 11	....	do.	105	do.

It is curious how the *mere visibleness of event and multitude*—the distant view of perpetually passing fleets of sails and steamers with which one has no communication breaks up the solitude of the country. It makes the difference (duly priced in the acre) between living on the river and away from it. The *beauty* of the view is of less value than the *companionship* there is in it. I find the eye can take in the needed food for this social craving. At my window, on this terrace of the Highlands, I sometimes look off, from a tired pen, upon the fleets of sails, crowded steamers and lines of tow-boats and barges, and feel, after a minute or two, as if I had been where people are. It does not need question and reply to exchange magnetism with others, nor does it need nearer neighborhood, I fancy, than the distance to which the eye can ever so indistinctly, follow the imagination. Many a traveller up the Hudson has helped to break the solitude of Idlewild, by what he gave to my thought—the thought that went to him as he passed, and came back from him to me. . . .

*　　*　　*　　*　　*　　*

We are wide awake, in this part of the country, with the idea of *becoming a seaport*. In the Report upon the great Diameter Railroad to and through the centre of the State (from NEWBURGH TO SYRACUSE, and so on to Detroit and San Francisco), *the Hudson, thus far*—to the broad expanse of deep water spread out before us, and which is encircled like a mountain dock by the Highlands—*is put down as an* "extension of the Bay of New York; and Newburgh (continues the Report) is located most favorably on that Bay, with the finest of harbors. Ships of war and vessels of every description can lie securely at anchor there, and moor at her wharves." And this saves near a hundred miles of river navigation (to reach the railroad at Albany), and saves the forty days' difference between Newburgh and Albany as to clearance from ice, saves the shallows of the Overslaugh, and sixty-four miles of absolute distance to Syracuse. The great belt of thoroughfare from the Eastern States is to be clasped to the Western belt by this same mountain seaport—the main road from Boston to the West, which is far towards completion, crossing the Hudson from Fishkill to Newburgh.

But Chamber street, in the City of New York, is also to be extended to

Newburgh, to meet this Diameter road—crossing directly to Hoboken, and then following the western bank of the Hudson—fifty miles of Chamber street! So Idlewild will be on Chamber street, four miles this side of Newburgh. We shall thank Heaven and enjoy, not a little, the relief which this direct crossing, from our side of the river to the centre of the city, will give us—a relief from an *alternative of nuisance,* viz.:—the tedious horse-car-ing from Thirty-first street *down town* (from the depot of the Hudson River Road), or the hour's delay of jamming, crowding, dodging and vexing *up town* (from the Erie depot at the blocked-up and struggling Babel of Jersey Ferry). It is perplexing and dangerous work to get self and belongings to a hotel from the arrival-point of either of the two present roads. I have lost temper and baggage in the two last attempts I have made at it—old traveller as I am, and quite at home as I ought to be, in New York and its "dodges."

It is a curious thing that the Western bank of the Hudson River, for the first fifty miles from New York, is as much a wilderness at the present moment, as many a river-bank of equal length in the far West. While the Eastern shore is a close-linked chain of villages which makes it an extension of the suburbs of the city for fifty miles, and land all along this thickening and crowded line of railroad is selling for one and two thousand dollars the acre, the opposite river-bank from Hoboken to West Point is mostly a vague desert, of which the chance traveller knows nothing, except that Cozzens's caravanserai makes one break in its long stretch of *terra incognitia.* Most of the land has been, hitherto, comparatively valueless. And it has been valueless and unknown *only because no railroad gave access to it.* Yet—within an hour of New York, and with all the navigation-advantages and scenery of the Hudson—*a continuation, as it soon will be, of Chamber street to West Point*—what a magical change is to take place on that fifty miles of river-bank! Villages and country-seats will multiply, we venture to predict, as they were never seen to multiply before. The "Report" expresses itself well on the general magic of railroad influence, to be tried here with such unprecedented opportunity:—

"The effect of railways everywhere has been the same, greatly enhancing all property within their influences, and especially within twenty or twenty-five miles of them on each side. Hon. D. D. Andrews, in his report to Congress, says:—'It is estimated by the President of the Nashville and Chattanooga Road that the increased value of a belt of land, ten miles wide, lying upon each side of its line, is equal at least to seven dollars and a half per acre, or ninety-six thousand dollars for every mile of road, which will cost only about twenty thousand dollars per mile.' 'It is believed that the construction of the three thousand miles of railway in Ohio will add to the value of the landed property in the State at least five times the cost of the roads, assuming this to be sixty million of dollars.' 'The valuation of Massachusetts went up from 1840 to 1850, from two hundred and ninety million to five hundred and eighty million dollars, and by far the greater part of it due to the numerous railroads she has constructed.' Seventy-two towns, not enjoying railway advantages, did not increase in population during that period."

The extension-quill of Chambers street for fifty miles, with its feather of ten-mile breadth of farms, will cipher up the market supplies to balance the other statistics of New York growth and commerce; but there is also a very possible SOCIAL RESULT, which is not likely to be put down with the cost and profit of the road, but which is as interesting a probability as it is purely a national one.

From the first settlement of the country, the Eastern shore of the Hudson has been a garden of Dutch aristocracy. It was divided up into the estates of "old families," from Manhattan to Albany—the Knickerbockers giving way reluctantly and grudgingly even to the well-paying intrusions of improvement; and, even still, strengthening their fences around what they can afford to retain, and raising signs of warning to trespassers, with the jealousy of dignity invaded. Railway stations have been built, contrary to their protest and will; villages have sprung up like mushrooms along the line of the opposed road; country-houses, school-houses, and churches have thickened like bubbles on a canal break—*and yet they rule*. Those of the thousands of new residents whose beautiful houses are acknowledged to "belong to the first people," have propitiated the Knickerbocracy. All others live isolated amid their fresh paint and shingles.

But the most American feature of our time is the successful voting of such aristocracy to be "old-fogey-ism," and the being merrily independent of it—anywhere out of its immediate neighborhood. While, in England, a new-comer's preference for the site of a villa would be *nearness* to an "old family" mansion, in our country (conveniences being equal), the preference would be *distance* from it. In the natural rivalry for consequence, every self-enriched man prefers fair play and a fresh start to any hitchings-on or borrowings by subserviency. To genial Geoffrey, at Sunnyside, of course, any home-seeker in the Republic would like to be a neighbor—and an honoring and deferential one—but he is a Knickerbocker and himself beside.

"Old-fogey-ism," however, is a growth of centuries. While the *Eastern* bank of the Hudson has been *two hundred* years in settling and embellishing, the *Western* bank will start new and overtake it in from five to twenty. There will be "first people" everywhere. There is no help for it. But it is "a fair field and no favor" on the Hoboken shore. It will be so rapid a settlement of neighborhoods, too, that there will be no time for mould to cover up false claims to "gentility"—none impregnably the first by grave-yard iteration. As soon as this extremity of the great Diameter Railroad is completed—as soon as Chambers street is extended to West Point, for its first link of fifty miles—the home-seeking crowd, who wish to be within an hour of the city with the families they are enriching, will divide up this now desert riverside into estates and villa-grounds, while farmers and gardeners will cluster behind them in the valleys and on the hills—a Minerva-birth of a rich and populous range of country without infancy or weakness. This will be new, even in our newest of histories. The *social contrast* of the two banks of the Hudson will be without a precedent in the world's progress—"old-fogeyism" on one side of a river exclusively, and start-fair-dom on the other.

LETTER V.

Reasons for Neighbors moving Off—Morals of Steamboat Landings—Class that is gradually taking Possession of the Hudson—Thought-property in a Residence—Horizon-clock of Idlewild—Society for the Eye, in a View.

April 23,1853.

I met one of my neighbors yesterday, seated in his wife's rocking-chair, on top of a wagon-load of tools and kitchen utensils, and preceded by his boys, driving a troop of ten or fifteen cows. As he was one I had always chatted with, in passing, and had grown to value for his good sense and kindly character, I inquired into his movements with some interest. He was going (to use his own phrase) "twenty miles farther back, where a man could afford to farm, at the price of the land." His corn-fields on the banks of the Hudson had risen in value, as probable sites for ornamental residences, and with the difference (between two hundred dollars the fancy acre, and sixty dollars the farming acre) in his pocket, he was transferring his labor and his associations to a new soil and neighborhood. With the market for his produce quite as handy by railroad, he was some four or five thousand dollars richer in capital, and only a loser in scenery and local attachments. A Yankee's pots and kettles will almost walk away on their own legs, with such inducement.

There is another "alluvial deposit," however, besides Taste and Wealth, which helps to drive the farmer from the banks of the river. The steamboat landings occurring every few miles, are nests of bad company, and constant temptations to the idle curiosity of laborers and children. It is a gay sight—at least contrasted with plough and barn-yard—to see the "day boat" sweep up with twice as many inhabitants as the nearest village; crowds of city-dressed people, leaning over the balustrades, and the whole a gaily painted and confusedly fascinating spectacle of life and movement. Then the "evening boat," with her long line of lights, her ringing bells, and the magical glide with which she comes through the darkness, touches the wharf, and is gone; the perpetual succession of freight-boats; the equipages from the surrounding villages; and all the "runners," coachmen, porters, and "loafers," who abound upon the docks, swarming the bar-rooms in the intervals of arrivals, contribute to keep up an excitement, within reach of which a farmer's customary reliances are made vexatiously uncertain. He would scarce need more than this to make him seek a different neighborhood. But for once, the "money down" also pays virtue's expenses, and it is not surprising that the migration of the river farmers to both cheaper lands and a more moral atmosphere, is general and lively. The "opening down the middle" of the Empire State's robe of agriculture, will soon be edged with velvet, and, for its common cloth, we must look to the sides and skirts, broad back and towering shoulders. *A class who can afford to let the trees grow* is getting possession of the Hudson; and it is at least safe to rejoice in this, whatever one may preach as to the displacement of the laboring tiller of the soil by the luxurious idler. With the bare fields fast changing into wooded lawns, the rocky wastes into groves, the angular farm-houses into shaded villas, and the naked uplands into waving forests, our great thoroughfare will soon be seen (as it has not been for many years) in something like its natural beauty. It takes very handsome men and mountains to look well bald.

Yet the mover-back from the banks of the Hudson soon finds, probably, that he has sold more than he meant to sell. The *farm that belonged to his thoughts* has gone with the other farm. He has parted, unintentionally, with what he was daily in the habit of looking for, measuring time by, thinking about, and finding society in—the rail-trains and steamers, schooners and barges, sloops, yachts and lumber-rafts, of one of the most lively thoroughfares in the world. Stupidly enough, he had included all this in the "scenery"—the mere trees, hills and running water, of which he expected to find plenty where he was going! But a mere landscape—and a landscape alive with moving objects of beauty and interest—are very different places in which even to be yourself solitary.

It is to this blindness as to the *un-fenceible property in a spot,* that Idlewild owes its name. It belonged to a valuable farm; but it was a side of it, which, from being little more than a craggy ravine—the bed of a wayward torrent—had always been left in complete wilderness. When I first fell in love with it, and thought of making a home amid its tangle of hemlocks, my first inquiry as to its price was met with the disparaging remark, that it was of little value—*"only an idle wild of which nothing could ever be made."* And that description of it stuck captivatingly in my memory. "Idle-wild!" "Idle-wild!" But let me describe what belongs to Idlewild, besides its acres of good-for-nothing torrent and unharvestable crags, and besides the mere scenery around them.

To begin with a trifling convenience, it supplies *a clock,* gratis. From the promontory on which stands my cottage, I see five miles of the Hudson River Railroad, and two miles of the Newburgh and Erie—a clock rimmed round with a mountain horizon, the loveliest of landscapes for a face, and half-mile streaks of smoke for the fingers. Once learn the startings of the trains, and every one that passes announces the time of day. The smoke-fingers serve also as a barometer—more or less white and distinct, depressed or elevated, in proportion to the dampness of the atmosphere. It is something of a luxury also to be *daily*

William H. Bartlett, self-portrait. Drawing by William H. Bartlett, from N. P. Willis, *American Scenery* (London: Virtue, 1836).

View from West Point. Drawing by William H. Bartlett, from N. P. Willis, *American Scenery* (London: Virtue, 1836).

astonished; and I feel no beginning, at present, of getting used to seeing a rail-train slide along the side of a mountain—the swift smoke-tails of the Newburgh and Erie cars slicing off the top of Skunnemunk several times a day, at an elevation of two hundred feet above the Hudson, and often, when there is a mist below or above it, looking more like a meteor shooting along the face of a cloud, than a mechanical possibility in which a mortal may take passage or send a parcel. To have these swift trains perpetually flying past, one on each side of the river, and meeting at right angles where the ferry-boat is seen continually to cross, varies a man's walk, even at the tail of a plough.

But the two railways, though the most wonderful features of the *movement* in my landscape, are the least beautiful. The spread of the river above the pass of the Highlands (upon which I look immediately down), might be a small lake of four or five miles in extent, embosomed in mountains. This would be fine "scenery" to be solitary amidst, though the birds and the tree-tops were the only stirrers. But to be just as picturesquely secluded, as to personal remoteness, and still see the lake beneath my lawn traversed daily by a hundred craft of one sort and another—steamers, tow-boats, sloops, rafts, yachts, schooners and barges— makes, as I said before, a different thing of solitude. I presume five thousand people, at least, pass daily under my library window; and as one looks out upon the crowded cars and flotillas which bear such multitudes along, it does not require poetry, in these days of animal magnetism, to express how the sense of society is thus satisfied. A man mingles in a crowd, or goes to the play, to satisfy the social craving which is irresistible—but he need not speak or be spoken to, to get rid of his lonely feeling altogether. He must have a certain amount of human life and motion within reach of his eye. And, just how near or distant these moving fellow-beings must needs be, to magnetize companionship into the air, would vary, probably, with each man's electric circle. Across the river and over to Skunnemunk is near enough for me.

From *American Scenery**

VIEW FROM WEST POINT.

Of the river scenery of America, the Hudson, at West Point, is doubtless the boldest and most beautiful. This powerful river writhes through the highlands in abrupt curves, reminding one, when the tide runs strongly down, of Laocoon in the enlacing folds of the serpent. The different spurs of mountain ranges which meet here, abut upon the river in bold precipices from five to fifteen hundred feet from the water's edge; the foliage hangs to them, from base to summit, with the tenacity and bright verdure of moss; and the stream below, deprived of the slant

*Nathaniel Parker Willis, *American Scenery* (London: George Virtue, 1836), with illustrations by William H. Bartlett.

lights which brighten its depths elsewhere, flows on with a sombre and dark green shadow in its bosom, as if frowning at the narrow gorge into which its broad-breasted waters are driven.

Back from the bluff of West Point extends a natural platform of near half a mile square, high, level, and beautifully amphitheatred with wood and rock. This is the site of the Military Academy, and a splendid natural parade. When the tents of the summer camp are shining on the field—the flag, with its blood-bright stripes, waving against the foliage of the hills—the trumpet echoing from bluff to bluff, and the compact batallion cutting its trim line across the greensward—there are few more fairy spots in this working-day world.

On the extreme edge of the summit, overlooking the river, stands a marble shaft, pointing like a bright finger to glory, the tomb of the soldier and patriot Kosciusko. The military colleges and other buildings skirt the parade on the side of the mountain; and forward, toward the river, on the western edge, stands a spacious hotel, from the verandahs of which the traveller gets a view through the highlands, that he remembers till he dies. Right up before him, with the smooth curve of an eagle's ascent, rises the "old cro' nest" of the culprit Fay, a bright green mountain, that thrusts its topmost pine into the sky; the Donderbarrak, or (if it is not sacrilege to translate so fine a name for a mountain,) the *Thunder-chamber*, heaves its round shoulder beyond; back from the opposite shore, as if it recoiled from these, leans the bold cliff of Breknock; and then looking out, as if from a cavern, into the sun-light, the eye drops beyond upon a sheet of wide-spreading water, with an emerald island in its bosom; the white buildings of Newburgh creeping back to the plains beyond, and in the far, far distance, the wavy and blue line of the Cattskills, as if it were the dim-seen edge of an outer horizon.

The passage through the highlands at West Point still bears the old name of Wey-gat, or Wind-gate; and one of the prettiest moving dioramas conceivable, is the working through the gorge of the myriad sailing-craft of the river. The sloops which ply upon the Hudson, by the way, are remarkable for their picturesque beauty, and for the enormous quantity of sail they carry on in all weathers; and nothing is more beautiful than the little fleets of from six to a dozen, all tacking or scudding together, like so many white sea-birds on the wing. Up they come, with a dashing breeze, under Anthony's Nose, and the Sugar-Loaf, and giving the rocky toe of West Point a wide berth, all down helm, and round into the bay; when—just as the peak of Crow Nest slides its shadow over the mainsail—slap comes the wind aback, and the whole fleet is in a flutter. The channel is narrow and serpentine, the wind baffling, and small room to beat; but the little craft are worked merrily and well; and dodging about, as if to escape some invisible imp in the air, they gain point after point, till at last they get the Donderbarrak behind them, and fall once more into the regular current of the wind.

THE PALISADES—HUDSON RIVER.

The first feature of the celebrated banks of the Hudson, which arrests the eye of the traveller after leaving New York, is this singular wall of rock, extending as far onward as he can see, and forming a bold barricade against the river on the side of New Jersey. This singular precipice varies in height from fifty to two hundred feet, and presents a naked front of columnar strata, which gives it its descriptive name. The small sloops which lie along under the shore, loading with building stone from its base, and an occasional shed, diminished to the size of a dog-kennel, across the breadth of the river, are the only marks of life and habitation it presents to the traveller's eye.

With most persons, to mention the Palisades is to recall only the confusion of a steamer's deck, just off from the wharf, with a freight of seven or eight hundred souls hoping to "take tea" in Albany. The scene is one of inextricable confusion, and it is not till the twenty miles of the Palisades are well passed, that the bewildered passenger knows rightly whether his wife, child, or baggage, whichever may be his tender care, is not being left behind at the rate of fifteen miles in the hour.

I have often, when travelling alone, (for "reflection with folded arms" consorts only with the childless and baggageless bachelor), I have often flung my valise into a corner, and sure that the whole of my person and personal effects are under way, watched the maniform embarrassments and troubles that beset the uninitiated voyager on the Hudson. Fifteen minutes before the starting of the boat, there is not a passenger on board; "time is moving," and the American counting it as part of the expense, determines to pay only "on demand." He arrives on the narrow pier at the same instant with seven hundred men, ladies, and children, besides lapdogs, crammed baskets, uncut novels, and baggage for the whole. No commissioner in the world would guarantee to get all this freight on board in the given time, and yet it is done, to the daily astonishment of newspaper hawkers, orange-women, and penny-a-liners watching for dreadful accidents. The plank is drawn in, the wheels begin to paw like foaming steeds impatient to be off, the bell rings as if it was letting down the steps of the last hackney-coach, and away darts the boat, like half a town suddenly slipping off and taking a walk on the water. The "hands," (who follow their nomenclature literally, and have neither eyes nor bowels) trip up all the little children and astonished maids, in coiling up the hawser; the black head-waiter rings a hand-bell as if he were crazy, exhorting "them passengers as hasn't settled to step to the Cap'n's office, *and* settle," and angry people who have lost sight of their portmanteaus, and selfish people who *will not* get up to let the young gentleman see if his penny trumpet is not under them, play in a real-life farce better than Keeley or Liston. A painted notice and a very fat black woman in the door-way, inform the gentleman who has not seen his wife since the boat started, and is not at all sure that she is on board, that "no gentleman is permitted to enter the ladies' cabin," and spite of his dreadful uncertainty, he is obliged to trust to this dark Hebe to find her, among three hundred ladies, by description, and amuses all the listeners with his inventory of her dress, features, and general appearance. The negress disappears, is called twenty ways in twenty seconds, and an hour after, the patient husband sees the faithless messenger pass with a glass of lemonade, having utterly forgotten him and the lady in the black bonnet and grey eyes, who may be, for ought he knows to the contrary, wringing her hands at that moment on the warf at New York. By this time, the young ladies are tired of looking at the Palisades, and have taken out their novels, the old gentlemen are poring over their damp newspapers, and the captain has received his fourteen hundred or two thousand dollars, locked up his office, and gone up to smoke with the black funnel and the engineer. The broad waters of the Tappan Sea open before the flying cut-water; those who have never been up the river before, think of poor André as they pass Tappan and Tarrytown, and those who love gentle worth and true genius begin to look out for Sleepy Hollow, and the house of Washington Irving. It is a quiet little spot, buried in trees, and marked with an old Dutch vane. May his latter days, when they shall come, find there the reverence and repose which are his due!

THE COLONNADE OF CONGRESS HALL (SARATOGA SPRINGS).

Congress Hall has for many years held the palm of fashion among the rival Hotels of Saratoga. It is an immense wooden caravanserai, with no pretensions to architecture beyond what is seen in the drawing, and built with the sole view of affording the average accommodations of packed herrings to an indefinite number of persons. The roominess and liberal proportions of the Colonnade are one of those lies of architecture common to the hotels of this country. The traveller passes from the magnificent promise of the outside, to a chamber ten feet by four, situated in a remote gallery, visited once a day by the "boots" and chambermaid. His bed, chair, and wash-stand, resemble those articles as seen in penitentiaries; and if he chance to be ill at night, he might die like a Pagan, "without bell or candle." The arrangements of the house are, of necessity, entirely gregarious. A bell rings at half-past seven in the morning, at which every body who intends to breakfast, *must* get up; another bell at eight, to the call of which, if he prefers hot omelette to cold, he must be punctual. Dinner and tea exact the same promptitude; and the latter, which in other countries is a thing of no circumstance or importance, becomes, where you dine at two, a meal not willingly missed. "Tea" is at six or half past, and consists of cold meats, hot rolls, Indian cakes, all other kinds of cakes, all kinds of berries, pies, sweetmeats, and jellies, coffee and tea.

This is not a matter to be slighted after a fast of four hours; and home hurry beaux and belles from their abbreviated drives, with a loss of sentiment and sunset, and with profit to the keepers of stables, who let their horses "by the afternoon."

After tea, the gentlemen who dressed for dinner and "undressed" for their drive, dress once more for the evening, and the spacious Colonnade is thronged with the five hundred guests of the house, who pace to and fro for an hour, or, if it is a ball night, till the black band have made an orchestra of the tables in the dining-room, and struck up "Hail, Columbia!" A hoop, bound with evergreens, and stuck full of candles, hangs in the centre of the hall (*ci-devant* dining-room); an audience of all the negroes in the establishment sweetens the breath of heaven as it steals in at the windows; and, as the triumphant music returns a second time to the refrain, the lady Patroness enters on the arm of the gentleman who has the most stock in the Bank, followed in couples by all the gentlemen and ladies who intend to dance or play wall-flower. The black musicians "vex their instruments," and keep time with their heads and heels, as if all their extremities had been hired; the beaux who were interrupted in their declarations by the last *chassé*, (if they wish to go on with it,) lead out their partners to take the air and a cold,—perhaps a heart,—on the Colonnade; and at eleven, champagne goes round for the ladies, and the gentlemen take "summat to drink" at "the bar;" after which the candles burn brighter, and every body is much more agreeable.

Congress Hall is built very near the principal Spring, which lies in the westerly edge of a swamp. It was first discovered by the tracks of the deer, who frequented it so much as to wear paths to it from the surrounding woods. The mineral water is highly medicinal, and is not unpleasant to the taste. It formerly rose in the bed of a small brook, but it is now hid under the floor of an open colonnade, and discharges nearly a gallon a minute. The disengaged gas breaks through in limpid globules, giving to the surface the appearance of an active simmer. Here, before breakfast, creep the few who come to Saratoga for health; and here, before dinner, saunter those who are in need of a walk, or who wish a tonic for the coming meal. A busy varlet, with a capital of a hooked stick and two tin tumblers, drives a thriving trade here, fishing up the sparkling waters at a cent a glass, for all comers. When the gentleman has swallowed his muriate and four carbonates* in proper quanitity, a smooth serpentine walk leads to the summit of a prettily wooded hill, where he may either grind himself round a circular rail-road in a self-moving chair, or ramble off to the shade, for a little meditation.

*The analysis of a gallon of Congress water is thus stated:—

Muriate of soda	471.6	grains.
Carbonate of lime	178.474	—
Carbonate of soda	16.5	—
Carbonate of magnesia	3.356	—
Carbonate of iron	6.168	—
Total	676.000	—

ALBANY.

Albany is the second city in the State of New York, in population, wealth, and commerce. It stands on the west bank of the Hudson, and about one hundred and forty-five miles from New York by the river, and near the head of sloop navigation. It is built just over the pitch of an extensive plain, lying between the Mohawk and the Hudson, and has very much the look of a city sliding down hill.

The history of Albany is not very definite, touching its first settlement. The probability seems, that, in 1614, the Dutch erected a fort and trading-house on an island just below the city; and also, in nine years after, a fort, which they called Fort Orange, on the present site. I would appear to have been canonically christened, and has been called at different periods Aurania, Beverwyck, and Williamstadt. "All this time," says the historian, "it was known also by the name of '*The Fuyck.*'" The Indian appellation in which it rejoiced was Schaunaugh-ta-da, or *Once the pine plains.*

Albany is the residence of several of the oldest and wealthiest families in the State; but except this, it is a mere centre of transit—the channel through which passes the vast tide of commerce and travel to the north and west. The Erie and Champlain canals here meet the Hudson; and that which is passed up by this long arm from the sea, is handed over to the great lakes by the other two,—as if old Enceladus had been turned into a "worky," and stood with his long arms between salt water and fresh.

The association most people have with Albany, is that of having lost a portmanteau there. The north-river steam-boats land you with from three to seven hundred passengers upon a narrow pier, in the dusk of the evening, where you find from three to seven hundred individuals (more or less), each of whom seems to have no other object in life, than to persuade you, at that particular instant, to go by a certain conveyance, or to stop at a certain hotel. Upon setting your foot on shore, you find yourself among five or six infuriated gentlemen, two or three of whom walk backward before you, and all talking at the pitch which is necessary to drown the deepening hiss of the escape-valve and each other's voices. If you attempt to reason, you have no sooner satisfied the aforesaid six, that your route, your baggage, and your choice of an hotel, are matters in which they cannot be of the slightest assistance to you, than six more take their places, who must be satisfied as well; and so on in the same order. If you resolutely shut your lips, silence is taken for consent; your baggage is seized, and disappears before you have recovered from your amazement; and your only course is to follow the most importunate of your remaining five persecutors to an hotel; advertise in the next morning's paper for your portmanteau; and wait in Albany till it returns from Canada or Lake Erie, or till you are reconciled to its loss.

One of the most amusing scenes in the world, if it were not so distressing, is to

Albany. Drawing by William H. Bartlett, from N. P. Willis, *American Scenery* (London: Virtue, 1836).

The steamer *Chauncey Vibbard* arriving at Cornwall Landing ca. 1886, reminiscent of the daily arrival of *Alida* of earlier vintage described by Willis in *Out-Doors at Idlewild*. Oil painting, 1988, by William G. Muller; a large detail is reproduced in full color on the front cover.

see a large family of rather respectable emigrants landed by the steamer in Albany. It is their first step inland; and with all the confidence of those who are accustomed to countries where a man's person and property are outwardly respected, they yield their children and baggage to the persuasive gentlemen who assure them that all is right; and if a passing wonder crosses the mind of the sufferer, that his route should be so immediately comprehended by a perfect stranger, it is chased away the next moment by his surprise at the scene of bustle and confusion. At the end of five minutes the crowd thins a little, and he looks about for his family and effects. A stage coach is dashing off at top-speed in one direction, with his eldest daughter stretching out of the window, and crying in vain that there is some mistake; his two youngest are on board a steam-boat just off from the pier, and bound eight miles further up the river: the respectable part of his baggage has entirely disappeared; and nothing but his decrepit grand-mother and the paternal bedstead (both indebted for their escape to being deaf, and not portable,) remain of his family and chattels. For his comfort, the gentry around inform him that his children may be got back in a day or two, and he may find his baggage somewhere on his route to the west—offering, for a considera-tion not very trifling, to send off an express for either one or the other.

Albany is the seat of government, and has a State House, of which the historian of New York remarks: "In the structure of this edifice, the rules of architecture, Composite, have been violated." Lately, however, a taste for a better style of architecture seems to prevail; and in North Pearl-street we lately noticed a façade (we think, of a new church,) in a very pure and beautiful style. The private houses of Albany are built, many of them, very expensively; and the city is remarkable for its hospitality.

CROW NEST, FROM BULL HILL, WEST POINT.

It is true of the Hudson, as of all other rivers, that, to be seen to advantage, it should form the middle, not the foreground of the picture. Those who go to Albany by steam have something the same idea of the scenery of West Point, that an inside passenger may have of the effect of the Brighton coach at top-speed. It is astonishing how much foreground goes for in landscape; and there are few passes of scenery where it is more naturally beautiful than those of the Hudson. In the accompanying drawing, the picturesque neighbourhood of Undercliff, the seat of Colonel Morris, lies between the river and the artist, and directly opposite stands the peak of Crow Nest, mentioned in the description of West Point.

Crow Nest is one of the most beautiful mountains of America for shape, verdure, and position; and when the water is unruffled, and the moon sits on his summit, he looks like monarch crowned with a single pearl. This is the scene of the first piece-work of fancy which has come from the practical brain of Amer-ica,—the poem of The Culprit Fay. The opening is so descriptive of the spot, that it is quite in place here; and to those who have not seen the poem (as most European readers have not) it will convey an idea of a production which, in my opinion, treads close on the heels of the Midsummer Night's Dream:—

> "'Tis the middle watch of a summer's night,—
> The earth is dark, but the heavens are bright
> Nought is seen in the vault on high,
> But the moon, and the stars, and the cloudless sky,
> And the flood which rolls its milky hue,—
> A river of light on the welkin blue.
> The moon looks down on old Crow Nest,
> She mellows the shades on his shaggy breast
>
> And seems his huge grey form to throw
> In a silver cone on the wave below;
> His sides are broken by spots of shade,
> By the walnut boughs and the cedar made,
> And through their clustering branches dark
> Glimmers and dies the firefly's spark,—
> Like starry twinkles that momently break
> Through the rifts of the gathering tempest rack.
>
> The stars are on the moving stream,
> And fling, as its ripples gently flow,
> A burnish'd length of wavy beam,
> In an eel-like, spiral line below.
> The winds are whist, and the owl is still,
> The bat in the shelvy rock is hid;
> And nought is heard on the lonely hill
> But the cricket's chirp and the answer shrill
>   Of the gauze-wing'd katy-did;
> And the plaints of the mourning whip-poor-will,
> Who mourns unseen,and ceaseless sings
> Ever a note of wail and wo,
> Till morning spreads her rosy wings,
> And earth and skies in her glances glow.
>
> 'Tis the hour of fairy ban and spell:
> The wood-tick has kept the minutes well;
> He has counted them all with click and stroke
> Deep in the heart of the mountain-oak;
> And he has awakened the sentry-elve,
> Who sleeps with him in the haunted tree,
> To bid him ring the hour of twelve,
> And call the fays to their revelry.

 *　　*　　*　　*　　*　　*
They come from beds of lichen green,
They creep from the mullen's velvet screen;
Some on the backs of beetles fly
From the silver tops of moon-touch'd trees,
Where they swing in their cob-web hammocks high,
And rock'd about in the evening breeze;
Some from the hum-bird's downy nest,
They had driven him out by elfin power,
And pillow'd on plumes of his rainbow breast,
Had slumber'd there till the charmed hour;
Some had lain in a scarp of the rock,
With glittering ising-stars inlaid,
And some had open'd the four-o'clock,
And stolen within its purple shade:
And now they throng the moonlight glade,
Above—below—on every side,
Their little minion forms arrayed
In the tricksy pomp of fairy pride."

The general assembly of the fairies is at last complete, and they proceed to the trial of the culprit fay, who has extinguished his elfin lamp and paralyzed his wings by a love for a mortal maid. He is condemned to penances, which are most exquisitely described, and constitute the greater part of the poem; and he finally expiates his sins, and is forgiven. There is a fineness of description, and a knowledge of the peculiarities of American nature, in birds, fishes, flowers, and the phenomena of this particular region, which constitute this little poem a book of valuable information as well as an exquisite work of fancy.

Just under Crow Nest, buried in the heavy leaves of a ravine, springs a waterfall like a Naiad from the depths of the forest, and plunges down into the river. The rambles in and about its neighbourhood are cool and retired; and it is a favourite place for lovers from New York, who run up in the steamer in three hours, and find the honeymoon goes swimmingly off there,—the excellent hotel within half a mile supplying the *real*, without which the *ideal* is found to be very trumpery. The marble tomb of a cadet, who was killed by the bursting of a gun, forms a picturesque object, and gives a story to the spot.

KOSCIUSKO'S MONUMENT.

A pretty marble shaft stands on the edge of the broad highland esplanade of West Point, overlooking the most beautiful scene on the most beautiful river of our country. It commemorates the virtues of Kosciusko, who, during his second sojourn in America, lived at West Point, and cultivated his little garden, near the site of this tribute to his memory. Kosciusko's first laurels were gained in this country under Washington. He was educated in the military school at Warsaw, whence he was sent, as one of four, to complete his education at Paris. On his return to Poland, he had a commission given him, but, being refused promotion, he determined to come to America, and join the colonies in their struggle for independence. With letters from Dr. Franklin to General Washington, he presented himself to the great patriot, and was immediately appointed his aid-de-camp, and later he received the appointment to the engineers, with the rank of colonel. At the close of the war, having distinguished himself by his courage and skill, he returned to Poland, was appointed major-general in the army of the diet, and served as general of division under the younger Poniatowski. Finding, however, his efforts for freedom paralysed by the weakness or treachery of others, he gave in his resignation, and went into retirement at Leipsic. He was still there in 1793, when the Polish army and people gave signs of being in readiness for insurrection. All eyes turned towards Kosciusko, who was at once chosen for their leader, and messengers were sent to him from Warsaw to acquaint him with the schemes and wishes of his compatriots. In compliance with the invitation, he proceeded towards the frontiers of Poland; but apprehensive of compromising the safety of those with whom he acted, he was about to defer his enterprise, and set off for Italy. He was fortunately persuaded to return, and, arriving at Cracow at the very time when the Polish garrison had expelled the Russian troops, he was chosen generalissimo, with all the power of a Roman dictator. He immediately published an act, authorizing insurrection against the foreign authorities, and proceeded to support Colonel Madalinski, who was pursued by the Russians. Having joined that officer, they gained their first victory, defeating the enemy with inferior numbers. His army now increased to nine thousand men, the insurrection extended to Warsaw, and in a few days the Russians were driven from the palatinate. He obtained some advantage over the enemy in one more contest, but the king of Prussia arriving to the assistance of the Russians, he was exposed to great personal danger, and suffered a defeat. From this period he waged a disadvantageous warfare against superior force, and at last at Maczienice (or Maniejornice), fifty miles from Warsaw, an overwhelming Russian force completely defeated Kosciusko. He fell from his horse wounded, saying *Finis Polaniæ,* and was made prisoner.

Kosciusko was sent to Russia, and confined in a fortress near St. Petersburgh, where he was kept till the accession of Paul I. This monarch, through real or affected admiration for the character of the great man, released him, and presented him with his sword: "*I have no longer occasion for a sword, since I have no longer a country,*" answered Kosciusko.

In 1797 he once more took his departure for the United States, where he was received with honour and warm welcome by the grateful people whose liberty he had aided to achieve. He was granted a pension by the government, and elected to

The Narrows, at Staten Island. Drawing by William H. Bartlett, from N. P. Willis, *American Scenery* (London: Virtue, 1836).

the society of the Cincinnati. He returned to Europe the following year, bought an estate near Fontainebleau, and lived there till 1814. He removed again to Switzerland, and established himself at Soleure, where he died, in consequence of a fall with his horse over a precipice near Vevay. Among the last acts of his life, were the emancipation of the slaves on his own estate in Poland, and a bequest for the emancipation and education of slaves in Virginia.

Kosciusko was never married. His body was removed to Cracow, and deposited with great state in the tomb of the kings beneath the cathedral. The oldest officers were his bearers; two beautiful young girls with wreathes of oak leaves and cypress followed, and then came a long procession of the general staff, senate, clergy, and people. Count Wodsiki delivered a funeral oration on the hill of Wavel, and a prelate delivered an eloquent address in the church. The senate decreed that a lofty mound should be erected on the heights of Bronislawad. For three years men of every age and class toiled gratuitously at this work, and at last the *Mogila Kosziuszki,* the mound of Kosciusko, was raised to the height of 3000 feet! A serpentine path leads to the top, from which there is a noble view of the Vistula, and of the ancient city of the Polish kings. The small monument at West Point has less pretension, but it is the exponent of as deep a debt of gratitude, and of as grateful and universal honour to his memory.

THE NARROWS, AT STATEN ISLAND.

Almost any land looks beautiful after a long voyage; and it would not be surprising if the Narrows, oftenest seen and described by those who have just come off the passage of the Atlantic, should have this reputation. It does not require an eye long deprived of verdure, however, to relish the bold shores, the bright green banks, the clustering woods, and tasteful villas, which make up the charms of this lovely strait.

Busier waters than the Narrows could scarcely be found; and it is difficult to imagine, amid so much bustle and civilisation, the scene that presented itself to Hendrick Hudson, when the little *Halve-Mane* stole in on her voyage of discovery two hundred years ago. *Hoofden,* or the Highlands, as he then named the hills in this neighbourhood, "were covered with grass and wildflowers, and the air was filled with fragrance." Groups of friendly natives, clothed in elk skins, stood on the beach, singing, and offering him welcome, and, anchoring his little bark, he explored with his boats the channel and inlets, and penetrated to the mouth of the river which was destined to bear his name. It appears, however, that the Indians on the Long Island side were less friendly; and in one of the excursions into the Bay of Manhattan, his boat was attacked by a party of twenty-nine savages of a ferocious tribe, and an English sailor, named Colman, was killed by an arrow-shot in the shoulder. Other unfriendly demonstrations from the same tribe, induced Hudson to leave his anchorage at Sandy Hook, and he drew in to the Bay of New York, which he found most safe and commodious, and where he still continued his intercourse with the Indians of Staten Island, receiving them on board his vessel, dressing them, to their extravagant delight, in red coats, and purchasing from them fish and fruits in abundance.

At this day there stands a villa on every picturesque point; a thriving town lies on the left shore; hospitals and private sanitary establishments extend their white edifices in the neighbourhood of the quarantine-ground; and between the little fleets of merchantmen, lying with the yellow flag at their peak, fly rapidly and skilfully a constant succession of steam-boats, gaily painted and beautifully modelled, bearing on their airy decks the population of one of the first cities of the world. Yet of Manhattan Island, on which New York is built, Hudson writes, only two hundred years ago, that "it was wild and rough; a thick forest covered the parts where anything would grow; its beach was broken and sandy, and full of inlets; its interior presented hills of stony and sandy alluvion, masses of rock, ponds, swamps, and marshes."

The gay description which an American would probably give of the Narrows,—the first spot of his native land seen after a tedious voyage,—would probably be in strong contrast with the impression it produces on the emigrant, who sees in it only the scene of his first difficult step in a land of exile. I remember noting this contrast with some emotion, on board the packet-ship in which I was not long ago a passenger from England. Among the crowd of emigrants in the steerage, was the family of a respectable and well-educated man, who had failed as a merchant in some small town in England, and was coming, with the wreck of his fortune, to try the back-woods of America. He had a wife, and eight or ten very fine children, the eldest of whom, a delicate and pretty girl of eighteen, had contributed to sustain the family under their misfortunes at home, by keeping a village school. The confinement had been too much for her, and she was struck with consumption—a disease which is peculiarly fatal in America. Soon after leaving the British Channel, the physician on board reported her to the captain as exceedingly ill, and suffering painfully from the close air of the steerage; and by the general consent of the cabin passengers, a bed was made up for her in the deck-house, where she received the kindest attention from the ladies on board; and with her gentle manners and grateful expressions of pleasure, soon made an interest in all hearts. As we made the land, the air became very close and hot; and our patient, perhaps from sympathy with the general excitement about her, grew feverish and worse, hourly. Her father, and younger sister, sat by her, holding her hands and fanning her; and when we entered the Narrows with a fair wind, and every one on board, forgetting her in their admiration of the lovely scene, mounted to the upper deck, she was raised to the window, and stood with the bright red spot deepening on her cheek, watching the fresh green land without the slightest expression of pleasure. We dropped anchor, the boats were lowered, and as the steerage passengers were submitted to a quarantine, we attempted to take leave of her before going on shore. A fit of the most passionate tears, the paroxysms of which seemed almost to suffocate her, prevented her replying to us; and we left the poor girl surrounded with her weeping family, trying in vain to comfort her. Hers were feelings, probably, which are often associated with a remembrance of the Narrows.

VIEW FROM FORT PUTNAM.

This fort, which commands the military position of West Point, and which was considered so important during the revolutionary war, is now in ruins, and is visited by all travellers for the superb view which it affords of the sublime pass of the Highlands. This was the great key which Arnold's treachery intended to give into the hands of the English; and, associated with the memory of the unfortunate André, and with other painful events of the conspiracy, it possesses an interest which is wanting to other objects of the same description in our country.

Washington's visit of inspection to Fort Putnam, and the other redoubts on this side the river, was made only two or three hours before his discovery of the treason of Arnold, at that moment as he supposed in command at West Point. The commander-in-chief was expected to arrive the evening before, and had he done so, Arnold would probably never have escaped. Having accidentally met the French minister, M. de Lucerne, at Fishkill, however (eight miles above), he was induced to pass the night there for the purpose of some conference, and set off early in the morning on horseback, sending on a messenger to Mrs. Arnold that himself and suite would be with her to breakfast. Arriving opposite West Point, near a small redoubt called Fort Constitution, Washington turned his horse from the road. Lafayette, who was then in his suite, called out, "General, you are going in the wrong direction; you know Mrs. Arnold is waiting breakfast for us." "Ah," answered Washington, "I know you young men are all in love with Mrs. Arnold, and wish to get where she is as soon as possible. Go and take your breakfast with her, and tell her not to wait for me: I must ride down and examine the redoubts on this side the river." Two of the aides rode on, found breakfast waiting, and sat down at once with General Arnold and his family. While they were at table, a messenger came in with a letter for Arnold, which announced the capture of André, and the failure and betrayal, of course, of the whole conspira-cy. Showing little or no emotion, though his life hung upon a thread, he merely said to one of his aides that his presence was required at West Point; and, leaving word for General Washington that he was called over the river, but would return immediately, he ordered a horse and sent for Mrs. Arnold to her chamber. He then informed her abruptly that they must part, possibly for ever, and that his life depended on his reaching the enemy's lines without delay. Struck with horror at this intelligence, she swooned and fell senseless. In that state he left her, hurried down stairs, mounted a horse belonging to one of his aides that stood saddled at the door, and rode with all speed to the bank of the river. A boat with six men was in waiting; and, pretending that he was going with a flag of truce, he pulled down the stream, and arrived safe on board the Vulture sloop of war, lying some miles below.

Having finished his inspection of the redoubt, Washington arrived at Arnold's house, received the message, and concluded to cross immediately and meet Arnold at West Point. As the whole party were seated in the barge moving smoothly over the water, with the majestic scenery of the highlands about them, Washington said, "Well, gentlemen, I am glad, on the whole, that General Arnold has gone before us, for we shall now have a salute; and the roaring of the cannon will have a fine effect among these mountains." The boat drew near to the beach, but no cannon were heard, and there was no appearance of preparation to receive them. "What!" said Washington, "do they not intend to salute us!" At this moment an officer was seen making his way down the hill to meet them, who seemed confused at their arrival, and apologized for not being prepared to receive such distinguished visitors. "How is this, Sir," said Washington, "is not General Arnold here?" "No, Sir," replied the officer, "he has not been here these two days, nor have I heard from him within that time." "This is extraordinary," said Washington; "we were told he had crossed the river, and that we should find him here. However, our visit must not be in vain. Since we have come, we must look round a little, and see in what state things are with you." He then ascended the hill, examined Fort Putnam and the other fortifications, and returned to Arnold's house, where the treason was at once revealed. This had occupied two or three hours, however, and Arnold was beyond pursuit. Washington retained his usual calmness, though Arnold was one of his favourite officers, and had been placed at West Point by his own personal influence with Congress. He called Lafayette and Knox, showed them the proofs, and only said to the former, "Whom can we trust now!"

VIEW FROM HYDE PARK.

The Hudson at Hyde Park is a broad, tranquil, and noble river, of about the same character as the Bosphorus above Roumeli-bissar, or the Dardanelles at Abydos. The shores are cultivated to the water's edge, and lean up in graceful, rather than bold elevations; the eminences around are crested with the villas of the wealthy inhabitants of the metropolis at the river's mouth; summer-houses, belvideres, and water-steps, give an air of enjoyment and refreshment to the banks, and, without any thing like the degree of the picturesque which makes the river so remarkable thirty or forty miles below, it is, perhaps, a more tempting character of scenery to build and live among.

All along, in this part of the river, occur the "landings," which are either considerable towns in themselves, or indicate a thickly settled country in the rear. The immense steamers that ply on the Hudson leave and receive passengers at all

View from Hyde Park. Drawing by William H. Bartlett, from N. P. Willis, *American Scenery* (London: Virtue, 1836).

these points, and, to a person maⁿ⸳ g the passage for the first time, the manner and expedition of this operation is rather startling. In the summer time, the principal steam boats average from five to seven hundred passengers, and there is usually a considerable number to go ashore and come off at each place. A mile or two before reaching the spot, a negro makes the tour of the boat, with a large hand-bell, and, in an amusing speech, full of the idioms of his own race, announces the approach, and requests those who are going ashore to select their baggage. This done, the steamer, gliding over the smooth water at the rate of fifteen or twenty miles in the hour, sheers in toward the shore, and the small boat is lowered, with the captain in her at the helm; the passengers are put on board, and away she shoots at the end of a line gradually loosened, but still kept tight enough to send her, like an arrow to her mark. The moment she touches the pier, the loose line is let out from the steamer, which still keeps on her way, and between that moment and the exhaustion of the line, perhaps thirty seconds, the baggage is thrown out, and taken in, passengers jump ashore, and embark, and away shoots the little boat again, her bow rising clear over the crest of her own foam, with the added velocity of the steamer at full speed, and the rapid hauling in of the crew. I never have failed to observe a look of astonishment on the part of the subjects of this hurried transfer, however used to it by frequent repetition; and a long sigh of relief, as they look about on the broad and steady deck, or tread the ground beneath them if they have gone ashore, follows as invariably. As the boat is hauled up again, the negro crier reappears with his bell, and, looking the newly arrived group close in the face, cries out, as if they were a mile off, "All pas'ng'rs as hasn't paid their passage, please walk to the cap'n's office and settLE-E-E!!"
—the whole sentence recited in the most monotonous tone till the last syllable, which rises suddenly to a ludicrous scream, prolonged as long as his breath will continue it.

Many fatal accidents occurred formerly from this practice; but there is now more care and time taken about it, and the accidents, if any, are rather ludicrous than serious. I was going to Albany, some years ago, on board a very crowded boat, and among the passengers were a German and his wife, emigrants of the lower class. They had been down stairs at dinner, and the husband came up in search of his wife, who had preceded him, just as a crowded boatful were going ashore at Poughkeepsie. Either fancying it the end of his journey, or misunderstanding the man who was busy with the baggage, he threw in his bundle, and was peeping through the crowd of ladies on the stern for his wife; when one of the men, impatient of his delay, drew him in, and away he flew to the pier. He sprang ashore with the rest, his bundle was thrown after him, and, as the steamer sped away, we saw him darting about in the crowd to find his *vrouw,* who by this time had missed him, and was running from side to side, in quite as great embarrassment on board. The poor woman's distress was quite pitiable, and when, at last, one of the passengers, who had observed them together, pointed out to her her husband, in his flat cap and foreign *bleuse,* standing on the receding pier, with his hands stretched out after the boat, her agony could no longer be controlled. She was put ashore at the next landing to return by the "down boat;" but as another boat up the river arrived soon after at Poughkeepsie, the probability was, that he would embark again to follow her, and they would thus cross each other by the way; with scarce a word of English, and probably very little money, they may be hunting each other to this day.

VILLAGE OF SING-SING.

Sing-Sing is famous for its marble, of which there is an extensive quarry near by; for its State prison, of which the discipline is of the most salutary character; and for its academy, which has a high reputation. It may be said, altogether, to do the State some service.

The county of West Chester, of which this is the principal village on the Hudson, has been made the scene of, perhaps, the best historical novel of our country, and, more than any other part of the United States, suffered from the evils of war. The character and depredations of the "cow-boys" and "skinners," whose fields of action were on the skirts of this neutral ground, are familiar to all who have read "the Essay" of Mr. Cooper. A distinguished clergyman gives the following very graphic picture of West Chester county in those days:—

"In the autumn of 1777, I resided for some time in this county. The lines of the British were then in the neighbourhood of Kingsbridge, and those of the Americans at Byram river. The unhappy inhabitants were, therefore, exposed to the depredations of both. Often they were actually plundered, and always were liable to this calamity. They feared every body whom they saw, and loved nobody. It was a curious fact to a philosopher, and a melancholy one to hear their conversation. To every question they gave such an answer as would please the inquirer; or, if they despaired of pleasing, such a one as would not provoke him. Fear was, apparently, the only passion by which they were animated. The power of volition seemed to have deserted them. They were not civil, but obsequious; not obliging, but subservient. They yielded with a kind of apathy, and very quietly, what you asked, and what they supposed it impossible for them to retain. If you treated them kindly, they received it coldly; not as a kindness, but as a compensation for injuries done them by others. When you spoke to them, they answered you without either good or ill nature, and without any appearance of reluctance or hesitation; but they subjoined neither question nor remarks of their own; proving to your full conviction that they felt no interest either in the conversation or yourself. Both their countenances and their motions had lost every trace of animation and of feeling. Their features were smoothed, not into serenity, but apathy; and, instead of being settled in the attitude of quiet thinking, strongly indicated, that all thought beyond what was merely instinctive, had fled their minds for ever.

"Their houses, meantime, were, in a great measure, scenes of desolation.

Their furniture was extensively plundered, or broken to pieces. The walls, floors, and windows were injured both by violence and decay, and were not repaired, because they had not the means to repair them, and because they were exposed to the repetition of the same injuries. Their cattle were gone. Their enclosures were burnt, where they were capable of becoming fuel; and in many cases thrown down where they were not. Their fields were covered with a rank growth of weeds and wild grass.

"Amid all this appearance of desolation, nothing struck my eye more forcibly than the sight of the high road. Where I had heretofore seen a continual succession of horses and carriages, life and bustle lending a sprightliness to all the environing objects, not a single, solitary traveller was seen, from week to week, or from month to month. The world was motionless and silent, except when one of these unhappy people ventured upon a rare and lonely excursion to the house of a neighbour no less unhappy, or a scouting party, traversing the country in quest of enemies, alarmed the inhabitants with expectations of new injuries and sufferings. The very tracks of the carriages were grown over, and obliterated; and where they were discernible, resembled the faint impressions of chariot wheels, said to be left on the pavements of Herculaneum. The grass was of full height for the scythe, and strongly realized to my own mind, for the first time, the proper import of that picturesque declaration in the Song of Deborah: 'In the days of Shamgar, the son of Anath, in the days of Jael, the highways were unoccupied, and the travellers walked through by-paths. The inhabitants of the villages ceased: they ceased in Israel.'"

West Chester is a rough county in natural surface, but since the days when the above description was true, its vicinity to New York, and the ready market for produce, have changed its character to a thriving agricultural district. It is better watered with springs, brooks, and mill-streams, than many other parts of New York, and, among other advantages, enjoys, along the Hudson, a succession of brilliant and noble scenery.

VIEW FROM RUGGLE'S HOUSE, NEWBURGH, HUDSON RIVER.

Newburgh stands upon a pretty acclivity, rising with a sharp ascent from the west bank of the Hudson; and, in point of trade and consequence, it is one of the first towns on the river. In point of scenery, Newburgh is as felicitously placed, perhaps, as any other spot in the world, having in its immediate neighbourhood every element of natural loveliness; and, just below, the sublime and promising Pass of the Highlands. From the summit of the acclivity, the view over Wateaman and Fishkill is full of beauty; the deep flow of the Hudson lying between, and the pretty villages just named, sparkling with their white buildings and cheerful steeples, beyond.

Newburgh has a considerable trade with the back country, and supports two or three steam-boats, running daily and exclusively between its pier and New York.

If there were wanting an index of the wondrous advance of enterprise and invention in our country, we need not seek farther than this simple fact—a small intermediate town, on one river, supporting such an amount of expensive navigation. Only thirty years ago Fulton made his first experiment in steam on the Hudson, amid the unbelief and derision of the whole country. Let any one stand for one hour on the pier at Newburgh, and see those superb and swift palaces of motion shoot past, one after the other, like gay and chasing meteors; and then read poor Fulton's account of his first experiment—and never again throw discouragement on the kindling fire of genius.

"When I was building my first steam-boat," said he to Judge Story, "the project was viewed by the public at New York either with indifference or contempt, as a visionary scheme. My friends, indeed, were civil, but they were shy. They listened with patience to my explanations, but with a settled cast of incredulity on their countenances. I felt the full force of the lamentation of the Poet:—

'Truths would you teach, to save a sinking land,
All shun, none aid you, and few understand.'

As I had occasion to pass daily to and from the building-yard while my boat was in progress, I have often loitered, unknown, near the idle groups of strangers gathering in little circles, and heard various inquiries as to the object of this new vehicle. The language was uniformly that of scorn, sneer, or ridicule. The loud laugh rose at my expense; the dry jest, the wise calculation of losses and expenditure; the dull but endless repetition of "*the Fulton folly.*" Never did a single encouraging remark, a bright hope, or a warm wish, cross my path.

"At length the day arrived when the experiment was to be made. To me it was a most trying and interesting occasion. I wanted many friends to go on board to witness the first successful trip. Many of them did me the favour to attend, as a matter of personal respect; but it was manifest they did it with reluctance, feigning to be partners of my mortification, and not of my triumph. I was well aware that, in my case, there were many reasons to doubt of my own success. The machinery was new, and ill-made; and many parts of it were constructed by mechanics unacquainted with such work; and unexpected difficulties might reasonably be presumed to present themselves from other causes. The moment arrived in which the word was to be given for the vessel to move. My friends were in groups on the deck. There was anxiety mixed with fear among them. They were silent, sad, and weary. I read in their looks nothing but disaster, and almost repented of my efforts. The signal was given, and the boat moved on a short distance, and then stopped, and became immovable. To the silence of the preceding moment, now succeeded murmurs of discontent and agitation, and whispers and shrugs. I could hear distinctly repeated, "I told you so,—it is a

View from the Telegraph Signal, New York Bay. Drawing by William H. Bartlett, from N. P. Willis, *American Scenery* (London: Virtue, 1836).

foolish scheme.—I wish we were well out of it." I elevated myself on a platform, and stated that I knew not what was the matter; but if they would be quiet, and indulge me for half an hour, I would either go on or abandon the voyage. I went below, and discovered that a slight maladjustment was the cause. It was obviated. The boat went on; we left New York; we passed through the Highlands; we reached Albany!—Yet even then, imagination superseded the force of fact. *It was doubted if it could be done again, or if it could be made, in any case, of any great value.*"

What an affecting picture of the struggles of a great mind, and what a vivid lesson of encouragement to genius, is contained in this simple narration!

VIEW FROM THE TELEGRAPH SIGNAL, NEW YORK BAY.

The first visitor to the Bay of New York, and the writer of the first description on record, was John de Verrazzano, a Florentine, in the service of Francis the First. This bold navigator had been for some time in command of four ships, cruising against the Spaniards. But his little fleet being separated in a storm, Verrazzano determined, with one of them, the Dauphin, to take a voyage in search of new countries. He arrived on the American coast, somewhere near North Carolina, and first proceeded south as far as "the region of palmtrees," probably Florida. He then turned, and proceeded north till he entered a harbour, which he describes thus, in a passage of a letter addressed by him to his Royal master:—

"This land is situated in the paralele of Rome, in forty-one degrees and two terces; but somewhat more colde by accidentall causes. The mouth of the haven lieth open to the south, half a league broad; and being entred within it, between the east and the north, it stretcheth twelve leagues, where it wareth broader and broader, and maketh a gulfe about twenty leagues in compass, wherein are five small islands, very fruitfull and pleasant, full of hie and broad trees, among the which islands any great navie may ride safe without any feare of tempest or other danger."

In this harbour Verrazzano appears to have remained about fifteen days. He and his men frequently went on shore to obtain supplies and see the country. He says in another part of his letter—"Sometimes our men stayed two or three daies on a little island neere the ship for divers necessaries. We were oftentimes within the land five or six leagues, which we found as pleasant as is possible to declare, very apt for any kind of husbandry, of corne, wine, and ayle. We entered afterwards into the woods, which we found so thicke that any army, were it never so great, might have hid itself therein; the trees whereof are okes, cypresse-trees, and other sortes unknown in Europe."

These were probably the first European feet that ever trod on any part of the territory now included in the State of New York. Verrazzano and his crew seem to have had considerable intercourse with the natives, and generally to have been treated well, though by his own account he did not always deserve it. Speaking of an excursion made by his men somewhere on the coast, he says:—"They saw only one old woman, with a young maid of eighteen or twenty yeeres old, which, seeing our companie, hid themselves in the grasse for feare. The old woman carried two infants on her shoulders, and the young woman was laden with as many. As soone as they saw us, to quiet them and win their favours, our men gave them victuals to eate, which the old woman received thankfully, but the young woman threw them disdainfully on the ground. *They took a child from the old woman to bring into France; and going about to take the young woman, which was very beautiful, and of tall stature,* they could not possibly, for the great outcries that she made, bring her to the sea; and especially having great woods to pass thorow, and being far from the ship, we proposed to leave her behind, *bearing away the child only.*"

In a subsequent part of his narrative, Verrazzano presents a very favourable picture, not only of the amenity, but of the discretion of the aborigines. "They came in great companies of their small boats unto the ship, with their faces all bepainted with divers colours, and bringing their wives with them, whereof they were very jealous; they themselves entring aboard the ship, and staying there a good space, but causing their wives to stay in their boats; and for all the entreatie that we could make, offering to give them divers things, we could never obtaine that they would suffer them to come aboard the ship. And oftentimes one of the two Kings comming with his Queene, and *many gentlemen* for their pleasure to see us, they all stayed on shore 200 paces from us, sending us a small boat to give us intelligence of their comming; and as soon as they had answere from us they came immediately, and wondered at hearing the cries and noyses of the mariners. The Queene and her maids staied in the very light boat at an island a quarter of a league off, while the King abode a long space in our ship, uttering divers conceits with gestures, viewing with great admiration the furniture of the shippe. And sometimes our men staying one or two days on a little island near the ship, he returned with seven or eight of *his gentlemen* to see what we did; then the King drawing his bow, and running up and down with *his gentlemen,* made much sport to gratify our men."

The sail-studded bay of New York at this day presents another scene; and one of these same "*gentlemen*" is now almost as much a curiosity here as was John de Verrazzano, only three centuries ago, to the rightful lords of this fair land and water.

PEEKSKILL LANDING.

Like most of the *landings* on the Hudson, Peekskill is a sort of outstretched hand from the interior of the country. It is about eighty* miles from New York, and

*Ed. Note: Peekskill is actually 40 miles from New York City.

Peekskill Landing. Drawing by William H. Bartlett, from N. P. Willis, *American Scenery* (London: Virtue, 1836).

the produce from the country behind is here handed over to the trading sloops, who return, into the waiting palm, the equivalent in goods from the city. A sort of town naturally springs up at such a spot, and, as a river-side is a great provocative of idleness, all the Dolph Heyligers of the country about seem to be collected at the landing.

The neighbourhood of this spot is interesting from its association with the history of the Revolution. The head-quarters of General Washington were just below, at Verplank's Point; and the town of Peekskill, half a mile back from the river, was the depôt of military stores, which were burnt by General Home in 1777. "On my return southward in 1782," says the translator of Chastellux, who has not given his name, "I spent a day or two at the American camp at Verplank's Point, where I had the honour of dining with General Washington. I had suffered severely from an ague, which I could not get quit of, though I had taken the exercise of a hard-trotting horse, and got thus far to the north in the month of October. The General observing it, told me he was sure I had not met with a good glass of wine for some time,—an article then very rare,—but that my disorder must be frightened away. He made me drink three or four of his silver camp cups of excellent Madeira at noon, and recommended to me to take a generous glass of claret after dinner; a prescription by no means repugnant to my feelings, and which I most religiously followed. I mounted my horse the next morning, and continued my journey to Massachusetts, without ever experiencing the slightest return of my disorder.

"The American camp here presented the most beautiful and picturesque appearance. It extended along the plain, on the neck of land formed by the winding of the Hudson, and had a view of this river to the south. Behind it, the lofty mountains, covered with wood, formed the most sublime back-ground that painting could express. In the front of the tents was a regular continued portico, formed by the boughs of the trees in full verdure, decorated with much taste and fancy. Opposite the camp, and on distinct eminences, stood the tents of some of the general officers, over which towered predominant that of Washington. I had seen all the camps in England, from many of which drawings and engravings have been taken; but this was truly a subject worthy the pencil of the first artist. The French camp, during their stay in Baltimore, was decorated in the same manner. At the camp at Verplank's Point we distinctly heard the morning and evening gun of the British at Knightsbridge."*

The curiosity seizes with avidity upon any accidental information which fills up the bare outline of history. The personal history of Washington more particularly, wherever it has been traced by those who were in contact with him, is full of interest. Some of the sketches given by the Marquis of Chastellux, who passed this point of the Hudson on his way to Washington's headquarters below, are very graphic.

*Ed. Note: More likely Kingsbridge.

"The weather being fair on the 26th," he says, "I got on horseback, after breakfasting with the General. He was so attentive as to give me the horse I rode on the day of my arrival. I found him as good as he is handsome; but, above all, perfectly well broke and well trained, having a good mouth, easy in hand, and stopping short in a gallop without bearing the bit. I mention these minute particulars, because it is the the General himself who breaks all his own horses. He is an excellent and bold horseman, leaping the highest fences, and going extremely quick without standing upon his stirrups, bearing on the bridle, or letting his horse run wild; circumstances which our young men look upon as so essential a part of English horsemanship, that they would rather break a leg or an arm than renounce them."

After passing some days at headquarters, this young nobleman thus admirably sums up his observations on Washington:—

"The strongest characteristic of this great man is the perfect union which reigns between his physical and moral qualities. Brave without temerity, laborious without ambition, generous without prodigality, noble without pride, virtuous without severity; he seems always to have confined himself within those limits beyond which the virtues, by clothing themselves in more lively but more changeable colours, may be mistaken for faults. It will be said of him hereafter, that *at the end of a long civil war he had nothing with which he could reproach himself.* His stature is noble and lofty, he is well made and exactly proportioned; his physiognomy mild and agreeable, but such as to render it impossible to speak particularly of any of his features; so that on quitting him, you have only the recollection of a fine face. He has neither a grave nor a familiar air; his brow is sometimes marked with thought, but never with inquietude; in inspiring respect he inspires confidence, and his smile is always the smile of benevolence."

LIGHTHOUSE NEAR CALDWELL'S LANDING.

This picturesque object is seen to great effect by the passenger in the evening boat from New York to Newburgh. Leaving the city at five in the summer afternoon, she makes the intervening forty* miles between that hour and twilight; and while the last tints of the sunset are still in the sky, the stars just beginning to twinkle through the glow of the west, the bright light of this lofty beacon rises up over the prow of the boat, shining apparently on the very face of the new-starred heaven. As he approaches, across the smooth and still purpled mirror of the silent river is drawn a long and slender line of light, broken at the foot of the beacon by the mild shrubbery of the rock on which it stands; and as he rounds the point, and passes it, the light brightens and looks clearer against the darker sky of the east, while the same cheering line of reflection follows him on his way, and is lost to sight as he disappears among the mountains.

*Ed. Note: Newburgh is 57 miles from New York City.

274

Lighthouse near Caldwell's Landing (Stony Point Light). Drawing by William H. Bartlett, from N. P. Willis, *American Scenery* (London: Virtue, 1836).

The waters of the river at this point were the scene of the brief and tragic drama enacted so fatally by poor André. Four or five miles below stands Smith's house, where he had his principal interview with Arnold, and where the latter communicated to him his plans for the delivery of West Point into the hands of the English, and gave him the fatal papers which proved his ruin.

At Smith's house Mrs. Arnold passed a night, on her way to join her husband at West Point, soon after he had taken command. The sufferings of this lady have excited the sympathy of the world, as the first paroxysms of her distress moved the kind but firm heart of Washington. There seems to have arisen a doubt, however, whether her long and well-known correspondence with André had not so far undermined her patriotism, that she was rather inclined to further than impede the treason of Arnold; and consequently could have suffered but little after Washington generously made every arrangement for her to follow him. In the "Life of Aaron Burr," lately published, are some statements which seem authentic on the subject. It is well known that Washington found Mrs. Arnold apparently frantic with distress at the communication her husband had made to her the moment before his flight. Lafayette, and the other officers in the suite of the commander-in-chief, were alive with the most poignant sympathy; and a passport was given her by Washington, with which she immediately left West Point to join Arnold in New York. On her way she stopped at the house of Mrs. Prevost, the wife of a British officer, who subsequently married Colonel Burr. Here "the frantic scenes of West Point were renewed," says the narrative of Burr's biographer, "and continued so long as strangers were present. As soon as she and Mrs. Prevost were left alone, however, Mrs. Arnold became tranquillized, and assured Mrs. Prevost that she was heartily sick of the theatrics she was exhibiting. She stated that she had corresponded with the British commander; that she was disgusted with the American cause, and those who had the management of public affairs; and that, through great persuasion and unceasing perseverance, she had ultimately brought the General into an arrangement to surrender West Point to the British. Mrs. Arnold was a gay, accomplished, artful, and extravagant woman. There is no doubt, therefore, that, for the purpose of acquiring the means of gratifying her vainty, she contributed greatly to the utter ruin of her husband, and thus doomed to everlasting infamy and disgrace all the fame he had acquired as a gallant soldier, at the sacrifice of his blood."

It is not easy to pass and repass the now peaceful and beautiful waters of this part of the Hudson, without recalling to mind the scenes and actors in the great drama of the revolution, which they not long ago bore on their bosom. The busy mind fancies the armed guard-boats, slowing pulling along the shore; the light pinnace of the Vulture plying to and fro on its errands of conspiracy; and not the least vivid picture to the imagination, is the boat containing the accomplished, the gallant André and his guard, on his way to his death. It is probable that he first admitted to his own mind the possibility of a fatal result, while passing the very spot presented in the drawing. A late biographer of Arnold gives the particulars of a conversation between André and Major Tallmadge, the officer who had him in custody, and who brought him from West Point down the river to Tappan, the place of his subsequent execution.

"Before we reached the Clove" (a landing just below the beacon represented in the drawing,) "Major André became very inquisitive to know my opinion as to the result of his capture. When I could no longer evade his importunity, I remarked to him as follows:—'I had a much-loved classmate in Yale College, by the name of Hale, who entered the army in 1775. Immediately after the battle of Long Island, Washington wanted information respecting the strength of the enemy. Hale tendered his services, went over to Brooklyn, and was taken, just as he was passing the outposts of the enemy on his return.' Said I, with emphasis, 'Do you remember the sequel of this story?' 'Yes,' said André, 'he was hanged as a spy. But you surely do not consider his case and mine alike?' I replied, 'Yes, precisely similar, and similar will be your fate.' He endeavoured to answer my remarks, but it was manifest he was more troubled in spirit than I had ever seen him before."

INDIAN FALL, OPPOSITE WEST POINT.

This is a secluded and delicious bit of nature, hidden amid rocks and woods, on the shore of the Hudson, but possessing a refinement and an elegance in its wildness which would almost give one the idea that it was an object of beauty in some royal park. One of the most secret streams that feed this finest of our rivers, finds its way down through a winding and almost trackless channel; and after fretting over rocks, and loitering in dark and limpid pools for several miles, suddenly bursts out over a precipice of fifty feet, and fills with its clear waters the sheltered basin seen in the drawing. Immense trees overhang it on every side, and follow the stream still on in its course; and, in the depth of summer, the foaming current scarcely catches a ray of the sun from its source to its outlet. The floor of the basin below the Fall is pebbly, the water is clear and cool, the spot secluded, and, in all respects, Nature has formed it for a bath. A fair and famous lady, residing a summer or two since at West Point, was its first known Musidora, and the limpid and bright basin is already called after her name.*

A large party visiting at a hospitable house, where the artist and his travelling companion were entertained during the heat of the last summer, proposed to accompany him on his visit to the Indian Fall. Excursions on the banks of the Hudson are usually made in boats; but it was necessary to see some points of view from the hills between, and we walked out to the stables to see what could be done for vehicles and cattle. A farm waggon, with its tail up in the air, built after an old Dutch fashion, which still prevails in New York,—a sort of loosely jointed, long,

*Ed. Note: Fanny Kemble's bath.

lumbering vehicle, which was meant to go over any rock smaller than a beer-barrel without upsetting—was the only "consarn," as the "help" called it, which would hold the party. With straw in the bottom, and straps put across from peg to peg, it would carry eleven, and the driver.

Horses were the next consideration; and here we were rather staggered. A vicious old mare, that kept a wheelwright and a surgeon in constant employ,—and a powerful young colt, half broken,—were the only steeds in stable. However either might be made to go alone, they had never been tried together; and the double waggon harness was the worse for service. The "help" suggested very sensibly that the load would be too heavy to run away with, and that if the mare kicked, or the colt bolted—or, in short, if any thing happened, except backing over a precipice, we had only to sit still and let them do their "darndest."

We cobbled the harness in its weak spots, shook down the straw for the ladies, nailed up the tail-board, which had lost its rods, got the cattle in, and brought up quietly to the door. The ladies and the champagne were put in, and the colt led off by the bit, shaking his head, and catching up his hind leg; while the demure old mare drew off tamely and steadily, "never wicked," as the ploughman said, "till you got her dander up with a tough hill." The driver had a chain with a list bottom, and, having had some practice in Charing Cross and Fleet Street, fingered his reins and flourished his maple whip through the village, evidently not thinking himself or his driving *de la petite bière.*

The road, which followed the ridges of the superb hills skirting the river opposite West Point, was, in some places, scarce fit even for a bridle-path; and, at every few paces, came a rock, which we believed passable when we had surged over it—not before. The two ill-matched animals drew to a wonder; and the ladies and the champagne had escaped all damage, till, as the enemy of mankind would have it, our ambitious whip saw stretching out before him a fair quarter of a mile of more even road. A slight touch of the whip sent off the colt in a jump, carrying away the off trace with the first spring; the old mare struck into a gallop, and, with the broken trace striking against the colt's heels, and whippletree parallel with the pole, away they went as nearly in a tandem as the remaining part of the harness would allow. The tail-board soon flew off, and let out two unsuspecting gentlemen, who had placed their backs and their reliance upon it; and the screams of the ladies added what was wanting to raise the "dander" of the old mare to its most unpleasant climax. The straps gave way, the ladies rolled together in the straw, the driver tossed about on his list-bottomed chain, the champagne corks flew,—and presently, as if we were driven by a battering-ram against a wall, we brought up with a tremendous crash, and stood still. We had come to a sharp turn in the road; and the horses, unable to turn, had leaped a low stone wall, and breaking clear of every thing, left us on one side, while they thrashed the ripe wheat with the whippletrees on the other.

The ladies were undamaged, fortunately; and, with one champagne bottle saved from the wreck, we completed the excursion to the Fall on foot, and were too happy to return by water.

View of the Ferry at Brooklyn, New York.

Brooklyn is as much a part of New York, for all purposes of residence and communication, as "the Borough" is of London. The steam ferry-boats cross the half-mile between it and the city every five minutes; and in less time than it usually takes to thread the press of vehicles on London Bridge, the elegant equipages of the wealthy cross to Long Island for the afternoon drive; morning visits are interchanged between the residents in both places—and, indeed, the east river is hardly more of a separation than the same distance in a street.

Brooklyn is the shire-town of King's County, and by this time, probably, is second in population only to New York. Land there, has risen in value to an enormous extent within the last few years; and it has become the fashion for business-men of New York to build and live on the fine and healthy heights above the river, where they are nearer their business, and much better situated than in the outskirts of the city itself. The town of Brooklyn is built on the summit and sides of an elevation springing directly from the bank of the river, and commanding some of the finest views in America. The prospect embraces a large part of East River, crowded with shipping, and tracked by an endless variety of steamers, flying through the channel in quick succession; of the city of New York, extending, as far as the eye can see, in closely piled masses of architecture; of the Hudson, and the shore of Jersey, beyond; of the bay and its bright islands, and of a considerable part of Long and Staten Islands, and the Highlands of Neversink. A more comprehensive, lively, and interesting view is nowhere to be found.

Historically, Brooklyn will long be remembered for the battle fought in its neighbourhood between the British and Hessians under the command of General Howe, and the Americans under the immediate command of Generals Putnam and Sullivan. It was a contest of a body of ill-disciplined militia against twice their number of regular troops, and ended in defeat; but the retreat conducted by General Washington saved the army, and relieved a little the dark fortunes of the day.

The American forces were composed of militia and raw recruits, and without even dragoons to serve as videts. They were stationed on a chain of eminences running from Yellow Hook towards Hempstead; and the British, from the Ferry between Staten and Long Island, through the level country to the village of Flatland. From the last-mentioned place, a strong column, led by General Clinton and Lord Percy, marched into the Jamaica Road, through an unoccupied pass in this chain of hills on the right, and turned the left of the American army. General Grant at the same time attacked the right of the Americans under the

View of the Ferry at Brooklyn, New York. Drawing by William H. Bartlett, from N. P. Willis, *American Scenery* (London: Virtue, 1836).

The Two Lakes and the Mountain House on the Catskills. Drawing by William H. Bartlett, from N. P. Willis, *American Scenery* (London: Virtue, 1836).

command of Lord Sterling, posted near the Ferry; while the fleet commenced a powerful cannonade upon a battery at Red Hook, to draw off the attention of the Americans from the main attack directed by Sir Henry Clinton.

As soon as the Americans perceived that the enemy had gained the rear, they were thrown into confusion, and attacks were made on the centre, commanded by General Sullivan, and the right, commanded by Lord Stirling, and both divisions completely routed. A gallant attempt was made by the latter officer, which, though unavailing, facilitated the retreat of part of the troops under his command. He was himself taken prisoner, as were also Generals Sullivan and Woodhull. The number of Americans killed is estimated at four hundred, and the wounded and prisoners at a thousand.

General Washington, who had passed over from New York to Brooklyn during the heat of the action, perceived that nothing could be done to turn the fortune of the day, and that the only thing to be accomplished was a retreat. The British were only waiting for a wind to move their shipping into the East River, and the next morning might find the ferry in their possession. The British were encamped within six hundred yards of him; and the wind, until eleven o'clock, was unfavourable. At that hour it lulled, and a thick fog covered the bosom of the river. The army commenced their embarkation under this fortunate protection; and the whole of the forces, with their ammunition, provision, horses, waggons, &c. crossed undisturbed. The retreat was discovered by the British half an hour after the evacuation. The sound of their pickaxes was distinctly heard within the American lines during the embarkation.

THE TWO LAKES AND THE MOUNTAIN HOUSE ON THE CATSKILLS.

At this elevation, you may wear woollen and sleep under blankets in midsummer; and that is a pleasant temperature where much hard work is to be done in the way of pleasure-hunting. No place so agreeable as Catskill, after one has been parboiled in the city. New York is at the other end of that long thread of a river, running away south from the base of the mountain; and you may change your climate in so brief a transit, that the most enslaved broker in Wall Street may have half his home on Catskill. The cool woods, the small silver lakes, the falls, the mountain-tops, are all delicious haunts for the idler-away of the hot months; and, to the credit of our taste, it may be said they are fully improved—Catskill is a "resort."

From the Mountain-House, the busy and all-glorious Hudson is seen winding half its silver length—towns, villas, and white spires, sparkling on the shores, and snowy sails and gaily-painted steamers, specking its bosom. It is a constant diorama of the most lively beauty; and the traveller, as he looks down upon it, sighs to make it a home. Yet a smaller and less-frequented stream would best fulfil desires born of a sigh. There is either no seclusion on the Hudson, or there is so much that the conveniences of life are difficult to obtain. Where the steamers come to shore, (twenty a day, with each from one to seven hundred passengers,) it is certainly far from secluded enough; yet, away from the landing-places, servants find your house too lonely, and your table, without unreasonable expense and trouble, is precarious and poor. These mean and *menus plaisirs* reach, after all, the very citadel of philosophy. Who can live without a cook or a chambermaid, and dine seven days in the week on veal, consoling himself with the beauties of a river-side?

On the smaller rivers these evils are somewhat ameliorated; for in the rural and uncorrupt villages of the interior, you may find servants born on the spot, and content to live in the neighbourhood. The market is better, too, and the society less exposed to the evils that result from too easy an access to the metropolis. No place can be rural, in all the *virtues* of the phrase, where a steamer will take the villager to the city between noon and night, and bring him back between midnight and morning. There is a suburban look and character about all the villages on the Hudson which seems out of place among such scenery. They are suburbs; in fact, steam has destroyed the distance between them and the city.

The Mountain-House on the Catskill, it should be remarked, is a luxurious hotel. How the proprietor can have dragged up, and keeps dragging up, so many superfluities from the river level to that eagle's nest, excites your wonder. It is the more strange, because in climbing a mountain the feeling is natural that you leave such enervating indulgences below. The mountain-top is too near heaven. It should be a monastery to lodge in so high—a St. Gothard, or a Vallambrosa. But here you may choose between Hermitages, "white" or "red," Burgundies, Madeiras, French dishes, and French dances, as if you had descended upon Capua.

VILLA ON THE HUDSON, NEAR WEEHAWKEN.

From this admirably chosen spot, the Bay of New York appears with every accessory of beauty. The city itself comes into the left of the picture to an advantage seen from no other point of view, the flocks of river-craft scud past in all directions, men-of-war, merchantmen, steamers, and ferry-boats, fill up the moving elements of the panorama; and far away beyond stretches the broad harbour, with its glassy or disturbed waters, in all the varieties of ever-changing sea-view. It was on this side that Hudson, who had felt the hostility of the Manhattan Indians, found a friendlier tribe, and made his first amicable visit on shore. The Indian tradition, springing from that visit,* and describing the first intoxication they had ever experienced, is extremely amusing.

"A long time ago, before men with a white skin had ever been seen, some

---

*It is disputed whether this scene of intoxication took place on the present site of New York, on the Jersey side, or at Albany.

The Catskill Mountain House. Drawing by William H. Bartlett, from N. P. Willis, *American Scenery* (London: Virtue, 1836).

Villa on the Hudson, near Weehawken. The home of James Gore King, Esq., also known as King's Bluff. Drawing by William H. Bartlett, from N. P. Willis, *American Scenery* (London: Virtue, 1836).

Indians, fishing at a place where the sea widens, espied something at a distance moving upon the water. They hurried ashore, collected their neighbours, who together returned and viewed intensely this astonishing phenomenon. What it could be, baffled all conjecture. Some supposed it to be a large fish or animal, others that it was a very big house, floating on the sea. Perceiving it moving towards land, the spectators concluded that it would be proper to send runners in different directions to carry the news to their scattered chiefs, that they might send off for the immediate attendance of their warriors. These arriving in numbers to behold the sight, and perceiving that it was actually moving towards them (*i.e.* coming into the river or bay), they conjectured that it must be a remarkably large house, in which the Manitto (or Great Spirit), was coming to visit them. They were much afraid, and yet under no apprehension that the Great Spirit would injure them. They worshipped him. The chiefs now assembled at York Island, and consulted in what manner they should receive their Manitto: meat was prepared for a sacrifice; the women were directed to prepare the best of victuals; idols or images were examined and put in order; a grand dance they thought would be pleasing, and, in addition to the sacrifice, might appease him, if angry. The conjurers were also set to work, to determine what this phenomenon portended, and what the result would be. To these, men, women, and children, looked up for advice and protection. Utterly at a loss what to do, and distracted alternately by hope and fear, in this confusion a grand dance commenced. Meantime fresh runners arrived, declaring it to be a great house, of various colours, and full of living creatures. It now appeared certain that it was their Manitto, probably bringing some new kind of game. Others arriving, declared it positively to be full of people, of different colour and dress from theirs, and that one, in particular, appeared altogether *red*. This then must be the *Manitto*. They were lost in admiration; could not imagine what the vessel was, whence it came, or what all this portended. They are now hailed from the vessel in a language they could not understand; they answer by a shout or yell in their way. The house (or large canoe, as some render it) stops. A smaller canoe comes on shore, with the red man in it; some stay by his canoe, to guard it. The chiefs and wise men form a circle, into which the red man and two attendants approach. He salutes them with friendly coutenance, and they return the salute after their manner. They are amazed at their colour and dress, particularly with him who, glittering in red, wore something (perhaps lace, or buttons) they could not comprehend. He *must* be the great Manitto, they thought; but why should he have a *white skin*? A large elegant *hockhack* (*gourd, i.e.* bottle, decanter, &c.) is brought by one of the supposed Manitto's servants, from which a substance is poured into a small cup or glass, and handed to the Manitto. He drinks, has the glass refilled, and handed to the chief near him; he takes it, smells it, and passes it to the next, who does the same. The glass in this manner is passed round the circle, and is about to be returned to the red-clothed man, when one of them, a great warrior, harangues them on the impropriety of returning the cup unemptied. It was handed to them, he said, by the Manitto, to drink out of as he had; to follow his example would please him—to reject it might provoke his wrath; and if no one else would, he would drink it himself, let what would follow; for it was better for one even to die, than a whole nation to be destroyed. He then took the glass, smelled at it, again addressed them, bidding adieu, and drank the contents. All eyes were now fixed (on the first Indian in New York who had tasted the poison which has since affected so signal a revolution in the condition of the native Americans). He soon began to stagger; the women cried, supposing him in fits; he rolled on the ground; they bemoan his fate; they thought him dying. He fell asleep. They at first thought he had expired, but soon perceived he still breathed. He awoke, jumped up, and declared he never felt more happy; he asked for more; and the whole assembly imitating him, became intoxicated."

In descending the river, after he had penetrated to Albany, Hudson ran his little craft ashore at Weehawken; but the ground was a soft ooze, and she was got off without damage, and proceeded to sea.

BALLSTON SPRINGS.

These celebrated springs rise in a valley formed by a branch of the Kayaderos-seras Creek. In this valley, and on its acclivities, is built the village called Ballston Spa. The medicinal character of the waters was discovered (as was said of Saratoga) by the beaten track of the deer to the springs at certain seasons. Ballston is now a populous village during the summer, and, since the rail-road has connected it with Saratoga, these two resorts have become like one, and, together, assemble, during certain months, the greater proportion of the moving population of the country. A description of the kind of life led at these springs accompanies another drawing in this Series.

At the time of the breaking out of the revolutionary war this part of the country was very thinly settled. The inhabitants for the most part took the continental side; but at the battle of Hoosac, a few miles from Ballston, a man was taken prisoner by the Americans, whose history exhibits some fine traits of character. He was a plain farmer from this neighbourhood, named Richard Jackson, and had conscientiously taken the British side in the contest. Feeling himself bound of course to employ himself in the service of his sovereign, he no sooner heard that Colonel Baum was advancing, than he saddled his horse and rode to Hoosac, intending to attach himself to this corps. Here he was taken, in such circumst-ances as proved his intention beyond every reasonable doubt. He was, besides, too honest to deny it. Accordingly he was transmitted to Great Barrington, then the shire-town of Berkshire, and placed in the hands of General Fellows, high sheriff of the county, who immediately confined him in the county gaol. This building was at that time so infirm, that without a guard no prisoner could be kept in it who wished to make his escape. To escape, however, was in no degree

Ballston Springs. Drawing by William H. Bartlett, from N. P. Willis, *American Scenery* (London: Virtue, 1836).

consonant with Richard's idea of right; and he thought no more seriously of making an attempt of this nature, than he would have done had he been in his own house. After he had lain quietly in gaol a few days, he told the sheriff that he was losing his time, and earning nothing, and wished that he would permit him to go out and work in the day time, promising to return regularly at evening to his quarters in the prison. The sheriff had become acquainted with his character, and readily acceded to his proposal. Accordingly Richard went out regularly during the remaining part of the autumn, and the following winter and spring, until the beginning of May, and every night returned at the proper hour to the gaol. In this manner he performed a day's work every day, with scarcely any exception beside the Sabbath, through the whole period.

In the month of May he was to be tried for high treason. The sheriff accordingly made preparations to conduct him to Springfield, where his trial was to be held; but he told the sheriff that it was not worth his while to take this trouble, for he could just as well go alone, and it would save both the expense and inconvenience of the sheriff's journey. The sheriff, after a little reflection, assented to his proposal, and Richard commenced his journey; the only one, it is believed, which was ever undertaken in the same manner for the same object. In the woods of Tyringham he was overtaken by the Hon. T. Edwards, from whom I had this story.—"Whither are you going?" said Mr. Edwards. "To Springfield, Sir," answered Richard, "to be tried for my life." Accordingly he proceeded directly to Springfield, surrendered himself to the sheriff of Hampshire, was tried, found guilty, and condemned to die.

The council of Massachusetts was at this time the supreme executive of the State. Application was made to this board for a pardon. The facts were stated, the evidence by which they were supported, and the sentence grounded on them. The question was then put by the president, "Shall a pardon be granted to Richard Jackson?" The gentleman who spoke first observed that the case was perfectly clear; the act alleged against Jackson was unquestionably high treason; and the proof was complete. If a pardon should be granted in this case, he saw no reason why it should not be granted in every other. In the same manner answered those who followed him. When it came to the turn of Mr. Edwards, he told this story with those little circumstances of particularity, which, though they are easily lost from the memory, and have escaped mine, give light and shade, a living reality, and a picturesque impressiveness, to every tale which is fitted to enforce conviction, or to touch the heart. At the same time he recited it without enhancement, without expatiating, without any attempt to be pathetic. As is always the case, this simplicity gave the narration its full force. The council began to hesitate. One fo the members at length observed—"Certainly such a man as this ought not to be sent to the gallows." To his opinion the members unanimously assented. A pardon was immediately made out and transmitted to Springfield, and Richard returned to his family.

Never was a stronger proof exhibited, that honesty is wisdom.

THE NARROWS, FROM FORT HAMILTON

Not quite one hundred years after Verrazzano's discovery of the Bay of New York, during all which period we have no account of its having been visited by an European vessel, Hudson made the Capes of Virginia on his third cruise in search of the north-west passage. Standing still on a northward course, he arrived in sight of the Narrows, distinguishing from a great distance the Highlands of Neversink, which his mate, Robert Juet, describes in the journal he kept as a "very good land to fall with, and a pleasant land to see."

The most interesting peculiarity of our country to a European observer, is the freshness of its early history, and the strong contrast it presents of most of the features of a highly civilized land, with the youth and recent adventure of a newly discovered one. The details of these first discoveries are becoming every day more interesting: and to accompany a drawing of the Narrows, or entrance to the Bay of New York, the most fit illustration is that part of the journal of the great navigator which relates to his first view of them. The following extracts describe the Narrows as they were two hundred years ago: the drawing presents them as they are.

"At three of the clock in the afternoone we came to three great rivers. So we stood along to the northernmost, thinking to have gone into it, but we found it to have a very shoald barre before it, for we had but ten foot water. Then we cast about to the southward, and found two fathoms, three fathoms, and three and a quarter, till we came to the souther side of them, then we had five or six fathoms, and anchored. So we sent in our boat to sound, and they found no less water than foure, five, six, and seven fathoms, and returned in an hour and a halfe. So we weighed and went in, and rode in five fathoms, ose ground, and saw many salmons, and mullets, and rayes very great.

"The fourth, in the morning, as soone as the day was light, we saw that it was good riding farther up. So we sent our boate to sound, and found that it was a very good harbour; then we weighed and went in with our ship. Then our boat went on land with our net to fish, and caught ten great mullets, of a foot and a half long apeece, and a ray as great as foure men could hale into the ship. So we trimmed our boat, and rode still all day. At night the wind blew hard at the north-west, and our anchor came home, and we drove on shore, but took no hurt, thanked bee God, for the ground is soft sand and ose. This day the people of the country came aboard of us, seeming very glad of our comming, and brought greene tobacco, and gave us of it for knives and beads. They go in deere skins loose, well dressed. They have yellow copper. They desire cloathes, and are very civill. They have great store of maise, or Indian wheate, whereof they make good bread. The country is full of great and tall oaks.

"The fifth, in the morning, as soone as the day was light, the wind ceased; so

The Narrows, from Fort Hamilton. Drawing by William H. Bartlett, from N. P. Willis, *American Scenery* (London: Virtue, 1836).

we sent our boate in to sound the bay. Our men went on land there and saw great store of men, women, and children, who gave them tobacco at their coming on land. So they went up into the woods, and saw great store of very goodly oakes, and some currants.

"The sixth, in the morning, was faire weather, and our master sent John Colman with foure other men in our boate over to the north side, to sound the other river," (the Narrows.) "They found very good riding for ships, and a narrow river to the westward," (probably what is now called the Kells, or the passage between Bergen-Neck and Staten Island,) "between two islands. The lands, they told us, were as pleasant, with grasse and flowers, and goodly trees, as ever they had seen, and very sweet smells came from them. So they went in two leagues and saw an open sea,* and returned; and as they came backe they were set upon by two canoes, the one having twelve, the other fourteen men. The night came on, and it began to raine, so that their match went out; and they had one man slain in the fight, which was an Englishman, named John Colman, with an arrow shot into his throat, and two more hurt. It grew so dark that they could not find the shippe that night, but laboured to and fro on their oares.

"The seventh was fair, and they returned aboard the ship, and brought our dead man with them, whom we carried on land and buried."

On the eighth, Hudson lay still, to be more sure of the disposition of the natives before venturing farther in. Several came on board, but no disturbance occurred, and on the ninth he got under weigh, passed the Narrows, and proceeded by slow degrees up the river destined to bear his name.

UNDERCLIFF (THE SEAT OF GENERAL MORRIS).

The pen of the poet and the pencil of the artist have so frequently united to record the grandeur and sublimity of the Hudson, and with such graphic fidelity, that little of interest remains unsaid or unsketched. But when every point of its bold and beautiful scenery might be made the subject of a picture, and every incident of its past history the theme of a poem, it requires no great research to discover new and prominent objects of attraction. Perhaps there is no portion of this beautiful river which partakes more of the picturesque, or combines more of the wild and wonderful, than the vicinity of the present View; and when time shall touch the history of the present with the wand of tradition, and past events shall live in the memory of the future as legends, romance will never revel in a more bewitching region. Fiction shall then fling its imaginative veil over the things we have seen—covering, but not concealing them—and, in the plenitude of poetic genius, people the drama of futurity with a thousand exquisite creations, clothed in the venerated garb of antiquity.

Undercliff, the mansion of General George P. Morris, which forms the

*Ed. Note: Probably Newark Bay.

principal object in the engraving, is situated upon an elevated plateau, rising from the eastern shore of the river; and the selection of such a commanding and beautiful position at once decides the taste of its intellectual proprietor. In the rear of the villa, cultivation has placed her fruit and forest trees with a profuse hand, and fertilized the fields with a variety of vegetable products. The extent of the grounds is abruptly terminated by the base of a rocky mountain, that rises nearly perpendicular to its summit, and affords in winter a secure shelter from the bleak blasts of the north. In front, a circle of greensward is refreshed by a fountain in the centre, gushing from a Grecian vase, and encircled by ornamental shrubbery; from thence a gravelled walk winds down a gentle declivity to a second plateau, and again descends to the entrance of the carriage road, which leads upwards along the left slope of the hill, through a noble forest, the growth of many years, until suddenly emerging from its sombre shades, the visitor beholds the mansion before him in the bright blaze of day. A few openings in the wood afford an opportunity to catch a glimpse of the water, sparkling with reflected light; and the immediate transition from shadow to sunshine is perculiarly pleasing.

Although the sunny prospects from the villa, of the giant mountains in their eternal verdure—the noble stream, when frequent gusts ruffle its surface into a thousand waves—the cluster of white cottages collected into the distant village, are glorious; it is only by the lovely light of the moon, when nature is in repose, that their magic influence is fully felt. We were fortunate in having an opportunity to contemplate the scene at such an hour: the moon had risen from a mass of clouds which formed a line across the sky so level that fancy saw her ascending from the dark sea, and her silvery light lay softened on the landscape; silence was over all, save where the dipping of a distant oar was echoed from the deep shadows of the rocks. Sometimes the white sail of a sloop would steal into sight from the deep gloom, like some shrouded spirit gliding from the confines of a giant's cavern, and recalled the expressive lines by Moore:—

> "The stream is like a silvery lake,
> And o'er its face each vessel glides
> Gently, as if it feared to wake
> The slumber of the silent tides."

VIEW OF NEW YORK, FROM WEEHAWKEN.

Weehawken is slighted by the traveller ascending to the bolder and brighter glories of the Highlands above; and few visit it except—

> "The prisoner to the city's pent-up air,"

who, making a blest holiday of a summer's afternoon, crosses thither to set his foot on the green grass, and mount the rocks for a view of our new-sprung

View of New York, from Weehawken. Drawing by William H. Bartlett, from N. P. Willis, *American Scenery* (London: Virtue, 1836).

Babylon and its waters. There is no part of "the country" which "God made" so blest in its offices of freshening the spirit, and giving health to the blood, as the rural suburb of a metropolis. The free breath drawn there, the green herb looked on before it is trodden down, the tree beautiful simply for the freedom of its leaves from the dust of the street, the humblest bird or the meanest butterfly, are dispensers of happiness in another measure than falls elsewhere to their lot. Most such humble ministers of large blessings have their virtue for "its own reward;" but it has fallen to the lot of Weehawken to find a minstrel, and no mean one, among those for whose happiness and consolation it seems made to bloom. A merchant-poet, whose "works" stand on shelves in Wall Street, but whose rhymes for pastime live in literature, and in the hearts of his countrymen, thus glorifies his suburban Tempe:—

> "Weehawken! in thy mount: ..1 scenery yet,
>   All we adore of Nature in her wild
> And frolic hour of infancy, is met,
>   And never has a summer morning smiled
> Upon a lovelier scene than the full eye
> Of the enthusiast revels on—when high

> "Amid thy forest-solitudes he climbs
>   O'er crags that proudly tower above the deep,
> And knows that sense of danger, which sublimes
>   The breathless moment—when his daring step
> Is on the verge of the cliff, and he can hear
> The low dash of the wave with startled ear,

> "Like the death music of his coming doom,
>   And clings to the green turf with desperate force,
> As the heart clings to life; and when resume
>   The currents in his veins their wonted course
> There lingers a deep feeling, like the moan
> Of wearied ocean when the storm is gone.

> "In such an hour he turns, and on his view
>   Ocean, and earth, and heaven, burst before him;
> Clouds slumbering at his feet, and the clear blue
>   Of summer's sky in beauty bending o'er him;
> The city bright below; and far away
> Sparkling in light, his own romantic bay.

> "Tall spire, and glittering roof, and battlement,
>   And banners floating in the sunny air,
> And white sails o'er the calm blue waters bent,
>   Green isle, and circling shore, are blended there

In wild reality. When life is old,
And many a scene forgot, the heart will hold

"Its memory of this; nor lives there one
  Whose infant breath was drawn, or boyhood's days
Of happiness were passed beneath that sun,
  That in his manhood's prime can calmly gaze
Upon that bay, or on that mountain stand,
Nor feel the prouder of his native land."*

Weehawken is the "Chalk Farm" of New York, and a small spot enclosed by rocks, and open to observation only from the river, is celebrated as having been the ground on which Hamilton fought his fatal duel with Aaron Burr. A small obelisk was erected on the spot, by the St. Andrew's Society, to the memory of Hamilton, but it has been removed. His body was interred in the churchyard of Trinity, in Broadway, where his monument now stands.

It is to be regretted that the fashion of visiting Hoboken and Weehawken has yielded to an impression among the "fashionable" that it is a vulgar resort. This willingness to relinquish an agreeable promenade because it is enjoyed as well by the poorer classes of society, is one of those superfine ideas which we imitate from our English ancestors, and in which the more philosophic continentals are so superior to us. What enlivens the Tuileries and St. Cloud at Paris, the Monte-Pincio at Rome, the Volksgarten at Vienna, and the Corso and Villa Reale at Naples, but the presence of innumerable "vulgarians?" They are considered there like the chorus in a pantomime, as producing all the back-ground effect as necessary to the *ensemble*. The place would be nothing—would be desolate, without them; yet in England and America it is enough to vulgarize any—the most agreeable resort, to find it frequented by the "people!"

Sing-Sing Prison, and Tappan Sea.

An American prison is not often a picturesque object, and, till late years, it suggested to the mind of the philanthropist only painful reflections upon the abuses and thwarted ends of penitentiary discipline. To the persevering humanity of Louis Dwight, and to the liberal association that sustained him, we owe the change in these institutions which enables us to look on them without pain and disgust as places of repentance and reformation, rather than as schools for vice, and abodes of neglect and idleness. It is a creditable thing to our country to have led the way in these salutary changes; and there are many who have felt their patriotism more flattered by the visits of persons from Europe sent out by their

*From "Fanny," a poem, by Fitz-Greene Halleck.

governments to study our systems of prison discipline, than by many an event sounded through the trumpet of national glory.

The Tappan Sea spreads its broad waters at this part of the Hudson, looking, like all scenes of pure natural beauty, as if it was made for a world in which there could neither exist crime nor pain. Yet there stands a vast and crowded prison on its shores to remind us of the first—and for the latter, who ever entered upon these waters without a recollection of poor André? It may be doubted whether in the history of our country the fate of an individual has ever excited more sympathy than his. The rare accomplishments which he possessed, the natural elegance of his mind, the unfitness of his open character for the degrading circumstances under which he was taken, and his mild constancy at the approach of his melancholy fate, endear him, without respect to party, to the memories of all who read his story. André was taken on the eastern shore of the river at Tarrytown, and executed on the opposite side, at Tappan.

The story of Captain Hale has been regarded as parallel to that of Major André. This young officer had received a university education, and had but recently taken his degree when the war of the revolution commenced. He possessed genius, taste, ardour, was a distinguished scholar, and to all this was added, in an eminent degree, the winning address and native grace of a gentleman. No young man of his years put forth a finer promise of usefulness and celebrity.

Upon the first news of the battle of Lexington, he obtained a commission in the army, and marched with his company to Cambridge, where his promptness, activity, and assiduous attention to discipline, were early observed. After considerable service, the theatre of action was changed, and the army was removed to the southward. The battle of Long Island was fought, and the American forces were drawn together in the city of New York. At this moment it became extremely important for Washington to know the situation of the British army on the heights of Brooklyn, its numbers, and the indications as to its future movements. Having expressed a wish to this effect, Colonel Knowlton called together the younger officers, stated to them the wish of the General, and left it to their reflections, without naming any individual for the service. The undertaking was particularly hazardous; but it was immediately determined upon by Hale, who resisted all opposition on the part of his friends, and crossed over the river to the enemy's ground. His disguise was well contrived, and he had obtained all necessary information, when he was arrested in the boat by which he was attempting to return. He was taken before the British commander, was condemned as a spy, and hanged the following morning. The circumstances of his death, however, were widely different from those of André. The Provost-marshal was a refugee, and behaved towards him in the most unfeeling manner, refusing him the attendance of a clergyman, and the use of a Bible in his last moments, and destroying the letters he had written to his mother and friends. In the midst of these barbarities Hale was collected and calm. To the last he displayed his native elevation of soul, and his dignity of deportment.

"But," says a distinguished writer of biography, "whatever may have been the parallel between these two individuals while living, it ceased with their death. A monument was raised and consecrated to the memory of André by the bounty of a grateful sovereign. His ashes have been removed from their obscure resting-place, transported across the ocean, and deposited with the remains of the illustrious dead in Westminster Abbey. Where is the memento of the virtues, the patriotic sacrifice, the early fate of Hale?"

VIEW OF HUDSON, AND THE CATSKILL MOUNTAINS.

A wedge-shaped promontory, or bluff, pushes forward to the river at this spot; and on its summit, which widens into a noble plain, stands the city of Hudson. The business of the place is chiefly done in a simple street, which runs at right angles from the river. Its growth at first was remarkably rapid; but the resources of the surrounding country were found inadequate to second its prosperity, and its trade has accordingly been nearly stationary for a number of years. The enterprise of the citizens, however, has found a new source of wealth in the whale fishery.

It is supposed that the Halve-Mane, the vessel in which the great discoverer made his first passage up the Hudson, reached no farther than two leagues above the city which bears his name, and that the remainder of the exploring voyage was made in the shallop. His reception here was in the highest degree hospitable. "He went on shore in one of their canoes, with an old Indian, who was the chief of forty men, and seventeen women: these he saw in a house made of the bark of trees, exceedingly smooth and well-finished within and without. He found a great quantity of Indian corn and beans, enough of which were drying near the house to have loaded three ships, besides what was growing on the fields. On coming to the house, two mats were spread to sit on, eatables were brought in, in red bowls, well made; and two men were sent off with bows and arrows, who soon returned with two pigeons. They also killed a fat dog, and skinned it with shells. They expected their visitors would remain during the night, but the latter determined to return on board. The natives were exceedingly kind and good-tempered; for when they discovered Hudson's determination to proceed on board, they, imagining it proceeded from fear of their bows and arrows, broke them to pieces, and threw them into the fire."

On his return down the river, Hudson stopped again for four days opposite the site of the future city. The historical collections give a very particular account of every day's movements in this interesting voyage. "On the report of those whom he had sent to explore the river," says the historian, "Hudson found that it would be useless to proceed with his ship any farther, or to delay his return. He had passed several days in a profitable traffic, and a friendly intercourse with the natives; among whom were probably those from each side of the river—the *Mahicanni*, as well as the Mohawks. At noon of the 23d of September, he therefore went down six miles to a shoal: having but little wind, the tide laid his ship on the bar until the flood came, when she crossed it, and was anchored for the night.

"The next day, after proceeding seven or eight leagues, she grounded on a bank of ooze in the middle of the river, where she was detained till the ensuing morning, when the flood, at ten o'clock, enabled Hudson to anchor her in deep water. Thus the ship once more was interrupted in her passage opposite the spot where a city now commemorates the name of Hudson.

"Here he remained, by reason of adverse winds, four days. On the day of his arrival, 'they went on land and gathered good store of chestnuts;' but whether on the east or west side of the river, is not mentioned. But the day following they went on land, 'to walk on the west side of the river, and found good ground for corn, and other garden herbs, with good store of goodly oaks and walnut-trees, and chestnut-trees, yew-trees, and trees of sweet wood, in great abundance, and great store of *slate for houses, and other good stones.*' Nothing is said of any inhabitants while they were thus visiting the site, which is now that of the village of Athens, opposite Hudson. But, next morning (26th), after the carpenter, mate, and four of the company, had gone on shore to cut wood, while the vessel lay at anchor, two canoes came up the river from the place where they first found 'loving people,' (Catskill landing,) and in one of them was the old chief whom Hudson had caused to be made intoxicated at Albany. He had followed our strange visitors thirty miles, to the base of the Catskill mountains, with the double view of again testifying to Hudson the sincerity of his friendship, and of gratifying the love of the marvellous, by relating his own adventures to the mountaineers, and drawing them from their retreat to witness the floating phenomenon. The old chief now introduced with him 'an old man, who brought more stropes of beads, and gave them to our master, and showed him all the country thereabout, as though it were at his command!' They tarried, greatly pleased with the unaccountable curiosities they discovered on board. Hudson 'made the two old men dine with him, and the old man's wife; for they brought two old women, and two young maidens of the age of sixteen or seventeen years with them, who behaved themselves very modestly.'

"After dinner, and upon exchange of presents, the guests retired, inviting Hudson by signs to come down to them; for the ship was within two leagues of the place where they dwelt."

VIEW FROM GOWAN'S HEIGHTS, BROOKLYN.

The Bay of New York and Staten Island, are, from this elevated point of view, laid out beautifully beneath the eye, but the picturesque interest of the spot yields to the historic. Directly below these heights was fought the battle so disastrous to the revolutionary forces, between the detachments commanded by Sullivan and Putman, and the English army, under Generals Howe and Clinton. As the defence of Long Island was intimately connected with that of New York, Washington had stationed a brigade at Brooklyn; and an extensive camp had been marked out and fortified, fronting the main land of Long Island, and stretching quite across the peninsula occupied by the village of Brooklyn. When the movements of General Howe threatened an immediate attack on this position, Major-General Putnam was directed to take the command, with a reinforcement of six regiments; and the day previous to the action Washington passed entirely at Brooklyn, inspecting the works, and encouraging the soldiers.

The Hessians, under General De Heister, composed the centre of the British army at Flatbush. Major-General Grant commanded the left wing, which extended to the coast, and the greater part of the forces under General Clinton. Earl Percy and Lord Cornwallis turned short to the right, and approached the opposite coast of Flatland.

On the night previous to the action, General Clinton was successful in seizing a pass through the heights, leading into the level country between them and Brooklyn. Before this movement was completed, General Grant advanced along the coast, at the head of the left wing, with ten pieces of cannon. As his first object was to draw the attention of the Americans from their left, he moved slowly, skirmishing as he advanced, with the light parties stationed on that road.

This movement was soon communicated to General Putnam, who reinforced the parties which had been advanced in front; and as General Grant continued to gain ground, still stronger detachments were employed in this service. About three in the morning, Brigadier-General Lord Stirling was directed to meet the enemy, with the two nearest regiments, on the road leading from the Narrows. Major-General Sullivan, who commanded all the troops without the lines, advanced at the head of a strong detachment on the road leading directly to Flatbush; while another detachment occupied the heights between that place and Bedford.

About the break of day, Lord Stirling reached the summit of the hills, where he was joined by the troops which had been already engaged, and were retiring slowly before the enemy, who almost immediately appeared in sight. A warm cannonade was commenced on both sides, which continued for several hours; and some sharp but not very close skirmishing took place between the infantry. Lord Stirling being anxious only to defend the pass he guarded, could not descend in force from the heights; and General Grant did not wish to drive him from them until that part of the plan which had been entrusted to Sir Henry Clinton should be executed.

About half-past eight, the British right having then reached Bedford, in the rear of Sullivan's left, General De Heister ordered Colonel Donop's corps to

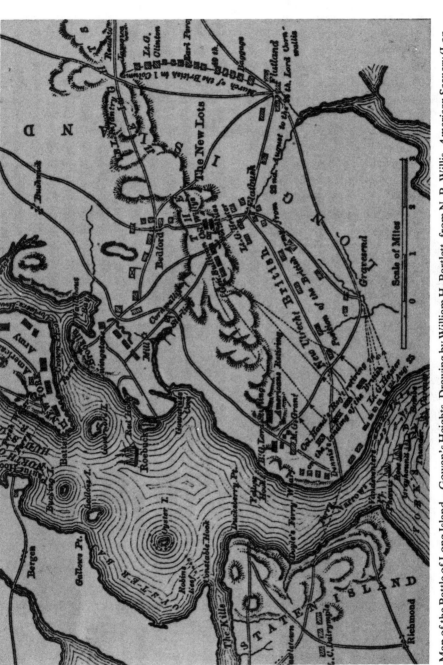

Map of the Battle of Long Island—Gowan's Heights. Drawing by William H. Bartlett, from N. P. Willis, *American Scenery* (London: Virtue, 1836).

Bridge at Glen's Falls, on the Hudson. Drawing by William H. Bartlett, from N. P. Willis, *American Scenery* (London: Virtue, 1836).

advance to the attack of the hill, following himself with the centre of the army. The approach of Clinton was now discovered by the American left, which immediately endeavoured to regain the camp at Brooklyn. While retiring from the woods by regiments, they encountered the front of the British. About the same time the Hessians advanced from Flatbush, against that part of the detachment which occupied the direct road to Brooklyn. Here General Sullivan commanded in person; but he found it difficult to keep his troops together long enough to sustain the first attack. The firing heard towards Bedford had disclosed the alarming fact that the British had turned their left flank, and were getting completely into their rear. Perceiving at once the full danger of their situation, they sought to escape it by regaining the camp with the utmost possible celerity. The sudden rout of this party enabled De Heister to detach a part of his force against those who were engaged near Bedford. In that quarter, too, the Americans were broken, and driven back into the woods; and the front of the column led by General Clinton continuing to move forward, intercepted and engaged those who were retreating along the direct road from Flatbush. Thus attacked both in front and rear, and alternately driven by the British on the Hessians, and by the Hessians back again on the British, a succession of skirmishes took place in the woods, in the course of which, some part of the corps forced their way through the enemy and regained the lines of Brooklyn, and several individuals saved themselves under cover of the woods; but a great proportion of the detachment was killed, or taken. The fugitives were pursued up to the American works; and such is represented to have been the ardour of the British soldiers, that it required the authority of their cautious commander to prevent an immediate assault.

The fire towards Brooklyn gave the first intimation to the American right that the enemy had gained their rear. Lord Stirling perceived the danger, and that he could only escape it by retreating instantly across the creek. After one other gallant attempt, however, upon a British corps under Lord Cornwallis, the brave men he commanded were no longer able to make opposition, and those who survived were, with their general, made prisoners of war.

The British army were masters of the field, but before morning, Washington had won one of his brightest military laurels in the safe withdrawal, unperceived by the enemy, of his defeated and dispirited troops to the opposite shore of New York.

BRIDGE AT GLEN'S-FALLS, ON THE HUDSON.

Few of our readers who will not consider this subject as one of the most picturesque in our collection, and yet many of them we fear have passed over the bridge in our View unconscious of the proximity of so extraordinary a scene as the Falls of the Hudson at this spot.

This was, at least, our own case when first visiting Lake George, from Saratoga; and we would counsel every one to steal a few moments, even if travelling by the stage, to descend from the covered bridge to the rocky bed of the river. Miss Martineau observes—"We were all astonished at the splendour of Glen's Falls. The full, though narrow Hudson, rushes along amidst enormous masses of rock, and leaps sixty feet down the chasms and precipices which occur in the passage, sweeping between dark banks of shelving rocks below, its current speckled with foam. The noise is so tremendous, that I cannot conceive how people can fix their dwellings in the immediate neighbourhood. There is a long bridge over the roaring floods, which vibrates incessantly; and clusters of saw-mills deform the scene. There is stone-cutting as well as planking done at these mills. The fine black marble of the place is cut into slabs, and sent down to New York to be polished. It was the busiest scene that I saw near any water-power in America."

Her description is excellent, but, as regards the mills, we cannot agree with her; they certainly add much to the picturesque effect of the scene.

VIEW FROM MOUNT IDA, NEAR TROY, NEW YORK.

The scenery in this neighbourhood is exceedingly beautiful. The junction of the Mohawk and Hudson, the Falls of the Cohoes, the gay and elegant town of Troy, Albany in the distance, and a foreground of the finest mixture of the elements of landscape, compose a gratification to the eye equalled by few other spots in this country. "Think," says one of our noblest and best writers, speaking of a similar scene—"think of the country for which the Indians fought! Who can blame them? As the river chieftains, the lords of the waterfalls and the mountains, ranged this lovely valley, can it be wondered at that they beheld with bitterness the forest disappearing beneath the settler's axe—the fishing-place disturbed by his saw-mills? Can we not fancy the feelings with which some strong-minded savage, who should have ascended the summit of the mountain in company with a friendly settler, contemplating the progress already made by the white man, and marking the gigantic strides with which he was advancing into the wilderness, should fold his arms and say, 'White man, there is eternal war between me and thee! I quit not the land of my fathers but with my life! In those woods where I bent my youthful bow, I will still hunt the deer; over yonder waters I will still glide unrestrained in my bark canoe. By those dashing water-falls I will still lay up my winter's food; on these fertile meadows I will still plant my corn. Stranger,the land is mine! I understand not these paper rights; I gave not my consent when, as thou sayest, those broad regions were purchased for a few baubles of my fathers. They could sell what was theirs; they could sell no more. How could my father sell that which the Great Spirit sent me into the world to live upon? They knew not what they did. The stranger came, a timid suppliant, few

View from Mount Ida, near Troy, New York. Drawing by William H. Bartlett, from N. P. Willis, *American Scenery* (London: Virtue, 1836).

and feeble, and asked to lie down on the red man's bear-skin, and warm himself at the red man's fire, and have a little piece of land to raise corn for his women and children; and now he is become strong, and mighty, and bold, and spreads out his parchment over the whole, and says, It is mine. Stranger, there is not room for us both. The Great Spirit has not made us to live together. There is poison in the white man's cup; the white man's dog barks at the red man's heels. If I should leave the land of my fathers, whither shall I fly? Shall I go to the south, and dwell among the groves of the Pequods? Shall I wander to the west? the fierce Mohawk—the man-eater—is my foe. Shall I fly to the east?—the great water is before me. No, stranger, here have I lived, and here will I die! and if here thou abidest, there is eternal war between me and thee! Thou hast taught me thy arts of destruction, for that alone I thank thee; and now take heed to thy steps; the red man is thy foe. When thou goest forth by day, my bullet shall whistle by thee; when thou liest down at night, my knife is at thy throat. The noon-day sun shall not discover thy enemy, and the darkness of midnight shall not protect thy rest. Thou shalt plant in terror, and I will reap in blood! thou shalt sow the earth with corn, and I will strew it with ashes! thou shalt go forth with the sickle, and I will follow after with the scalping-knife! thou shalt build, and I will burn, till the white man or the Indian shall cease from the land. Go thy way for this time in safety, but remember, stranger, there is eternal war between me and thee!'"

As the same writer afterwards observes, however, the Pilgrim Fathers "purchased the land of those who claimed it, and paid for it—often, more than once. They purchased it for a consideration, trifling to the European, but valuable to the Indian. There is no overreaching in giving but little for that which, in the hands of the original proprietors, is worth nothing."

VIEW NEAR ANTHONY'S NOSE, HUDSON HIGHLANDS.

This mountain, "known to fame," serves as a landmark to the industrious craft plying upon the Hudson, and thus fulfils a more useful destiny than is commonly awarded to spots bright in story. It stands amid a host of interesting localities, marked with the events of the Revolution, and has witnessed, with less damage than other noses, many a conflict by land and water.

On the opposite side of the river from the base of the mountain, lie the two forts Montgomery and Clinton, taken by the British in October, 1777. The commander-in-chief at New York was prompted to this expedition by two objects: to destroy a quantity of military stores which the Americans had collected in this neighbourhood, and to make a diversion in favour of General Burgoyne. For these purposes Sir Henry Clinton embarked between three and four thousand troops at New York, and sailed with them up the Hudson. On the 5th of October they landed at Verplank's Point, a few miles below the entrance to the Highlands. The next morning, a part of the force landed on Stony Point, which projects into the river on the western side, just below the mountains; hence they marched into the rear of the fortresses.

General Putnam commanded at that time in this quarter. He had one thousand continental troops, a part of which only were effective, and a small body of militia. He believed the principal design of the enemy to be the destruction of the stores; and when he was informed of their main purpose, it was too late for him to resist with success. He supposed that they were aiming at Fort Independence, and directed his attention to its defence; the heavy firing on the other side of the river gave him the first decisive information of their real intentions. Mr. Clinton, at that time governor of the state, placed himself at this post on the first notice that he received of the enemy's advancing. Having made the best disposition for the defence of the forts, he despatched an express to General Putnam to acquaint him with his situation; but when it reached his head quarters, that officer and General Parsons were reconnoitering the position of the enemy on the east side of the river.

Lieut.-Col. Campbell, in the mean time, proceeded with nine hundred men by a circuitous march to the rear of Fort Montgomery; while Sir Henry Clinton, with Generals Vaughan and Tryon, moved onwards towards Fort Clinton. Both fortresses were attacked at once, between four and five in the afternoon: they were defended with great resolution. This will be readily admitted, when it is remembered that the whole garrison consisted of but six hundred men. The conflict was carried on till dark, when the British had obtained absolute possession, and such of the Americans as were not killed or wounded had made their escape. The loss of the two garrisons amounted to about two hundred and fifty. Among the killed on the enemy's side was Lieut.-Col. Campbell.

It has been thought that an addition of five or six hundred men to these garrisons would have saved the works; the correctness of this opinion may be doubted. Fifteen hundred soldiers would have been barely sufficient completely to man Fort Montgomery alone. The works themselves were imperfect, and the ground was probably chosen rather for the defence of the river, than because it was itself defensible.

Governor Clinton and his brother, General James Clinton, escaped after the enemy had possession of the forts; the former by crossing the river. The latter had been wounded in the thigh by a bayonet.

On the 8th, the English forces proceeded to the eastern side, where they found Fort Independence evacuated. A party then burnt the continental village, as it was called, a temporary settlement raised up by the war for the accommodation of the army. Here had been gathered a considerable number of those artisans, whose labours are particularly necessary for military purposes; and a considerable quantity of military stores. They then removed a chain which was stretched across the river at Fort Montgomery, and advancing up the river, removed another which was extended from Fort Constitution to the opposite shore at West

Point. General Vaughan then advanced still further up the Hudson, and on the 13th reached the town of Kingston, which he burnt. On the 17th, took place the surrender of Burgoyne, and he returned down the Hudson with his fleet to New York.

Count Grabouski, a Polish nobleman, was killed in the assault on Fort Clinton, while acting as aid-de-camp to the British commander. He was buried on the spot, but his grave is now undiscoverable.

CHAPEL OF "OUR LADY OF COLD SPRING".

The Hudson bends out from Crow-Nest into a small bay; and, in the lap of the crescent thus formed, lies snug and sheltered, the little village of Cold Spring. It is not much of a place for its buildings, history, or business; but it has its squire and post-master, its politics and scandal, and a long disappointed ambition to become a regular landing-place for the steamers. Then there are cabals between the rival ferrymen, on which the inhabitants divide; the vote for the president, on which they agree (for Van Buren); and the usual religious sects, with the usual schisms. The Presbyterians and Methodists, as usual, worship in very ugly churches; and the Catholics, as usual, in a very picturesque and beautiful one. (*Vide* the Drawing.)

It is a pity (picturesquely speaking) that the boatmen on the river are not Catholics; it would be so pretty to see them shorten sail off Our Lady of Cold Spring, and uncover for an Ave-Maria. This little chapel, so exquisitely situated on the bluff overlooking the river, reminds me of a hermit's oratory and cross which is perched similarly in the shelter of a cliff on the desolate coast of Sparta. I was on board a frigate, gliding slowly up the Ægean, and clinging to the shore for a land-wind, when I descried the white cross at a distance of about half a mile, strongly relieved against the dark rock in its rear. As we approached, the small crypt and altar became visible; and, at the moment the ship passed, a tall monk, with a snow-white beard, stepped forth like an apparition upon the cliffs, and spread out his arms to bless us. In the midst of the intense solitude of the Ægean, with not a human dwelling to be seen on the whole coast from Moron to Napoli, the effect of this silent benediction was almost supernatural. He remained for five minutes in this attitude, his long cowl motionless in the still air, and his head slowly turning to the ship as she drew fast around the little promontory on her course. I would suggest to Our Lady of Cold Spring, that a niche under the portico of her pretty chapel, with a cross to be seen from the river by day, and a lamp by night, would make at least a catholic impression on the passer by, though we are not all children of St. Peter.

Half way between the mountain and our Lady's shrine, stands, on a superb natural platform, the romantic estate of Undercliff, the seat of Colonel Morris. Just above it rises the abrupt and heavily wooded mountain, from which it derives its name; a thick grove hides it from the village at its foot; and, from the portico of the mansion, extend views in three directions unparalleled for varied and surprising beauty. A road, running between high-water mark and the park gate, skirts the river in eccentric windings for five or six miles; the brows of the hills descending to the Hudson in the west and north, are nobly wooded and threaded with circuitous paths, and all around lies the most romantic scenery of the most romantic river in the world.

The only fault of the views from West Point, is, that West Point itself is lost as a feature in the landscape. The traveller feels the same drawback which troubled the waiting-maid when taken to drive by the footman in her mistress's chariot— "How I wish I could stand by the road side and see myself go by!" From Undercliff, which is directly opposite, and about at the same elevation, the superb terrace of the Military School is seen to the greatest advantage. The white barracks of Camptown, the long range of edifices which skirt the esplanade, the ruins half way up the mountain of old Fort Putnam, and the waving line of wood and valley extending to Mr. Cozzen's estate of "Stoney Lonesome," form a noble feature in the view from Undercliff.

I had forgotten that Cold Spring "plucks a glory on its head" from being honoured with the frequent visits of Washington Irving, Halleck, and other lesser stars in the literary firmament; when these first lights above the horizon shall have set, (Hesperus-like—first and brightest!) there will linger about this little vil-lage—by that time, perhaps, arrived at the dignity of a landing-place—many a tale of the days when Geoffrey Crayon talked in his gentle way with the ferryman who brought him to Cold Spring; or the now plethoric post-master, who, in his character of librarian to the village, enjoyed the friendship of Irving and Halleck, and received from their own hands the "authors' copies," since curiously pre-served in the execrable print and binding then prevalent in America. Perhaps even old Lipsey the ferryman, and his rival Andrews, will come in for their slice of immortality, little as they dream now, pulling close in for the counter-current under our Lady's skirts, of working at that slow oar for posthumous reputation.

Evert Augustus Duyckinck

Evert Augustus Duyckinck (1816-78) was born in New York City and was graduated from Columbia University in 1835. He studied law, but never prac-ticed. He edited *Arcturus, a Journal of Books and Opinion* from 1840 to 1842. With his brother, George Long Duyckinck (1823-63), he owned and edited *Literary World*, a weekly, between 1848 and 1853. Together, they also edited much of the copy for the *Cyclopedia of American Literature* (1855). He edited the first American editions of the novels of William Makepeace Thackeray and many other classics. He compiled *Irvingiana* in 1860 and wrote the text for the *National Portrait Gallery of Eminent Americans* (1861-62) in two volumes. He also wrote the text for the *National History of the War for the Union* (1861-65) in three volumes. He had a library of 17,000 volumes.

Gulian Crommelin Verplanck

Gulian Crommelin Verplanck (1786-1870) was born in New York City and attended Columbia University, from which he was graduated in 1801. In 1807 he was admitted to the bar and actively took part in politics. His verse-satire, "The Bucktail Bards" (1819) was written against the Clinton faction. He served in the New York Legislature from 1825 until 1833 and also in the U. S. House of Representatives. Between 1821 and 1824, he was a professor at the General Theological Seminary. He wrote *Essays on the Nature and Uses of the Various Evidences of Revealed Religion* in 1824. Between 1828 and 1830, he was associated with William Cullen Bryant and R. C. Sands in writing the annual *Talisman*. He spent much time at his estate near Beacon, where he edited Shakespeare's plays, which came out in three volumes in 1847, and remains a standard commentary.

PART IV

Nineteenth-Century Personalities

Henry Wheeler Shaw

Henry Wheeler Shaw (1818-85), better known by his pen name of Josh Billings, was born in Lanesboro, Massachusetts. He attended Hamilton College until he was expelled for removing the clapper from the campus bell. He married his childhood sweetheart Zilpha Bradford in 1845 and settled in Poughkeepsie in 1858 after a roving life as farmer, explorer, and coal miner. In Poughkeepsie he established himself as an auctioneer and real estate dealer.

In 1860, he began writing humorous sketches in rural dialect. Between 1870 and 1880, he issued an annual *Allminax*. Other writings include *Josh Billings On Ice, and Other Things* (1868), *Everybody's Friend* (1874), *Josh Billings' Thrump Kards* (1887), *Old Probability: Perhaps Rain-Perhaps Not* (1879), *Josh Billings' Struggling With Things* (1881), and *Josh Billings' Spice Box* (1882).

John Bigelow

John Bigelow (1817-1911) was born at Malden, New York, and was graduated from Union College in 1835. He was admitted to the New York bar in 1838. Between 1848 and 1860, he was joint owner and editor of the New York *Evening Post* with William Cullen Bryant when he was known for advocating free trade and being against slavery. He was appointed Consul General at Paris in 1861, and Minister to France from 1865 to 1866 and is given large credit for preventing French recognition of the Confederacy.

Returning to the United States, he served as Secretary of State of New York from 1875 to 1877. His literary works include a *Life of Franklin* (1874), *France and the Confederate Navy 1862-68* (1888), *Retrospections of an Active Life* (1909-13) in five volumes, and works on Swedenborgianism. He also edited the *Complete Works of Benjamin Franklin* (1887-88) in ten volumes.

Frederick Swartwout Cozzens

Frederick Swartwout Cozzens (1818-69) was born in New York City. He is remembered for *Yankee Doodle* (1847), *Prismatics* (1853), *The Tike Sparrow-grass Papers* (1856), *Acadia, or a Month with the Bluenoses* (1859), and *The Slayings of Dr. Bushwacker and Other Learned Men* (1867).

Edgar Allan Poe

While he could not be strictly considered as a Hudson River author, Edgar Allan Poe (1809-49) attended West Point in 1830 and 1831 until he was dismissed for minor deliberate infractions of the rules. The Hudson River had some influence upon his imagination. This can be seen in the extracts from *The Domain of Arnheim* and the short essay "Landor's Cottage." The former is reminiscent of both Shelley's "Alastor" and the scenery on the Hudson near West Point and Kosciusko's Garden. "Landor's Cottage" is a remarkable description of a Dutch Colonial home, such as may still be found in Rockland County. It is possible that Frederick Church's home, Olana, was influenced by *The Domain of Arnheim*.

From The Domain of Arnheim*

The visitor, shooting suddenly into this bay from out the gloom of the ravine, is delighted but astounded by the full orb of the declining sun, which he had supposed to be already far below the horizon, but which now confronts him, and forms the sole termination of an otherwise limitless vista seen through another chasm-like rift in the hills.

But here the voyager quits the vessel which has borne him so far, and descends into a light canoe of ivory, stained with arabesque devices in vivid scarlet, both within and without. The poop and beak of this boat arise high above the water, with sharp points, so that the general form is that of an irregular crescent. It lies on the surface of the bay with the proud grace of a swan. On its ermined floor reposes a single feathery paddle of satin-wood; but no oarsmen or attendant is to be seen. The guest is bidden to be of good cheer—that the fates will take care of him. The larger vessel disappears, and he is left alone in the canoe, which lies apparently motionless in the middle of the lake. While he considers what course to pursue, however, he becomes aware of a gentle movement in the fairy bark. It slowly swings itself around until its prow points toward the sun. It advances with a gentle but gradually accelerated velocity, while the slight ripples it creates seem to break about the ivory side in divinest melody—seem to offer the only possible explanation of the soothing yet melancholy music for whose unseen origin the bewildered voyager looks around him in vain.

The canoe steadily proceeds, and the rocky gate of the vista is approached, so that its depths can be more distinctly seen. To the right arise a chain of lofty hills rudely and luxuriantly wooded. It is observed, however, that the trait of exquisite *cleanness* where the bank dips into the water, still prevails. There is not one token

Works of Edgar Allan Poe (New York: Walter J. Black, Inc., 1927).

304

Edgar Allan Poe, photo by S. W. Hartshorne. Editor's collection.

of the usual river *debris*. To the left the character of the scene is softer and more obviously artificial. Here the bank slopes upward from the stream in a very gentle ascent, forming a broad sward of grass of a texture resembling nothing so much as velvet, and of a brilliancy of green which would bear comparison with the tint of the purest emerald. This *plateau* varies in width from ten to three hundred yards; reaching from the river-bank to a wall, fifty feet high, which extends, in an infinity of curves, but following the general direction of the river, until lost in the distance to the westward. This wall is of one continuous rock, and has been formed by cutting perpendicularly the once rugged precipice of the stream's southern bank; but no trace of the labor has been suffered to remain. The chiselled stone has the hue of ages, and is profusely overhung and overspread with the ivy, the coral honeysuckle, the eglantine, and the clematis. The uniformity of the top and bottom lines of the wall is fully relieved by occasional trees of gigantic height, growing singly or in small groups, both along the *plateau* and in the domain behind the wall, but in close proximity to it; so that frequent limbs (of the black walnut especially) reach over and dip their pendent extremities in the water. Farther back within the domain, the vision is impeded by an impenetrable screen of foliage.

These things are observed during the canoe's gradual approach to what I have called the gate of the vista. On drawing nearer to this, however, its chasm-like appearance vanishes; a new outlet from the bay is discovered to the left—in which direction the wall is also seen to sweep, still following the general course of the stream. Down this new opening the eye cannot penetrate very far; for the stream, accompanied by the wall, still bends to the left, until both are swallowed up by the leaves.

The boat, nevertheless, glides magically into the winding channel; and here the shore opposite the wall is found to resemble that opposite the wall in the straight vista. Lofty hills, rising occasionally into mountains, and covered with vegetation in wild luxuriance, still shut in the scene.

Floating gently onward, but with a velocity slightly augmented, the voyager, after many short turns, finds his progress apparently barred by a gigantic gate or rather door of burnished gold, elaborately carved and fretted, and reflecting the direct rays of the now fast-sinking sun with an effulgence that seems to wreath the whole surrounding forest in flames. This gate is inserted in the lofty wall; which here appears to cross the river at right angles. In a few moments, however, it is seen that the main body of the water still sweeps in a gentle and extensive curve to the left, the wall following it as before, while a stream of considerable volume, diverging from the principal one, makes its way, with a slight ripple, under the door, and is thus hidden from sight. The canoe falls into the lesser channel and approaches the gate. Its ponderous wings are slowly and musically expanded. The boat glides between them, and commences a rapid descent into a vast amphitheatre entirely begirt with purple mountains, whose bases are laved by a gleaming river throughout the full extent of their circuit. Meantime the whole Paradise of Arnheim bursts upon the view. There is a gush of entrancing melody; there is an oppressive sense of strange sweet odor;—there is a dream-like intermingling to the eye of tall slender Eastern trees—bosky shrubberies—flocks of golden and crimson birds—lily-fringed lakes—meadows of violets, tulips, poppies, hyacinths, and tuberoses—long intertangled lines of silver streamlets— and, upspringing confusedly from amid all, a mass of semi-Gothic, semi-Saracenic architecture, sustaining itself by miracle in mid-air; glittering in the red sunlight with a hundred oriels, minarets, and pinnacles; and seeming the phantom handiwork, conjointly, of the Sylphs, of the Fairies, of the Genii, and of the Gnomes.

LANDOR'S COTTAGE*

A PENDANT TO "THE DOMAIN OF ARNHEIM".

During a pedestrian trip last summer, through one or two of the river counties of New York, I found myself, as the day declined, somewhat embarrassed about the road I was pursuing. The land undulated very remarkably; and my path, for the last hour, had wound about and about so confusedly, in its effort to keep in the valleys, that I no longer knew in what direction lay the sweet village of B———, where I had determined to stop for the night. The sun had scarcely *shone*— strictly speaking—during the day, which nevertheless, had been unpleasantly warm. A smoky mist, resembling that of the Indian summer, enveloped all things, and of course, added to my uncertainty. Not that I cared much about the matter. If I did not hit upon the village before sunset, or even before dark, it was more than possible that a little Dutch farmhouse, or something of that kind, would soon make its appearance—although, in fact, the neighborhood (perhaps on account of being more picturesque than fertile) was very sparsely inhabited. At all events, with my knapsack for a pillow, and my hound as a sentry, a bivouac in the open air was just the thing which would have amused me. I sauntered on, therefore, quite at ease—Ponto taking charge of my gun—until at length, just as I had begun to consider whether the numerous little glades that led hither and thither, were intended to be paths at all, I was conducted by one of them into an unquestionable carriage track. There could be no mistaking it. The traces of light wheels were evident; and although the tall shrubberies and overgrown undergrowth met overhead, there was no obstruction whatever below, even to the passage of a Virginian mountain wagon—the most aspiring vehicle, I take it, of its kind. The road, however, except in being open through the wood—if wood be

The Works of Edgar Allan Poe (New York: Walter J. Black, Inc., 1927).

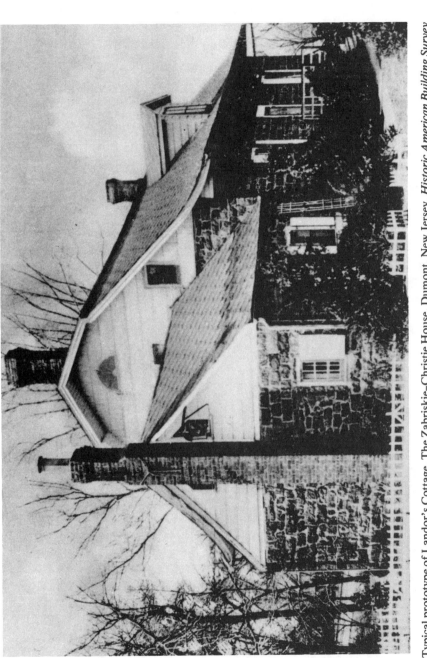

Typical prototype of Landor's Cottage. The Zabriskie–Christie House, Dumont, New Jersey. *Historic American Building Survey* (Washington: Government Printing Office, 1937). The small wing was the original house. Dormer windows were a much later addition.

not too weighty a name for such an assemblage of light trees—and except in the particulars of evident wheel-tracks—bore no resemblance to any road I had before seen. The tracks of which I speak were but faintly perceptible—having been impressed upon the firm, yet pleasantly moist surface of—what looked more like green Genoese velvet than any thing else. It was grass, clearly—but grass such as we seldom see out of England—so short, so thick, so even, and so vivid in color. Not a single impediment lay in the wheel-route—not even a chip or dead twig. The stones that once obstructed the way had been carefully *placed*—not thrown—along the sides of the lane, so as to define its boundaries at bottom with a kind of half-precise, half-negligent, and wholly picturesque definition. Clumps of wild flowers grew everywhere, luxuriantly, in the interspaces.

What to make of all this, of course I knew not. Here was *art* undoubtedly—*that* did not surprise me—all roads, in the ordinary sense, are works of art; nor can I say that there was much to wonder at in the mere *excess* of art manifested; all that seemed to have been done, might have been done *here*—with such natural "capabilities" (as they have it in the books on Landscape Gardening)—with very little labor and expense. No; it was not the amount but the *character* of the art which caused me to take a seat on one of the blossomy stones and gaze up and down this fairy-like avenue for half an hour or more in bewildered admiration. One thing became more and more evident the longer I gazed: an artist, and one with a most scrupulous eye for form, had superintended all these arrangements. The greatest care had been taken to preserve a due medium between the neat and graceful on the one hand, and the *pittoresque,* in the true sense of the Italian term, on the other. There were few straight, and no long uninterrupted lines. The same effect of curvature or of color appeared twice, usually, but not oftener, at any one point of view. Everywhere was variety in uniformity. It was a piece of "composition," in which the most fastidiously critical taste could scarcely have suggested an emendation.

I had turned to the right as I entered this road, and now, arising, I continued in the same direction. The path was so serpentine, that at no moment could I trace its course for more than two or three paces in advance. Its character did not undergo any material change.

Presently the murmur of water fell gently upon my ear—and in a few moments afterward, as I turned with the road somewhat more abruptly than hitherto, I became aware that a building of some kind lay at the foot of a gentle declivity just before me. I could see nothing distinctly on account of the mist which occupied all the little valley below. A gentle breeze, however, now arose, as the sun was about descending; and while I remained standing on the brow of the slope, the fog gradually became dissipated into wreaths, and so floated over the scene.

As it came fully into view—thus *gradually* as I describe it—piece by piece, here a tree, there a glimpse of water, and here again the summit of a chimney, I could scarcely help fancying that the whole was one of the ingenious illusions sometimes exhibited under the name of "vanishing pictures."

By the time, however, that the fog had thoroughly disappeared, the sun had made its way down behind the gentle hills, and thence, as if with a slight *chassez* to the south, had come again fully into sight, glaring with a purplish lustre through a chasm that entered the valley from the west. Suddenly, therefore—and as if by the hand of magic—this whole valley and every thing in it became brilliantly visible.

The first *coup d'œil*, as the sun slid into the position described, impressed me very much as I have been impressed, when a boy, by the concluding scene of some well-arranged theatrical spectacle or melodrama. Not even the monstrosity of color was wanting; for the sunlight came out through the chasm, tinted all orange and purple; while the vivid green of the grass in the valley was reflected more or less upon all objects from the curtain of vapor that still hung overhead, as if loth to take its total departure from a scene so enchantingly beautiful.

The little vale into which I thus peered down from under the fog-canopy could not have been more than four hundred yards long; while in breadth it varied from fifty to one hundred and fifty or perhaps two hundred. It was most narrow at its northern extremity, opening out as it tended southwardly, but with no very precise regularity. The widest portion was within eighty yards of the southern extreme. The slopes which encompassed the vale could not fairly be called hills, unless at their northern face. Here a precipitous ledge of granite arose to a height of some ninety feet; and, as I have mentioned, the valley at this point was not more than fifty feet wide; but as the visitor proceeded southwardly from the cliff, he found on his right hand and on his left, declivities at once less high, less precipitous, and less rocky. All, in a word, sloped and softened to the south; and yet the whole vale was engirdled by eminences, more or less high, except at two points. One of these I have already spoken of. It lay considerably to the north of west, and was where the setting sun made its way, as I have before described, into the amphitheatre, through a clean cut natural cleft in the granite embankment; this fissure might have been ten yards wide at its widest point, so far as the eye could trace it. It seemed to lead up, up like a natural causeway, into the recesses of unexplored mountains and forests. The other opening was directly at the southern end of the vale. Here, generally, the slopes were nothing more than gentle inclinations, extending from east to west about one hundred and fifty yards. In the middle of this extent was a depression, level with the ordinary floor of the valley. As regards vegetation, as well as in respect to every thing else, the scene *softened and sloped* to the south. To the north—on the craggy precipice—a few paces from the verge—up sprang the magnificent trunks of numerous hickories, black walnuts, and chestnuts, interspersed with occasional oak; and the strong lateral branches thrown out by the walnuts especially, spread far over the edge of the cliff. Proceeding southwardly, the explorer saw, at first, the same class of trees, but less and less lofty and Salvatorish in character; then he saw the gentler elm, succeeded by the sassafras and locust—these again by the softer linden, red-bud, catalpa, and maple—these yet again by still more graceful and more modest varieties. The whole face of the southern declivity was covered with wild shrubbery alone—an occasional silver willow or white poplar excepted. In the bottom of the valley itself—(for it must be borne in mind that the vegetation hitherto mentioned grew only on the cliffs or hillsides)—were to be seen three insulated trees. One was an elm of fine size and exquisite form: it stood guard over the southern gate of the vale. Another was a hickory, much larger than the elm, and altogether a much finer tree, although both were exceedingly beautiful: it seemed to have taken charge of the northwestern entrance, springing from a group of rocks in the very jaws of the ravine, and throwing its graceful body, at an angle of nearly forty-five degrees, far out into the sunshine of the amphitheatre. About thirty yards east of this tree stood, however, the pride of the valley, and beyond all question the most magnificent tree I have ever seen, unless, perhaps, among the cypresses of the Itchiatuckanee. It was a triple-stemmed tulip-tree— the *Liriodendron Tulipiferum*—one of the natural order of magnolias. Its three trunks separated from the parent at about three feet from the soil, and diverging very slightly and gradually, were not more than four feet apart at the point where the largest stem shot out into foliage: this was at an elevation of about eighty feet. The whole height of the principal division was one hundred and twenty feet. Nothing can surpass in beauty the form, or the glossy, vivid green of the leaves of the tulip-tree. In the present instance they were fully eight inches wide; but their glory was altogether eclipsed by the gorgeous splendor of the profuse blossoms. Conceive, closely congregated, a million of the largest and most resplendent tulips! Only thus can the reader get any idea of the picture I would convey. And then the stately grace of the clean, delicately-granulated columnar stems, the largest four feet in diameter, at twenty from the ground. The innumerable blossoms, mingling with those of other trees scarcely less beautiful, although infinitely less majestic, filled the valley with more than Arabian perfumes.

The general floor of the amphitheatre was *grass* of the same character as that I had found in the road; if any thing, more deliciously soft, thick, velvety, and miraculously green. It was hard to conceive how all this beauty had been attained.

I have spoken of two openings into the vale. From the one to the northwest issued a rivulet, which came, gently murmuring and slightly foaming, down the ravine, until it dashed against the group of rocks out of which sprang the insulated hickory. Here, after encircling the tree, it passed on a little to the north of east, leaving the tulip tree some twenty feet to the south, and making no decided alteration in its course until it came near the midway between the eastern and western boundaries of the valley. At this point, after a series of sweeps, it turned off at right angles and pursued a generally southern direction—meandering as it went—until it became lost in a small lake of irregular figure (although roughly oval), that lay gleaming near the lower extremity of the vale. This lakelet was, perhaps, a hundred yards in diameter at its widest part. No crystal could be clearer than its waters. Its bottom, which could be distinctly seen, consisted altogether of pebbles brilliantly white. Its banks, of the emerald grass already described, *rounded,* rather than sloped, off into the clear heaven below; and *so* clear was this heaven, so perfectly, at times, did it reflect all objects above it, that where the true bank ended and where the mimic one commenced, it was a point of no little difficulty to determine. The trout, and some other varieties of fish, with which this pond seemed to be almost inconveniently crowded, had all the appearance of veritable flying-fish. It was almost impossible to believe that they were not absolutely suspended in the air. A light birch canoe that lay placidly on the water, was reflected in its minutest fibres with a fidelity unsurpassed by the most exquisitely polished mirror. A small island, fairly laughing with flowers in full bloom, and affording little more space than just enough for a picturesque little building, seemingly a fowl-house—arose from the lake not far from its northern shore—to which it was connected by means of an inconceivably light-looking and yet very primitive bridge. It was formed of a single, broad and thick plank of the tulip wood. This was forty feet long, and spanned the interval between shore and shore with a slight but very perceptible arch, preventing all oscillation. From the southern extreme of the lake issued a continuation of the rivulet, which, after meandering for, perhaps, thirty yards, finally passed through the "depression" (already described) in the middle of the southern declivity, and tumbling down a sheer precipice of a hundred feet, made its devious and unnoticed way to the Hudson.

The lake was deep—at some points thirty feet—but the rivulet seldom exceeded three, while its greatest width was about eight. Its bottom and banks were as those of the pond—if a defect could have been attributed, in point of picturesqueness, it was that of excessive *neatnesses.*

The expanse of the green turf was relieved, here and there, by an occasional showy shrub, such as the hydrangea, or the common snowball, or the aromatic seringa; or, more frequently, by a clump of geraniums blossoming gorgeously in great varieties. These latter grew in pots which were carefully buried in the soil, so as to give the plants the appearance of being indigenous. Besides all this, the lawn's velvet was exquisitely spotted with sheep—a considerable flock of which roamed about the vale, in company with three tamed deer, and a vast number of brilliantly-plumed ducks. A very large mastiff seemed to be in vigilant attendance upon these animals, each and all. Along the eastern and western cliffs—where, toward the upper portion of the amphitheatre, the boundaries were more or less precipitous—grew ivy in great profusion—so that only here and there could even a glimpse of the naked rock be obtained. The northern precipice, in like manner, was almost entirely clothed by grape-vines of rare luxuriance; some springing from the soil at the base of the cliff, and others from ledges on its face.

The slight elevation which formed the lower boundary of this little domain, was crowned by a neat stone wall, of sufficient height to prevent the escape of the deer. Nothing of the fence kind was observable elsewhere, for nowhere else was an artificial enclosure needed:—any stray sheep, for example, which should attempt to make its way out of the vale by means of the ravine, would find its progress arrested, after a few yards' advance, by the precipitous ledge of rock over which tumbled the cascade that had arrested my attention as I first drew near the domain. In short, the only ingress or egress was through a gate occupying a rocky pass in the road, a few paces below the point at which I stopped to reconnoitre the scene.

I have described the brook as meandering very irregularly through the whole of its course. Its two *general* directions, as I have said, were first from west to east, and then from north to south. At the *turn*, the stream, sweeping backward, made an almost circular *loop* so as to form a peninsula which was *very* nearly an island, and which included about the sixteenth of an acre. On this peninsula stood a dwelling-house—and when I say that this house, like the infernal terrace seen by Vathek, "*etait d'une architecture inconnue dans les annales de la terre,*" I mean, merely, that its *tout ensemble* struck me with the keenest sense of combined novelty and propriety—in a word, of *poetry*—(for, than in the words just employed, I could scarcely give, of poetry in the abstract, a more rigorous definition)—and I do *not* mean that merely *outre* was perceptible in any respect.

In fact nothing could well be more simple—more utterly unpretending than this cottage. Its marvellous *effect* lay altogether in its artistic arrangement *as a picture*. I could have fancied, while I looked at it, that some eminent landscape-painter had built it with his brush.

The point of view from which I first saw the valley, was not *altogether*, although it was nearly, the best point from which to survey the house. I will therefore describe it as I afterwards saw it—from a position on the stone wall at the southern extreme of the amphitheatre.

The main building was about twenty-four feet long and sixteen broad—certainly not more. Its total height, from the ground to the apex of the roof, could not have exceeded eighteen feet. To the west end of this structure was attached one about a third smaller in all its proportions:—the line of its front standing back about two yards from that of the larger house; and the line of its roof, of course, being considerably depressed below that of the roof adjoining. At right angles to these buildings, and from the rear of the main one—not exactly in the middle—extended a third compartment, very small—being, in general, one-third less than the western wing. The roofs of the two larger were very steep—sweeping down from the ridge-beam with a long concave curve, and extending at least four feet beyond the walls in front, so as to form the roofs of two piazzas. These latter roofs, of course, needed no support; but as they had the *air* of needing it, slight and perfectly plain pillars were inserted at the corners alone. The roof of the northern wing was merely an extension of a portion of the main roof. Between the chief building and western wing arose a very ´all and rather slender square chimney of hard Dutch bricks, alternately black and red:—a slight cornice of projecting bricks at the top. Over the gables the roofs also projected very much:—in the main building about four feet to the east and two to the west. The principal door was not exactly in the main division, being a little to the east— while the two windows were to the west. These latter did not extend to the floor, but were much longer and narrower than usual—they had single shutters like doors—the panes were of lozenge form, but quite large.The door itself had its upper half of glass, also in lozenge panes—a moveable shutter secured it at night. The door to the west wing was in its gable, and quite simple—a single window looked out to the south. There was no external door to the north wing, and it also had only one window to the east.

The blank wall of the eastern gable was relieved by stairs (with a balustrade) running diagonally across it—the ascent being from the south. Under cover of the widely projecting eave these steps gave access to a door leading into the garret, or rather loft—for it was lighted only by a single window to the north, and seemed to have been intended as a store room.

The piazzas of the main building and western wing had no floors, as is usual; but at the doors and at each window, large, flat irregular slabs of granite lay imbedded in the delicious turf, affording comfortable footing in all weather. Excellent paths of the same material—not *nicely* adapted, but with the velvety sod filling frequent intervals between the stones, led hither and thither from the house, to a crystal spring above five paces off, to the road, or to one or two out-houses that lay to the north, beyond the brook, and were thoroughly concealed by a few locusts and catalpas.

Not more than six steps from the main door of the cottage stood the dead trunk of a fantastic pear-tree, so clothed from head to foot in the gorgeous bignonia blossoms that one required no little scrutiny to determine what manner of sweet thing it could be. From various arms of this tree hung cages of different kinds. In one, a large wicker cylinder with a ring at top, revelled a mocking bird; in another an oriole; in a third the impudent bobolink—while three or four more delicate prisons were loudly vocal with canaries.

The pillars of the piazza were enwreathed in jasmine and sweet honeysuckle; while from the angle formed by the main structure and its west wing, in front, sprang a grape-vine of unexampled luxuriance. Scorning all restraint, it had clambered first to the lower roof—then to the higher; and along the ridge of this latter it continued to writhe on, throwing out tendrils to the right and left, until at length it fairly attained the east gable, and fell trailing over the stairs.

The whole house, with its wings, was constructed of the old-fashioned Dutch shingles—broad, and with unrounded corners. It is a peculiarity of this material to give houses built of it the appearance of being wider at bottom than at top—after the manner of Egyptian architecture; and in the present instance, this exceedingly picturesque effect was aided by numerous pots of gorgeous flowers that almost encompassed the base of the buildings.

The shingles were painted a dull gray; and the happiness with which this neutral tint melted into the vivid green of the tulip tree leaves that partially overshadowed the cottage, can readily be conceived by an artist.

From the position near the stone wall, as described, the buildings were seen at great advantage—for the southeastern angle was thrown forward—so that the eye took in at once the whole of the two fronts, with the picturesque eastern gable, and at the same time obtained just a sufficient glimpse of the northern wing, with parts of a pretty roof to the spring-house, and nearly half a light bridge that spanned the brook in the near vicinity of the main buildings.

I did not remain very long on the brow of the hill, although long enough to make a thorough survey of the scene at my feet. It was clear that I had wandered from the road to the village, and I had thus good travellers' excuse to open the gate before me, and inquire my way, at all events; so, without more ado, I proceeded.

The road, after passing the gate, seemed to lie upon a natural ledge, sloping gradually down along the face of the north-eastern cliffs. It led me on to the foot of the northern precipice, and thence over the bridge, round by the eastern gable to the front door. In this progress, I took notice that no sight of the out-houses could be obtained.

As I turned the corner of the gable, the mastiff bounded towards me in stern silence, but with the eye and the whole air of a tiger. I held him out my hand, however, in token of amity—and I never yet knew the dog who was proof against such an appeal to his courtesy. He not only shut his mouth and wagged his tail, but absolutely offered me his paw—afterward extending his civilities to Ponto.

As no bell was discernible, I rapped with my stick against the door, which stood half open. Instantly a figure advanced to the threshold—that of a young woman about twenty-eight years of age—slender, or rather slight, and somewhat above the medium height. As she approached, with a certain *modest decision* of step altogether indescribable, I said to myself, "Surely here I have found the perfection of natural, in contradistinction from artificial *grace*." The second impression which she made on me, but by far the more vivid of the two, was that of *enthusiasm*. So intense an expression of *romance*, perhaps I should call it, or of unworldliness, as that which gleamed from her deep-set eyes, had never so sunk into my heart of hearts before. I know not how it is, but this peculiar expression of the eye, wreathing itself occasionally into the lips, is the most powerful, if not absolutely the *sole* spell, which rivets my interest in woman. "*Romance*," provided my readers fully comprehended what I would here imply by the word—"romance" and "womanliness" seem to me convertible terms: and, after all, what man truly *loves* in woman, is simply her *womanhood*. The eyes of Annie (I heard someone from the interior call her "Annie, darling!") were "spiritual gray;" her hair, a light chestnut: this is all I had time to observe of her.

At her most courteous of invitations, I entered—passing first into a tolerably wide vestibule. Having come mainly to *observe*, I took notice that to my right as I stepped in, was a window, such as those in front of the house; to the left, a door leading into the principal room; while, opposite me, an *open* door enabled me to see a small apartment, just the size of the vestibule, arranged as a study, and having a large *bow* window looking out to the north.

Passing into the parlor, I found myself with *Mr. Landor*—for this, I afterwards found, was his name. He was civil, even cordial in his manner; but just then, I was more intent on observing the arrangements of the dwelling which had so much interested me, than the personal appearance of the tenant.

The north wing, I now saw, was a bed-chamber; its door opened into the parlor. West of this door was a single window, looking toward the brook. At the west end of the parlor, were a fireplace, and a door leading into the west wing—probably a kitchen.

Nothing could be more rigorously simple than the furniture of the parlor. On the floor was an ingrain carpet, of excellent texture—a white ground, spotted with small circular green figures. At the windows were curtains of snowy white jaconet muslin: they were tolerably full, and hung *decisively*, perhaps rather formally in sharp, parallel plaits to the floor—*just* to the floor. The walls were prepared with a French paper of great delicacy, a silver ground, with a faint green cord running zig-zag throughout. Its expanse was relieved merely by three of Julien's exquisite lithographs *a trois crayons*, fastened to the wall without frames. One of these drawings was a scene of Oriental luxury, or rather voluptuousness; another was a "carnival piece," spirited beyond compare; the third was a Greek female head—a face so divinely beautiful, and yet of an expression so provokingly indeterminate, never before arrested my attention.

The more substantial furniture consisted of a round table, a few chairs (including a large rocking-chair), and a sofa, or rather "settee;" its material was plain maple painted a creamy white, slightly interstriped with green; the seat of cane. The chairs and table were "to match," but the *forms* of all had evidently been designed by the same brain which planned "the grounds;" it is impossible to conceive anything more graceful.

On the table were a few books, a large, square, crystal bottle of some novel perfume, a plain ground-glass *astral* (not solar) lamp with an Italian shade, and a large vase of resplendently-blooming flowers. Flowers, indeed, of gorgeous colours and delicate odour formed the sole mere *decoration* of the apartment. The fireplace was nearly filled with a vase of brilliant geranium. On a triangular shelf in each angle of the room stood also a similar vase, varied only as to its lovely contents. One or two smaller *bouquets* adorned the mantel, and late violets clustered about the open windows.

Walt Whitman, anonymous photo. From *Famous Americans* (Washington: Columbia Press, 1910).

It is not the purpose of this work to do more than give in detail, a picture of Mr. Landor's residence *as I found it.*

Walt Whitman

Another author of national scope, some of whose works have Hudson River topical interest, was Walt Whitman (1819-92). Lack of detailed biographical material on him and Poe is not to be construed as belittling their importance, but this information is readily available elsewhere. Whitman's poems "Mannahatta" and "Crossing Brooklyn Ferry" provide lively portraits of activities on the river.

MANNAHATTA*

I was asking for something specific and perfect for my city,
Whereupon lo! upsprang the aboriginal name.

Now I see what there is in a name, a word, liquid, sane, unruly, musical, self-sufficient,
I see that the word of my city is that word from of old,
Because I see that word nested in nests of water-bays, superb,
Rich, hemmed thick all around with sail ships and steam ships, an island sixteen miles long, solid-founded,
Numberless crowded streets, high growths of iron, slender, strong, light, splendidly uprising toward clear skies,
Tides swift and ample, well-loved by me, towards sundown,
The flowing sea-currents, the little islands, larger adjoining islands, the heights, the villas,
The countless masts, the white shore-steamers, the lighters, the ferry-boats, the black sea-steamers well-modelled,
The down-town streets, the jobbers' houses of business, the houses of business of the ship-merchants and money-brokers, the river-streets,
Immigrants arriving, fifteen or twenty thousand in a week,
The carts hauling goods, the manly race of drivers of horses, the brown-faced sailors,
The summer air, the bright sun shining, and the sailing-clouds aloft,
The winter snows, the sleigh-bells, the broken ice in the river, passing along up, or down with the flood-tide or ebb-tide,

*Walt Whitman in *An American Anthology,* edited by Edmund Clarance Stedman (Cambridge: Houghton Mifflin Company, The Riverside Press, 1900).

The mechanics of the city, the masters, well-formed, beautiful-faced, looking you straight in the eyes,

Trottoirs thronged, vehicles, Broadway, the women, the shops and shows,

A million people—manners free and superb—open voices—hospitality—the most courageous and friendly young men,

City of hurried and sparkling waters! city of spires and masts!

City nested in bays! my city!

CROSSING BROOKLYN FERRY*

I

Flood-tide below me! I see you face to face!

Clouds of the west-sun there half an hour high—I see you also face to face.

Crowds of men and women attired in the usual costumes, how curious you are to me!

On the ferry-boats the hundreds and hundreds that cross, returning home, are more curious to me than you suppose,

And you that shall cross from shore to shore years hence are more to me, and more in my meditations, than you might suppose.

2

The impalpable sustenance of me from all things at all hours of the day,

The simple, compact, well-join'd scheme, myself disintegrated, every one disintegrated yet part of the scheme,

The similitudes of the past and those of the future,

The glories strung like beads on my smallest sights and hearings, on the walk in the street and the passage over the river,

The current rushing so swiftly and swimming with me far away,

The others that are to follow me, the ties between me and them,

The certainty of others, the life, love, sight, hearing of others.

Others will enter the gates of the ferry and cross from shore to shore,

Others will watch the run of the flood-tide,

Others will see the shipping of Manhattan north and west, and the heights of Brooklyn to the south and east,

Others will see the islands large and small;

Fifty years hence, others will see them as they cross, the sun half an hour high,

A hundred years hence, or ever so many hundred years hence, others will see them,

Will enjoy the sunset, the pouring-in of the flood-tide, the falling-back to the sea of the ebb-tide.

*Walt Whitman in *American Poetry and Prose*, edited by Norman Foerster (New York: Houghton Mifflin Company, 1947).

3

It avails not, time nor place—distance avails not,

I am with you, you men and women of a generation, or ever so many generations hence,

Just as you feel when you look on the river and sky, so I felt,

Just as any of you is one of a living crowd, I was one of a crowd,

Just as you are refresh'd by the gladness of the river and the bright flow, I was refresh'd,

Just as you stand and lean on the rail, yet hurry with the swift current, I stood yet was hurried,

Just as you look on the numberless masts of ships and the thick-stemm'd pipes of steamboats, I look'd.

I too many and many a time cross'd the river of old,

Watched the Twelfth-month sea-gulls, saw them high in the air floating with motionless wings, oscillating their bodies,

Saw how the glistening yellow lit up parts of their bodies and left the rest in strong shadow,

Saw the slow-wheeling circles and the gradual edging toward the south,

Saw the reflection of the summer sky in the water,

Had my eyes dazzled by the shimmering track of beams,

Look'd at the fine centrifugal spokes of light round the shape of my head in the sunlit water,

Look'd on the haze on the hills southward and south-westward,

Look'd on the vapor as it flew in fleeces tinged with violet,

Look'd toward the lower bay to notice the vessels arriving,

Saw their approach, saw aboard those that were near me,

Saw the white sails of schooners and sloops, saw the ships at anchor,

The sailors at work in the rigging or out astride the spars,

The round masts, the swinging motion of the hulls, the slender serpentine pennants,

The large and small steamers in motion, the pilots in their pilot-houses,

The white wake left by the passage, the quick tremulous whirl of the wheels,

The flags of all nations, the falling of them at sunset,

The scallop-edged waves in the twilight, the ladled cups, the frolicsome crests and glistening,

The stretch afar growing dimmer and dimmer, the gray walls of the granite storehouses by the docks,

On the river the shadowy group, the big steam-tug closely flank'd on each side by the barges, the hay-boat, the belated lighter,

On the neighboring shore the fires from the foundry chimneys burning high and glaringly into the night,

Casting their flicker of black contrasted with wild red and yellow light over the tops of houses, and down into the clefts of streets.

4

These and all else were to me the same as they are to you,
I loved well those cities, loved well the stately and rapid river,
The men and women I saw were all near to me,
Others the same—others who look back on me because I look'd forward to them,
(The time will come, though I stop here to-day and to-night.)

5

What is it then between us?
What is the count of the scores or hundreds of years between us?

Whatever it is, it avails not—distance avails not, and place avails not,
I too lived, Brooklyn of ample hills was mine,
I too walk'd the streets of Manhattan island, and bathed in the waters around it,
I too felt the curious abrupt questionings stir within me,
In the day among crowds of people sometimes they came upon me,
In my walks home late at night or as I lay in my bed they came upon me,
I too had been struck from the float forever held in solution,
I too had receiv'd identity by my body,
That I was I knew was of my body, and what I should be I knew I should be of my
    body.

6

It is not upon you alone the dark patches fall,
The dark threw its patches down upon me also,
The best I had done seem'd to me blank and suspicious,
My great thoughts as I supposed them, were they not in reality meagre?
Nor is it you alone who know what it is to be evil,
I am he who knew what it was to be evil,
I too knitted the old knot of contrariety,
Blabb'd, blush'd, resented, lied, stole, grudg'd,
Had guile, anger, lust, hot wishes I dared not speak,
Was wayward, vain, greedy, shallow, sly, cowardly, malignant,
The wolf, the snake, the hog, not wanting in me,
The cheating look, the frivolous word, the adulterous wish, not wanting,
Refusals, hates, postponements, meanness, laziness, none of these wanting,
Was one with the rest, the days and haps of the rest,
Was call'd by my nighest name by clear loud voices of young men as they saw me
    approaching or passing,
Felt their arms on my neck as I stood, or the negligent leaning of their flesh
    against me as I sat,

Saw many I loved in the street or ferry-boat or public assembly, yet never told
them a word,
Lived the same life with the rest, the same old laughing, gnawing, sleeping,
Play'd the part that still looks back on the actor or actress,
The same old role, the role that is what we make it, as great as we like,
Or as small as we like, or both great and small.

7

Closer yet I approach you,
What thought you have of me now, I had as much of you—I laid in my stores in
advance,
I consider'd long and seriously of you before you were born.

Who was to know what should come home to me?
Who knows but I am enjoying this?
Who knows, for all the distance, but I am as good as looking at you now, for all
you cannot see me?

8

Ah, what can ever be more stately and admirable to me than mast-hemm'd
Manhattan?
River and sunset and scallop-edg'd waves of flood-tide?
The sea-gulls oscillating their bodies, the hay-boat in the twilight, and the belated
lighter?
What gods can exceed these that clasp me by the hand, and with voices I love call
me promptly and loudly by my nighest name as I approach?
What is more subtle than this which ties me to the woman or man that looks in my
face?
Which fuses me into you now, and pours my meaning into you?

We understand then do we not?
What I promis'd without mentioning it, have you not accepted?
What the study could not teach—what the preaching could not accomplish is
accomplish'd, is it not?

9

Flow on, river! flow with the flood-tide, and ebb with the ebb-tide!
Frolic on, crested and scallop-edg'd waves!
Gorgeous clouds of the sunset! drench with your splendor me, or the men and
women generations after me!
Cross from shore to shore, countless crowds of passengers!
Stand up, tall masts of Manhattan! stand up, beautiful hills of Brooklyn!

Throb, baffled and curious brain! throw out questions and answers!
Suspend here and everywhere, eternal float of solution!
Gaze, loving and thirsting eyes, in the house or street or public assembly!
Sound out, voices of young men! loudly and musically call me by my nighest name!
Live, old life! play the part that looks back on the actor or actress!
Play the old role, the role that is great or small according as one makes it!
Consider, you who peruse me, whether I may not in unknown ways be looking upon you!
Be firm, rail over the river, to support those who lean idly, yet haste with the hasting current;
Fly on, sea-birds! fly sideways, or wheel in large circles high in the air;
Receive the summer sky, you water, and faithfully hold it till all downcast eyes have time to take it from you!
Diverge, fine spokes of light, from the shape of my head, or any one's head, in the sunlit water!

Come on, ships from the lower bay! pass up or down, white-sail'd schooners, sloops, lighters!
Flaunt away, flags of all nations! be duly lower'd at sunset!
Burn high your fires, foundry chimneys! cast black shadows at nightfall! cast red and yellow light over the tops of the houses!
Appearances, now or henceforth, indicate what you are,
You necessary film, continue to envelop the soul,
About my body for me, and your body for you, be hung our divinest aromas,
Thrive, cities—bring your freight, bring your shows, ample and sufficient rivers,
Expand, being than which none else is perhaps more spiritual,
Keep your places, objects than which none else is more lasting.
You have waited, you always wait, you dumb, beautiful ministers,
We receive you with free sense at last, and are insatiate henceforward,
Not you any more shall be able to foil us, or withhold yourselves from us,
We use you, and do not cast you aside—we plant you permanently within us,
We fathom you not—we love you—there is perfection in you also
You furnish your parts toward eternity,
Great or small, you furnish your parts toward the soul.

Susan Bogert Warner and Anna Bartlett Warner

The Warner Sisters—Susan Bogert Warner (1819-85), who wrote under the name Elizabeth Wetherell, and Anna Bartlett Warner (1827-1915)—had unusual lives. Both were born in New York City. Their father, Henry Warner, was a lawyer who had purchased Constitution Island in 1836 as a summer retreat. After suffering financial reverses, he retired there with his sister and his two daughters. Their home, Wood Crag, was built of stone and clapboard, with parts dating back to before the Revolution. A large addition was put on about 1845. The family lived a simple life, and the girls, who were very religious, never married. For many years they conducted Bible classes for the neighboring West Point cadets, and they befriended many of the homesick ones. Aside from a rare trip to New York City or Boston, they never left the island.

Despite this relative seclusion, they attained wide fame. In 1850 G.P. Putnam published a novel by Susan Warner entitled *The Wide Wide World*, under the pen name of Elizabeth Wetherell. This melancholy story is the sentimental unfolding of a young girl's moral character. It went through thirty editions and was second in sales for its time only to Harriet Beecher Stowe's *Uncle Tom's Cabin*. *Queechy,* a second novel published in 1852 was almost as successful. From then on Susan Warner was launched on a successful literary career. Other novels followed regularly: *The Old Helmet* (1863); *Melbourne House* (1864); *Daisy* (1868); *Diana* (1877); *My Desire* (1879); *Nobody* (1882) and *Stephen M. D.* (1883).

Her sister, Anna Warner, also took up the pen under the name Amy Lothrop. She specialized in childrens' books and wrote thirty-one novels. Her most popular novel was *Dollars and Cents* in 1852. Others included: *Gold of Chickaree, Stories of Blackberry Hollow, Stories of Vinegar Hill* (1872) and *In West Point Colors* (1904). She also wrote a *Biography of Susan B. Warner* in 1909. The sisters collaborated on several novels including *Wych Hazel, Mr. Rutherford's Children* (1853-55) and *The Hills of the Shatemuc* (1856). Their home is now part of the grounds of the United States Military Academy and is preserved as a museum.

Joel Benton

Joel Benton (1832-1911) was born in Amenia, New York, and died in Poughkeepsie. He is remembered for *Emerson As A Poet* (1882); *The Truth About Protection* (1892); *Greeley On Lincoln* (1893); and *In the Poe Circle* (1899).

Amelia Edith Barr

Amelia Edith Barr (1831-1919) was born Amelia Huddleston at Ulverston, England. She came to America with her husband Robert Barr in 1853. Barr was a clergyman, and they moved to Texas in 1854 where he and three sons died of yellow fever. She returned to New York City to earn a living and became associated with Henry Ward Beecher. She was a good story teller and had a sense of history, which redeems her rather sentimental novels. She wrote seventy-six of them! Among the more popular were: *Jan Vedder's Wife* (1885); *A Bow of Orange Ribbon* (1886); *Remember the Alamo* (1898); *The Maid of Maiden Lane* (1900); *The Strawberry Handkerchief* (1908); and *An Orkney Maid* (1917). Her autobiography, *All the Days of My Life,* was written in 1913.

Lyman Abbott

Lyman Abbott (1835-1922) was a clergyman turned editor and writer. He was born at Roxbury, Massachusetts, the son of Jacob Abbott. He attended New York University and graduated in 1853. In 1856 he was admitted to the bar, and in 1860 he was ordained a minister. He held various pastorates, and in 1888 succeeded Henry Ward Beecher as pastor of the Plymouth Congregational Church in Brooklyn. In 1899 he resigned his church in favor of editorial duties.

In 1876, Abbott joined Beecher in editing the *Christian Union,* the name of which was changed to *Outlook* in 1893. Abbott was an exponent of the "New Theology" with emphasis on the social gospel as applied to modern American Christianity. His books, of which he wrote forty, include: *The Theology of an Evolutionist* (1897); *Henry Ward Beecher* (1903); *The Spirit of Democracy* (1910) and his *Reminiscences* (new edition 1923). Although Abbott did not write directly about the Hudson, he spent considerable time in the Hudson Valley and was considered a major local personage.

Edward Payson Roe

Edward Payson Roe (1838-88) was born at Windsor, New York. He attended Williams College for two years and Auburn Theological Seminary for one. He

Lyman Abbott. Photo by Sophie Chapman, courtesy of
Beatrice Abbott Duggan.

John Burroughs, seated on "Boyhood Rock," Roxbury, New York. Editor's collection.

was Chaplain to the Second New York Cavalry stationed at the hospital at Fortress Monroe, Virginia, during the Civil War. He then became pastor of the Highland Falls Presbyterian Church from 1865 to 1874, after which he devoted all his efforts to literature. After N. P. Willis's death in 1867, Roe purchased Idlewild, his Cornwall estate. Here he wrote his seventeen best-selling novels and practiced and wrote about horticulture. His books include the novels *Near to Nature's Heart* (1876); *A Knight of the Nineteenth Century* (1877); *Without A Home* (1881); *He Fell In Love With His Wife* (1886); and *The Earth Trembled* (1887). On horticulture he wrote *Play and Profit In My Garden* (1873); *A Manual On The Culture of Small Fruits* (1876); *Success With Small Fruits* (1880); *Nature's Serial Story* (1885); and *The Home Acre* (1889).

John Burroughs

John Burroughs (1837-1921) is the most important regional writer to live and work in the mid-Hudson Valley. He was born at Roxbury, New York, in the Catskills, the son of a farmer. As young man he taught school in Olive Bridge and worked as a treasury clerk in Washington, and later as a journalist. In 1874 he settled on his farm at West Park, which he called Riverby. Here he devoted himself to horticulture, pomology, and writing. He built a rustic retreat up in the Plattekill Hills, which he called Slabsides, and also had another summer home in the Catskills, near Roxbury, which he called Woodchuck Lodge. He was an avid explorer and among the first to make a recorded visit to the summit of Slide Mountain, highest of the Catskills.

He wrote on a broad range of subjects—philosophy, ornithology, nature, history, agriculture, horticulture, and literary criticism—and was also a poet. He numbered Walt Whitman, Henry Ford, and Theodore Roosevelt among his close personal friends. The scope of his interests can be measured by the titles of his books: *Wake Robin* (1871); *Winter Sunshine* (1875); *Birds and Poets* (1877); *Locust and Wild Honey* (1879); *Pepacton* (1881); *Fresh Fields* (1884); *Signs and Seasons* (1886); *Riverby* (1894); *Far and Near* (1904); *Ways of Nature* (1905); *Indoor Studies* (1894); *Camping and Tramping with Roosevelt* (1907); and *Leaf and Tendril* (1908). He also wrote numerous magazine articles and a volume of verse entitled *Bird and Bough* in 1906 and collected an anthology of his writings entitled *In The Heart of the Southern Catskills*.

"Our River" by John Burroughs*

"Rivers are as various in their forms as forest trees. The Mississippi is like an oak with enormous branches. What a branch is the Red River, the Arkansas, the Ohio, the Missouri! The Hudson is like the pine or poplar—mainly trunk. From New York to Albany there is only an inconsiderable limb or two, and but few gnarls and excrescences. Cut off the Rondout, the Esopus, the Catskill and two or three similar tributaries on the east side, and only some twigs remain. There are some crooked places, it is true, but, on the whole, the Hudson presents a fine, symmetrical shaft that would be hard to match in any river in the world. Among our own water-courses it stands preëminent. The Columbia—called by Major Winthrop the Achilles of rivers—is a more haughty and impetuous stream; the Mississippi is, or course, vastly larger and longer; the St. Lawrence would carry the Hudson as a trophy in his belt and hardly know the difference; yet our river is doubtless the most beautiful of them all. It pleases like a mountain lake. It has all the sweetness and placidity that go with such bodies of water, on the one hand, and all their bold and rugged scenery on the other. In summer, a passage up or down its course in one of the day steamers is as near an idyl of travel as can be had, perhaps, anywhere in the world. Then its permanent and uniform volume, its fullness and equipoise at all seasons, and its gently-flowing currents give it further the character of a lake, or of the sea itself. Of the Hudson it may be said that it is a very large river for its size,—that is for the quantity of water it discharges into the sea. Its water-shed is comparatively small—less, I think, than that of the Connecticut. It is a huge trough with a very slight incline, through which the current moves very slowly, and which would fill from the sea were its supplies from the mountains cut off. Its fall from Albany to the bay is only about five feet. Any object upon it, drifting with the current, progresses southward no more than eight miles in twenty-four hours. The ebb-tide will carry it about twelve miles and the flood set it back from seven to nine. A drop of water at Albany, therefore, will be nearly three weeks in reaching New York, though it will get pretty well pickled some days earlier. Some rivers by their volume and impetuosity penetrate the sea, but here the sea is the aggressor, and sometimes meets the mountain water nearly half way. This fact was illustrated a couple of years ago, when the basin of the Hudson was visited by one of the most severe droughts ever known in this part of the State. In the early winter after the river was frozen over above Poughkeepsie, it was discovered that immense numbers of fish were retreating up stream before the slow encroachment of salt water. There was a general exodus of the finny tribes from the whole lower part of the river; it was like the spring and fall migration of the birds, or the fleeing of the population

*John Burroughs, *Scribners Magazine*, August, 1880.

of a district before some approaching danger: vast swarms of cat-fish, white and yellow perch and striped bass were en route for the fresh water farther north. When the people along shore made the discovery, they turned out as they do in the rural districts when the pigeons appear, and, with small gill-nets let down through holes in the ice, captured them in fabulous numbers. On the heels of the retreating perch and cat-fish came the denizens of the salt water, and codfish were taken ninety miles above New York. When the February thaw came and brought up the volume of fresh water again, the sea brine was beaten back, and the fish, what were left of them, resumed their old feeding-grounds.

It is this character of the Hudson, this encroachment of the sea upon it, that led Professor Newberry to speak of it as a drowned river. We have heard of drowned lands, but here is a river overflowed and submerged in the same manner. It is quite certain, however, that this has not always been the character of the Hudson. Its great trough bears evidence of having been worn to its present dimensions by much swifter and stronger currents than those that course through it now. Hence, Professor Newberry has recently advanced the bold and striking theory that in pre-glacial times this part of the continent was several hundred feet higher than at present, and that the Hudson was then a very large and rapid stream, that drew its main supplies from the basin of the Great Lakes through an ancient river-bed that followed, pretty nearly, the line of the present Mohawk; in other words, that the waters of the St. Lawrence once found an outlet through this channel debouching into the ocean from a broad, littoral plain, at a point eighty miles south-east of New York, where the sea now rolls 500 feet deep. According to the soundings of the coast survey, this ancient bed of the Hudson is distinctly marked upon the ocean floor to the point indicated. To the gradual subsidence of this part of the continent, in connection with the great changes wrought by the huge glacier that crept down from the north during what is called the ice period, is owing the character and aspects of the Hudson as we see and know them. The Mohawk Valley was filled up by the drift, the Great Lakes scooped out, and an opening for their pent-up waters found through what is now the St. Lawrence. The trough of the Hudson was also partially filled and has remained so to the present day. There is, perhaps, no point in the river where the mud and clay are not from two to three times as deep as the water. That ancient and grander Hudson lies back of us several hundred thousand years—perhaps more, for a million years are but as one tick of the time-piece of the Lord; yet even *it* was a juvenile compared with some of the rocks and mountains which the Hudson of to-day mirrors. The Highlands date from the earliest geological race—the primary; the river—the old river—from the latest, the tertiary; and what that difference means in terrestrial years hath not entered into the mind of man to conceive. Yet how the venerable mountains open their ranks for the stripling to pass through. Of course, the river did not force its way through this barrier, but has doubtless found an opening there of which it has availed itself, and which it has enlarged. In thinking of these things, one only has to allow time enough, and the most stupendous changes in the topography of the country are as easy and natural as the going out or the coming in of spring or summer. According to the authority above referred to, that part of our coast that flanks the mouth of the Hudson is still sinking at the rate of a few inches per century, so that in the twinkling of a hundred thousand years or so, the sea will completely submerge the city of New York, the top of Trinity Church steeple alone standing above the flood. We who live so far inland, and sigh for the salt water, need only to have a little patience, and we shall wake up some fine morning and find the surf beating upon our door-steps."

Henry Abbey

Henry Abbey (1842-1911) was born at Rondout, New York. For some years he was a journalist in New York City, but returned to Kingston in 1864, where he became a merchant. He wrote a considerable body of verse: *May Dreams* (1862), *Ballads of Good Deeds* (1872), *The City of Success* (1883) and collected poems in 1886 and 1895. He was particularly influenced by the Hudson in "By Hudson's Tide" and "Onteora."

By Hudson's Tide.*

What pleasant dreams, what memories rise,
When filled with care, or priced in pride,
I wander down in solitude
And reach the beach by Hudson's tide!
I wandered on the pebble beach,
And think of boyhood's careless hours . . .

I woke; and since, long years have passed;
By Hudson's tide my days go by;
Its varied beauty fills my heart.

Onteora.†

Moons on moons ago
In the sleep, or night, of the moon,

*By Henry Abbey in *Picturesque Catskills—Greene County*, by R. Lionel De Lisser (Northampton, Mass.: Picturesque Publishing Company, 1894).
†By Henry Abbey in *Picturesque Catskills—Greene County*, by R. Lionel De Lisser (Northampton, Mass.: Picturesque Publishing Company, 1894).

"By Hudson's Tide," view of Kaaterskill High Peak from Cruger's Island, ca. 1870. Drawing by Harry Fenn. Editor's collection.

When evil spirits have power,
The monster, Onteora,
Came down in the dreadful gloom.
The monster came stalking abroad,
On his way to the sea, for a bath,
For a bath in the salt, gray sea.

In Onteora's breast
Was the eyrie of the winds,
Eagles of measureless wing,
Whose screeching, furious swoop,
Startled the sleeping dens.
His hair was darkness unbound,
Thick, and not mooned nor starred.
His head was plumed with rays
Plucked from the sunken sun.

To him the forest of oak,
Of maple, hemlock and pine,
Were as grass that a bear treads down.
He trod them down as he came,
As he came from his white-peak'd tent,
At whose door, ere he started abroad,
He drew a flintless arrow
Across the sky's striped bow,
And shot at the evening star.

He came like a frowning cloud,
That fills and blackens the west.
He was wroth at the bright-plumed sun,
And his pale-faced wife, the moon,
With their twinkling children, the stars.

But he hated the red men all,
The Iroquois, fearless and proud,
The Mohegans, stately and brave,
And trod them down in despite,
As a storm treads down the maize,
He trod the red men down,
And drove them out of the land,
As winter drives the birds.

When near the King of Rivers,
The river of many moods,
To Onteora thundered
Manitou out of a cloud.
Between the fountain's crystal
And the waters that reach to the sky
Manitou, spirit of God,
To the man-shaped monster spoke:

"You shall not go to the sea,
But be into mountains changed,
And wail to the last, and weep
For the red men you have slain.
You shall lie on your giant back
While the river rises and falls,
And the tide of years on years
Flows in from a depthless sea."

Then Onteora replied:
"I yield to the heavy doom;
Yet what am I but a type
O a people who are to come?
Who as with a bow will shoot
And bring the stars to their feet
And drive the red man forth
To the land of the setting sun."

So Onteora Wild,
By eternal silence touched,
Fell backward in a swoon,
And was changed into lofty hills,
The mountains of the sky.

This is the present sense
Of Onteora's name,
"The mountains of the sky."
His bones are rocks and crags,
His flesh is rising ground,
His blood is the sap of trees.

On his back, with one knee raised,
He lies, with his face to the sky,

A monstrous human shape
In the Catskills high and grand,
And from the valley below,
Where the slow tide ebbs and flows,
You can mark his knee and breast,
His forehead, beetling and vast,
His nose and retreating chin,
But his eyes, they say, are lakes,
Whose tears flow down in streams
That seam and wrinkle his cheeks,
For the fate he endures, and for shame
Of the evil he did, as he stalked
In the vanquished and hopeless moon,
Moons on moons ago.

Wallace Bruce

Wallace Bruce (1844-1914), sometimes known by his pen name, Thrusty McQuill, was born in Hillsdale, New York, in Columbia County, of Scottish ancestry. He was keenly aware of his Scottish heritage, and this is reflected in his later writings. He received a bachelor's degree from Yale in 1867 and immediately thereafter he commenced the study of law at Troy. On June 29, 1870, he married Annie Becker. From that time forward he was engaged in literary work and lecturing. This was the great age of travel writers such as Bayard Taylor, N.P. Willis, Mark Twain, and the Stoddards—Charles Warren Stoddard (1843-1909), Richard Henry Stoddard (1825-1903) and John Lawson Stoddard (1850-1931). Nearer to home, Walton Van Loan was issuing annual Catskill Mountain Guides. Wallace Bruce followed with his *Hudson By Daylight*, which ran through many editions and became the standard guide to the Hudson.

He was also a popular lecturer and after-dinner speaker. His works of the middle period were *The Land of Burns* (1878); *The Yosemite* (1879); *The Hudson* (1882, with major revisions in 1907); *From The Hudson to The Yosemite* (1884); *Old Homestead Poems* (1887); *The Hudson Panorama* (1888), with an annotated strip photograph of the river banks; and *In Clover and Heather* (1889), a volume of verse.

Bruce gives us an interesting glimpse of his life at that period in his *The Hudson* of 1882:

It may seem antiquated and old-fashioned in the midst of elevated railroads to speak of mountain roads, but that to Palenville, as we last saw it, was a beautiful piece of engineering—as smooth as a floor and securely built. It looks as if it were intended to last for a century, the stone work is so thoroughly finished. The views from this road are superior to anything we have seen in the Catskills, and the great sweep of the mountain clove is as grand and beautiful as the Sierra Nevadas on the way to Yosemite. [He is describing the present Route 23-A in Kaaterskill Clove.]

We must not forget, moreover, another Catskill drive that we took a few years ago. Starting one morning with a pair of mustang ponies from Phoenicia, we called at the Kaaterskill, The Catskill Mountain House, and the Laurel House, took supper at Catskill Village, and reached New York that evening at eleven o'clock. It is unnecessary to say that we were on business—our Guide Book was on the press—and we went as if one of the printer's best-known companions was on our tail.

This conjures up a vision of a very busy and urbane young man who possibly had Burns' "Tam O'Shanter" in the back of his mind—or perhaps Irving's "Headless Horseman."

Bruce was invited to act as "Poet of the day" at the great Centennial Celebration of the Proclamation of Peace after the Revolution at Newburgh in 1783 and the disbanding of Washington's Army. This great celebration was held at Newburgh on October 18, 1883, at which time the Belvidere Monument to Washington, on the grounds of the Hasbrouck House, was dedicated. One hundred and fifty thousand people attended, including an entire squadron of United States Battle Ships that anchored in the Bay and offered numerous salutes and displays of fireworks. Bruce's poem was entitled "The Long Drama—From '76 to '83."

This Centennial event brought Bruce to the attention of many notables, and in 1889 he was appointed U. S. Consul at Edinburgh, Scotland, a post for which he was uniquely well suited. That same year he produced a volume entitled *In Clover and Heather*. The year of 1886 was the centennial of the first publication of Robert Burns' poems at Kilmarnock. Bruce was invited to give the principal anniversary address on that occasion and also at similar ceremonies at Ayr, Burns' birthplace, and at Edinburgh. He gave an address on Washington Irving at the Grammar School in Stratford-On-Avon. While at Edinburgh, Bruce was voted honarary president of the Shakespeare Society of Edinburgh. Upon returning home from Scotland he settled in Brooklyn where he was a member of the Reformed Church and an active Republican. Among his other activities, he was president of the Florida Chatauqua at De Funiak Springs. He died in Brooklyn in 1914. His later literary works include *Here's A Hand* (1893), *Wayside Poems* (1894), *Scottish Poems* (1907), *Leaves of Gold* (1907), and *Wanderers* (1907).

In a late edition of his *Hudson River* Bruce offers us a very short foreword, which is quite poetic. It develops his conception of the Hudson as the "Queen of Rivers," as he calls her in the "Long Drama."

Greeting: The Hudson, more than any other river, has a distinct personality—an absolute soul-quality. With moods as various as the longings of human life she responds to our joys in sympathetic sweetness, and soothes our sorrows as by a gentle companionship. If the Mississippi is the King of Rivers, the Hudson is, par excellence, the Queen, and continually charms by her "Infinite variety." It often seems that there are in reality four separate Hudsons—the Hudson of Beauty, the Hudson of History, the Hudson of Literature, and the Hudson of Commerce. To blend them all into a loving cable reaching from heart to heart is the purpose of the writer. It has been his privilege to walk again and again every foot of its course from the wilderness to the sea, to linger beside her fountains and dream amid her historic shrines, and from many braided threads of memory it has been his hope to set forth with affectionate enthusiasm what the student or traveler wishes to see and know of her majesty and glory.

THE LONG DRAMA.*

With banners bright, with roll of drums,
  With pride and pomp and civic state
A nation, born of courage, comes
  The closing act to celebrate.

We've traced the drama, page by page,
  From Lexington to Yorktown field;
The curtain drops upon the stage,
  The century's book to-day is sealed.

A cycle grand-with wonders fraught
  That triumph over time and space—
In woven steel its dreams are wrought,
  The nations whisper face to face.

But in the proud and onward march
  We halt an hour for dress parade,
Remembering that fair freedom's arch
  Springs from the base our fathers laid.

*By Wallace Bruce in "The Centennial Celebration and Washington Monument at Newburgh, N. Y.," Report of the Joint Select Committee (Washington, D. C.: Government Printing Office, 1889).

With cheeks aglow with patriot fire
   They pass in long review again,
We grasp the hand of noble sire
   Who made two words of "noblemen."

In silence now the tattered band—
   Heroes in homespun worn and gray—
Around the old Headquarters stand
   As in that dark, uncertain day.

That low-roofed dwelling shelters still
   The phantom tenants of the past;
Each garret beam, each oaken sill
   Treasures and holds their memories fast.

Ay, humble walls! the manger-birth
   To emphasize this truth was given:
The noblest deeds are nearest earth,
   The lowliest roofs are nearest heaven.

We hear the anthem once again,
   "No king but God!" to guide our way—
Like that of old, "Good will to men"—
   Unto the shrine where freedom lay.

One window looking toward the east,
   Seven doors wide open every side;
That room revered proclaims at least
   An invitation free and wide.

Wayne, Putnam, Knox and Heath are there,
   Steuben, proud Prussia's honored son,
Brave La Fayette from France the fair,
   And chief of all, our Washington.

Serene and calm in peril's hour,
   An honest man without pretense,
He stands supreme to teach the power
   And brilliancy of common sense.

Alike disdaining fraud and art,
   He blended love with stern command;

The Winter-Cantonment of the American Army and its Vicinity for 1783. From *The Centennial Celebration and Washington Monument at Newburgh, N.Y.* (Washington: Government Printing Office, 1889).

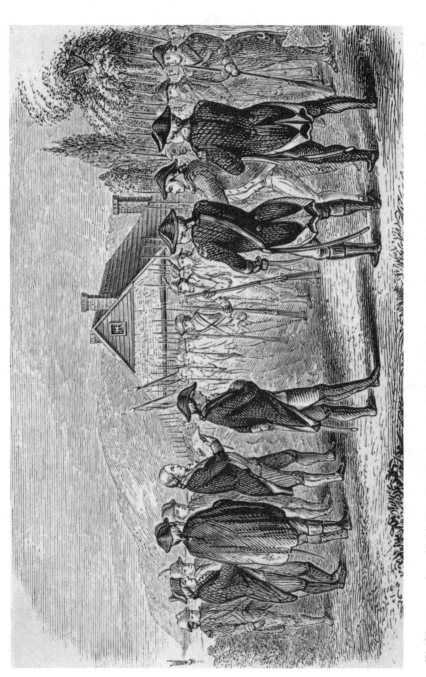

Washington parting with his Guard at Headquarters, June 7, 1783. From *The Centennial Celebration and Washington Monument at Newburgh, N.Y.* (Washington: Government Printing Office, 1889).

He bore his country in his heart,
   He held his army by the hand.

Hush, carping critic! read aright
   The record of his fair renown;
A leader by diviner right
   Than he who wore the British crown.

With silvered locks and eyes grown dim,
   As victory's sun proclaimed the morn,
He pushed aside the diadem
   With stern rebuke and patriot scorn.

He quells the half-paid mutineers,
   And binds them closer to the cause;
His presence turns their wrath to tears,
   Their muttered threats to loud applause.

The Great Republic had its birth
   That hour beneath the Army's wing,
Whose leader taught by native worth
   The man is grander than the king.

The stars on that bright azure field,
   Which proudly wave o'er land and sea,
Were fitly taken from his shield
   To be our common heraldry.

We need no trappings worn and old,
   No courtly lineage to invoke,
No tinseled plate, but solid gold,
   No thin veneer, but heart of oak.

No aping after foreign ways
   Becomes a son of noble sire;
Columbia wins the sweetest praise
   When clad in simple, plain attire.

In science, poesy, and art,
   We ask the best the world can give;
We feel the throb of Britain's heart.
   And will while Burns and Shakespeare live.

But oh! the nation is too great
   To borrow emptiness and pride;
The queenly Hudson wears in state
   Her robes with native pigments dyed.

October lifts with colors bright
   Its mountain canvas to the sky;
The crimson trees, aglow with light,
   Unto our banners wave reply.

Like Horeb's bush, the leaves repeat
   From lips of flame with glory crowned:
"Put off thy shoes from off thy feet,
   The place they trod is holy ground."

O fairest stream beneath the sun!
   Thy Highland portal was the key,
Which force and treason well-nigh won,
   Like that of famed Thermopylae.

That Ridge along our eastern coast,
   From Carolina to the Sound
Opposed its front to England's host,
   And heroes at each pass were found.

A vast primeval palisade,
   With bastions bold and wooded crest,
A bulwark strong, by nature made,
   To guard the valley of the West.

Along its heights the beacons gleamed,
   It formed the nation's battle-line,
Firm as the rocks and cliffs, where dreamed
   The soldier-seers of Palestine.

These hills shall keep their memory sure;
   The blocks we rear shall fall away;
The mountain fastnessess endure,
   And speak their glorious deeds for aye.

And oh! while mornihg's golden urn
   Pours amber light o'er purple brim,

"The New Colossus—Statue of Liberty," photo from *Smith's New York Harbor Guide* (New York, ca. 1900).

And rosy peaks, like rubies burn
Around the emerald valley's rim;

So long preserve our hearth-stone warm!
Our reverence, O God, increase!
And let the glad centennials form
One long Millennial of Peace.

Hamilton Wright Mabie

Hamilton Wright Mabie (1845-1916) was born in Cold Spring, New York. He graduated from Williams College in 1867, and from Columbia University Law School in 1869. He practiced law until 1879, when he joined the staff of the *Christian Union* and *Outlook*. He later served as an exchange professor in Japan. His specialty was literary criticism. His books include: *William Shakespeare—Poet, Dramatist and Man* (1900); *Backgrounds of Literature* (1903); *Myths Every Child Should Know* (1905); *Fairy Tales Every Child Should Know* (1905); *Legends Every Child Should Know* (1906); *American Ideals, Character and Life* (1913); and *Japan Today and Tomorrow* (1914). He spent his later years in Summit, New Jersey, where he died in 1916.

Emma Lazarus

Emma Lazarus (1849-87) was born in New York City and was privately educated. Her *Poems and Translations* (1867) was followed by *Admetus and Other Poems* (1871) dedicated to Ralph Waldo Emerson. Her prose romance *Alide* was published in 1874, and her poetic drama *The Spagnoletto* in 1876. During the 1880s she devoted herself to helping Russian Jewish refugees in America. She also translated the works of Heine in 1881 and wrote her *Songs of a Semite* in 1882. She is best remembered for her short sonnet to the Statue of Liberty, entitled "The New Colossus" (1886), which was carved inside the statue's pedestal.

THE NEW COLOSSUS.*

Not like the brazen giant of Greek fame,
With conquering limbs astride from land to land;

*By Emma Lazarus in *Masterpieces of Religious Verse*, James Dalton Morrison, Ed. (New York: Harper and Brothers, 1948).

NINETEENTH-CENTURY PERSONALITIES

Here at our sea-washed, sunset gates shall stand
A mighty woman with a torch, whose flame
Is the imprisoned lightning, and her name
Mother of Exiles. From her beacon-hand
Glows world-wide welcome; her mild eyes command
The air-bridged harbor that twin cities frame.
"Keep, ancient lands, your storied pomp!" cries she
With silent lips. "Give me your tired, your poor,
Your huddled masses yearning to breathe free,
The wretched refuse of your teeming shore.
Send these, the homeless, tempest-tost to me
I lift my lamp beside the golden door!"

Richard Burton

Richard Burton (1861-1940) was born in Hartford, Connecticut. He received his A. B. Degree from Trinity College in 1883 and his Ph.D. from Johns Hopkins University in 1888. He was a poet and lecturer whose principal works are: "Dumb in June" (1895), "Memorial Day" (1897), *Lyrics of Brotherhood* (1899), *Life of Whittier* (1900), *Message and Melody—A Book of Verse* (1903), *Rahab—A Poetic Drama* (1906), and *From the Book of Life* (1909). His poem "On A Ferry Boat" is particularly evocative.

ON A FERRY BOAT. *

The river widens to a pathless sea
  Beneath the rain and mist and sullen skies.
  Look out the window; 'tis a gray emprise,
The piloting of massed humanity
  On such a day, from shore to busy shore,
  And breeds the thought that beauty is no more.

But see yon woman in the cabin seat,
  The Southland in her face and foreign dress;
  She bends above a babe, with tenderness
That mothers use; her mouth grows soft and sweet.
  Then, lifting eyes, ye saints in heaven, what pain
  In that strange look of hers into the rain!

*By Richard Burton in *An American Anthology,* edited by Edmund Clarance Stedman (Cambridge: Houghton Mifflin Co., Riverside Press, 1900).

John
Sloan
*American
Artist
1871–1951*
United
States
8 cents

"On the Ferry," painting by John Sloan (1871–1951). From a commemorative postage stamp.

Erie Railroad Ferryboat *Meadville*, ca. 1954. Photo by Raymond J. Baxter.

There lies a vivid band of scarlet red
  With careless grace across her raven hair;
  Her cheek burns brown; and 'tis her way to wear
A gown where colors stand in satin's stead.
  Her eye gleams dark as any you may see
  Along the winding roads of Italy.

What dreamings must be hers of sunny climes,
  This beggar woman midst the draggled throng!
  How must she pine for solaces of song,
For warmth and love to furnish laughing-times!
  Her every glance upon the waters gray
  Is piteous with some lost yesterday.

I've seen a dove, storm-beaten, far at sea;
  And once a flower growing stark alone
From out a rock; I've heard a hound make moan,
Left masterless: but never came to me
  Ere this such sense of creatures torn apart
  From all that fondles life and feeds the heart.